Historical Dictionary
of the
Great Depression,
1929–1940

Historical Dictionary
of the
Great Depression,
1929–1940

JAMES S. OLSON

GREENWOOD PRESS
Westport, Connecticut • London

Library of Congress Cataloging-in-Publication Data

Historical dictionary of the Great Depression, 1929–1940 / [edited] by James S. Olson.
    p. cm.
  Includes bibliographical references (p.   ) and index.
  ISBN 0–313–30618–4 (alk. paper)
  1. United States—Civilization—1918–1945—Dictionaries. 2. United States—Economic
conditions—1918–1945—Dictionaries. 3. United States—Social
conditions—1933–1945—Dictionaries. 4. Depressions—1929—United States—Dictionaries.
I. Olson, James Stuart, 1946–
E801 .H57 2001
973.91—dc21   2001019988

British Library Cataloguing in Publication Data is available.

Library of Congress Catalog Card Number: 2001019988
ISBN: 0–313–30618–4

First published in 2001

Greenwood Press, 88 Post Road West, Westport, CT 06881
An imprint of Greenwood Publishing Group, Inc.
www.greenwood.com

Printed in the United States of America

The paper used in this book complies with the
Permanent Paper Standard issued by the National
Information Standards Organization (Z39.48–1984).

10 9 8 7 6 5 4 3 2 1

CONTENTS

PREFACE

As Americans wallow in turn-of-the-century prosperity, the Great Depression seems to recede farther back into the historical memory. Those who remember the depression firsthand are also disappearing, since any meaningful recollection of the 1930s requires at least a birthday in the 1920s. What's left for younger Americans are Shirley Temple videos, posters of Babe Ruth swinging a bat, reruns of *The Wizard of Oz*, and re-releases of *Gone With the Wind*, along with archaic reminiscences by grandparents and great-grandparents.

But for scholars, the Great Depression remains a seminal event in U.S. history, one of only a few occasions when the economy completely failed us and our legendary confidence went dormant. Ever since the first colonists arrived in the New World, Americans had nurtured a boundless, naive faith in the future, as if God intended for the United States to succeed. They came to believe in success as a birthright and economic progress as destiny. But when the stock market crashed in October 1929 and the economy settled into the Great Depression, American optimism, for a short time at least, cratered as well.

The years of the Great Depression also changed American public policy forever. Until the 1930s, most Americans believed that the economy regulated itself according to impersonal natural, economic laws, and they were comfortable leaving economic matters to those market forces. But President Franklin D. Roosevelt and the New Deal made the government a key player in the economy, and eventually Americans gave to Washington, D.C., the responsibility of maintaining full employment and stable prices. The advent of Keynesian economics during the 1930s also gave the federal government unprecedented tools for controlling the economy.

In the *Historical Dictionary of the Great Depression*, I have provided more than 500 entries on life during the Great Depression. Because economic issues consumed most public attention during the 1930s, the dictionary especially emphasizes economic problems, economic events, and the individuals most directly involved with them. But hundreds of other entries revolve around popular culture—sports, films, radio, and books—and diplomacy, technology, and litera-ture. An asterisk next to an item indicates that a fully essay on that topic can be found in the text. I am indebted to the professional librarians of the Newton Gresham Library of Sam Houston State University for their assistance and to Cynthia Harris, my editor at the Greenwood Publishing Group.

A

ABBOTT, GRACE. Grace Abbott was born in Grand Island, Nebraska, on November 17, 1878. As a child, she was raised on a steady diet of politics, since her father was active in local Nebraska politics and her mother a committed suffragette and abolitionist. But while her parents concerned themselves with the major issues in nineteenth-century liberal reform politics, Abbott's focus revolved around twentieth-century urban problems. She graduated from Grand Island College in 1898 and then earned a master's degree in political science at the University of Chicago. Poverty, immigration, blighted housing, and family instability—all endemic to modern urban society—troubled Abbott, and she decided to spend her life working to ameliorate those problems.

Coming out of the University of Chicago with an interest in urban challenges inevitably brought Abbott to Hull House, where social worker and reformer Jane Addams had pioneered the settlement house movement. Abbott remained there until 1917, when she headed to Washington, D.C., to work in the Children's Bureau of the Department of Labor. At the time, the Children's Bureau was leading the way in promoting the federal government as an agent in improving the lives of mothers and children. In 1919 Abbott returned to Chicago to work for the Illinois State Immigrants Commission, but in 1921 she returned to Washington, D.C., when President Woodrow Wilson, at the end of his administration, appointed her to head the Children's Bureau. From that post, she also actively campaigned to promote the causes of the Women's Trade Union League and the National Consumers League. In 1923 and 1924, Abbott reached the peak of her profession when she was elected president of the National Conference of Social Work.

When the Great Depression engulfed the United States, the plight of the urban poor deteriorated dramatically, and Grace Abbott's influence increased. She had long been close to Eleanor Roosevelt,* the wife of Governor Franklin D. Roosevelt* of New York, and when Roosevelt became president of the United States in 1933, Abbott found herself with a voice in Washington, D.C. She became one of the most influential women of the New Deal,* serving on the Consumers

Advisory Board of the National Recovery Administration* and on the Committee on Economic Security,* which drafted the Social Security Act of 1935.* The Social Security Act was the crowning achievement of Abbott's life, something she had long been advocating. Grace Abbott died in Chicago on June 19, 1939.

SUGGESTED READINGS: Lela B. Costin, *Two Sisters for Social Justice: A Biography of Grace and Edith Abbott*, 1983; *New York Times*, June 20, 1939; Susan Ware, *Beyond Suffrage: Women in the New Deal*, 1981.

ADJUSTED COMPENSATION ACT OF 1936. See BONUS ARMY.

AGRICULTURAL ADJUSTMENT ACT OF 1933. Throughout the 1920s, a severe depression afflicted American agriculture. During World War I, to take advantage of high European demand for American commodities, farmers went deep into debt and expanded production. Enticed by unusually high prices, American farmers bought land and modern equipment and invested the capital necessary to make marginal land more productive. Between 1914 and 1918, production boomed and farmers enjoyed an unprecedented era of prosperity. Although farmers had heavy debt burdens, income and cash flow were strong because of high commodity prices. They had little difficulty making debt payments.

But with the armistice in November 1918, European farmers went back into production. They planted their fields in the spring of 1919 and harvested them in the summer. By the fall of 1919, with so much new production on line around the world, commodity prices began to fall, and American farmers sustained serious losses in income. Bankruptcy and foreclosures became all too common. Politicians and farm leaders came up with a variety of solutions—marketing cooperatives, foreign dumping of surpluses, and government-backed commodity storage programs—but nothing seemed to work. Discontent in rural America reached epidemic proportions.

Late in the 1920s, momentum began to mount for an acreage reduction plan. William Spillman's *Balancing the Farm Output* (1927) proposed inducing individual farmers, under government allotment programs, to reduce the number of acres they planted. In 1929, Professor John Black* of the University of Minnesota wrote *Agricultural Reform in the United States*, which further developed that idea. Professor Milburn Wilson, an agricultural economist at Montana State College, then proposed his "Voluntary Domestic Allotment Plan" in which the federal government, by taxing the processing of food and fiber, would generate money to pay farmers to reduce commodity production. Reducing production, so the argument went, would wipe out the large surpluses and stimulate increases in commodity prices and farm income. In 1933, when Henry A. Wallace* became secretary of agriculture in the Franklin D. Roosevelt* administration, the idea gained a powerful advocate. Under the sponsorship of Democrat Marvin

Jones of Texas, Congress passed the Agricultural Adjustment Act in May 1933, during the famous "Hundred Days."* The legislation authorized the secretary of agriculture to enter into "marketing agreements" with wheat, cotton, corn, hog, tobacco, and milk producers to reduce their production. Later other commodities were added to the list. Henry Wallace established the Agricultural Adjustment Administration* (AAA) to administer the program. By early 1934, more than 3 million farmers had signed on to the program. They received government checks for not planting.

Controversy dogged the AAA from the very beginning. Because some of the marketing agreements were signed late in the season, sows had already farrowed and cotton had already been planted. Rather than see those commodities go on the market in the fall and force prices down even more, Wallace authorized the destruction of 6 million piglets and 200,000 sows and ordered 10 million acres of cotton to be plowed under. Critics assailed the decision, even though logic was on Wallace's side. If the long-term goal of administration policy was to reduce surpluses so that prices could be raised, destroying pigs and cotton achieved it.

The plight of poor sharecroppers and tenant farmers in the South also produced criticism. In the South, approximately 725,000 farms were managed by sharecroppers and tenant farmers who did not own the land. When landlords signed the marketing agreements, tens of thousands of tenant and sharecropping families were thrown off the land. The people who really benefitted from the AAA checks were well-to-do landlords, not small, needy farmers.

Conservatives criticized the AAA as "socialistic agriculture," and their voices resonated with the U.S. Supreme Court. William Butler and several associates had purchased the bankrupt Hoosac Mills Corporation, and they refused to pay the AAA processing taxes on cotton. The federal government sued for recovery of the taxes, and the case of *United States v. Butler** went all the way to the Supreme Court. On January 6, 1936, the Court declared the Agricultural Adjustment Act unconstitutional. Farm problems, the Court ordered, were essentially state and local, not national, issues, and therefore the federal government had no jurisdiction. The AAA violated the Tenth Amendment to the Constitution.

SUGGESTED READINGS: Dean Albertson, *Roosevelt's Farmer. Claude R. Wickard and the New Deal*, 1961; David Conrad, *The Forgotten Farmers: The Story of Sharecroppers in the New Deal*, 1965; Van L. Perkins, *Crisis in Agriculture: The Agricultural Adjustment Administration and the New Deal*, 1969; Edward L. Schapsmeier and Frederick H. Schapsmeier, *Henry A. Wallace of Iowa: The Agrarian Years, 1910–1940*, 1968.

AGRICULTURAL ADJUSTMENT ACT OF 1938. In its decision in *United States v. Butler* (1936),* the Supreme Court declared the Agricultural Adjustment Act of 1933* unconstitutional on the grounds that the tax imposed on food processors and middlemen was not really a tax but a camouflage for federal regulation of agricultural production. With funds from the processor tax, the Agricultural Adjustment Administration* had paid farmers to reduce production in hopes of solving the dual problem of overproduction and falling commodity prices. By a 6 to 3 vote, the justices decided that regulating agricultural production did not come under the general welfare clause of the U.S. Constitution.

In the wake of the decision, farm production skyrocketed. In 1936 American farmers produced more than 18 million bales of cotton, and cotton prices fell. Similar gains occurred in wheat, corn, rice, and tobacco production. In response, Congress passed the Agricultural Adjustment Act of 1938, which allowed the secretary of agriculture to establish marketing quotas on a particular crop when surplus production sent its price below a benchmark. The Commodity Credit Corporation* would loan farmers money on their surplus crops just below the parity* levels of 1909–1914. If prices fell below that level, the Commodity Credit Corporation would seize the crops and absorb the loss. If, on the other hand, prices rose above parity levels, farmers could sell and keep the increase. The legislation also established the Federal Crop Insurance Corporation to ensure wheat crops and a Surplus Reserve Loan Corporation to provide loans to needy farmers. Although the Agricultural Adjustment Act of 1938 survived the scrutiny of federal courts, it did little to rein in crop surpluses. Not until the outbreak of World War II in Europe did increased demand for American commodities bring about substantial increases in crop prices.

SUGGESTED READINGS: 297 U.S. 1 (1936); Dean Albertson, *Roosevelt's Farmer. Claude R. Wickard and the New Deal,* 1961; Van L. Perkins, *Crisis in Agriculture: The Agricultural Adjustment Administration and the New Deal,* 1969; Edward L. Schapsmeier and Frederick H. Schapsmeier, *Henry A. Wallace of Iowa: The Agrarian Years, 1910–1940,* 1968.

AGRICULTURAL ADJUSTMENT ADMINISTRATION. Ever since the late nineteenth century, it had become obvious that the real problem in American agriculture was overproduction, which kept commodity prices so low that many farmers had difficulty staying in business. During the 1920s, that problem became especially acute. A variety of solutions were proposed. In the McNary-Haugen Bill, which Congress passed twice and President Calvin Coolidge vetoed twice, the federal government would have purchased farm surpluses at domestic market prices and then sold them on the world market, with any losses being made up by a tax on farmers and consumers. Other proposals included federal assistance in establishing farm marketing cooperatives to assist farmers in selling products in a timely manner and shipping them at cheap, bulk prices. But nothing seemed to work. As commodity prices steadily declined during the 1920s, farmers simply produced more to generate the income necessary to cover their fixed costs, and the result was greater surpluses and lower prices.

In 1929, a new proposal began gaining converts. John Black,* an economics professor at Harvard, wrote the book *Agricultural Reform in the United States,* which argued in favor of government-directed acreage reductions that would reduce crop surpluses and increase commodity prices. In other words, the federal government would pay farmers to reduce production, which would, Black claimed, lead to higher commodity prices. Black's ideas were first implemented when Congress passed the Agricultural Adjustment Act of 1933,* which became the heart and soul of New Deal* agricultural policy. The legislation created the Agricultural Adjustment Administration (AAA) to implement Black's ideas.

The AAA's long-range goal was to achieve parity* for farmers—an economic equilibrium between the prices received for farm commodities and the prices paid for manufactured goods equivalent to the balance that had existed in the 1909–1914 period, a time of general prosperity for farmers. Under the Agricultural Adjustment Act, the AAA would negotiate "marketing agreements" in which individual farmers agreed to reduce production. The legislation defined wheat, cotton, hogs, corn, rice, tobacco, and milk as "basic commodities" subject to the law. Parity would be achieved, New Dealers hoped, by raising the prices of basic commodities. The entire program would be financed by federal taxes on middlemen and food and fiber processors.

The AAA was barely under way when it became embroiled in controversy. Cotton had been planted during the debates over the law, and sows had farrowed, which meant the legislation would have no impact on 1933 prices. Huge surpluses were anticipated in those commodities, so the AAA ordered the slaughter of 6 million little pigs and 200,000 sows and the plowing under of approximately 10 million acres of cotton. Although the decision made economic sense, given the AAA's objectives, it brought about a storm of protest. Since so many Americans were out of work and having trouble buying food and clothing, the destruction of those commodities gave Republican conservatives potent ammunition to criticize the Roosevelt administration.

The AAA also found itself the object of criticism from such farm groups as the National Farmers' Union and the National Farmers' Holiday Association, both of which represented the interests of small farmers. They were convinced that the AAA was actually a tool of the American Farm Bureau Federation,* which represented large commercial farmers likely to reap the most from AAA policies. They accused the AAA of ignoring the needs of millions of small farmers. When AAA acreage reductions led to the layoffs of migrant farm laborers and sharecroppers, many of those criticisms gained credibility.

In spite of the criticism, the AAA aggressively recruited participating farmers, and by early 1934, more than 3 million farmers had signed the marketing agreements. With the depression worsening in 1933, tens of thousands of farmers kept their economic heads above water in 1934 only because of the AAA checks they received. The AAA program then expanded in 1934 when the Jones-Connally Farm Relief Act* added barley, rye, peanuts, flax, cattle, and sorghum to the list of basic commodities. AAA workers then began recruiting those farmers and ranchers as well into the program.

But the AAA also encountered problems implementing the program because the farm economy remained plagued by huge surpluses. Farmers would often sign their marketing agreements, accept the government checks, and then try to squirm around the production limits of their contracts. Congress decided to tighten the program through more regulation. The Bankhead Cotton Control Act of 1934* gave cotton farmers tax-exempt certificates for their contracted crop, with the total of all the tax-exempt certificates equaling a national crop quota of 10 million 500-pound bales. Stiff taxes were imposed on ginned cotton in excess of the quota. Subsequent legislation, such as the Kerr-Smith Tobacco Control Act of 1934* and the Warren Potato Control Act of 1935,* extended such regulations to other commodities.

Although conservative critics lambasted the AAA, its greatest challenge came in the federal courts, where its constitutionality was questioned. The food and fiber processors claimed that the taxes they had to pay were unconstitutional. William H. Butler, owner of the Hoosac Mills Corporation, refused to pay the tax, and the federal government sued him. The case of *United States v. Butler** wound its way through the federal courts, and on January 6, 1936, the U.S. Supreme Court rendered its decision, declaring the AAA an unconstitutional violation of the Tenth Amendment to the Constitution. Farm problems, the Court claimed, were inherently local in nature, not national, and therefore were not within the realm of congressional authority. The Court also claimed that the AAA's voluntary marketing agreements were not voluntary at all and involved considerable coercion of farmers.

The Roosevelt administration responded almost immediately, and on February 29, 1936, Congress passed the Soil Conservation and Domestic Allotment Act,* which allowed for government payments to farmers who would agree to practice soil conservation by taking acreage out of production. Participating farmers would lease the land not in production to the AAA, which would then make rent payments to them. It was, of course, little more than legal maneuvering to work around the Supreme Court's constitutional objections. Even then the program did not work well. In 1936, the nation's cotton crop exceeded 18 million bales, a record bumper crop, and cotton prices collapsed. Wheat, corn, and tobacco production was also up and prices similarly down.

In 1938, Congress passed a new Agricultural Adjustment Act,* which eliminated all of the processing taxes and funded the program through general revenues. The new law allowed the AAA to establish compulsory production quotas once two-thirds of farmers raising a particular commodity had agreed to participate. Finally, the legislation allowed the Commodity Credit Corporation* to make loans on surplus crops at prices just below parity levels and to allow farmers to store the crops at government expense until market prices hit or exceeded parity levels. The law also established the Federal Crop Insurance Corporation. Even then, however, the AAA never really solved the problem of commodity surpluses. Not until the outbreak of World War II, and the consequent huge increases in demand for food and fiber, did the surpluses disappear and commodity prices rise.

SUGGESTED READINGS: David Conrad, *The Forgotten Farmers: The Story of Sharecroppers in the New Deal*, 1965; James S. Olson, *Saving Capitalism: The Reconstruction Finance Corporation and the New Deal, 1933–1940*, 1988; Van L. Perkins, *Crisis in Agriculture: The Agricultural Adjustment Act and the New Deal*, 1969; Theodore Saloutos and John D. Hicks, *Agricultural Discontent in the Midwest, 1900–1939*, 1951; James Shideler, *Farm Crisis, 1919–1923*, 1957.

AIR MAIL ACT OF 1934. In 1918, Congress first authorized the U.S. Post Office to ship mail by air, and in 1925, air mail was privatized to commercial airlines. To assist the companies in covering high operating costs, Congress began subsidizing them in the late 1920s and 1930s. But when it became known publically in 1931 that contracts were not being awarded on the basis of competitive bidding, a congressional investigation ensued. In response to the scandal, President Franklin D. Roosevelt* handed over the job of carrying the mail to the U.S. Army Air Corps. The decision generated a host of Republican criticism alleging that the New Deal* was taking the country down the path to socialism, and when a series of well-publicized crashes killed several pilots, the Republicans added incompetence to their critique. In June 1934, Congress entered the fray with the Air Mail Act, which returned the business to private contractors but mandated competitive bidding for contracts, established maximum rates and standards for mail loads, and awarded some regulatory authority over the business to the Interstate Commerce Commission. The legislation also outlawed monopolies among commercial air mail carriers.

SUGGESTED READING: Thomas T. Spencer, "The Air Mail Controversy of 1934," *Mid-America*, 62 (1980), 161–72.

ALASKA REORGANIZATION ACT OF 1936. See **INDIAN REORGANIZATION ACT OF 1934**.

ALBANIA. Albania, traditionally the poorest and weakest country in Europe, fell under Italian control in 1939. Italian dictator Benito Mussolini, not wanting to be outdone by Adolf Hitler's political and military triumphs in Austria* and Czechoslovakia,* decided to invade Albania. Compared to the efficiency of Hitler's victory in Austria and Czechoslovakia, Mussolini's invasion of Albania was laughably incompetent, and he prevailed only because the Albanians were even more incompetent. On April 16, 1939, Albanian diplomats essentially ceded sovereignty to Italy, and Albania became a province of Italy.

SUGGESTED READINGS: Bernard J. Fisher, *Albania at War, 1939–1945*, 1999; *New York Times*, April 17–19, 1939.

ALLEN, FRED. Fred Allen was born as John Florence Sullivan in Cambridge, Massachusetts, on May 31, 1894. Orphaned at the age of eleven, he was raised by an aunt. He developed a juggling act when he was eighteen and began making the circuit of New England amateur act contests. He soon combined juggling with jokes and storytelling, and his bookings began to improve. In 1916 he added ventriloquism to his repertoire, telling jokes through a dummy named Jake. Allen broke into radio in 1932, and in 1934 the comedy and variety show *Town Hall Tonight* premiered on NBC radio. Nothing was sacred, but Allen had an endearing quality about him that let him get away with comedy that might have seemed too edgy coming from another performer. Beginning in 1937, Jack Benny* began appearing on some of the broadcasts, and the two developed a repartee of jokes and insults that became extremely popular. Millions of listeners tuned in each week. Fred Allen remained a popular radio figure until 1949.

SUGGESTED READING: Robert Taylor, *Fred Allen: His Life and Wit*, 1989.

ALTMEYER, ARTHUR JOSEPH. Arthur J. Altmeyer was born on May 8, 1891, in De Pere, Wisconsin. In 1914 he graduated from the University of Wisconsin and went to work first as a teacher and then as a principal. Blessed with a keenly analytical mind and a gift for applied mathematics, Altmeyer in 1920 became chief statistician for the Wisconsin Tax Committee. With the publication of his books *The Industrial Commission* (1932) and *General Accident Statistics for Wisconsin* (1933), and his commitment to unemployment insurance, workmen's compensation, and old-age pensions, Altmeyer became nationally known in the social work community. In 1933, President Franklin D. Roosevelt* appointed Altmeyer to head the National Recovery Administration's* (NRA) compliance division, a post Altmeyer filled until the Supreme Court declared the NRA unconstitutional. Roosevelt then named Altmeyer to the Committee on Economic Security,* a government body exploring the merits of creating social security. Once Social Security became law in 1935 under the Social Security Act,* Altmeyer was named a member of the Social Security Board. In 1937, he became chairman of the board and remained in the position until 1946.

From that post, Altmeyer lobbied for more comprehensive federal social insurance programs. He called for more careful coordination of state unemployment insurance programs and state employment agencies, expanding Social Security coverage to include disability, lowering the retirement age for women to sixty, and expanding coverage to domestic workers, the self-employed, and employees of religious institutions, which had not been included in the original legislation. Between 1946 and 1953, Altmeyer served as commissioner of Social Security. He retired from the federal government in 1953 and spent the rest of his life teaching, in succession, at the University of Utah, the University of Chicago, and the University of Wisconsin and consulting with a number of international social insurance commissions. Altmeyer died on October 17, 1972.

SUGGESTED READING: *New York Times*, October 17, 1972.

AMERICAN CHRISTIAN DEFENDERS. The American Christian Defenders was one of many anti-Semitic, fascist lobbying groups during the 1930s. It was headed by Eugene Nelson Sanctuary and accused President Franklin D. Roosevelt* of conspiring to bring "about a Jewish state where only Jews will own property and reap profits." The American Christian Defenders made a great deal of noise, to little effect, during the 1930s.

SUGGESTED READING: George Wolfskill and John A. Hudson, *All But the People. Franklin D. Roosevelt and His Critics, 1933–1939*, 1969.

AMERICAN FARM BUREAU FEDERATION. During the years of the Great Depression, the American Farm Bureau Federation (AFBF) became one of the strongest lobbies in the United States. Ever since the late nineteenth century, American agriculture had been plagued by the problem of chronic overproduction, which drove commodity prices down and sent millions of small farmers into bankruptcy. Farm advocates had promoted a series of ideas to raise prices, but none seemed to work. During the 1920s, the problem of overproduction became specially severe and the crisis on the farms especially acute.

The AFBF had its beginnings in 1911 when its first county bureau was opened, and in 1915, the first state federation of county bureau offices was organized. Other state federations soon appeared. At first, the local bureaus simply worked at disseminating new scientific information about farming, but when the Smith-Lever Act of 1914 created the Federal-State Agricultural Extension Service, with county agricultural extension agents, the AFBF offices found themselves working in close cooperation with the agents. In 1919, the formal organization of the American Farm Bureau Federation united all of the state federations.

By 1929, when the country slipped into the Great Depression, the AFBF had a membership of 163,000 people. But Americans suffering in rural areas were desperate for help, and many joined the AFBF because of its commitment to parity*—having the federal government guarantee that farmer purchasing power would be restored to its 1909–1914 levels. Large commercial farmers became especially influential in the AFBF. In order to achieve this, the AFBF backed the voluntary domestic allotment program, in which farmers would be paid to reduce their production. During the 1930s the AFBF supported all federal programs designed to achieve parity through voluntary production controls, including the Agricultural Adjustment Act of 1933,* the Soil Conservation and Domestic Allotment Act of 1936,* and the Agricultural Adjustment Act of 1938.* When World War II broke out in 1940, AFBF membership exceeded 1 million people.

SUGGESTED READINGS: Samuel R. Berger, *Dollar Harvest: The Story of the Farm Bureau*, 1971; Christina M. Campbell, *The Farm Bureau and the New Deal: A Study of* *the Making of National Farm Policy, 1933–1940*, 1962; David Conrad, *The Forgotten Farmers: The Story of Sharecroppers in the New Deal*, 1965.

AMERICAN FEDERATION OF LABOR. The first successful national labor union in U.S. history, the American Federation of Labor (AFL) was founded in 1886 when thirteen national craft unions joined together. They elected Samuel Gompers as the AFL's first president. By focusing its attention only on the organization of skilled workers, the union secured real leverage over employers. Previous national labor unions, such as the National Labor Union and the Knights of Labor, had failed in part because they tried to organize unskilled workers as well. It was relatively easy for management to bring in strikebreakers to fill in for striking unskilled workers. Gompers knew that replacing skilled workers would be far more difficult. Gompers also insisted that the AFL focus only on what he called the "bread and butter" issues—better wages, shorter workweeks, and safer working conditions—and eschew all forms of radicalism. Under Gompers's leadership, the AFL gained ground steadily. AFL membership went from 297,000 members in 1897 to 1,676,000 in 1904 to 2,865,000 in 1924 when Gompers died.

William Green* then assumed the helm of the AFL, but hard times faced him. Business leaders during the 1920s took special aim at the major labor unions, and when the Great Depression struck the nation, unions lost much of their leverage. Between 1929 and 1933, AFL membership fell by 865,000 members. The other threat to the AFL came in 1935 when John L. Lewis,* head of the United Mine Workers, an AFL member union, founded the Committee for Industrial Organization to organize unskilled and semiskilled mass production workers in the automobile, steel, mining, and rubber industries. Such a plan undermined the AFL's commitment to skilled workers. Lewis was undeterred, however, and in 1936 the committee became the Congress of Industrial Organizations* (CIO), with Lewis as president. The AFL promptly expelled the CIO constituent unions and their 561,000 members.

The AFL soon recovered, however, from the losses. New Deal* labor legislation, particularly the National Industrial Recovery Act of 1933 and the National Labor Relations Act of 1935,* had made it much easier for unions to organize, recruit members, and engage in collective bargaining with employers, and AFL leadership vigorously signed up new members. By 1940, AFL membership exceeded 4 million members, and World War II, with its huge demand for labor, made the union only stronger.

SUGGESTED READINGS: David Montgomery, *The Fall of the House of Labor: The Workplace, the State, and American Labor Activism, 1865–1925*, 1987; David R. Roediger and Philip S. Foner, *Our Own Time: A History of American Labor and the Working Day*, 1989; Philip Taft, *The A.F. of L. from the Death of Gompers to the Merger*, 1959; Philip Taft, *The A.F. of L. in the Time of Gompers*, 1957.

AMERICAN GOTHIC. Grant Wood's painting *American Gothic* first appeared in 1930 at the Art Institute of Chicago. Wood posed his sister and his dentist as two somber-faced, straitlaced, austere farmers, standing in front of their Gothic-style farmhouse, with the balding, bespeckled farmer holding a pitchfork with his expressionless wife at his side. The painting portrayed the drabness of rural life but also the stoic strength of the people who inhabited those regions. Critics proclaimed Wood a successor to Thomas Hart Benton as an "American regionalist." Given the depth of the depression in rural America during the 1930s, *American Gothic* had a particularly poignant appeal to many Americans.

SUGGESTED READINGS: James M. Dennis, *Grant Wood: A Study in American Art and Culture*, 1975; Darrell Garwood, *Artist in Iowa: A Life of Grant Wood*, 1944.

AMERICAN GUARD. The American Guard, also known as the White Man's Party, was founded by Olov E. Tietzow, a bitter anti-Semite who believed Franklin D. Roosevelt* and the New Deal* were synonymous with communism. He predicted a civil war between Jews and New Dealers on one side and what he called "Gentile Americans" on the other. His ideas had little appeal beyond the right-wing lunatic fringe in the United States.

SUGGESTED READING: George Wolfskill and John H. Hudson, *All But the People. Franklin D. Roosevelt and His Critics, 1933–1939*, 1969.

AMERICAN LABOR PARTY. By 1936, President Franklin D. Roosevelt* enjoyed the complete support of organized labor, primarily because of the New Deal's* relief programs and because of the National Labor Relations Act of 1935.* John L. Lewis* of the United Mine Workers had established the Labor's Non-Partisan League* to support FDR's reelection campaign, and in New York, David Dubinsky* of the International Ladies' Garment Workers' Union and Sidney Hillman* of the Amalgamated Clothing Workers formed the American Labor Party. Dubinsky also resigned from the Socialist Party* because he feared socialist votes for Norman Thomas* might drain votes from FDR and help elect Republican candidate Alf Landon.* In New York, the American Labor Party named Roosevelt as its nominee, and he won 274,924 votes, compared to only 187,720 for Thomas, the Socialist Party candidate.

SUGGESTED READING: Max D. Danish, *The World of David Dubinsky*, 1957.

AMERICAN LIBERTY LEAGUE. The American Liberty League (ALL) was the most influential of the conservative, anti-Roosevelt, anti–New Deal* groups of the 1930s. Composed primarily of well-to-do representatives from industry, business, and banking, it had none of the anti-Semitic, fascist overtones of many conservative groups. Among the American Liberty League's most influential leaders were such conservative Democrats as John W. Davis, Democratic presidential nominee in 1924; Al Smith,* Democratic presidential nominee in 1928; and businessman Irenee du Pont. The ALL was organized on August 22, 1934, to "defend and uphold the Constitution . . . to teach the necessity of respect for the rights of persons and property . . . to preserve the ownership and lawful use of property when acquired." The ALL condemned the New Deal's proclivity for big budgets, deficit spending, and large government bureaucracies. Between 1934 and 1940, the ALL raised $1.2 million and spent it on anti–New Deal advertising, most of it during the presidential election of 1936.* The ALL endorsed the candidacy of Republican Alf Landon.* The ALL warned that the New Deal would ruin capitalism and produce socialism or, even worse, a communist dictatorship. Roosevelt's landslide victory in the election of 1936 doomed the American Liberty League, and it disbanded after Franklin Roosevelt's* reelection victory in 1940.

SUGGESTED READING: George Wolfskill, *The Revolt of the Conservatives: A History of the American Liberty League, 1933–1940,* 1962.

AMERICAN VIGILANT INTELLIGENCE FEDERATION. Like the American Guard, the American Vigilant Intelligence Federation was an anti-Semitic, anti–New Deal* lobbying group during the 1930s. It was led by Harry A. Jung, a man obsessed with notions of Jewish conspiracies to take over the world. Jung and the American Vigilant Intelligence Federation distributed millions of copies of the "Protocols of the Elders of Zion," a fictitious document that purported to be evidence of a global Jewish conspiracy. Jung considered Franklin D. Roosevelt* to be a co-conspirator. When the United States declared war on Germany* in December 1941, the American Vigilant Intelligence Federation disappeared.

SUGGESTED READING: George Wolfskill and John H. Hudson, *All But the People. Franklin D. Roosevelt and His Critics, 1933–1939,* 1969.

AMOS 'N' ANDY SHOW. The *Amos 'n' Andy Show* was radio's most popular program during the years of the Great Depression. On vaudeville, Freeman Gosden had played "Amos," and Charles J. Correll had played "Andy." The two white men, in black face, played African Americans. In 1926, they took the act to WGN Radio in Chicago, where they added exaggerated, malapropism-loaded black dialogue for comic effect. They took the show to NBC Radio in New York in 1929, where it became known as the *Amos 'n' Andy Show.* The show revolved around the characters of Amos Jones and Andrew Brown, two Harlem residents who owned and managed the Fresh Air Taxi Company, a company that operated a single, all-but-broken-down jalopy that masqueraded as a taxi. Amos was a hardworking, well-mannered, conservative family man, while Andy was a playful, irresponsible ne'er-do-well always searching for the pot of gold at the end of the proverbial rainbow but never managing to find it or to even come close.

During the years of the Great Depression, the *Amos 'n' Andy Show* was broadcast every night, Monday through Friday, for fifteen minutes as a serial, and the audiences grew steadily larger as the program went out over the NBC Radio Network. Pepsodent toothpaste was one of its key sponsors, and Campbell Soup the other. Both companies enjoyed growing market shares because of the program. *Amos 'n' Andy* was so popular that movie theaters would stop their projectors when the show began and broadcast it to the theater audiences. Otherwise, people would have stayed home in order to hear the program. Historians today recognize *Amos 'n' Andy* as the first radio program to achieve a truly national audience, and as such, it occupies a unique place in the rise of a mass culture in the United States.

SUGGESTED READINGS: Charles Correll and Freeman Gosden, *All About Amos 'n' Andy*, 1929; Melvin Patrick Ely, *The Adventures of Amos 'n' Andy*, 1991.

ANDERSON, MARIAN. See **THE MARIAN ANDERSON INCIDENT**.

ANDY HARDY. "Andy Hardy" was a popular character in a series of highly successful Hollywood films in the late 1930s and 1940s. The first of the "Andy Hardy" films—*Love Finds Andy Hardy*—was released in 1938 and featured Mickey Rooney as Andy Hardy, a happy-go-lucky teenager from a beautiful small town in middle America. Lana Turner and Judy Garland played his teenage heartthrobs, but it was Garland who continued the role in subsequent Andy Hardy films. The two eventually made fifteen Andy Hardy films together—and the series proved to be box-office gold. In a world troubled by depression and then war, the Andy Hardy films seemed to reconfirm the American virtues of common sense, hard work, loyalty, and honesty.

SUGGESTED READING: Andrew Bergman, *We're in the Money: Depression America and Its Films*, 1971.

ANNA CHRISTIE. When the era of talking films began in the late 1920s, studio executives were extremely worried about whether Greta Garbo* could make the transition from the silent era. The star of such films as *The Temptress*, *Flesh and the Devil*, and *Love*, she was the world's sexual icon, but a host of other silent screen stars, because of foreign accents or light-sounding voices, had flopped in the early "talkies." Because of poor, low-fidelity sound technology, high-pitched voices or heavily accented voices could be difficult to understand. But Garbo also had mystery and a smoldering sexuality going for her. Still, there were doubts and concerns. On March 14, 1930, Garbo's film *Anna Christie*, an adaptation of Eugene O'Neill's hit play, premiered in New York. The film revolved around a Swedish-born, American-raised prostitute who works the bars and cheap hotels of the waterfront. She falls in love with a sailor, and her first words on screen were: "Gimme a visky. Ginger ale on the side. And don't be stingy." The dialogue worked, and Garbo made the jump from one film era to another. One critic wrote, "When Garbo spoke, the world breathed again."

SUGGESTED READING: Andrew Bergman, *We're in the Money: Depression America and Its Films*, 1971.

ANSCHLUSS. See **AUSTRIA**.

APPEASEMENT. The term "appeasement" became synonymous in 1939 with diplomatic vacillation in the face of a military bully. British Prime Minister Neville Chamberlain believed that Adolf Hitler in Germany* and Benito Mussolini in Italy* could be "appeased," or stopped from further military aggression, by a policy of concession. His response to the Italian invasion of Ethiopia* was tepid at best, and in 1938, he refused to join hands with the French in denouncing Hitler's takeover of Austria* in the *Anschluss*. He immediately extended diplomatic recognition to Hitler's puppet government in Austria. He then acknowledged Italian sovereignty in Ethiopia in return for Mussolini's promise to withdraw Italian troops from Spain at the conclusion of the civil war (Spanish Civil War*) there. Finally, in September 1938, when Adolf Hitler announced his intentions of seizing the Sudetenland in western Czechoslovakia,* Chamberlain flew to Munich and negotiated with the German dictator. When Hitler promised to discontinue his aggressive military policies in central Europe, Chamberlain signed the Munich Pact, announcing to the world that it meant "peace in our time."

That peace proved to be short-lived. In 1939, when Hitler took over the rest of Czechoslovakia, journalists in Great Britain and the United States became hypercritical of Chamberlain, painting him as a naive, shortsighted, weak leader who had tried to "appease" the dictator. Even Chamberlain acknowledged his mistake. Throughout the rest of the twentieth century, Western leaders looked to Chamberlain's "appeasement" policy as the one way *not* to treat a military bully. Aggressors, so the logic went, understood only brute military power, and that idea dominated U.S. national security policy throughout the second half of the twentieth century.

SUGGESTED READING: Frederick Marks III, *Wind and Sand: The Diplomacy of Franklin Roosevelt*, 1988.

"ARKIES." The term "Arkies" first appeared in California during the 1930s as an epithet to describe the tens of thousands of poor farmers who had lost their land in Arkansas and had headed west to California hoping to find work, land, or both. The migration had actually started in the 1920s when the nation's farm economy went into depression, but it accelerated during the 1930s. More common was the term "Okies,"* which was used more generically in California to describe migrants from Texas, Oklahoma, Missouri, and Arkansas.

ARNOLD, THURMAN WESLEY. Although Thurman Arnold was relatively unknown outside government legal experts and academics, he wielded tremendous influence over public policy during the 1930s. Arnold was born in Laramie, Wyoming, on June 2, 1891. In 1911 he graduated from Princeton and then three years later took a law degree from Harvard. Arnold practiced law privately for several years in Chicago, but when the United States declared war on Germany* in 1917, he resigned and enlisted in the 101st Field Artillery. After the war, Arnold returned to Laramie, Wyoming, where he practiced law, raised sheep, taught law at the University of Wyoming, and eventually served as mayor of the city. In 1922 he won a seat as the only Democrat in the state legislature.

Arnold left Wyoming in 1927 to become dean of the law school at the University of West Virginia. He spent only three years there before joining the law faculty at Yale, where he wrote *The Symbols of Government* (1935) and *The Folklore of Capitalism* (1937), both of which analyzed the influence of large corporations on the economy and the relationship between large business enterprises and the federal government. Arnold became convinced that mere size did not constitute a relevant issue in considering antitrust action. He instead wanted to apply the "rule of reason," which had been at the core of Theodore Roosevelt's New Nationalism and part of the later Woodrow Wilson administration, in dealing with potential and real restraints of trade. His books were well received in academic circles, giving Arnold a national legal reputation.

In 1938 Arnold left Yale to head up the Justice Department's antitrust division. In spite of his belief in the rule of reason and the need to discriminate between large corporations that behaved irresponsibly and those that competed with integrity, Arnold proved to be indefatigable in filing antitrust lawsuits. During his tenure at the Justice Department (1938–1943), he filed 230 antitrust suits and made liberal use of consent decrees, national investigations, and careful evaluations of prospective cases. In 1943 Arnold was appointed to the Court of Appeals for the District of Columbia, a post he held for two years. Arnold then began practicing law privately in Washington, D.C. He died on November 7, 1969.

SUGGESTED READINGS: Thurman W. Arnold, *Fair Fights and Foul: A Dissenting Lawyer's Life*, 1965; Ellis W. Hawley, *The New Deal and the Problem of Monopoly: A Study in Economic Ambivalence*, 1966; *New York Times*, November 8, 1969.

ASHWANDER V. TENNESSEE VALLEY AUTHORITY (1936). During the years of the Great Depression, Americans found themselves in the midst of a ferocious debate over the Constitution and the reach of the federal government.

The Supreme Court, tradition bound and dominated by conservative justices, was not prepared for the New Deal* and its unprecedented expansion in the powers of Congress and the executive branch. One of the Court's most important decisions came in *Ashwander v. Tennessee Valley Authority*. The case was argued on December 1935 and decided on February 17, 1936.

Minority shareholders in a southern utility contested the company's decision to purchase electricity from the Tennessee Valley Authority* (TVA), a large federal bureaucracy created by Congress in 1933 to provide hydroelectric power, flood control, and irrigation throughout the Tennessee River Valley. Many private utility companies resented the competition provided by TVA because they feared it would impose downward pressure on electricity rates. The minority stockholders argued that TVA was an unconstitutional expansion of governmental power.

In the end, the Court upheld the constitutionality of the Tennessee Valley Authority. Since the case was an internal matter within a company, it did not possess an adversarial context, nor had anybody been injured. As a result, the justices declined to interfere in the case. In their decision not to interfere, the Supreme Court helped legitimize a new role for the federal government in national economic affairs.

SUGGESTED READING: 297 U.S. 288 (1936).

ASTAIRE, FREDERICK AUSTERLITZ. Fred Astaire, one of Hollywood's leading men during the 1930s and 1940s, was born in Omaha, Nebraska, on May 10, 1899. His older sister Adele broke into show business in New York City, and in 1917, he began performing with her. They spent ten years dancing together on vaudeville stages, making ballroom and tap dancing very popular. They won some spots in several Broadway musicals. Adele retired in 1932 and Fred went to Hollywood to make movies. He teamed up with several dance partners in Hollywood musicals, but when he began performing with Ginger Rogers, the two became national icons. The dance partnership of Fred Astaire and Ginger Rogers became one of Hollywood's most magical musical film combinations. Beginning in 1934 with the film *The Gay Divorcee*,* they danced their way through seven more films, winning the hearts of every American who nurtured romantic notions. Astaire exhibited an elegant, extraordinary style and athleticism in the dance numbers, while Rogers exuded a subdued sexuality. During the years of the Great Depression and World War II, Astaire's relaxed, care-free persona reassured audiences that in spite of the nation's problems all was going to be well. He radiated confidence, tranquility, and happiness. During the 1950s and 1960s, Astaire's dance partners included Lucille Bremer, Cyd Charisse, and Barrie Chase. As his physical skills declined in the 1970s, Astaire took character roles in a number of popular films. When he died on June 22, 1987, Fred Astaire was one of Hollywood's most beloved figures.

SUGGESTED READINGS: Fred Astaire, *Steps in Time*, 1967; Stanley Grewn and Burt Goldblatt, *Starring Fred Astaire*, 1973; *New York Times*, June 23, 1987; Bob Thomas, *Astaire: The Man, the Dancer*, 1984.

AUSTRIA. For a variety of complex personal, cultural, and geopolitical reasons, Adolf Hitler became determined to bring Austria within the orbit of Germany.* In his vision of a new world order, Hitler believed that all German-speaking people should be united under his Third Reich, and Austria, second only to Germany in the number of its German population, became a natural target. He also considered control of Austria to be central to his designs on the rest of central Europe. Finally, he still loathed his long-dead father, who had been an Austrian patriot.

Hitler preferred the takeover to be peaceful, but he was ready to employ violence if necessary. Hitler called his policy *Anschluss*, or unity. His task was made easier by large numbers of Nazi sympathizers in Austria, especially among younger people, who demanded German unification as a means of restoring Austria to greatness. Austria, of course, had neither the military nor the economy to resist. In 1936 Hitler had forced Austrian chancellor Kurt von Schuschnigg to acknowledge Austria as a "German state." The German takeover was under way.

In February 1938, Hitler extracted from Schuschnigg a promise to extend "moral, diplomatic, and press support to Germany," to stop political prosecution of all Nazi sympathizers, and to appoint Nazi attorney Arthur Seyss-Inquart as minister of the interior. In March 1938, when Schuschnigg refused to vacate the chancellorship in favor of Inquart, Hitler moved in with Nazi troops and took control of the country peacefully. In fact, when he drove in a motorcade through the streets of Vienna, crowds numbering in the tens of thousands hailed him. In an April 1938 plebiscite, 99.75 percent of Austrian voters, supposedly, approved the German takeover of their country. Austria was Hitler's first great conquest.

SUGGESTED READING: Radomin Luza, *Austro-German Relations in the Anschluss Era*, 1975.

AWALT, FRANCIS GLOYD. Francis G. Awalt, a leading figure during the banking crisis* of the 1930s, was born in Laurel, Maryland, in 1895. In 1914 he graduated from the Baltimore Polytechnic Institute, and three years later he received a law degree from the University of Maryland. For several years he practiced law privately in Baltimore, and in 1921, he became special assistant to Secretary of the Treasury Andrew Mellon.* During the Hoover administration, Awalt served as deputy comptroller of the currency, and he was acting comptroller during the banking panic of 1932–1933. In March 1933, Awalt argued that the only way of saving the banking system from absolute collapse was a complete, nationwide bank holiday.* President Herbert Hoover* was reluctant to take such a step, but newly inaugurated President Franklin D. Roosevelt* accepted the idea and declared such a holiday on March 6, 1933. Awalt remained in Washington, D.C., for several months advising the Roosevelt administration on how to handle the certification and reopening of the banks. He then returned to private life and died on December 30, 1966.

SUGGESTED READINGS: Francis G. Awalt, "Recollections of the Banking Crisis of 1933," *Business History Review*, 43 (Autumn 1969), 347–71; *New York Times*, December 31, 1966.

AXIS POWERS. During World War II, the term "Axis Powers" referred to a political and diplomatic alliance between Germany,* Italy,* and Japan.* Late in the 1920s, Hitler had developed a profound admiration for Benito Mussolini and his fascist control of Italy, and for a time, Hitler tried to model his own political model after that of his Italian counterpart. By the mid-1930s, however, the German economy had far eclipsed Italy's and Hitler had emerged as the world's most influential fascist leader. In 1936, when Italy's invasion of Ethiopia* alienated Great Britain and France, Mussolini fell into Hitler's orbit. In July 1936, Mussolini signed a diplomatic accord with Germany that journalists dubbed the "Rome-Berlin Axis." The two countries identified the Soviet Union* as a common enemy, awarded common trade preferences in Ethiopian markets, and promised to come to one another's assistance during times of crisis.

On November 25, 1936, Germany concluded the "Anti-Comintern Pact" with Japan, promising one another mutual assistance in any confrontation with the Soviet Union. One year later, Mussolini signed Italy on the agreement, essentially forming the Rome-Berlin-Tokyo Axis, or the Axis Powers. Those loyalties would form the battle lines of World War II against the Allied Powers.

SUGGESTED READING: R. Lee Ready, *The Forgotten Axis: Germany's Partners and Foreign Volunteers in World War II*, 1987.

B

BAILEY, JOSIAH. Josiah Bailey was born in Warrenton, North Carolina, on September 14, 1873. In 1893 he graduated from Wake Forest College and took a job as editor of *The Biblical Recorder*, a Baptist magazine. He remained there until 1907. Bailey studied law during his last years at the magazine, and in 1908, he went into private practice in Raleigh, North Carolina. His activity and loyalty to the Democratic Party earned him an Internal Revenue collectorship from President Woodrow Wilson, and he kept that job until 1921. He continued his legal practice and in 1930 was elected to the U.S. Senate. Bailey became an implacable enemy of the New Deal* during the 1930s. He felt that deficit spending, large federal bureaucracies, and the growing legislative power of many New Deal agencies were bad for the country. Bailey also interpreted Franklin D. Roosevelt's* court-packing scheme* of 1937 and Reorganization Act of 1939* as bald attempts at achieving dictatorial power. Bailey also opposed the administration's attempts to get a federal anti-lynching bill* passed. But with the Japanese attack on Pearl Harbor, Bailey did an about-face and became one of FDR's strongest supporters. Bailey was reelected to the Senate in 1936 and 1942 and died in office on December 15, 1946.

SUGGESTED READING: John Robert Moore, *Senator Josiah William Bailey of North Carolina: A Political Biography*, 1968.

BALLANTINE, ARTHUR ATWOOD. Arthur Ballantine was born in Oberlin, Ohio, on August 3, 1883. He took undergraduate and law degrees from Harvard (1904 and 1907) and then practiced law privately in Boston. He specialized in tax policy and in 1918 joined the federal government as solicitor of Internal Revenue. It was the beginning of a distinguished career in government finance. In 1927 Ballantine became a consultant to the Joint Committee of Congress on Internal Revenue Taxation. President Herbert Hoover* named him undersecretary of the treasury in 1929. During the banking crisis* of 1932–1933, Ballantine played a key role in shaping government policy, urging Hoover to declare a national bank holiday* as a means of stopping the panic and the draining of bank reserves. He also urged Hoover to promote a plan in which the Reconstruction Finance Corporation* could be authorized to invest in the preferred stock of banks as a means of providing them with long-term liquidity. Neither of those proposals became reality during Hoover's administration, but Ballantine remained on in Washington, D.C., during the transition to the Franklin D. Roosevelt* administration, and within weeks, both had been implemented. Economic historians now credit Ballantine with playing a major role in the reconstruction of the banking system in the early 1930s. He returned to a private law practice in 1933 and died on October 10, 1960.

SUGGESTED READINGS: Arthur Ballantine, "When All the Banks Closed," *Harvard Business Review*, 26 (1948), 129–43; *New York Times*, October 11, 1960; James S. Olson, *Saving Capitalism: The Reconstruction Finance Corporation and the New Deal, 1933–1940*, 1988.

BANKHEAD COTTON CONTROL ACT OF 1934. Congress passed the Bankhead Cotton Control Act on April 21, 1934, to promote farmer participation in the Agricultural Adjustment Administration's* (AAA) programs, which were designed to reduce cotton production in the United States so that prices would rise and give farmers a living wage. Ever since the early 1920s, cotton prices had fluctuated widely on world markets, but the long-term trend was steadily lower, just as the long-term production trend had been higher and higher.

At first, the AAA required farmers to sign contracts agreeing to plow under from 25 to 50 percent of their 1933 crops. In return, the AAA would pay them in cash. In 1934–1935, a new series of contracts required farmers to plant only 45 to 55 percent of their usual acreage. The AAA cotton program, however, was voluntary, and many did not sign up; many of those who did sign up did not comply with their contracted acreage reductions, planting large crops anyway. Cotton production continued to climb, in spite of the AAA cotton program, and prices remained too low.

The Bankhead Cotton Control Act was designed to address the problems of enforcing AAA contracts and inducing more farmers into the program. Under the Bankhead law, individual farmers received tax-exempt certificates for their contracted crop. The total of all tax-exempt certificates would equal the predetermined crop quota of 10 million 500-pound bales. Such a total crop, the AAA had determined, would help raise cotton prices. A tax would be levied on "the ginning of cotton equal to 50 percent of the average price of the standard grade on the 10 principal spot markets, but not under 5 cents per pound." In doing so, the tax penalized any cotton ginned in excess of an individual farmer's allotment. It proved more successful in imposing limits on cotton production. When the Supreme Court declared the Agricultural Adjustment Act* unconstitutional, the Bankhead Cotton Control Act had to be repealed, which Congress did on February 10, 1936.

SUGGESTED READINGS: Sidney Baldwin, *Poverty and Politics: The Rise and Decline of the Farm Security Administration*, 1968; Irvin M. May, Jr., *Marvin Jones: The Public Life of an Agrarian Advocate*, 1980; Theodore Saloutos, *The American Farmer and the New Deal*, 1983.

BANKHEAD-JONES FARM TENANCY ACT OF 1937. During the 1920s, the problems in the farm economy became acute. To finance acreage and production expansions during the World War I years, farmers went heavily into debt, and they put their farms up as collateral for the loans. Increasing numbers of farmers lost their land when they failed to make mortgage payments, and increasingly large numbers of American farms were run by tenants. Also contributing to the rise of farm tenancy was the high capital requirements needed to survive economically, especially in purchases of heavy equipment. By 1935, a total of 42 percent of American farms were operated by tenants. The cotton economy of the South was the region where farm tenancy increased the most dramatically.

To address the problem of farm tenancy, President Franklin D. Roosevelt* in November 1935 established a Special Committee on Farm Tenancy. He also asked Senator John Bankhead of Alabama and Congressman Marvin Jones of Texas to begin work on federal legislation to ameliorate the suffering of farm tenants. Jones felt that the key to the problem involved the availability of credit. If local communities could use government funds to purchase available land, they could then resell the land at low interest rates to the tenants working the land. Jones's ideas became the Bankhead-Jones Farm Tenancy Act of 1937. The legislation authorized such rehabilitation loans, which tenants could also use for education and operating expenses, and appropriated $50 million for conservation programs on marginal lands. The Bankhead-Jones Farm Tenancy Act also established the Farm Security Administration* to administer the legislation. The long-term consequences of the Bankhead-Jones Farm Tenancy Act were modest but real. Between 1937 and 1947, the Farm Security Administration made loans of $293 million to 47,104 farmers.

SUGGESTED READINGS: Sidney Baldwin, *Poverty and Politics: The Rise and Decline of the Farm Security Administration*, 1968; Irvin M. May, Jr., *Marvin Jones: The Public Life of an Agrarian Advocate*, 1980; Theodore Saloutos, *The American Farmer and the New Deal*, 1983.

BANK HOLIDAY. Perhaps the most dramatic economic and political event of the Great Depression was President Franklin D. Roosevelt's* decision to proclaim a national bank holiday to deal with the crisis in the money markets. During the 1920s—because of weak farm loans and undercapitalization—the banking system experienced severe problems. Thousands of banks failed, undermining depositors' confidence and precipitating runs on the banks, which forced bankers to liquidate assets in order to generate cash. The liquidation process further eroded assets and further weakened depositors confidence, creating a vicious, self-reinforcing cycle.

During the last weeks of February 1933, as the Hoover administration was winding down and Franklin D. Roosevelt was preparing to take the oath of office as president, the banking system collapsed. With 95 percent of the nation's banks threatening to shut down amidst a huge wave of panic-stricken depositors, President Herbert Hoover* and his advisers considered a banking holiday, but they could get little cooperation from the incoming New Dealers and decided not to act. On March 6, 1933, President Franklin D. Roosevelt signed a proclamation declaring a moratorium on all banking operations in the United States. The proclamation was later confirmed by the Emergency Banking Act,* which Congress passed on March 9.

Although the Roosevelt administration had only the vaguest notions of what to do about the crisis, they did know that when the holiday ended, only sound banks should reopen. Even a few failures could trigger another panic and liquidity crisis. The administration decided to make sure that each reopened bank was safe and secure and to inform the public of its safety. Bank examiners from the Reconstruction Finance Corporation* (RFC), the Treasury Department, the comptroller of the currency, and the Federal Reserve System launched a crash program to examine the basic solvency of every national bank in the country. Healthy banks were licensed to reopen. Weaker banks could receive investment capital and loans from the RFC and then reopen. The weakest banks were not allowed to reopen at all but were forced into bankruptcy or into consolidation with stronger institutions. State banking officials used similar procedures to examine state banks.

On March 14, 1933, the night before the first banks were to reopen, President Roosevelt addressed the nation by radio in what was labeled a "fireside chat."* He explained that Americans could rest assured that the banks that reopened the next day were safe and could be trusted. Money deposited in any of those reopened banks would be completely safe. On March 15, 1933, federal and state officials allowed 12,756 banks to reopen, compared to the 18,390 banks in operation before the holiday. The bank holiday was a success, and the financial panic ended.

SUGGESTED READINGS: Susan Estabrook Kennedy, *The Banking Crisis of 1933*, 1973; James S. Olson, *Saving Capitalism: The Reconstruction Finance Corporation and the New Deal, 1933–1940*, 1988.

BANKING ACT OF 1933. During the 1920s, as tens of thousands of banks failed in the United States, critics and economists began proposing major reforms to protect depositors and to stabilize the money markets. Some actually called for creation of a single federal banking system and scrapping of the decentralized Federal Reserve System, with its twelve regional banks and weak central board in Washington, D.C. Radicals even demanded federal nationalization of the entire banking system. Some state banking authorities argued that state regulation of their individual banking systems would be sufficient and that all forms of federal regulation should be scrapped.

In 1931, the investigation into banking practices by Congressman Ferdinand Pecora (Pecora Committee*) exposed serious problems in the banking system, none more important than the fact that the lines between commercial banking and investment banking had become hopelessly blurred, with bankers siphoning money from commercial bank depositors and channeling them into speculative new securities offerings. When the stock market crashed in 1929–1930, millions of depositors saw their savings wiped out. Small bankers were also concerned about the trend for large commercial banks to establish small branches in smaller cities and towns. Such an invasion of local markets, they were convinced, would send small, independent banks toward bankruptcy. Many economists worried that the failure of more than 5,600 banks during the 1920s had ominous implications for the future and that the federal government needed to provide a system of guaranteeing bank deposits so that panic-stricken depositors would not make runs on troubled financial institutions. When several thousand more banks failed during the financial meltdown of 1931–1932, demands for some type of federal deposit insurance escalated.

Throughout 1932, several bills surfaced in Congress to address these problems, and the most influential among them was sponsored by Senator Carter Glass* of Virginia and Congressman Henry Steagall* of Alabama. The bill called for a liberalization of Federal Reserve rediscounting regulations but said nothing about other problems in the money markets, and the Hoover administration was paralyzed anyway, unable to achieve anything politically because of its complete loss of credibility. When the banking system virtually collapsed in 1932–1933, the administration of newly elected President Franklin D. Roosevelt* enjoyed, or faced, overwhelming support and overwhelming pressure to do something about the banking system.

In March and April of 1933, New Deal* officials carefully studied the problem, and in mid-May, Carter and Glass submitted new legislation to Congress. It was an omnibus measure that made the nation's banking system stronger and less vulnerable to foreign manipulation and domestic panic. The bill called for an increase in Federal Reserve control over bank credit and more careful coordination of Federal Reserve open market operations, and it awarded official legal recognition to the Federal Open Market Committee. The bill gave control to the Federal Reserve Board* of all the foreign operations of its member banks. To prevent future speculative manias and protect depositors' savings, the bill separated investment banking from commercial banking and outlawed a mixing of the two functions within the same bank. Banks would have to define themselves as commercial banks or investment banks. Commercial banks could underwrite the securities only of state and local governments and had one year to divest themselves of their securities affiliates. Officers of national banks could no longer accept loans from their own banks. Also, national banks could establish branch banks but only in states that had authorized them to do so by law. To regulate chain and group banking, the comptroller of the currency had power to regulate the stock voting rights of the holding company affiliate of national banks. The legislation also raised the capital requirements of national banks to give them more power and resiliency during times of financial crisis. Finally, the law established a Federal Deposit Insurance Corporation* (FDIC) to insure bank deposits. The FDIC received $150 million in capital from the federal government and operating funds from each member bank participating in the insurance program. The FDIC would begin operations on July 1, 1936. In mid-June, the Glass-Steagall Banking Act, or Banking Act, of 1933 passed in both houses of Congress, and President Franklin D. Roosevelt signed it into law.

SUGGESTED READINGS: Helen M. Burns, *The American Banking Community and New Deal Banking Reforms, 1933–1935*, 1974; James S. Olson, *Saving Capitalism: The Reconstruction Finance Corporation and the New Deal, 1933–1940*, 1988.

BANKING ACT OF 1935. By late 1934, a number of financial challenges faced the American banking system. First, the Banking Act of 1933* had required the officers of all national banks, by July 1, 1935, to divest themselves of all loans extended to them by their own banks. The logic, of course, was to make sure that bank officers made decisions consistent with the interests of all of their depositors and creditors and not just for their own individual interests. Many bank officers, however, felt that the July 1, 1935, deadline was approaching too quickly and that they would need more time to complete the divestiture. They wanted the federal government to give them a time extension. Second, the Federal Deposit Insurance Corporation* (FDIC), also authorized by the Banking Act of 1933, was set to begin operation on January 1, 1935, but many bankers who wanted to participate in FDIC insurance felt that its proposed charges, or dues, were exorbitant and wanted them reduced. Finally, Marriner Eccles,* newly appointed head of the Federal Reserve Board* in Washington, D.C., felt that existing federal law relating to the Federal Reserve System was outdated and rendered the Federal Reserve Board largely ineffective in dealing with the Great Depression. Eccles was an early convert to the fiscal policy ideas of English economist John Maynard Keynes,* who believed that the federal government, through its taxation and spending policies, could play a key role in stimulating the economy. Eccles wanted to shift the base of power in the Federal Reserve System from the regional Federal Reserve Banks to the Federal Reserve Board in Washington, D.C. In a national economy, the idea of twelve regional banks pursuing contradictory monetary policies seemed ludicrous to Eccles. He wanted the Federal Reserve Banks raising or lowering interest unitedly or engaging in the same open market operations, buying or selling government securities on the open market at the same time and in the same volumes. Only then could the Federal Reserve System truly engage in national economic policymaking.

President Franklin D. Roosevelt* and his economic staff put together an omnibus bill that addressed all these concerns. He realized that private commercial bankers would resist the centralization of Federal Reserve powers, but he suspected that he could get them to swallow the proposal in return for reducing FDIC membership charges and giving national bank officers a time extension in divesting themselves of loans for their own banks. The legislation made its way through the House and the Senate and then through a conference committee in the summer of 1935, and on August 23, 1935, President Roosevelt signed the legislation into law.

The Banking Act of 1935 was divided into three separate titles. Title I pleased private commercial bankers by substantially reducing annual membership fees in the Federal Deposit Insurance Corporation and allowed the FDIC to begin formal operations as scheduled. Title II implemented many of Eccles's proposals. It dismantled the Federal Reserve Board and replaced it with a board of governors of the Federal Reserve System. The board would consist of seven members, each appointed by the president and confirmed by the U.S. Senate. The first appointments to the board were for terms ranging from two to fourteen years, so that board members would be rotated off on a steady schedule and the board would be more able to maintain policy continuity. At each regional Federal Reserve Bank, the office of governor was replaced by a president who served a five-year term. Each president was selected by the board of directors of the regional bank. The president's nomination had to be confirmed by the board of governors in Washington, D.C. Title II scrapped the old Federal Open Market Committee, which had consisted of the twelve governors of the regional Federal Reserve Banks, and replaced it with a new Federal Open Market Committee that was composed of the board of governors of the Federal Reserve System and five presidents from the regional Federal Reserve Banks. The legislation gave complete control of open market operations to the new Federal Open Market Committee. Finally, Title II liberalized Federal Reserve discount policies by allowing local Federal Reserve Banks, with the permission of the board of governors, to advance cash to local commercial banks on a broader range of collateral. Title III of the Banking Act of 1935 extended the deadline for national bank officers to refinance loans from their own banks with loans from other national banks.

Historians look back upon the Banking Act of 1935 as a turning point in U.S. financial and economic history. The Federal Reserve System now had dramatically increased powers for controlling the flow of credit to banks, businesses, and consumers, and it had at its head a man—Marriner Eccles—who was a confirmed Keynesian. For the first time in U.S. history, commercial banks had become part of a coordinated banking system. Since the Banking Act of 1935, the federal government has played a key role in the functioning of the money markets.

SUGGESTED READINGS: Helen M. Burns, *The American Banking Community and New Deal Banking Reforms, 1933–1935,* 1974; James S. Olson, *Saving Capitalism: The Reconstruction Finance Corporation and the New Deal, 1933–1940,* 1988.

BANKING CRISIS. During the Great Depression, the money markets constituted the weakest sector of the economy, and within the money markets, the
banking system was the most fragile. During the 1920s, a catastrophe had
stricken the money markets. At the beginning of the decade, there were more
than 30,000 commercial banks as well as thousands of savings banks, building
and loan associations, investment companies, private banks, industrial banks,
credit unions, and finance companies, for a total of more than 50,000 financial
institutions. Most of the banks were undercapitalized, and in rural areas, there
were simply too many banks and not enough business. It was not unusual for
a community with only 500 people to be served by two banks, neither one of
which could produce sufficient profits. To put it simply, America was badly
overbanked.

Rural banks also suffered from the decline of the farm economy. Overproduction and low commodity prices had long plagued American agriculture,
and during the 1920s, both problems intensified. Many rural banks had loaned
heavily to expand agricultural production during World War I, and bankruptcies
increased during the 1920s. When banks had to foreclose on bankrupt property,
they lost assets, and the number of bank failures increased. Between 1921 and
1929, more than 5,400 rural banks went out of business in the United States.
Another 4,100 had to merge with other banks in order to survive.

The stock market crash of 1929 then sent banks into a tailspin. Those banks
that had invested in or loaned heavily to brokers to buy stocks discovered that
their assets were badly eroded, and a tidal wave of panic-stricken depositors
showed up demanding their cash. When bankers had to liquidate assets to generate the cash, stock prices fell further, only making matters worse. In 1929,
641 American banks closed their doors, and in 1930, the number jumped to
1,350. In 1931 a total of 1,700 banks went belly up. Bad agricultural loans,
collapsing stock values, and defaults on business loans had made life all but
impossible for bankers. The disaster culminated in the bank holiday* of 1933,
when newly inaugurated President Franklin D. Roosevelt* closed all the nation's
banks to stop a universal run on financial institutions throughout the country.
When the holiday was over, only 13,500 of the 30,000 banks open in 1920
remained in business.

Dealing with the banking crisis became a preoccupation of the Hoover and
Roosevelt administrations. In 1932 Congress passed and President Hoover*
signed legislation creating the Reconstruction Finance Corporation* (RFC) to
loan money to troubled banks, but loans proved insufficient. It was not until
1933, when Congress authorized the RFC to purchase the preferred stock of
American banks, that the crisis eased. With investment capital instead of loans,
bankers had time to deal with depositors and did not have to engage in panic
sales of stocks or loan calls that so damaged the money markets. Throughout
the rest of the 1930s, the annual number of bank failures registered in dozens,
not the hundreds or thousands as before.

SUGGESTED READINGS: James S. Olson, *Herbert Hoover and the Reconstruction Finance Corporation, 1931–1933*, 1977; James S. Olson, *Saving Capitalism: The Reconstruction Finance Corporation and the New Deal, 1933–1940*, 1988.

BARRYMORE, JOHN. John Barrymore, one of America's most distinguished film actors during the years of the Great Depression, was born John Sydney Blythe on February 15, 1882, in Philadelphia, Pennsylvania. His parents and grandparents constituted one of the country's most famous theatrical families, and Barrymore followed in the tradition. During the early 1900s, he won parts in a number of Broadway plays, but in 1913 he left the stage for the silver screen, signing a contract with Fox Studio (William Fox*). Barrymore became an international star because of his performance in *Dr. Jekyll and Mr. Hyde* (1920). He remained with Fox until 1922, when he signed with Warner Brothers. That contractual relationship lasted until 1926 when Barrymore jumped to United Artists. By that time he was a matinee idol, nicknamed "The Great Profile" by journalists and magazine writers. When the transition to sound films came in the late 1920s, Barrymore made the transition easily, primarily because of his strikingly handsome looks and his deep, resonant voice. In 1932, Barrymore went to MGM Studios, and by that time he was commanding $150,000 per film. Throughout most of the decade, Barrymore became the country's most bankable star. He was also an alcoholic and a womanizer, and both obsessions took their toll on his health. Barrymore died on May 29, 1942.

SUGGESTED READINGS: Lionel Barrymore, *We Barrymores*, 1951; James Card, *The Films of John Barrymore*, 1969; James Hotsilibas-Davis, *The Barrymores: The Royal Family in Hollywood*, 1981; *New York Times*, May 30, 1942; Alma Power-Waters, *John Barrymore: The Legend and the Man*, 1941.

BARRYMORE, LIONEL. Lionel Barrymore, the elder brother of actor John Barrymore,* was born Lionel Blythe on April 28, 1878, to the country's most famous theatrical family. After studying at Seton Hall University and then the Art Students League in New York, he worked on Broadway in a series of prominent plays. In 1911, he had a starring role in his first film—*The Battle*—and during the 1920s he starred in dozens of films, several under the direction of D. W. Griffith, including *America* and *Sadie Thompson*. Later in the decade, Barrymore abandoned the romantic, leading-man role, primarily because age militated against it. Instead, he became a character actor and won an Academy Award in 1931 for his performance in *A Free Man*. During the years of the Great Depression, however, Barrymore was best remembered for his role as Judge Hardy in the Andy Hardy* film series and as Dr. Gillespie in the Dr. Kildare series of movies. In both roles, Barrymore radiated inner strength, wisdom, and confidence, characteristics that Americans admired during the hard times of the 1930s. By the time of his death on November 15, 1954, Barrymore had made more than 300 films.

SUGGESTED READINGS: Lionel Barrymore, *We Barrymores*, 1951; James Hotsilibas-Davis, *The Barrymores: The Royal Family in Hollywood*, 1981; *New York Times*, November 16, 1954.

BARUCH, BERNARD. Bernard Baruch, a leading figure in the Democratic Party during the early twentieth century, was born to a Jewish family in Camden, South Carolina, on August 19, 1870. In 1881, the Baruch family moved to New York City. He graduated from the City College of New York in 1889, and after trying his hand at a number of jobs, he joined A. A. Hausman and Company, a Wall Street brokerage firm. Within a few years, Baruch was a full partner in the firm and owned his own seat on the New York Stock Exchange. He was also a multimillionaire because of shrewd investments in the sulfur, gold, rubber, and copper industries.

A faithful Democrat, Baruch contributed generously to the party and soon became an influential broker in political issues at the state and national levels. In the election of 1916, he was a major contributor to the reelection campaign of President Woodrow Wilson, and in 1918 Wilson named him to head the War Industries Board, a powerful government agency charged with organizing the business community to guarantee enough industrial production to achieve a military victory in Europe. Baruch proved to be an able administrator. By the end of World War I, Baruch had become one of the most influential people in the country.

During the 1920s, Baruch became closely connected with the political career of Governor Franklin D. Roosevelt,* and he was an economic and political adviser to the American Farm Bureau Federation* and the U.S. Grain Growers Corporation, both of which gave Roosevelt some caché in the farming community. When Roosevelt won the presidential election of 1932,* Baruch fully expected to get a major cabinet appointment, perhaps even secretary of state. But Roosevelt, always politically astute, knew that having a person of Baruch's stature in Washington, D.C., might eclipse some of his own influence. Baruch was profoundly disappointed when Roosevelt passed him by. He spent the rest of his life as an elder statesman of the Democratic Party, although he was troubled by the drift of the New Deal* and its geometric increases in the size and power of the federal government. Bernard Baruch died on June 20, 1965.

SUGGESTED READING: Jordan A. Schwarz, *The Speculator: Bernard M. Baruch in Washington, 1917–1965*, 1981.

BATHTUB GIN. The term "bathtub gin" was a popular expression during the years of Prohibition between 1921 and 1933. It referred to alcoholic beverages illegally manufactured in people's homes. The term generally fell out of use after ratification of the Twenty-first Amendment* to the Constitution ended Prohibition.

SUGGESTED READING: Paul Sann, *The Lawless Decade*, 1957.

BATMAN. The popular comic book superhero Batman was created in 1939 by eighteen-year-old graphic artist Bob Kane. He sold the character and the story line to Detective Comics, and it proved to be nearly as popular as the Superman* hero. Batman and his sidekick Robin, the "Boy Wonder," battled modern-day, urban desperadoes to protect peace-loving damsels and families. Nineteen-thirty-nine was an auspicious year for Batman's debut, since the problems America faced seemed so intransigent. The economy remained sluggish and mired in the Great Depression, and Europe was hurtling toward war. The ease with which Batman solved problems appealed to the battered American people.

SUGGESTED READINGS: Michael Benton, *The Comic Book in America*, 1989; Will Jacobs and Gerard Jones, *The Comic Book Heroes*, 1985.

BEER TAX ACT OF 1932. In the election of 1932,* the Democratic Party platform called for an end to Prohibition by repeal of the Eighteenth Amendment. When Franklin D. Roosevelt* won the presidential election, and with the Twenty-first Amendment* rapidly approaching ratification, he urged Congress to pass the Beer Tax Act, which would legalize the production and distribution of alcoholic beverages with no more than 3.2 percent alcohol. Congress passed the measure, and it became law on March 22, 1933.

SUGGESTED READINGS: Joseph M. Rowe, Jr., "The Beer Tax Act of 1932," in James S. Olson, ed., *Historical Dictionary of the New Deal*, 1985; *U.S. Statutes at Large*, 48 (1933), 16–20.

BELIEVE IT OR NOT. *Believe It or Not* was one of radio's popular programs during the 1930s. It premiered on NBC Radio on April 14, 1930, and remained on the air until 1948, alternating back and forth from NBC to the Blue Network, CBS, and Mutual Broadcasting. The brainchild of Robert L. Ripley, *Believe It or Not* featured bizarre facts and freak shows. Ripley used dramatizations and location broadcasts to enliven the stories. Part circus and part journalism, *Believe It or Not* garnered a loyal radio audience throughout its existence.

SUGGESTED READING: Bob Consodine, *Ripley, the Modern Marco Polo: The Life and Times of the Creator of "Believe It or Not,"* 1961.

BELL, DANIEL WAFENA. Daniel Bell was born on July 23, 1891, in Kinderhook, Illinois. Soon after finishing high school and a bookkeeping course, he went to work as a bookkeeper for the Department of the Treasury, and he spent the rest of his life in Washington, D.C. Bright and hardworking, he rose through the ranks of the civil service, and in 1919 he became the accountant in charge of foreign loans. One year later, Bell was appointed assistant to the assistant secretary of the treasury, and his influence in the department grew. He became assistant commissioner of accounts and deposits in 1924 and commissioner of accounts and deposits in 1931. In 1933, President Franklin D. Roosevelt* created the Bureau of the Budget to centralize government financial operations, and he named Bell as director of the bureau. At the same time, he became an assistant to Secretary of the Treasury Henry Morganthau, Jr.* Bell insisted, however, that he be named acting director of the budget, since he did not want to give up his civil service status with the federal government. Jobs were hard to come by during the Great Depression, and Bell realized that a civil service appointment was almost a guarantee of permanent employment.

It was an auspicious time to be director of the budget because of the increasing role that federal spending was playing in the American political economy. During the 1930s, federal spending increased exponentially, especially when Keynesian ideas came to the forefront of economic policy. Bell found himself on central stage during a period of intellectual revolution. Bell served as director of the budget until 1939. In 1940, Bell became undersecretary of the treasury. After World War II, Bell left government service and served as president of the American Security and Trust Company in Washington, D.C., from 1946 to 1959. He died on October 3, 1971.

SUGGESTED READING: *New York Times*, October 4, 1971.

BELL, JAMES "COOL PAPA." James "Cool Papa" Bell was born in Starkville, Mississippi, on May 17, 1903. When he was thirteen his family moved to St. Louis, where Bell dropped out of school and went to work slaughtering cattle in a packinghouse. He made small change playing sandlot baseball and quickly became recognized for his extraordinary talent. Bell signed a contract with the St. Louis Stars of the Negro National League in 1922, and he spent eleven years with the Stars. He combined extraordinary speed on the base paths with the ability to consistently hit at over a .400 batting average. Playing in the Negro Leagues was not easy. The season often exceeded 200 games a year, and players traveled by bus and stayed in cheap hotels, when they could afford that. Eventually, he played for the Kansas City Monarchs, the Homestead Grays, and the Chicago American Giants. In the black community, and among whites who watched the Negro Leagues, Bell was considered one of the finest players— white or black—of the era. He also brought poor southern and northern blacks out to ballparks during the 1930s where they could forget, if only temporarily, their economic troubles. Bell retired in 1946, spent several years scouting for a number of major league teams, and then worked as a night watchman. He was inducted into the Baseball Hall of Fame in 1974. James "Cool Papa" Bell died on June 12, 1991.

SUGGESTED READING: Martin Appel and Burt Goldblatt, *Baseball's Best: The Hall of Fame Gallery*, 1980.

BENNY, JACK. Jack Benny was born Benjamin Kubelsky on February 14, 1894, in Chicago, Illinois. He was the son of immigrant Jews from Lithuania. A talented violinist, he began going on local tours, and during a stint in the U.S. Navy during World War I, he added jokes and a deadpan delivery to his act. He took Jack Benny as his professional stage name. During the 1920s, he became a hit on the vaudeville circuit, and in 1932 he got a break and hosted for CBS *The Canada Dry Program*, a comedy and variety show. Benny's radio show became *The Chevrolet Program* for NBC in 1933, the *General Tire Show* for NBC in 1934, and *The Jell-O Program* for NBC from 1935 to 1942. The cast came to include wisecracking Phil Harris, Eddie Anderson as the irreverent black valet Rochester Van Jones, and Dennis Day. The program became famous for Benny's good-natured, on-the-air arguing with other cast members, his deadpan self-deprecating humor, his classic tight-fisted stinginess, and his lighthearted ridiculing of his sponsors. From that base on network radio, Benny launched a career that eventually made him America's most beloved comic. Jack Benny died on December 26, 1974.

SUGGESTED READINGS: Joan Benny and Jack Benny, *Sunday Nights at Seven: The Jack Benny Story*, 1990; Mary Livingstone Benny and Hilliard Marks, with Marcia Borie, *Jack Benny: A Biography*, 1978; Irving Fein, *Jack Benny: An Intimate Biography*, 1976.

BERGEN, EDGAR. Edgar Bergen was born on February 16, 1903, in Chicago, Illinois, to Swedish immigrant parents. The family later moved to Iowa to run a dairy farm. A natural-born entertainer, the younger Bergen, at age eleven, ordered through the mail a book titled *The Wizard's Manual*, from which he learned the art of the ventriloquist. He also developed magic tricks, sang and danced, and told funny stories. Then he built himself a dummy/doll and began performing for family members and friends. In high school, he paid a woodcarver to create a more realistic dummy for him, and Bergen then performed skits in which he satirized teachers, friends, and public figures. Since the voice of the dummy seemed to be making the comments, he became quite popular.

After high school, Bergen attended Northwestern University as a pre-med student, but he dropped out to hit the road with his act—"Edgar Bergen, the Voice Illusionist." Bergen saw the world, performing throughout Europe, South America, the United States, and Canada, and he then ended up doing vaudeville in New York City. In 1936, Bergen landed an appearance on Rudy Vallee's* *Royal Gelatin Hour* on NBC Radio, and he was an immediate hit. NBC gave him his own show in 1937.

Bergen remained on the air for the next twenty years, with either *The Edgar Bergen/Charlie McCarthy Show* or what was sometimes known as *The Charlie McCarthy Show*. The show brought the biggest stars of radio, vaudeville, Broadway, and film to visit with Bergen and his sarcastic dummy Charlie McCarthy. McCarthy flirted with the women guests and insulted the men. Bergen's daughter Candice, who would become a film and television star in her own right in the 1980s and 1990s, began appearing on the show when she was six years old. During the 1950s, Americans revered Bergen as the godfather of comedy-variety shows. After a performance at Caesar's Palace in Las Vegas, Bergen died quietly on October 1, 1978.

SUGGESTED READINGS: *New York Times*, October 2, 1978; Skip Press, *Candice and Edgar Bergen*, 1995.

BERLE, ADOLF AUGUSTUS. Adolf Augustus Berle, one of the least-well-known but most influential Americans during the Great Depression, was born on January 29, 1895, in Boston, Massachusetts. His father was a Congregational minister, but the younger Berle had little interest in the ministry. A child prodigy, he graduated from Harvard when he was eighteen years old, then earned a law degree there three years later. Brilliant, highly analytical, and very hardworking, Berle impressed everybody around him with the quality of his intellect. During World War I, he served in several U.S. Army intelligence units, and he continued that role on assignment to the Paris Peace Conference in 1919. After the war, Berle became a professor of law at Columbia University and practiced as a corporation attorney.

During the 1920s, he carefully studied the operation of the economy and began writing about it. In 1932, with his coauthor Gardiner Means, Berle published *The Modern Corporation and Private Property*, which many economists credit as being one of the most influential books of the 1930s. In the book, Means and Berle described an economy in which the 200 largest corporations were becoming increasingly influential as more and more economic power became concentrated in them. At the same time, these corporations were becoming increasingly divorced from stockholder or public control. The onset of the Great Depression made *The Modern Corporation* especially influential among economists and public policymakers because much of America was holding the large corporations responsible for the economic debacle. When Franklin D. Roosevelt* and the Democrats took control of Congress and the White House in 1932, Berle's star in America rose commensurately. He served as a member of Roosevelt's so-called Brains Trust,* which had great influence on early New Deal* policies, and Berle wrote FDR's Commonwealth Club speech, which set out a progressive, activist agenda for the New Deal.

Except for a brief role with the Reconstruction Finance Corporation* in 1933, Berle never held an official position in Washington, D.C. He remained in New York City and at Columbia University. Between 1934 and 1937, Berle served as chamberlain of New York City under Mayor Fiorello La Guardia.* He also played a key role in 1934–1935 formulating the plan to refinance New York City's bonded indebtedness to stave off bankruptcy. Throughout the 1930s,

Berle kept up a chatty but intellectual correspondence with President Franklin D. Roosevelt, always beginning his letters with "Dear Caesar." In 1938, Roosevelt finally brought him to Washington, D.C., as an assistant secretary of state, but the president primarily used him as an adviser concerning the federal government's approach to the recession of 1937–1938.

Two of Berle's ideas played key roles in the New Deal. During the first Roosevelt administration, Berle insisted that the nation's money markets needed to be stabilized so that credit could flow to worthy business borrowers; otherwise, the economy would never get out of the depression. Berle's ideas could be found in the Reconstruction Finance Corporation, the Emergency Banking Act of 1933,* the Banking Acts of 1933* and 1935,* and such New Deal agencies as the Federal Deposit Insurance Corporation* and the Commodity Credit Corporation.* Second, Berle always voiced opposition to the antitrust movement, especially when it gained momentum in the late 1930s. He believed that the rise of large corporations was inevitable and that antitrust policy per se made little economic sense. Instead, Berle argued, the federal government should regulate and direct larger economy through planning.

Berle remained at his post as assistant secretary of state until 1944, when FDR appointed him U.S. ambassador to Brazil. In 1946, Berle returned to the United States. He continued to advise the Harry Truman administration in hemispheric affairs, and in 1961, he helped draft the John F. Kennedy administration's Latin American initiative that became known as the Alliance for Progress. Between 1949 and 1971, Berle also served as president of the Twentieth Century Fund. He died on February 18, 1971.

SUGGESTED READINGS: Elliot A. Rosen, *Hoover, Roosevelt, and the Brains Trust: From Depression to New Deal*, 1977; *New York Times*, February 19, 1971; Jordan Schwarz, *Liberal: Adolf A. Berle and the Vision of an American Era*, 1987.

BERLIN, IRVING. Irving Berlin was born Israel Baline on May 11, 1888, in Temun, Russia. When he was twelve years old, the family immigrated to New York City, and Berlin was raised on the Lower East Side of Manhattan. Berlin's father died after their arrival in the United States, and the younger Berlin had to go to work to help support his family. He sold newspapers and sang and danced in clubs and saloons, but his musical talents were obvious, and in 1909 he began writing songs professionally, even though he could not read music or play the piano except in F sharp on the black key. His first hit—"Alexander's Ragtime Band" (1911)—was a huge hit, selling 2 million copies in four years. During World War I, he wrote *Yip, Yap, Yaphank* (1918) and then "Oh How I Hate to Get Up in the Morning."

When the war ended, Berlin founded his own publishing house—Irving Berlin, Inc.—and built the Music Box Theater in New York. He was extraordinarily successful and became an American icon. During the 1930s, Berlin wrote a series of highly successful musicals and musical comedies. Among them were

As Thousands Cheer (1933), *Top Hat* (1935), *Follow the Fleet*, (1936) and *Louisiana Purchase* (1939). Film musicals were extremely popular during the years of the Great Depression, and Berlin was for all intents and purposes the architect of the genre. Eventually, Berlin published nearly 800 songs, and many of them—such as "Easter Parade," "White Christmas," and "This Is the Army"—became a permanent part of American popular culture. By the time of his death on September 22, 1989, Berlin had become an icon in his own right, the godfather of American popular music.

SUGGESTED READINGS: Philip Furia, *Irving Berlin: A Life in Song*, 1998; *New York Times*, September 23, 1989; Barbara Salsini, *Irving Berlin: Master Composer of Twentieth Century Songs*, 1972.

BETHUNE, MARY McLEOD. Mary McLeod Bethune was born in South Carolina in 1875. Her parents were emancipated slaves. She received her education at the Scotia Seminary in Concord, North Carolina, and at the Moody Bible Institute in Chicago. She then returned to the South to teach school. In 1904, she established an industrial school for black industrial workers, and the school eventually evolved into Bethune-Cookman College. Bethune served as president of the college, and it gave her a forum that eventually helped give her a national profile on education and civil rights. She also played key leadership roles in the National Council of Negro Women, the National Urban League, and the National Association for the Advancement of Colored People.* In 1935, President Franklin D. Roosevelt* named Bethune his special adviser on minority affairs, and as such she became the most influential black woman in the country and a member of the so-called black cabinet.* The fact that she was a close friend of First Lady Eleanor Roosevelt* only enhanced her influence. Bethune died in 1955.

SUGGESTED READING: Rackman Holt, *Mary McLeod Bethune. A Biography*, 1964.

BETTY AND BOB. *Betty and Bob* was one of radio's soap operas during the 1930s. Dripping with melodrama, the show was the story of lower-class working girl Betty who worked as a secretary to tycoon Bob Drake. The plot lines revolved around love, hate, hubris, jealousy, greed, betrayal, divorce, and madness, just what an escapist America wanted to hear during the Great Depression. *Betty and Bob* premiered on the Blue Network on October 10, 1932, as a daily, weekday, fifteen-minute program. General Mills sponsored the program, and its target audience was housewives. Over the years, the leads were played by such prominent actors and actresses as Don Ameche, Agnes Moorhead, Edmond O'Brien, and Arlene Francis. The last network broadcast of *Betty and Bob* was on March 15, 1940.

SUGGESTED READING: John Dunning, *On the Air: The Encyclopedia of Old-Time Radio*, 1998.

BLACK, EUGENE ROBERT. Eugene Black was born in 1872 in Atlanta, Georgia. He graduated from the University of Georgia and then attended the University of Georgia law school without graduating. Black read law privately and was admitted to the Georgia bar. He then practiced law privately for twenty years, and in 1921 he became president of the Atlanta Trust Company. In 1927, President Calvin Coolidge appointed him governor of the Federal Reserve Bank of Atlanta. A fiscal and business conservative, Black warned throughout the decade that the banking system in particular and the economy in general were headed for a colossal liquidity crisis, but few people listened to him. When the banking system collapsed in 1932–1933, Black's caché rose, and in May 1933, President Franklin D. Roosevelt* appointed him to head the Federal Reserve Board* in Washington. There he played critical roles in the bank holiday,* the reconstruction of the banking system, the Securities Act of 1933,* the Banking Act of 1933,* and the broadening of the powers of the Reconstruction Finance Corporation.* Black suddenly fell ill and died on December 19, 1934.

SUGGESTED READINGS: Helen M. Burns, *The American Banking Community and New Deal Banking Reforms, 1933–1935*, 1974; *New York Times*, December 20, 1935.

BLACK, HUGO LAFAYETTE. Hugo Black was born in Harlan, Alabama, on February 27, 1886. Blessed with a keen intellect and an indefatigable sense of determination, Black came to transcend his roots in rural Clay County. He studied law for two years at the University of Alabama and then went into private practice. He became active in local Democratic Party politics and in 1926 parlayed that into a seat in the U.S. Senate. A populist in his political views, Black became during the 1920s an inveterate opponent of big business and during the 1930s an ardent backer of President Franklin D. Roosevelt* and the New Deal.*

In 1937, as part of his plan to reorient the Supreme Court, Roosevelt nominated Black as an associate justice. Soon after his appointment, a storm of controversy erupted when it became widely known that between 1923 and 1926 Black had been a member of the Ku Klux Klan. Although Black claimed that Klan membership had been a prerequisite to practicing law in Alabama in the 1910s and 1920s, liberals coined the term "Black Day" to describe his first day on the Supreme Court. During the rest of his career, however, Black proved to be a foe of laissez-faire and a proponent of individual civil liberties. He took a literalist approach to the First Amendment and felt it was not the business of the courts to overturn the work of Congress and the state legislatures when they acted in the public interest. During the late 1930s he became part of the liberal majority that allowed New Deal legislation to stand and permitted the emergence of a modern political economy. Black remained a justice of the Supreme Court until his death on September 25, 1971.

SUGGESTED READINGS: Howard Ball, *Hugo Black: Cold Steel Warrior*, 1996; Howard Ball, *The Vision and the Dream of Hugo L. Black: An Examination of a Judicial Philosophy*, 1975; Gerald T. Dunne, *Hugo Black and the Judicial Revolution*, 1977; Tinsley E. Yarbrough, *Mr. Justice Black and His Critics*, 1988.

BLACK, JOHN DONALD. John Donald Black was the intellectual architect of New Deal* farm policy. He was born in Jefferson County, Wisconsin, on June 6, 1883. Between 1909 and 1918, Black earned bachelor's, master's, and Ph.D. degrees at the University of Wisconsin, specializing in agricultural economics. He specialized in the relationship between the federal government and the farm economy and worked diligently at developing policy approaches to the problem of chronic overproduction, which kept commodity prices too low. In 1927 Black joined the economics faculty at Harvard, and with the 1929 publication of his book *Agricultural Reform in the United States*, he became a leading light in the field of agricultural economics. Black argued in the book for government-directed acreage reductions that would reduce crop surpluses and increase commodity prices.

Black's ideas proved to be extremely popular among liberal agricultural economists but anathema to conservatives, who preferred to let market forces do their work. In 1933, when Franklin D. Roosevelt* won the presidency and named liberal Henry Wallace, Jr.,* as secretary of agriculture, Black's ideas found a powerful venue. They became the basis for the Agricultural Adjustment Act of 1933.* The legislation created the Agricultural Adjustment Administration* (AAA), which paid farmers to reduce the number of acres they put into production. Black continued to teach and write. His book *The Dairy Industry and the AAA* appeared in 1935, and in 1938, *Three Years of the AAA* appeared. In 1942 he wrote *Parity, Parity, Parity*. Black taught at Harvard until his retirement in 1956. He died on April 12, 1960.

SUGGESTED READING: *New York Times*, April 13, 1960.

BLACK CABINET. Journalists first coined the term "black cabinet" to refer to a small circle of black people centered around Frederick Douglass, who had some influence in the Republican Party during the 1870s and 1880s. The term was revived during the 1930s and sometimes referred to as the "black brains trust," a group of African Americans influential in the New Deal.* President Franklin D. Roosevelt* was interested in completing the shift of black voters away from the Republican Party and to the Democratic Party. In order to do that, he needed to develop policies that would benefit black people, and he needed to raise his profile among them.

Secretary of the Interior Harold Ickes* played a key role in assembling the so-called black cabinet. Ickes had once served as head of the Chicago chapter of the National Association for the Advancement of Colored People,* and because of that experience, he became the president's liaison between the administration and the black community. As a first step, Ickes ended segregation in the Department of the Interior. He next hired a contingent of black engineers, accountants, architects, and attorneys. He named William Hastie, a black lawyer, as assistant solicitor in the department, and he appointed Robert C. Weaver* as his adviser on black problems. Mary McLeod Bethune* was appointed as director of minority affairs in the National Youth Administration,* and Robert L. Vann,* editor of the *Pittsburgh Courier*, worked as a special assistant in the Justice Department.

All of these individuals met informally and periodically to discuss the challenges of the black community, and they exerted all the pressure they could to make sure that African Americans received their fair share of government jobs and their fair share of government grants and loans. First Lady Eleanor Roosevelt* also cultivated a close relationship with members of the black cabinet, and in doing so she helped elevate the New Deal in the minds of most black people. In the end, the New Deal's initiatives for the black community were not much more than symbolic gestures, but it was enough to accelerate the conversion of most African Americans to the Democratic Party.

SUGGESTED READINGS: Robert H. Brisbane, *The Black Vanguard: Origins of the Negro Social Revolution, 1900–1960*, 1970; John B. Kirby, *Black Americans in the Roosevelt Era: Liberals and Race*, 1980; Patricia Sullivan, *Days of Hope: Race and Diversity in the New Deal Era*, 1996.

"BLACK MONDAY" (October 28, 1929). Journalists and economists used the term "Black Monday" to describe October 28, 1929, when the stock market dropped an unprecedented 49 points on a high volume of 9,250,000 shares. Economic historians look back to "Black Monday" as the day in which the Great Crash* of 1929 went into full speed.

SUGGESTED READING: John Kenneth Galbraith, *The Great Crash 1929*, 1955.

"BLACK MONDAY" (May 27, 1935). Journalists used the term "Black Monday" to describe May 27, 1935, when three Supreme Court decisions gutted much of Franklin D. Roosevelt's* early New Deal* legislation. In *Louisville Joint Stock Land Bank v. Radford*, the Court declared the Frazier-Lemke Act unconstitutional because it violated the contract clause of the Constitution by extending mortgage relief to debt-ridden farmers. The Court then attacked the president's ability to replace the members of government regulatory agencies in order to make the federal bureaucracy more amenable to New Deal policies. In a unanimous decision, the Court ruled in *Humphrey's Executor v. United States* that the president did not possess such summary authority. Finally, in *Schechter Poultry Corporation v. United States*,* the Court invalidated the National Recovery Administration* on the grounds that it was trying to regulate intrastate commerce when Congress possessed authority only over interstate commerce.

The three decisions enraged President Roosevelt, who accused the justices of employing a "horse-and-buggy definition of interstate commerce" and led to his ill-fated court-packing scheme* of 1937.

SUGGESTED READING: *New York Times*, May 28, 1935.

BLACKSTONE PLANTATION. *Blackstone Plantation* was a popular radio program of the 1930s. It starred husband and wife Frank Crumit and Julia Sanderson and premiered on CBS Radio in 1929. Blackstone Cigars sponsored the program, which consisted of talk, benign humor, music, and an endearing give and take between Crumit and Sanderson. *Blackstone Plantation* remained on the air until 1944.

SUGGESTED READING: John Dunning, *Tune in Yesterday: The Ultimate Encyclopedia of Old-Time Radio, 1925–1976*, 1976.

"BLACK THURSDAY." Journalists and economists used the term "Black Thursday" to describe October 24, 1929, when the stock market traded a record 12,894,000 shares. Although the major stock index only fell from 384 to 372, the number of shares indicated the onset of a panic. Four days later, on Monday, October 28, 1929, the stock market fell dramatically, setting in motion the Great Crash.*

SUGGESTED READING: John Kenneth Galbraith, *The Great Crash 1929*, 1955.

"BLACK TUESDAY." Journalists and economists refer to October 29, 1929, as "Black Tuesday" because the stock market fell a stunning 43 points on more than 16 million of traded shares. Economic historians cite that day as the formal beginning of the Great Crash* of 1929.

SUGGESTED READINGS: John Kenneth Galbraith, *The Great Crash 1929*, 1955; Robert Sobel, *The Great Bull Market: Wall Street in the 1920s*, 1968.

THE BLUE ANGEL. In 1930 German filmmaker Josef von Sternberg made *Der blaue Engel*, or *The Blue Angel*, starring Marlene Dietrich, a relatively unknown actress outside of Germany. Dietrich's performance as Lola Lola—an unredeemable, amoral, sensuous cabaret singer—launched her to international film stardom. Late in 1930, Paramount Studios in Hollywood brought Dietrich to the United States, where she starred in an English version of the film. Lola Lola's blonde, sultry, self-centered demeanor became that of Dietrich herself, who became one of the world's great actresses but who never escaped the confines of Lola Lola's character.

SUGGESTED READINGS: Steven Bach, *Marlene Dietrich: Life and Legend*, 1992; *New York Times*, April 2, 1930.

BLUE EAGLE. The "Blue Eagle" became a symbol of the early New Deal.* It was a symbol of businesses that were voluntarily cooperating with the National Recovery Administration's* program to stimulate an economic recovery.

BOMBSHELL. The film *Bombshell* debuted in New York on October 20, 1931, starring Jean Harlow* as Lola Burns and Lee Tracy as Space Hanlon. A comedic farce, the film revolved around Lola Burns, a platinum-blonde film star nick-named "Bombshell," who lives in a Hollywood mansion and refuses to be seen outdoors without her three sheepdogs and two black maids. She is insufferably self-indulgent and narcissistic, except when the possibility looms of adopting a baby. Lee Tracy is her publicity agent who will do anything to get Burns's name in print, and much of the comedy in the film emanates from his antics and her reactions to them. *Bombshell* was a big hit for Metro-Goldwyn-Mayer in 1931.

SUGGESTED READING: *New York Times*, October 21, 1933.

BONNEVILLE POWER ADMINISTRATION. Once construction on Bon-neville Dam in Oregon was completed, President Franklin D. Roosevelt* created the Bonneville Power Administration (BPA) to handle the sale of electrical power generated by the new government plant. In 1940, Roosevelt gave the BPA authority to market the power produced by the Grand Coulee Dam. Trans-mission lines were built by the Public Works Administration,* another govern-ment agency. In just a matter of a few years, the BPA was the largest producer of electrical power in the Pacific Northwest. Private utility companies could not compete, and the government program terminated construction of new private power projects in the region for the next twenty years.

SUGGESTED READING: Richard Lowitt, *The New Deal and the West*, 1984.

BONNIE AND CLYDE. During a twenty-one-month crime spree in 1933 and 1934, Bonnie and Clyde captured the ghoulish imaginations of millions of Americans. Clyde Barrow, a small-time hoodlum with a few short prison terms in Texas under his belt, teamed up with waitress Bonnie Parker, and together they cut a swath of crime through Missouri, Kansas, Oklahoma, and Texas, robbing banks, gas stations, luncheonettes, restaurants, and bars. Their exploits, exaggerated in the public mind by an uncanny ability to slip through roadblocks and police dragnets, made them pop culture antiheroes. In an age when bankers in suits were foreclosing on farms, homes, and businesses throughout the coun-try, Bonnie and Clyde robbed and killed them, endearing themselves to a certain element of American society. Along with the likes of John Dillinger,* Pretty Boy Floyd, Baby Face Nelson, and Ma Barker, Bonnie and Clyde even devel-oped a Robin Hood persona, occasionally robbing the rich and distributing a few dollars to the poor. Given the fact that none of their heists ever pulled in more than $1,500, they managed to generate an extraordinary volume of newspaper coverage.

But the twelve people they murdered extacted their own revenge. The Federal Bureau of Investigation, the Texas Rangers, and county sheriffs and police chiefs throughout the Midwest made getting Bonnie and Clyde a top priority. They succeeded on May 23, 1934, outside Gibsland, Louisiana. With a tip from the father of one of Bonnie and Clyde's gang members, a Texas Ranger and several duty sheriffs set an ambush for Bonnie and Clyde, virtually executing them in a hail of gunfire.

SUGGESTED READING: E. R. Milner, *The Lives and Times of Bonnie and Clyde*, 1996.

BONUS ARMY. As a payment for their loyal service to the nation during World War I, veterans learned in 1924 that Congress had issued to them compensation, or bonus, certificates. The certificates were due to mature in 1945, at which time the veterans could trade them in for cash or convert them into a pension. But the onset of the Great Depression threw millions of veterans out of work, and many of them demanded early payment of the bonuses. Veterans groups like the American Legion lobbied Congress for enabling legislation, and in February 1931, Congress complied, allowing the veterans to borrow up to 50 percent of the amount of their certificates. But President Herbert Hoover* vetoed the bill for fiscal reasons, claiming that it would bust the federal budget. Congress overrode the veto. Later in the year, sensing a popular political issue, Democrats in Congress began preparing legislation for a complete payout of the bonus.

In May and June 1932, more than 17,000 veterans arrived in Washington, D.C., to demonstrate their support for the legislation. The Hoover administration opposed the law. The veterans, dubbed the "Bonus Expeditionary Force" or the "Bonus Army" by the press, camped out at Anacostia Flats on the outskirts of Washington, D.C. Some of them also took up residence in abandoned government buildings. President Hoover supported, and Congress passed, legislation providing $100,000 for the protestors to use in going home. By early July 1932, all but 2,000 protestors had departed the city. But those left behind were militant about the issue and refused to leave without action of cash redemptions of the bonus certificates.

Near the end of the month, District of Columbia police tried to evict the protestors from government buildings, and a riot ensued in which two policemen and two rioters were killed. The president asked General Douglas MacArthur to use army troops to evict the protestors, and MacArthur accepted the assignment with excessive zeal. On July 29, using tanks, tear gas, sabers, rifle fire, and torches, the troops attacked the veterans and drove them from the buildings and from Anacostia Flats. It was a political nightmare for Hoover, since headlines and photographs of the maneuver found their way into the next day's newspapers. Americans were horrified at the sight of army troops attacking poor veterans. Hoover was appalled at what had happened, and it cost him dearly politically, convincing most Americans that he was an uncaring man detached from the problems of everyday people. Franklin D. Roosevelt,* the Democratic candidate for president in the upcoming November elections, remarked on hearing the news of the attack, "Well, this will elect me."

In 1935 Congressman Wright Patman of Texas, a supporter of veterans groups, sponsored a new bonus bill, but it did not see the light of day until 1936, when the upcoming congressional elections gave it a great deal of political currency. In January 1936, Congress passed the Adjusted Compensation Act, which provided for full payment of the bonuses by allowing the Treasury to issue nine-year, interest-bearing bonds redeemable in cash at any time. President Roosevelt vetoed the measure, but Congress overrode the veto. On June 15, 1936, more than $1.5 billion in bonus bonds were distributed to more than 3 million World War I veterans.

SUGGESTED READINGS: Roger Daniels, *The Bonus March: An Episode of the Great Depression*, 1971; Donald J. Lisio, *The President and Protest: Hoover, Conspiracy, and the Bonus Riot*, 1974.

BOONDOGGLING. During the 1930s, the term "boondoggling" was employed by critics of the New Deal* to describe the uselessness of many government programs and construction projects. Critics were especially likely to use the term in reference to projects by the Civil Works Administration* and the Works Progress Administration,* particularly the work of the Federal Writers' Project,* the Federal Art Project,* the Federal Music Project,* and the Federal Dance Project.*

SUGGESTED READING: Henry G. Leach, "In Praise of Boondoggling," *Forum*, 93 (1935), 321–22.

BOOTLEGGER. The term "bootlegger" emerged in the nineteenth-century American frontier to describe an individual who hid a flask of alcohol by hiding it in his boot. During the years of Prohibition during the 1920s and 1930s, the term "bootlegger" was commonly employed to describe individuals who defied the Eighteenth Amendment to the Constitution by illegally manufacturing and distributing alcohol. Once the Twenty-first Amendment* in 1933 again legalized alcohol, "bootlegger" referred to individuals who continued to manufacture alcohol in defiance of state and local ordinances.

SUGGESTED READING: Norman H. Clark, *Deliver Us from Evil: An Interpretation of American Prohibition*, 1976.

BORAH, WILLIAM EDGAR. William Borah was born on June 29, 1865, near Fairfield, Illinois. He was raised in Kentucky, Illinois, and Kansas, and he briefly attended the University of Kansas. He read law privately and in 1887 was admitted to the bar. Borah then moved to Idaho, where he practiced criminal law and became active in local Republican Party politics. He also served in a number of very high profile prosecutions, including those of William "Big Bill" Haywood, George Pettibone, and Charles Moyer. In 1906 he was elected to the U.S. Senate and quickly proved himself as a progressive Republican in domestic affairs and a confirmed isolationist in foreign policy.

During the 1930s, Borah provided a good deal of support to President Franklin D. Roosevelt* and the Democrats in forging the New Deal.* In particular, he helped push through Congress the Tennessee Valley Authority,* the Securities Exchange Act of 1934, the National Labor Relations Act of 1935,* the Wealth Tax Act of 1935,* the Silver Purchase Act of 1934,* and the Public Utility Holding Company Act of 1935.* At the same time, he fought the president's court-packing scheme* in 1937, and he opposed FDR's interventionist foreign policy. Borah played the leading role in getting the Neutrality Acts* passed. He died on January 19, 1940.

SUGGESTED READINGS: Claudius O. Johnson, *Borah of Idaho*, 1965; Marian C. McKenna, *Borah*, 1961.

BRAINS TRUST. During his tenure as governor of New York (1929–1933), Franklin D. Roosevelt* had displayed a willingness, even enthusiasm, to seek out the counsel of academics in trying to formulate public policy. He did not always take their counsel because he had a shrewd sense of what was politically possible, but more than any other political figure in the United States, he sought to generate programs to solve social and economic problems. That continued during his run for the presidency in 1932 and during the transition months before his inauguration.

In 1932, Governor Roosevelt, like most other Americans, was baffled by the tenacity of the Great Depression. He needed campaign suggestions that would allow him to criticize the Herbert Hoover* administration and to offer policy alternatives of his own. In March 1932, Samuel Rosenman, Roosevelt's general counsel, suggested that a team of academics and intellectuals be formed to develop campaign themes and programs to stimulate an economic recovery. He turned first to Raymond Moley,* a political scientist at Columbia University who had written speeches occasionally for Governor Roosevelt. As a specialist on agriculture policy, Rosenman tabbed Professor Rexford Tugwell,* also of Columbia. Professor Adolf Berle* of the Columbia University Law School was recruited for his expertise on corporate and economic issues. Roosevelt's long-time law partner, Basil O'Conner, also joined the group. Moley served as the de facto head of the group, and they met weekly throughout 1932 to discuss issues and formulate policy. Periodically, the governor sat in on the meetings.

In September 1932, *New York Times* columnist James Kieran dubbed the group the "Brains Trust."

The Brains Trust possessed a definite philosophical bias. They rejected completely the Woodrow Wilson–Louis Brandeis* version of progressivism that defined bigness in business as inherently bad. Instead, Berle, Tugwell, and Moley accepted large corporations as a modern economic reality. The government should not try to break up big business but merely prevent abuse of the public by concentrated corporate power. Regulation, not antitrust, should be the focus of government activity. They recognized that bigness could bring economies of scale to the market and drive down prices. Tugwell went even farther than Berle or Moley in calling for national economic planning, with the federal government, not the market, acting as the arbiter.

During the campaign, Governor Roosevelt had the good sense *not* to let the Brains Trust go public with their proposals. Conservatives would have been up in arms over the proposals, and Roosevelt knew that the election was his to lose. Avoiding controversy was the key to victory since public disillusionment with Hoover ran so deep. But when Roosevelt won the election in November 1932, the Brains Trust played the central role in formulating the administration's policies, and during the "Hundred Days,"* they found expression in such proposals as the National Recovery Administration,* the bank holiday,* and the Agricultural Adjustment Administration.*

SUGGESTED READING: Elliot A. Rosen, *Hoover, Roosevelt, and the Brains Trust: From Depression to New Deal*, 1977.

BRANDEIS, LOUIS DEMBITZ. Louis Dembitz Brandeis was born in Louisville, Kentucky, on November 13, 1856. His parents were economically prosperous immigrants from Bohemia in the Austro-Hungarian Empire. His father ran a very successful wholesale grain storage and marketing business. Brandeis was raised on a steady diet of upper-middle-class, bourgeois German values, with the household full of talk about politics, philosophy, history, and current events. He attended Harvard Law School and then went into private practice in St. Louis, Missouri.

Brandeis was unhappy in St. Louis, however, and he soon returned to Boston where he opened his own law office. Along with Samuel Warren, his friend and partner, Brandeis built one of the city's most successful commercial legal practices. He earned a reputation for his brilliance—an attorney unrivaled as a litigator and one who knew more about his clients' businesses than they did.

Brilliant and blessed with a streak of intellectual pragmatism, Brandeis rejected all forms of ideology and tradition, insisting that ideas and values be tested in the real world. He became a particular opponent of laissez-faire—the notion that government should not concern itself with the operations of the economy. On the contrary, Brandeis became a leading judicial and intellectual light in the progressive movement of the early 1900s. In particular, Brandeis backed the antitrust movement and argued that the powers of the federal government should be employed to guarantee the preservation of a competitive economy.

In 1908, he argued the case of *Muller v. Oregon* before the Supreme Court, defending a state law mandating a maximum ten-hour workday for women. In doing so, Brandeis laid the foundation for what became known as "sociological jurisprudence," the belief that jurists, in deciding cases, should take social and economic issues into account and not be tightly bound to legal tradition. He also urged lawyers to work to achieve independence from major corporations.

Brandeis's reputation among progressive reformers steadily increased, and in 1916, President Woodrow Wilson nominated him to the Supreme Court. Brandeis soon emerged as the heart and soul of the Court's liberal minority. Although the Court's conservative majority during the 1920s and early 1930s consistently limited the power of Congress and the state legislatures to regulate business practices, Brandeis's minority opinions built a foundation for the activist federal bench that emerged in the late 1930s.

During the early 1930s, when the Supreme Court, in such cases as *United States v. Butler* (1936)* and *Schechter Poultry Corporation v. United States* (1935),* systematically tried to dismantle the reforms of the early New Deal,* Brandeis consistently argued in favor of the power of Congress to regulate the affairs of the economy. He was also a close adviser to President Franklin D. Roosevelt,* even though he did so surreptitiously. By the late 1930s, when several conservative justices retired and Roosevelt replaced them with liberals, Brandeis frequently found himself in the majority, and his belief that the federal courts should defer to Congress and the state legislatures in matters of economic policy soon became judicial dogma in the United States. Louis Brandeis died in Washington, D.C., on October 5, 1941.

SUGGESTED READINGS: Alpheus T. Mason, *Brandeis: A Free Man's Life*, 1946; Bruce A. Murphy, *The Brandeis/Frankfurter Connection*, 1982; Philippa Strum, *Louis D. Brandeis: Justice for the People*, 1984; Melvin I. Urofsky and David W. Levy, *Letters of Louis D. Brandeis*, 5 vols., 1971–1979.

BRAVE NEW WORLD. In 1932 Aldous Huxley published his book *Brave New World*. The book was a unique combination of faith in the world's technological future with despair about the prospects for a concomitant spiritual progress. Huxley's novel described the world in the year 632 AF (which meant "After Ford"). The world had been cleansed of its chronic, historical problems— poverty, disease, and war, and through eugenics, a new class structure had been created. New drugs had eliminated depression, anxiety, loneliness, doubt, and insecurity, while the study of art and history had been eliminated as irrelevant. Sexual promiscuity had become an object of government sponsorship. Of course,

Huxley was not endorsing such a future. On the contrary, he viewed such a brave new world as not brave at all but a new form of slavery.

Brave New World became a bestseller in Great Britain, but its secular materialism and endorsement of sexual promiscuity generated heated protest in the United States, at least during the 1930s. In the post–World War II era, however, when American intellectuals became concerned about the social and cultural implications of mass conformity, *Brave New World* acquired a new caché, and the book became required reading in college courses throughout the country.

SUGGESTED READINGS: Aldous Huxley, *Brave New World*, 1932; Harold H. Watts, *Aldous Huxley*, 1969.

BREADLINES. After 1929, the term "breadline" was used by journalists to describe the lines of unemployed men and women waiting outside soup kitchens, urban missions for the homeless, and government relief stations for food.

SUGGESTED READING: Paul Sann, *The Lawless Decade*, 1957.

BROWDER, EARL. Earl Browder, America's leading communist, was born in Wichita, Kansas, on May 20, 1891. Politically precocious, he joined the Socialist Party in 1906, and in 1914 he formed the League for Democratic Control to keep the United States out of World War I. He eventually served time in state and federal penitentiaries for evading the draft and for conspiring to block the draft. In 1920 he joined the Communist Party and then traveled widely in the Soviet Union and China, where he received ideological training and worked with labor union organization. In 1936, Browder ran for president on the Communist Party ticket, but he received only 80,159 votes. In the election of 1940,* that number went down to 46,251. That year, Browder was sentenced to four years in prison for passport violations. Concerned that Browder's civil rights had been violated, President Franklin D. Roosevelt* pardoned him in 1943. Browder died on June 27, 1973.

SUGGESTED READINGS: Art Casciato, "Earl Browder," in James S. Olson, ed., *Historical Dictionary of the New Deal*, 1985; James Gilbert Ryan, "The Making of a Native Marxist: The Early Career of Earl Browder," *Review of Politics*, 39 (1977), 332–62; James Ryan, *Earl Browder: The Failure of American Communism*, 1997.

BROWN V. MISSISSIPPI (1936). *Brown v. Mississippi* was an early victory for the civil rights movement in the United States. Three African American tenant farmers had been convicted of murdering a well-to-do white cotton planter, but the only evidence against them had been their own confessions, which had been extracted by a Mississippi sheriff after brutal jail-house beatings. During the trial, even though prosecution witnesses readily admitted to the beatings, the presiding judge allowed the confessions to be admitted into evidence.

A jury unanimously convicted the defendants and sentenced them to death. On appeal, the Mississippi Supreme Court upheld the convictions.

The National Association for the Advancement of Colored People* helped finance an appeal, arguing that the defendants' Fourteenth Amendment right to due process of law had been denied them. In a unanimous opinion written by Chief Justice Charles Evans Hughes,* the U.S. Supreme Court ruled on February 17, 1936, that confessions extracted after physical brutality on the part of law enforcement officials could not be admitted into evidence; otherwise, the right of criminal defendants to due process would be violated.

SUGGESTED READING: 297 U.S. 278 (1936).

BUCK ROGERS IN THE TWENTY-FIFTH CENTURY. *Buck Rogers in the Twenty-fifth Century* was a popular juvenile science fiction serial that premiered on CBS Radio on November 7, 1932. It was based on the popular comic strip of John F. Dille, Phil Nowlan, and Dick Calkins. The plot revolved around the young Buck Rogers, who while surveying an abandoned mine is trapped by a strange gas that keeps him in a state of suspended animation for 500 years. He awakes to become an adventurer in the space age, fighting and foiling galactic villains.

SUGGESTED READING: John Dunning, *On the Air: The Encyclopedia of Old-Time Radio*, 1998.

BULL MARKET. During the 1920s, the stock market underwent unprecedented growth in a mania of speculation. In 1921, the New York Stock Exchange composite index stood at 54. It then increased to 65 in 1923, 106 in 1924, 245 in 1927, and 449 in 1929. These extraordinary gains were not tied, however, to improving dividends and corporate profits. American investors had dumped World War I profits into the stock market, and because the war had brought about an enormous transfer of wealth from Europe to the United States, those funds were huge. Republican policies during the 1920s—tax cuts on the wealthy and reductions in the federal debt—directed even more money into the securities markets. Corporations began directing profits into the market, as did small investors who pumped money from savings accounts into Wall Street. The result of such an infusion of cash was the greatest bull market in history. When the crash came in October 1929, it was an abrupt drop that became a free fall. The greatest bull market in history became the greatest bear market in history. By 1931 the New York Stock Exchange composite index stood at only 51, and it fell to 37 in 1932, more than wiping out the gains of the previous decade and sending the country into the Great Depression.

SUGGESTED READINGS: John Kenneth Galbraith, *The Great Crash 1929*, 1955; Robert Sobel, *The Great Bull Market: Wall Street in the 1920s*, 1968.

BURNS AND ALLEN. The comedy team of George Burns and his wife Gracie Allen was among the most popular entertainment acts of the 1930s. Gracie was born in San Francisco on July 26, 1905, and George was born as George Birnbaum in New York, on January 20, 1896. They met at a Union Hill, New Jersey, vaudeville theater and decided to form a comedy team. At first, Allen played the straight man and Burns delivered the comedy lines, but audiences happened to find Allen's lines hilariously funny, and the two soon switched roles. They married on January 27, 1926. In 1929, during a vaudeville tour in London, a BBC producer noticed their act and put them on radio, and they were a hit. They returned to New York, and in 1932, CBS gave them a Monday evening prime-time spot. Gracie played the wacky, hare-brained woman and George the long-suffering foil. In one form or another, their radio program remained on the air for nearly twenty years, making Burns and Allen the country's most well-known comedy act.

SUGGESTED READINGS: Cheryl Blythe and Susan Sackett, *Say Goodnight Gracie! The Story of Burns and Allen*, 1986; George Burns, *Gracie: A Love Story*, 1988.

BUSINESS ADVISORY COUNCIL. In June 1933 Secretary of Commerce Daniel Roper* established the Business Advisory and Planning Council, later known as the Business Advisory Council (BAC), to provide President Franklin D. Roosevelt* with input from the business community on how to best stimulate the economy. The BAC included forty-one of the most powerful businessmen in the country, including Arthur Sloan of General Motors, Robert Wood of Sears Roebuck, Walter Gifford of American Telephone and Telegraph, and Pierre du Pont. Gerard Swope of General Motors chaired the BAC.

There was a brief political honeymoon between the BAC and the Roosevelt administration, but the direction of the New Deal* soon troubled them. Such laws as the Securities Act of 1933* and the Securities Exchange Act of 1934 alienated most big businessmen, who believed that the New Deal had brought about a dangerous accumulation of power in the federal government. Many BAC members resigned in 1934 and 1935, and in 1935 and 1937, the BAC called for fiscal retrenchment and a balanced federal budget. By that time, of course, Roosevelt considered them completely irrelevant. The rise of Keynesian economics, in which the federal government used tax and spending techniques to stimulate the economy, alienated the remaining members of the Business Advisory Council. At the same time, however, the Business Advisory Council did not represent any ideological, laissez-faire point of view. They supported the Banking Acts of 1933* and 1935* and the Social Security Act of 1935* and were not averse to the idea of national economic planning.

SUGGESTED READING: Robert M. Collins, "Positive Business Responses to the New Deal: The Roots of the Committee for Economic Development, 1933–1942," *Business History Review*, 52 (1978), 369–91.

BUSINESS CONFERENCES OF 1929. When the stock market crashed in October 1929, President Herbert Hoover* was convinced that the economic pain would be short term. In fact, he believed that the crash might actually be good in the long term for the economy because it would pop the speculative bubble and redirect investment capital back into more productive enterprises, which he was convinced would stimulate the economy. For Hoover, the key to economic recovery was the restoration and preservation of confidence. To convince major corporations not to cut jobs and spending in a panicky mode, the president convened a series of conferences for executives in manufacturing, finance, railroads, construction, and public utilities. The conferences were held during November 19–23, 1929, and when they were concluded, three initiatives had been launched. The National Business Survey Conference consisted of 170 trade associations that, through the national Chamber of Commerce, would work to maintain wages and stimulate new investment. The National Building Survey Conference would work to stimulate new construction. Finally, a new division of public construction in the Department of Commerce would try to accelerate federal public works construction projects.

The long-term achievements of the business conferences were paltry, to say the least. Individual corporate leaders did not have Hoover's vision, or at least they could not afford his vision. They had to meet the needs of stockholders and could not afford to maintain wages or increase investment spending in the face of declining sales. In 1930, terrible quarterly earnings reports forced them into massive retrenchment and downsizing, cutting the workforce and new spending. It was exactly what President Hoover had hoped to avoid, and it strengthened the assumptions of some that only the federal government would have the authority and the resources to have a significant impact on the economy.

SUGGESTED READINGS: Martin L. Fausold, *The Presidency of Herbert C. Hoover*, 1985; Ellis W. Hawley, *The Great War and the Search for a Modern Order: A History of the American People and Their Institutions, 1917–1933*, 1979; *New York Times*, November 20–24, 1930.

C

CAGNEY, JAMES FRANCIS, JR. James "Jimmy" Cagney was born on July 17, 1899, on the Lower East Side of Manhattan in New York City. He was of Irish-Norwegian descent and grew up poor in a tough neighborhood. Cagney graduated from Stuyvesant High School and enrolled briefly at Columbia University, but he had to drop out to work and help support his widowed mother and four brothers and sisters. A talented athlete and dancer, Cagney found work on vaudeville, and in 1920 he landed a role in the Broadway musical *Pitter Patter*. At five feet eight inches, he was chunky, muscular, and ethnic, able to speak with Irish and Yiddish accents, and he could play a gangster as well as a comedian. Throughout the 1920s, Cagney worked the vaudeville circuit and Broadway, taking any part that would put some money in his pocket.

Cagney's break came in 1930 when he won a starring role in the melodrama *Penny Arcade*, playing a cowardly killer, and Warner Brothers made the film *Sinners' Holiday* out of the play. Cagney signed a film contract. In 1931, he became a Hollywood star with his portrayal of a gangster in *The Public Enemy*.* The film was a blockbuster that launched in Hollywood the new genre of gangster movies. He followed that up with a series of films, including *Footlight Parade* (1933), *Midsummer Night's Dream* (1935), *Frisco Kid* (1935), *Boy Meets Girl* (1938), *City of Conquest* (1940), and *The Strawberry Blonde* (1941). During the 1930s, Cagney was also a devoted Democrat and supporter of Franklin D. Roosevelt* and the New Deal.*

His subsequent career was just as distinguished. He won an Academy Award for his portrayal of George M. Cohan in *Yankee Doodle Dandy* (1942), and audiences especially remember him in such films as *Mister Roberts* (1955), *Man of a Thousand Faces* (1957), *Shake Hands with the Devil* (1959), and *The Gallant Hours* (1960). A leading light of Hollywood's golden age, Cagney died on March 30, 1986.

SUGGESTED READINGS: James Cagney, *Cagney on Cagney*, 1976; *New York Times*, March 31, 1986.

CALDWELL, ERSKINE. Erskine Caldwell was born in White Oak, Georgia, in 1903. He studied at Erskine College in South Carolina and the University of Virginia and then went to work as a reporter for *The Atlanta Journal*. Caldwell wrote short stories on the side and in 1926 moved to Maine, where he could spend more time writing fiction. *Scribner's Magazine* began publishing some of his work and then Scribner's published Caldwell's two most important works— *American Earth* (1930) and *Tobacco Road** (1932). Both novels dealt with poverty-stricken Georgia sharecropping families. So did Caldwell's third novel, *God's Little Acre* (1933). With his wife Margaret Bourke-White, the renowned photographer, Caldwell wrote *You Have Seen Their Faces* (1937), which depicted the poverty-stricken misery of poor black and white southern farmers. The body of Caldwell's work during the 1930s brought to the attention of millions of Americans the depth of southern poverty and helped lead to the Resettlement Administration* and the Farm Security Administration.* Although Caldwell continued to write until his death on April 11, 1987, his post-1940 work did not have nearly the influence.

SUGGESTED READINGS: Donald V. Coers, "Erskine Caldwell," in James S. Olson, ed., *Historical Dictionary of the New Deal*, 1985; James Korges, *Erskine Caldwell*, 1969; Scott MacDonald, *Critical Essays on Erskine Caldwell*, 1981.

CALLING ALL CARS. *Calling All Cars* was one of radio's first programs to dramatize crime stories. It premiered on CBS Radio on November 29, 1933, and remained on the air until September 8, 1939. The program had no superstar cast, and each weekly program tracked a crime, its investigation, and punishment of the perpetrators. Its only continuing character was Sgt. Jesse Rosenquist of the Los Angeles Police Department.

SUGGESTED READING: John Dunning, *On the Air: The Encyclopedia of Old-Time Radio*, 1998.

CANTOR, EDDIE. Eddie Cantor was born Edward Israel Iskowitz on January 31, 1892, in New York City. His talent for entertaining—singing, dancing, and storytelling—was obvious even when he was a child, and by the time of World War I he had already won a number of juicy roles on Broadway, usually playing an innocent young man who suddenly discovers women, alcohol, ideas, and culture. During the 1920s, Cantor appeared in a string of Ziegfeld Follies productions and became one of show business's key performers. During the early 1930s, he made the move to cinema, starring in such Busby Berkeley productions as *Whoopee* (1930), *Palmy Days* (1931), *The Kid from Spain* (1932), and *Roman Scandal* (1933).

But Cantor found his greatest fame during the 1930s on radio. In 1930 he made several appearances on the *Rudy Vallee Show*, singing and telling jokes, and audiences responded so well that in 1931 he got his own show. *The Eddie Cantor Show* premiered on NBC Radio and within months was the most popular radio show in the country. Cantor's mix of talk, comedy, and singing proved endearing during the bleak years of the Great Depression. By the 1950s, Cantor had made the move to television, transplanting his talk format and variety to Hollywood. Eddie Cantor died on October 10, 1964.

SUGGESTED READINGS: Eddie Cantor, *My Life Is in Your Hands*, 1932; Eddie Cantor, *Take My Life*, 1957; *New York Times*, October 11, 1964; John Dunning, *Tune in Yesterday: The Ultimate Encyclopedia of Old-Time Radio, 1925–1976*, 1976.

CARDOZO, BENJAMIN NATHAN. Benjamin Nathan Cardozo was born in New York City on May 24, 1877. A descendant of Spanish and Portuguese Jews, Cardozo possessed a great respect for learning and academics. He graduated from Columbia College and then took his law degree there. After leaving Columbia, Cardozo practiced law privately in New York City until being appointed to the New York Court of Appeals. He soon generated a reputation for brilliance that made him one of the country's premier jurists. In 1920 he delivered the Storrs Lectures at Yale, which were published a year later as *The Nature of the Judicial Process*. The book became a landmark in the development of what Cardozo termed "sociological jurisprudence"—the obligation of judges to balance the demands of legal tradition and case precedence with contemporary social and economic needs. In 1932, President Herbert Hoover* appointed Cardozo to the U.S. Supreme Court.

On the Court, Cardozo replaced Oliver Wendell Holmes and joined the liberal minority of Harlan Fiske Stone* and Louis D. Brandeis.* Like his liberal associates, Cardozo believed in the principle of judicial restraint—that Congress and the state legislatures had the right to determine economic policy and regulate economic matters. Cardozo voted to uphold New Deal* economic legislation, even while the majority overturned the legislation creating the Agricultural Adjustment Administration* and the National Recovery Administration.* When President Franklin D. Roosevelt* reshaped the Court by appointing liberal justices, Cardozo became the linchpin of a new majority that upheld the power of Congress and the state legislatures to ameliorate social and economic problems by governmental activism. Cardozo died in Port Chester, New York, on July 9, 1938.

SUGGESTED READINGS: Andrew L. Kaufman, *Cardozo*, 1998; *New York Times*, July 10–11, 1938.

CARTER V. CARTER COAL COMPANY (1936). During the Great Depression of the 1930s, wages and working conditions in the bituminous coal industry were scandalously low. To stem overproduction and cutthroat competition in the industry, Congress passed the Bituminous Coal Conservation Act of 1935 as part of President Franklin D. Roosevelt's* New Deal.* The legislation empowered the federal government to establish local boards that could set the price of coal above market levels. It also mandated collective bargaining arrangements to raise wages and improve working conditions. Several coal companies filed lawsuits against the measure, arguing that it was an unconstitutional increase in the power of the federal government in what would normally be a state matter. The Bituminous Coal Conservation Act of 1935, so their legal argument went, violated the Tenth Amendment to the Constitution. In a decision handed down on March 18, 1936, by a narrow 5 to 4 vote, the U.S. Supreme Court ruled against the New Deal, agreeing that the legislation violated the Tenth Amendment. Outrage in Congress and the White House over the decision was so intense that it helped inspire President Roosevelt's infamous court-packing scheme* in 1937.

SUGGESTED READING: 298 U.S. 238 (1936).

CHANDLER ACT OF 1938. During the 1930s, the unprecedented number of corporate bankruptcies wrecked havoc in the corporate bond markets and weakened the portfolios of thousands of banks. In addition, the bankruptcy proceedings often discriminated against small investors who held limited amounts of corporate debt. The Chandler Act of 1938 amended existing federal bankruptcy law and gave the Securities and Exchange Commission* power to participate in corporate reorganizations in order to protect the interests of small and inarticulate investors. The bill also allowed wage earners to extend debt payments over longer periods of time.

SUGGESTED READING: *New York Times*, June 17, 1938.

CHARLIE McCARTHY. Charlie McCarthy was one of radio's most popular personalities during the 1930s and 1940s. The dummy of ventriloquist Edgar Bergen,* McCarthy was a wisecracking, irreverent figure whom listeners found obnoxious and outrageously funny. He was a master of the double entendre and could get away with sexual innuendos that would be impossible in other settings. McCarthy was supposedly dressed in a tuxedo and white tie, with a monocle, and he engaged in hilarious repartee with visiting guests. The Charlie McCarthy character debuted on NBC in May 1937 as part of *The Chase and Sanborn Hour*. Largely because of McCarthy, the show remained number one in audience ratings until 1940.

SUGGESTED READING: "The Man Who Talks to Himself," *Colliers*, 97 (March 20, 1937), 24.

CHINA. Many historians identify Japan's* invasion of Manchuria* in 1931 as the beginning of World War II. In their drive to achieve political and economic parity with the West, Japanese leaders in the 1920s decided that they could no longer tolerate being resource dependent on Europe and the United States. Since their own country was resource poor, Japan looked longingly on Manchuria, with its abundant deposits of coal and iron ore. Japan also looked at Manchuria, which was relatively underpopulated, as a place where Japan's surplus population could be settled. Back in 1905, as a result of its victory in the Russo-Japanese War, Japan had won treaty rights to control and to militarily defend the South Manchurian Railway. In 1931, needing a pretext to justify an invasion of Manchuria, Japan charged Chinese forces with bombing the railroad depot at Mukden.

Japan's Kwangtung Army, without authorization of the government in Tokyo, marched on Mukden (Mukden Incident*), seized the Chinese military barracks there, and then assumed control of the city. From there, Japanese armies pushed north rapidly, seizing a number of other Manchurian cities. In the wake of the invasion, Japanese engineers, accountants, and transportation specialists poured into Manchuria and began organizing the extraction of coal and iron ore.

The Chinese government protested the invasion and appealed to the League of Nations for support, but the League was pathetically weak and in no position, economically or militarily, to defy the Japanese invasion. The other major powers—France, Great Britain, and the United States—denounced the invasion and offered moral support to China, but Chinese leaders received nothing more than platitudes. Secretary of State Henry Stimson* of the United States announced the so-called Stimson Doctrine, which condemned the invasion and refused to extend diplomatic recognition to the new Manchukuo government of Manchuria. But that was the extent of the American opposition to the invasion of Chinese territory. It would take another ten years, and the Japanese bombing of Pearl Harbor, before the United States would take up arms.

The unwillingness of the world's major powers to do anything about the Japanese invasion of Manchuria only emboldened Japan in its determination to create its own zone of control—or "Greater East Asia Co-Prosperity Sphere." On January 28, 1932, Tokyo's military forces attacked Shanghai, killing thousands of people. A few months later, Japanese forces were withdrawn from Shanghai at the insistence of Great Britain, but the world now realized that Japan had become the greatest power in East Asia and the western Pacific.

In February 1933, claiming that China's army posed a threat to the recently established Manchukuo government in Manchuria, the Japanese army invaded Jehol province, which China considered part of its traditional territory and not a part of Manchuria. The invasion left Japanese troops just 100 miles from Beijing, the Chinese capital. In response to a hostile reaction from the United States, France, and Great Britain, Japan announced its withdrawal from the League of Nations.

Japan bided its time, waiting for the opportunity to strike at the rest of China. The opportunity arose when a Japanese soldier stationed outside Beijing disappeared. Japan blamed the Chinese government for the incident and in July 1937 launched an offensive against Beijing. By the end of July, Japanese forces controlled a wide corridor running from Beijing in the east to Tianjin on the Gulf of Chihli. The Japanese army then turned south and attacked Shanghai. The Chinese put up a ferocious resistance, losing more than 250,000 soldiers in the fighting, but Shanghai fell in October. From there Japanese troops headed inland for Nanjing, seat of Chiang Kai-shek's government. Nanjing fell in December. Chiang Kai-shek then relocated the government to Chongqing in distant Sichuan Province. In Nanjing, Japanese troops went on a rampage, raping thousands and slaughtering hundreds of thousands of Chinese. They also leveled 70 percent of the buildings in the city. Western journalists dubbed the atrocity the "Rape of Nanjing," making Japan even more malignant in the eyes of the West.

Late in 1938, Japanese troops conquered Wuhan, the industrial heartland of east central China and with its conquest controlled much of eastern China. Chiang Kai-shek relocated his Nationalist government farther west of Chongqing. The location, though safe from Japanese invasion, was cut off, in terms of communications and transportation systems, from the rest of China. The Japanese invasion then stalled. Chiang and Mao Zedong, head of the Chinese Communist Party, suspended their civil war and joined forces against Japan. Both men knew that Japan could not occupy all of China, so they decided on a guerrilla war. To make it difficult, if not impossible, for Japan to move troops through Henan Province to southern China, Chiang's engineers dynamited the dykes holding back the waters of the Yellow River. The mass flooding killed tens of thousands of Chinese peasants and destroyed millions of homes, but it also stopped the southern advance of the Japanese army.

Safely isolated on the western side of the Henan flood plain, Chiang's forces began construction of the 715-mile-long Burma Road linking Kunming, China, with Mandalay, Burma. The huge construction project took the labor of hundreds of thousands of Chinese workers, who built the road largely by hand. It opened in the summer of 1939, which allowed Chiang's army to receive supplies from the Allied powers. Those Allies consisted of Great Britain after the formal outbreak of World War II in Europe in September 1939 and the United States after the Japanese bombing of Pearl Harbor on December 7, 1941.

SUGGESTED READING: You-li Sun, *China and the Origins of the Pacific War*, 1993.

CHRYSLER BUILDING. At the time of its opening in Midtown Manhattan in 1930, the Chrysler Building was considered the most spectacular piece of architecture in the world. The genius of architect William van Alen, it was financed by William P. Chrysler of automobile fame. He intended the building to be a monument to American capitalism. At 1,048 feet, it was the tallest building in the world. Alen decorated the exterior in art deco style, complete with nickel-plated steel radiator caps and gargoyles with eagle faces. The building tapered to a point in the upper stories, giving it a rocketlike quality. Its tenure as the tallest building on earth was short-lived, however, because the Empire State Building,* at 1,250 feet, opened in 1931.

SUGGESTED READING: "Chrysler's Pretty Baubble," *Nation*, 131 (October 22, 1936), 450–51.

CITIZENS' RECONSTRUCTION ORGANIZATION. During the late 1920s and early 1930s, the nation's banking system entered a period of instability and collapse. Millions of depositors lost faith in the system and began converting their deposits into cash, a phenomenon that created serious liquidity problems for bankers and a credit crunch for borrowers. In January 1932, President Herbert Hoover* and Congress created the Reconstruction Finance Corporation* to make loans to troubled banks, and in February 1932, the president established the Citizens' Reconstruction Organization (CRO) as a voluntary group to launch and sustain an anti–currency hoarding publicity campaign. Frank Knox, owner of the *Chicago Daily News*, headed the CRO, and a conference of more than forty public relations and journalist groups was convened in Washington, D.C., to promote the campaign. Local CRO groups were established at the state and local levels, and the publicity campaign continued throughout 1932.

But the CRO proved to be too little, too late. As more and more banks failed in 1932, bank depositors discounted CRO propaganda and continued to withdraw their money, exacerbating the banking system's liquidity problems. The absolute collapse of the banking system late in 1932 and early in 1933 made the Citizens' Reconstruction Organization a symbol of the impotency of the Hoover administration.

SUGGESTED READING: James S. Olson, *Herbert Hoover and the Reconstruction Finance Corporation, 1931–1933*, 1977.

CITY LIGHTS. The film *City Lights* premiered in New York City on February 6, 1931, starring Charlie Chaplin once again as the "Little Tramp"—with his derby hat, baggy pants, cane, and mustache—the character he had made so famous in his silent film comedies of the 1920s. Chaplin had built his screen persona on a disarming combination of mirth and pathos, and in *City Lights*, he resurrected that role. In an age of sound movies, *City Lights* was a nondialogue film, Chaplin's way of proving that he could nonverbally convey the entire range of human emotions. The plot revolves around the Little Tramp's crusade to raise enough money for an operation that will restore the vision of a sightless flower girl. He succeeds, of course, but the restoration of her sight is painful, too, because she had always imagined him as a tall, strong, and handsome man, not the tiny, vulnerable image her restored sight beheld. *City Lights* was not unlike

American life during the years of the Great Depression—difficult, poignant, frightening, and yet somehow meaningful.

SUGGESTED READINGS: Charlie Chaplin, *My Life in Pictures*, 1974; Pierre Leprohon, *Charles Chaplin*, 1970; Roger Manvell, *Chaplin*, 1974; *New York Times*, February 7, 1931.

CIVILIAN CONSERVATION CORPS. One of the real problems facing the country in the early 1930s was unemployment among urban young men. Early in 1933 more than 50 percent of all men between the ages of fifteen and twenty-four were unemployed or had only part-time jobs. To deal with that problem as well as to promote some conservation work, President Franklin D. Roosevelt* asked Congress to establish the Civilian Conservation Corps (CCC). Congress created the CCC on March 31, 1933. Robert Fechner was named director of the CCC. It offered jobs at $30 a month to young men between the ages of seventeen and twenty-four. They were placed under the authority of U.S. Army supervisors, and the CCC had all the trappings of military authority. Organized into companies of approximately 200 men, CCC workers constructed national park facilities, fought forest fires, built roads in national forests, and worked intensively in reforestation projects, planting more than 200 million trees. During the 1930s, the CCC employed more than 2.5 million men, with more than 500,000 employed at the same time during the peak year of 1935. In 1942, with World War II well under way, Congress stopped funding the CCC.

SUGGESTED READINGS: Robert S. Browning, Jr., "The Civilian Conservation Corps," in James S. Olson, ed., *Historical Dictionary of the New Deal*, 1985; Percy H. Merrill, *Roosevelt's Forest Army: A History of the Civilian Conservation Corps, 1933–1942*, 1981; John A. Salmond, *The Civilian Conservation Corps, 1933–1942: A New Deal Case Study*, 1967.

CIVIL WORKS ADMINISTRATION. The Civil Works Administration (CWA) was created by an executive order of President Franklin D. Roosevelt* on November 9, 1933. He appointed Harry Hopkins,* head of the Federal Emergency Relief Administration,* to head the CWA. Instead of just handing out checks to the unemployed, Hopkins believed in work relief because "able-bodied people should work for their existence." By February 1934 the CWA was employing 4.2 million workers and paying them minimum wage and putting them to work on a variety of public construction projects, disaster relief, and historic preservation. Those individuals then spent their wages, and their purchasing power helped stimulate the economy. CWA workers constructed more than 40,000 schools, 469 airports, and 255,000 miles of streets and roads. Eventually, the CWA was absorbed into the much larger and more comprehensive Works Progress Administration.*

SUGGESTED READINGS: J. Christopher Schnell, "The Civil Works Administration," in James S. Olson, ed., *Historical Dictionary of the New Deal*, 1985; Bonnie Schwartz, *The Civil Works Administration, 1933–1934*, 1984; Forrest A. Walker, *The Civil Works Administration: An Experiment in Federal Work Relief*, 1979.

COHEN, BENJAMIN VICTOR. Benjamin Cohen, one of the most influential if unseen figures in the New Deal,* was born on September 23, 1894, in Muncie, Indiana. His parents were Jewish immigrants from Poland.* Precocious and brilliant, Cohen was an honors graduate of the University of Chicago and then earned the highest grades in the history of the University of Chicago Law School. Cohen did graduate work at the Harvard Law School, where his brilliance was soon manifest to the entire faculty. He became a protégé of Professor Felix Frankfurter* there. Between 1916 and 1933 Cohen practiced law privately in New York City. In 1933, Cohen came to Washington, D.C., to assist James Landis in drafting the Securities Act of 1933.* When he met Thomas Corcoran,* a counsel for the Reconstruction Finance Corporation,* the two became fast friends and formed one of the most important legal partnerships in the history of American public policy.

During the next several years, Cohen and Corcoran drafted the legislation that eventually became the Securities Exchange Act of 1934, the Federal Housing Administration,* the Tennessee Valley Authority,* and the Public Utility Holding Company Act of 1935.* They earned sterling reputations for the tightness of the legal language they employed in drafting complex legislation, and they then played central roles in shepherding the legislation through Congress. He spent most of the rest of his life in public service. Cohen died on September 4, 1983.

SUGGESTED READINGS: Joseph P. Lash, *Dealers and Dreamers: A New Look at the New Deal*, 1988; William Lasser, "Benjamn Victor Cohen," in James S. Olson, ed., *Historical Dictionary of the New Deal*, 1985; Katie Louchheim, ed., *The Making of the New Deal. The Insiders Speak*, 1983; *New York Times*, September 5, 1983.

COLBERT, CLAUDETTE. Claudette Colbert was born Lily Claudette Chauchoin in Paris, France, on September 13, 1905. Her family immigrated to the United States in 1910 and settled in New York City. After graduating from high school, Colbert planned a career in fashion design, but she soon became interested in theater. During the 1920s she had a number of bit parts on Broadway, including a fine performance in *The Barker* (1927), which she reprised on the London stage in 1928. In 1929 she signed a film contract with Paramount and appeared with Edward G. Robinson in *The Hole in the Wall*. During the next eighteen months, Colbert also appeared in *The Lady Lies* (1929), *The Big Pond* (1930), *Young Man of Manhattan* (1930), and *Manslaughter* (1930). Known as a woman with a "million dollar smile," who radiated innocence and virtue,

Colbert was not really taken seriously as an actress until her riveting performances in Cecil B. DeMille's *The Sign of the Cross* (1932) and *Cleopatra* (1934), where she epitomized sex appeal. Her big break came in 1934, when she appeared with Clark Gable* in the comedy hit *It Happened One Night** and won an Academy Award. During the rest of the decade, Colbert appeared in *Imitation of Life* (1934), *The Gilded Lily* (1935), *Private Worlds* (1935), *Maid of Salem* (1937), and *Drums along the Mohawk* (1939). By the end of the decade, Colbert was one of Hollywood's superstars, and she continued to be a prominent fixture in the film industry for the rest of her life. She died on July 30, 1996.

SUGGESTED READING: *New York Times*, July 31, 1996.

COLLIER, JOHN. John Collier was born in Atlanta, Georgia, on May 4, 1884. He attended Columbia University, where he developed a keen interest in social work, and between 1904 and 1906, he worked as a journalist and social worker in Atlanta. After a tour of Europe in 1907, Collier settled in New York City and went to work for the People's Institute, a social work organization dedicated to improving the lot of recent immigrants. He also became active in the national community center movement, although he was its greatest critic as well. While most people in the community center movement wanted to use community centers to assimilate immigrants, Collier was an avowed multiculturalist who haled ethnic diversity as a national asset. In 1919 Collier moved to California to take a teaching post at San Francisco State Teachers' College. He also served as director of the state adult education program.

Collier became a victim of the Red Scare in 1920. State education authorities considered him too liberal for the general political climate of the time, and they eliminated his job. Collier then moved to New Mexico and lived for several months with the Pueblo Indians. What astonished Collier about the Pueblos was their success in maintaining their culture even while American society was trying to assimilate them. They seemed to be a symbol of diversity. Collier spent the rest of his life working in Indian affairs.

In 1922, Collier became research agent for the Indian Welfare Committee of the General Conference of Women's Clubs. One year later, he founded and became executive director of the American Indian Defense Association (AIDA). The AIDA soon became outspoken of the Dawes Severalty Act of 1887, which had launched the movement to separate Indians from their land and to destroy tribal culture. Collier was committed to preservation of Indian cultures and civil rights for Native Americans.

When Franklin D. Roosevelt* and the Democrats won the election of 1932,* the movement to reform government policy gained momentum, and Collier was at the forefront. He became the architect of the so-called Indian New Deal when Roosevelt named him commissioner of Indian affairs. Collier remained in the position until 1945. During his tenure, he dismantled the legacy of the Dawes Act, drafted and implemented the Indian Reorganization Act of 1934,* restored hundreds of thousands of acres of land to Native Americans, and defined the legal and political status of hundreds of Indian tribes.

Collier remained at the helm of the Bureau of Indian Affairs until 1945, when he returned to private life. He accepted a teaching post at the City College of New York and later at Knox College. At the time of his death on May 8, 1968, Collier was widely recognized as the most influential figure in the history of federal government Indian policy.

SUGGESTED READINGS: Lawrence C. Kelly, *The Assault on Assimilation: John Collier and the Origins of Indian Policy Reform*, 1983; Kenneth R. Philp, *John Collier's Crusade for Indian Reform, 1920–1954*, 1977.

COMIC BOOK. The first comic strip appeared in the *New York World* in 1896, and they became newspaper staples during the early 1900s. In 1934, George Delacorte of Dell Publishing Company marketed the first so-called comic book—a sixty-eight-page booklet that featured public comic strip characters and sold for ten cents. The first printing of 35,000 copies sold out in a few weeks. Other companies soon entered the market. The McKay Company in 1936 released comic books based on the exploits of Flash Gordon and Popeye, and in June 1938, Action Comics introduced the character of Superman.* The comic book business soon became a nationwide industry.

SUGGESTED READINGS: Michael Benton, *The Comic Book in America*, 1989; Will Jacobs and Gerard Jones, *The Comic Book Heroes*, 1985.

COMMITTEE FOR THE NATION. The Committee for the Nation to Rebuild Prices and Purchasing Power, commonly referred to as the Committee for the Nation, was formed early in 1933 by Frank Vanderlip and a number of other prominent businessmen and economists, including James H. Rand, Jr., of Remington, Rand; Robert E. Wood* and Lessing Rosenwald of Sears, Roebuck; newspaperman Frank Gannett; and economists Irving Fischer* and George Warren.* They promoted the idea of the "commodity dollar," or stimulating price increases in the economy through manipulation of gold and silver prices and the money supply. They hoped that inflation would create new investment capital and raise commodity prices. The committee endorsed Franklin D. Roosevelt's* gold-buying scheme of 1933–1934, the Silver Purchase Act of 1934* the Banking Acts of 1933* and 1935,* the Agricultural Adjustment Act of 1933,* the Reciprocal Trade Agreements Act of 1934,* and the Securities Exchange Act of 1934.

But the Committee for the Nation broke ranks with Roosevelt in 1935 when they decided that the focus of the New Deal* had changed dramatically. Such legislation in 1935 as the National Labor Relations Act,* the Public Utility Holding Company Act,* and the Wealth Tax Act* alienated the businessmen on the committee, and in the presidential election of 1936,* the committee formally endorsed the candidacy of Republican Alf Landon.*

SUGGESTED READING: H. M. Banter, "The Committee for the Nation," *Journal of Political Economy*, 49 (1941), 531–53.

COMMITTEE ON ECONOMIC SECURITY. Ever since the early 1900s, social welfare advocates in the United States had promoted the idea of federal pensions for senior citizens, and in the early 1930s, the idea gained momentum from labor unions and especially from the increasing popularity of Francis Townsend's* Old-Age Revolving Pensions, Ltd. To satisfy liberals in his own party and to steal some thunder from Townsend, President Franklin D. Roosevelt* in June 1934 established the Committee on Economic Security. The committee was chaired by Secretary of Labor Frances Perkins* and charged with developing a federal insurance plan before the end of the year. Proposals for national health insurance, federal unemployment insurance, and old-age pensions were all considered.

The committee had two difficult issues to resolve. First, they had to decide whether a system of unemployment compensation should be a single, federal government program or a state-based plan. The committee decided to promote the state-based plan, with the federal government setting certain minimum standards. The second issue to be resolved was how to finance old-age pensions. Liberals wanted the federal government simply to finance it out of general revenues, which would have the effect of redistributing national income. Conservatives wanted a financing system based on payroll deductions from employees and employers. The committee recommended the more conservative proposal. The committee also recommended supplemental benefits for the indigent elderly, for the blind, and for dependent children. Committee members decided not to make any proposals concerning national health insurance. The committee handed its report over to President Roosevelt on January 15, 1935, and the president quickly turned it over to Congress. Senator Robert Wagner* of New York and Congressmen David J. Lewis and Robert Doughton sponsored the legislation. The Social Security Act* became law on August 14, 1935.

SUGGESTED READING: Roy Lubove, *The Struggle for Social Security 1900–1935*, 1968.

COMMODITY CREDIT CORPORATION. One of the great challenges facing farmers in the 1920s and 1930s revolved around their difficulties in marketing their commodities. Overproduction and depressed prices had become chronic problems, and it was an even worse problem during harvest time, when cash-poor farmers all dumped certain commodities on the market at the same time, depressing prices even more. On a seasonal basis, prices were artificially low because crops hit the market at the same time. Farmers asked the Roosevelt administration for federal assistance in creating more stable marketing conditions.

On October 18, 1933, President Franklin D. Roosevelt* by executive order created the Commodity Credit Corporation (CCC), which had its origins in three subtreasury schemes of the Populists. The Commodity Credit Corporation assumed control of a Reconstruction Finance Corporation* (RFC) loan program established during the Herbert Hoover* administration. The RFC loaned money to banks and agricultural credit corporations for the orderly marketing of commodities. Such loans allowed farmers to hold their crops off the market until more favorable marketing conditions had materialized. In order to avoid making too many loans directly and undermining local financial institutions, the CCC agreed to buy up all such loans private bankers made. When banks refused to make such loans, the CCC made them directly.

Between 1933 and 1935 the Commodity Credit Corporation was a subsidiary of the Reconstruction Finance Corporation. It then became an independent agency. The CCC made loans on cotton, corn, wheat, turpentine, rosin, figs, peanuts, raisins, butter, dates, cowhides, wool, and tobacco. By 1936 CCC loans—the vast majority of them made originally through private banks—totaled $628 million. By 1939 they had reached $900 million and helped stabilize commodity prices. The outbreak of World War II, with its huge demand for farm products, brought about a dramatic increase in commodity prices and farm profits.

SUGGESTED READINGS: Jesse Jones, *Fifty Billion Dollars*, 1951; James S. Olson, *Saving Capitalism: The Reconstruction Finance Corporation and the New Deal, 1933–1940*, 1988.

COMMODITY DOLLAR. See GOLD RESERVE ACT OF 1934.

COMMUNICATIONS ACT OF 1934. See FEDERAL COMMUNICATIONS COMMISSION.

CONGRESS OF INDUSTRIAL ORGANIZATIONS. One reason for the long-term success of the American Federation of Labor* (AFL) had been Samuel Gompers's commitment to organizing only skilled workers in the craft unions. His logic was simple: When skilled workers went on strike, they enjoyed leverage because company profits would fall rapidly. When unskilled workers struck, they could easily be replaced. The AFL did have some mass production workers as members, but Gompers and his successor William Green* treated them as second-class citizens. But the Industrial Revolution's millions of semiskilled and unskilled mass production workers also wanted the protection of labor unions. At the 1934 convention of the American Federation of Labor, a group of AFL members demanded that the union try to organize mass production workers. John L. Lewis,* head of the United Mine Workers (UMW), spearheaded the request. The AFL denied the request. Lewis renewed the request at the 1935 convention, but again he was voted down, this time by a vote of 18,464 to 10,987.

To further the cause of mass production workers, John L. Lewis joined with Sidney Hillman* of the Amalgamated Clothing Workers, David Dubinsky* of the International Ladies' Garment Workers' Union, Thomas McMahon of the Textile Workers, and Charles Howard of the Typographers' Union and formed the Committee for Industrial Organization within the AFL. The AFL suspended the member unions of the committee, and in 1938, after years of legal wrangling, Lewis formed the Congress of Industrial Organizations (CIO).

The CIO soon became a powerful force in the labor movement and the American economy because of the protections offered labor unions in the National Labor Relations Act of 1935.* In the 1936 presidential election, the CIO contributed $1 million to Franklin D. Roosevelt's reelection campaign and established the Labor's Non-Partisan League* and the American Labor Party* to back him.

The CIO also actively campaigned to organize industrial workers. In June 1936 Philip Murray, who served as Lewis's assistant in the UMW, established the Steel Workers Organizing Committee (SWOC), and Sidney Hillman formed the Textile Workers Organizing Committee. Late in 1936, the United Automobile Workers staged their sit-down strikes against the major automobile companies, and in February 1937 General Motors agreed to bargain with the union. UAW membership jumped from 30,000 workers to 400,000 workers. In March 1937, United States Steel Corporation recognized the Steel Workers Organizing Committee, and within a few months, SWOC membership exceeded 350,000 workers. Other industrial unions that enjoyed similar success in 1937 included the United Rubber Workers, United Electrical and Radio Workers, and the Textile Workers Organizing Committee. By 1940, the CIO unions had a total membership of 2,654,000 workers.

SUGGESTED READINGS: Irving Bernstein, *Turbulent Years: A History of the American Worker, 1933–1941*, 1970; Robert H. Zieger, *The CIO, 1935–1955*, 1995.

CONNALLY ACT OF 1935. See **"LITTLE NRA."**

CORCORAN, THOMAS GARDINER. Thomas Corcoran, nicknamed "The Cork," was born in Pawtucket, Rhode Island, on December 29, 1900. In 1922 he graduated from Brown University, and he then went on to Harvard Law School, where he impressed Professor Felix Frankfurter* with his brilliance. Corcoran earned a doctorate of juristic science in 1926 and then clerked for Supreme Court Justice Oliver Wendell Holmes, Jr. A loyal Democrat because of his Irish Catholic roots, Corcoran practiced law privately in New York City between 1927 and 1932, specializing in corporate reorganization. In 1932 he joined the staff of the Reconstruction Finance Corporation* (RFC), and in 1933, at Felix Frankfurter's suggestion, Franklin D. Roosevelt* hired Corcoran as an assistant to Secretary of the Treasury William Woodin.* One year later, Corcoran returned to the RFC as special counsel and remained there until 1941.

During his stay in Washington, D.C., Corcoran formed an informal partnership with Benjamin Cohen,* and together they drafted and shepherded through Congress some of the New Deal's* most important legislation, including the Securities Exchange Act of 1934, the Public Utility Holding Company Act of 1935,* and the legislation creating the Tennessee Valley Authority* and the Federal Housing Administration.* Corcoran and Cohen shared an apartment in Georgetown and worked ninety-hour weeks for years, earning the nickname "the gold dust twins" or "Frankfurter's two chief little hot dogs." Although Corcoran's job was special counsel to the RFC, he actually ranged very widely throughout Washington, D.C., and was known by everyone to enjoy the ear of the president. In 1941, Corcoran resigned and launched a highly lucrative legal career in Washington. By that time, he was probably the most well-connected lawyer in the country and remained so for the rest of his life. Corcoran died on December 6, 1981.

SUGGESTED READINGS: Peter Irons, *The New Deal Lawyers*, 1982; Joseph P. Lash, *Dealers and Dreamers: A New Look at the New Deal*, 1988; *New York Times*, December 7, 1981.

COUGHLIN, CHARLES EDWARD. Charles Coughlin was born on October 25, 1891, and raised in Hamilton, Ontario, Canada. After studying theology at the University of Toronto, Coughlin became a Roman Catholic priest. After teaching for ten years at Assumption College in Windsor, Ontario, he was transferred in 1926 to a parish in Royal Oaks, Michigan. Coughlin had only been at his new assignment for two weeks when a local Ku Klux Klan group burned a cross in front of the parish church. In reaction, Coughlin started a radio broadcast from his "Shrine of the Little Flower," which quickly became very popular in the local area. Coughlin soon figured out that his warnings about the dangers of communism resonated especially well, and by 1930, his weekly radio show began reaching a national audience.

Soon, however, Coughlin began peddling hate and hyperbole. He blamed the depression on international bankers, Jews, and communists. Because he had invested all of his own money in silver mines, he began advocating the remonetization of silver. Coughlin also praised the early accomplishments of Benito Mussolini in Italy* and Adolf Hitler in Germany.* He was an early supporter of Franklin D. Roosevelt* and the New Deal,* telling his millions of listeners that the "New Deal is Christ's Deal."

But in 1934 Coughlin broke with the Roosevelt administration, criticizing the large bureaucracies created by the National Recovery Administration* and the

Agricultural Adjustment Administration,* labeling the "New Deal the Jew Deal," and even suggesting the need for Franklin D. Roosevelt to be assassinated. In November 1934, Coughlin formed the National Union for Social Justice to promote his commitment to inflationary monetary policies and redistribution of the national income. By early 1935, the National Union for Social Justice had a membership of more than 500,000 people.

In the summer of 1935, Coughlin threw in his lot with Senator Huey P. Long* and Francis Townsend,* and together they planned formation of the Union Party.* They hoped to run Long as a Union Party presidential candidate in the presidential election of 1936,* but after Long's assassination, the Union Party nominated William Lemke.* Lemke proved to be not only anti-Semitic but anti-Catholic, splitting the coalition. Coughlin became increasingly hostile to Roosevelt, so much so that Roman Catholic prelates intervened to suppress Coughlin's broadcasts. Lemke ended up with only 2 percent of the vote in 1936.

Coughlin's vitriol only worsened. He became so blatantly anti-Roosevelt, anti-Semitic, and pro-Hitler that the Vatican formally condemned him. In 1942, when he described World War II as a "Roosevelt-Jewish-British" conspiracy, the Church ended his radio broadcasts. The National Union for Social Justice disbanded in 1944. Father Coughlin died on October 27, 1979.

SUGGESTED READINGS: David H. Bennett, *Demagogues in the Depression. American Radicals and the Union Party, 1932–1936*, 1969; Charles J. Tull, *Father Coughlin and the New Deal*, 1965.

COURT-PACKING SCHEME. As soon as President Franklin D. Roosevelt* took the oath of office on March 4, 1933, the federal government aggressively attacked the economic problems associated with the Great Depression. With unemployment skyrocketing and prices plunging, with the money markets frozen into paralysis, and with the industrial and farm economies in a state of meltdown, the New Deal* embarked on a remarkable expansion in the power and scope of the federal government.

But the U.S. Supreme Court, dominated by conservative justices appointed in the 1910s and 1920s, could not tolerate the New Deal. It seemed to crush states' rights in the name of federal power and ran rough-shod over the property rights of corporations. In a series of highly controversial decisions, the Court systematically dismantled much of the early New Deal. The Court declared unconstitutional, in *Louisville Joint Stock Bank v. Radford* (1935), a law providing mortgage relief to farmers. In *Schechter Poultry Corporation v. United States* (1935),* the justices destroyed the National Recovery Administration.* The Agricultural Adjustment Administration* was declared unconstitutional in the Supreme Court's *United States v. Butler* (1936)* decision.

Enraged that the Supreme Court seemed bent on thwarting the will of Congress, the president, and the people, Franklin D. Roosevelt decided to redesign the Court. He waited until after his landslide victory in the election of 1936.* The president asked Attorney General Homer Cummings to come up with a plan that would reduce the Court's conservative majority to a minority. At first Cummings proposed a constitutional amendment increasing the number of justices on the Court, but New Dealers felt the amendment process would be too time-consuming. Roosevelt wanted more immediate action. Instead, the administration proposed to Congress a measure that would add one justice to the Supreme Court for every other justice who had reached the age of seventy, up to a maximum of six new appointments. The plan also called for forty-four new justices at the district and court of appeals levels.

The proposal, when it was made public on February 7, 1937, generated a storm of protest. Republicans denounced the measure, but so did moderate and conservative Democrats, newspapers, and bar associations. Although he had badly miscalculated the political fallout of the proposal, Roosevelt refused to back down, and a constitutional crisis loomed. Congress refused to approve the measure. But the standoff dissipated when the Court upheld the constitutionality of a minimum wage law and of the National Labor Relations Act of 1935,* legal battles that New Dealers had expected to lose. A series of resignations during the next two years also gave the president the opportunity to replace conservatives with liberals. The president had lost a battle but won the war. One year later, however, when voters went to the polls in the congressional elections of 1938,* the court-packing scheme cost Roosevelt badly. Republicans staged huge gains in Congress, dramatically reducing Roosevelt's Democratic majorities in the House and the Senate.

SUGGESTED READINGS: William E. Leuchtenburg, "The Origins of Franklin D. Roosevelt's 'Court-Packing' Plan," *The Supreme Court Review*, (1966), 347–400; William E. Leuchtenburg, *The Supreme Court Reborn: The Constitutional Revolution in the Age of Roosevelt*, 1995.

COUZENS, JAMES JOSEPH, JR. James Couzens, known during the 1930s as a "New Deal Republican," was born in Chatham, Ontario, Canada, on August 26, 1872. After high school, Couzens worked for a time in the family soap manufacturing and coal and ice delivery business, but in 1890 he moved to Detroit. He went to work for the Michigan Central Railroad, and in 1895 Couzens joined the Malcomson Fuel Company. Couzens soon became secretary to Alex Malcomson, who had already invested money with Henry Ford's* automobile manufacturing business. Couzens saw the company's potential and became one of the original shareholders in Ford Motor Company. He became business manager of Ford Motor Company and by 1915 was a multimillionaire. Unable to get along well with Henry Ford, Couzens resigned that year.

He then made politics his career, becoming police commissioner of Detroit in 1916 and mayor of Detroit in 1918. In 1922, Couzens was elected as a Republican to the U.S. Senate. In spite of his phenomenal wealth, Couzens proved to be a progressive Republican, supporting the proposal for federal development of Muscle Shoals and the McNary-Haugen plan for farmers and opposing Secretary of the Treasury Andrew Mellon's* tax cuts on the rich. During the years of the New Deal,* Couzens backed federal relief programs, Social Security, the National Industrial Recovery Act, the National Labor Relations Act of 1935,* and the Public Utility Holding Company Act of 1935.* Couzens consistently defended President Franklin D. Roosevelt* and the New Deal from attacks by conservatives. His backing of Roosevelt cost him his political career. Couzens was defeated in the Republican senatorial primary of 1936. He died on October 22, 1936.

SUGGESTED READING: Harry Barnard, *Independent Man: The Life of Senator James Couzens*, 1958.

CREDIT ANSTALT. Credit Anstalt was the largest bank in Austria and a key financial institution for all of central Europe. During the 1920s, because of mismanagement and too much political interference, Credit Anstalt had absorbed a number of weaker financial institutions in order to prevent their default and bankruptcy. But when the Great Depression settled on the world late in 1929, Credit Anstalt found itself burdened with hundreds of millions of dollars of bad assets. Since more than 70 percent of the Austrian economy depended upon the bank, the financial crisis affected the entire country. The government of Austria, still reeling economically from the effects of World War I, was in no position to bail out Credit Anstalt.

But when the government headed to France, Great Britain, and the United States in search of funds to rescue the bank, the efforts generated rumors that struck many depositors with panic. They began withdrawing funds from Credit Anstalt. In July 1930, Danat Bank, one of Germany's* largest, declared bankruptcy, triggering more panic throughout central Europe. Credit Anstalt tried to stave off the inevitable, but in the spring of 1931, the bank went under, closing its doors and precipitating a run on banks throughout Europe. In the wake of Credit Anstalt's failure, Great Britain abandoned the gold standard,* and banks throughout the United States witnessed runs by panic-stricken depositors. The failure of Credit Anstalt played a key role in the meltdown of world financial markets in 1932 and 1933.

SUGGESTED READING: James S. Olson, *Herbert Hoover and the Reconstruction Finance Corporation, 1931–1933*, 1977.

CROSBY, BING. Bing Crosby was born Harry Lillis Crosby on May 2, 1904, in Tacoma, Washington. He studied law at Gonzaga University but quit to pursue his real love—big band music. Blessed with a mellow, "crooner" voice, Crosby spent the 1920s singing with a number of dance bands. In 1931, after a radio appearance from the Coconut Grove night club in Los Angeles, he became a popular radio star on CBS. At a time when most Americans were preoccupied by bad economic times, Crosby exuded in his songs a "Don't Worry" attitude that most people found soothing and endearing. He also sold millions of records and became the most popular entertainer in the country. During the 1940s, Crosby turned to filmmaking, where he proved to be equally successful. Along with Bob Hope, he made seven of the so-called Road films, each a box-office hit. For his portrayal of a Catholic priest in *Going My Way* (1944), Crosby won an Academy Award. In the 1942 film *Holiday Inn*, Crosby sang the song "White Christmas," written by Irving Berlin,* and made it the most famous song in the history of popular music. He died on October 14, 1977.

SUGGESTED READINGS: Gary Giddins, *Bing Crosby: A Pocketful of Dreams—The Early Years 1903–1940*, 2000; *New York Times*, October 15, 1977; Barry Ulanov, *The Incredible Crosby*, 1948.

CRUSADERS FOR ECONOMIC LIBERTY. The Crusaders for Economic Liberty was an anti-Roosevelt, anti–New Deal* organization that accused President Franklin D. Roosevelt* of leading the country down the road to communism. Founded in 1934 by George W. Christians, they called themselves "White Shirts" and attacked deficit-spending government bureaucracies and the centralization of power in the federal government. Like other extreme, right-wing groups in the 1930s, the Crusaders for Economic Liberty had little impact on voters.

SUGGESTED READING: George Wolfskill and John A. Hudson, *All But the People. Franklin D. Roosevelt and His Critics, 1933–1939*, 1969.

CURRIE, LAUCHLIN. Lauchlin Currie was born in West Dublin, Nova Scotia, Canada, on October 8, 1902. In 1925 he graduated from the London School of Economics and then became an economics instructor at Harvard. While finishing his Ph.D. in economics at Harvard, he taught at the Fletcher School of Law and Diplomacy. In 1934 Currie went to Washington, D.C., to work in the Treasury Department, and he soon became a close friend of Marriner Eccles,* head of the Federal Reserve Board.* In November 1934, Currie came to work for Eccles as assistant director of the Federal Reserve Board's research and statistics division. He played a key role in drafting the Banking Act of 1935.* In 1936 Currie received his Ph.D. in economics from Harvard.

As a New Dealer, Currie was an early advocate of Keynesian economics— that through government spending and taxation policies the federal government should engage in deficit spending to lift the country out of the depression. He played a central role in converting Marriner Eccles to such ideas, and Eccles in turn lobbied President Franklin D. Roosevelt* to implement Keynesian policies.

Although Currie was for the most part a "behind the scenes" player in the New Deal,* he had tremendous influence. After World War II, Currie served as president of the International Bank for Reconstruction and Development.

SUGGESTED READINGS: Byrd L. Jones, "The Role of Keynesians in Wartime and Postwar Planning," *American Economic Review*, 62 (1972), 166–33; Dean May, *From New Deal to New Economics*, 1982; Patrick D. Reagan, "Lauchlin Currie," in James S. Olson, ed., *Historical Dictionary of the New Deal*, 1985.

CZECHOSLOVAKIA. The nation of Czechoslovakia was a political invention of the Paris Peace Conference of 1919–1920. President Woodrow Wilson of the United States, who believed in national and ethnic self-determination, wanted to respond to the minorities of central Europe, each of whom wanted its own nation–state. The Austro-Hungarian Empire had disintegrated as a result of World War I, and rather than create an independent country for each of its ethnic minorities, coalitions of minorities were formed into new countries. One of them was Czechoslovakia, a mix primarily of Germans, Bohemians, Moravians, Slovaks, and Carpatho-Ruthenians. It was an unstable political mix that would not survive the twentieth century.

Adolf Hitler was the first European politician to work on the disintegration of Czechoslovakia. At first he set his sight on the Sudetenland, the portion of western Czechoslovakia that was home to millions of ethnic Germans. Hitler was committed to the notion that all of the German-speaking people of Europe should be under the sovereign control of his Third Reich. The Sudetenland was also home to the Czech army's strongest fortifications, and Hitler wanted them neutralized. Finally the Sudetenland was the industial heartland of Czechoslovakia. To bring the Sudetenland under German control, Hitler instructed pro-Nazi Germans in the Sudetenland to begin to demand regional independence. He falsely accused the Czech government of a systematic campaign of terror against the country's German minority, and in a huge propaganda barrage, he convinced French and German leaders that his desire for territorial aggrandizement would stop with the Sudetenland.

In September 1938, British Prime Minister Neville Chamberlain and French Premier Edouard Daladier met with Hitler in Munich. Italian dictator Benito Mussolini acted as the mediator, although his sympathies with Hitler were overwhelming. Daladier and Chamberlain caved into Hitler's demands and more, awarding him the Sudetenland and all other areas of Czechoslovakia where ethnic Germans were the majority. President Eduard Benes of Czechoslovakia resigned in protest. Chamberlain naively announced that the Munich Pact guaranteed "peace in our time." On October 1, German troops moved into the Sudetenland.

With the Munich agreement, Germany* asserted sovereignty over the Sudentenland, and the dismemberment of Czechoslovakia began. Actually, Hitler was interested in neutralizing Czechoslovakia's army, one of the strongest in central

Europe. In mid-March 1939, Hungarian troops occupied Carpathia-Ruthenia in eastern Czechoslovakia, and on March 14, Slovakia declared its independence and its loyalty to Germany. Early the next day, the Czech Republic signed surrender documents and German troops occupied the country.

SUGGESTED READING: William V. Wallace, *Czechoslovakia*, 1976.

D

DARROW, CLARENCE. Clarence Darrow, one of the greatest trial lawyers in American history, was born in Kinsman, Ohio, on April 18, 1857. After studying at Allegheny College for two years, he matriculated to the University of Michigan Law School, graduating there in 1878. He was quickly admitted to the Ohio bar and began practicing. Darrow moved to Chicago in 1887, where he joined the law firm of John Peter Altgeld. Known for his civil liberties proclivities, Altgeld became a mentor for Darrow, who quickly developed a lifelong, passionate opposition to capital punishment. During the 1900s and 1910s, Darrow became the best-known trial lawyer in the country, successfully defending such prominent political radicals as Socialist head Eugene V. Debs and International Workers of the World leader William "Big Bill" Haywood. During the 1920s, his defense of convicted murderers Richard Loeb and Nathan Loeb and of John Scopes, the Tennessee teacher accused of teaching evolution in the public schools, made Darrow a household world.

Once the United States slipped into the Great Depression, Darrow's liberal political views turned radical, and he became a confirmed socialist and defender of the poor and the oppressed. When the New Deal's* National Recovery Administration* (NRA) became mired in controversy, Darrow was picked to head up a special investigative commission, and he concluded that the NRA had become dominated by large monopolistic and oligopolistic corporations. He called for the scrapping of the NRA and its replacement with a more powerful federal government agency empowered to plan and direct the development of the national economy. For Darrow, the only real answer to the Great Depression was the abandonment of capitalism and the rise of socialism.

SUGGESTED READING: Arthur Weinberg and Lola Weinberg, *Clarence Darrow: A Sentimental Rebel*, 1980.

DAVIS, BETTE. During the 1930s, Bette Davis emerged as one of Hollywood's most gifted and popular actresses. She was born on April 5, 1908, in

Lowell, Massachusetts. Infatuated with the theater, she moved to New York and worked her way into a number of Broadway plays. Davis burst upon the Hollywood scene and into American popular culture during the 1930s, portraying strong-willed, unpredictable women who had an edge to them. In her 1931 screen debut in *Bad Sister*, she demonstrated her acting range. She paid her dues in the studio system, appearing in twenty-two films before scoring in 1934 as the sharp-tongued waitress Mildred in *Of Human Bondage*. The next year, Davis won a best actress Oscar for her performance in *Dangerous*. With her round face, headlight eyes, and extraordinary emotional range, she was equally comfortable portraying lust and innocence or vulnerability and viciousness.

Despite such success, Davis was dissatisfied with the Hollywood studio system, which contractually bound actors to single studios and forced them to perform in whatever film or whatever role that was selected for them by studio executives. In 1936, Davis left Hollywood and moved to London. Warner Brothers Studio sued her for breach of contract, and she lost the lawsuit. But in the end, Davis won the war. When she returned to the United States in 1938, she was given better roles. In *Jezebel*, she played the strong-willed, charismatic Southern belle and won another Academy Award. Davis followed up those performances with *Dark Victory* (1939), *All This and Heaven Too* (1940), and *Now Voyager* (1942). Her characters were always quick with a wisecrack, unwilling to be intimidated by men or women, and sassy and brazen. At a time when the country was mired in depression, Davis portrayed strength and confidence. She went on to receive eight more Oscar nominations during her distinguished career. Bette Davis died on October 6, 1989.

SUGGESTED READING: Roy Moseley, *Bette Davis: An Intimate Memoir*, 1989.

DAWES, CHARLES GATES. Charles G. Dawes was born on August 27, 1865, in Marietta, Ohio. In 1884 he graduated from Marietta College and earned a master's degree there in 1887. At the same time, he studied at the University of Cincinnati Law School, graduating there in 1886. Dawes practiced law in Lincoln, Nebraska, and became active in Republican Party politics. In 1896, he became particularly prominent in the party by successfully managing William McKinley's 1896 presidential campaign in Illinois. As a reward, McKinley appointed Dawes comptroller of the currency, which launched Dawes's career in banking and finance.

Dawes left Washington, D.C., in 1902 to become president of the Central Republic Bank and Trust Company of Chicago. He remained active in Republican activities, and in 1921 newly elected President Warren G. Harding named him director of the budget. In that position, Dawes earned an international reputation for developing what became known as the Dawes Plan, a restructuring of Germany's* World War I reparations that restored some stability to the global economy. Dawes's work earned him the 1925 Nobel Peace Prize. In 1924,

Calvin Coolidge picked Dawes as his vice-presidential running mate, and they achieved an easy victory in the election.

Dawes retired from public life in 1929, returning to Chicago and Central Republic Bank, but he soon became embroiled in one of the Great Depression's most publicized scandals. When the money markets all but collapsed in 1931, Congress created the Reconstruction Finance Corporation* (RFC), a federal agency, to bail out private banks, and President Herbert Hoover* appointed Dawes as RFC president. Dawes remained there for several months before resigning and returning to Central Republic. But when the RFC made a $50 million loan to Central Republic, Democrats howled in protest and journalists began searching for a scandal. Actually, the RFC loan was necessary to prevent the bank from declaring bankruptcy, which almost certainly would have affected thousands of banks in the Midwest. But to many Americans, such a large loan to one bank, while millions of people were out of work, was obscene. The controversy tarnished Dawes's reputation. He remained active in banking and finance until his death on April 23, 1951.

SUGGESTED READINGS: Stephen A. Schuker, *The Ends of French Predominance in Europe: The Financial Crisis of 1924 and the Adoption of the Dawes Plan*, 1976; Bascom N. Timmons, *Portrait of an American: Charles G. Dawes*, 1953.

DDT. The initials "DDT" are an acronym for dichlorodiphenyltrichloroethane. Developed by Paul Muller, a Swiss chemist, the chemical was a marvelous pesticide—inexpensive, rapid working, and long lasting. Muller introduced DDT in 1939, and soon farmers throughout the developed world were using it to destroy a great range of pests. It was also used by warring powers to dust and fumigate the clothing and bedding of soldiers. In the short term, use of DDT dramatically improved crop yields. In the long term, however, it wreaked environmental damage. Over time, insects gradually developed resistance to DDT, and because of its wide-ranging killing effects, it wiped out beneficial species as well as bad ones. Also, DDT would prove to be carcinogenic for humans, especially when residues ended up in water supplies.

SUGGESTED READING: Rita Beatty, *The DDT Myth*, 1973.

DEATH VALLEY DAYS. *Death Valley Days* was one of America's most popular radio programs during the years of the Great Depression. It debuted in 1930 on NBC radio and enjoyed a continuous weekly run for eleven years, when CBS picked it up. *Death Valley Days* was set in late-nineteenth- and early-twentieth-century California, where traders and settlers were trying to settle the west. The stories revolved around the hard scrabble life of the desert frontier, and perhaps that explained its appeal. In an American economy suffering the effects of the Great Depression, with millions of families out of work, the courage and perseverance of the Death Valley pioneers inspired them with hope. Pacific Coast Borax Company sponsored *Death Valley Days*.

SUGGESTED READING: John Dunning, *Tune in Yesterday: The Ultimate Encyclopedia of Old-Time Radio, 1925–1976*, 1976.

DeJONGE V. OREGON **(1937).** In 1935, as part of a meeting to protest police shootings of striking longshoremen in Portland, Oregon, Clark DeJonge attended meetings of the Communist Party. DeJonge distributed Communist Party literature at the meeting. The meeting was peaceful, with no disorderly conduct. Nevertheless, DeJonge was arrested, prosecuted, and convicted of "criminal syndicalism" and advocating the overthrow of the U.S. government. He appealed the conviction in Oregon, but the Oregon Supreme Court upheld the state's case. *DeJonge v. Oregon* reached the U.S. Supreme Court, which decided the case on January 4, 1937. In a unanimous opinion, the Court declared that the conviction violated DeJonge's First Amendment right to peaceably assemble. Civil liberties historians consider the case a landmark in U.S. history.

SUGGESTED READING: 299 U.S. 353 (1937).

DENNIS, LAWRENCE. Lawrence Dennis was born on December 25, 1893, in Atlanta, Georgia. During his childhood he became a locally prominent child evangelist, but in 1913, he entered Exeter Academy and then graduated from Harvard in 1920. He joined the State Department as a foreign service officer and had postings in Romania, Nicaragua, Haiti, and Paris. During those years abroad, Dennis became increasingly frustrated about how the diplomatic corps seemed to exist to underwrite U.S. corporate expansion. Incongruously, he left the foreign service in 1927 to become an investment banker with J. & W. Seligman and Company. He resigned in 1930, and in 1932, he published *Is Capitalism Doomed* in which he argued that investment bankers were ruining the country. During the Pecora Committee* hearings in 1933–1934, Dennis testified against his former colleagues in the securities industry. Dennis's *The Coming of American Fascism* (1936) took a different approach to the country's problems, arguing that capitalism was doomed and that Americans would inevitably face a choice between communism and fascism. He urged them to choose fascism.

Dennis's formula to save America called for nationalization of the banks, destruction of monopolies, banning women from the workforce, federal guarantees of employment through public works construction, abolition of state's rights, and legalization of only one political party. Few people were listening to Dennis, although he did enjoy some brief intellectual vogue. In 1937 he returned to the investment banking business. In 1940 he wrote *The Dynamics of War and Revolution*, but his fascist sympathies doomed him as a serious public figure after the United States went to war against Germany* and Italy.* Dennis died on August 20, 1977.

SUGGESTED READINGS: *New York Times*, August 21, 1977; *Who Was Who in America*, vol. 150, 1978.

DePRIEST, OSCAR STANTON. Oscar DePriest, perhaps the early twentieth century's most prominent African American politician, was born in Florence, Alabama, on March 9, 1871. He was born to working-class parents. DePriest's father was a farm laborer and teamster, and his mother was a laundress. The family left Alabama for Kansas when the younger DePriest was eight years old, and in 1889, Oscar left home and moved to Chicago. He found work in the construction business and became active in Cook County Republican Party politics. DePriest won a seat on the Cook County Commission and served there for four years. In 1908 he went into the real estate business. In 1915, DePriest became Chicago's first African American alderman. Thirteen years later, black voters sent him to Congress.

DePriest served three terms in Congress and made a name for himself in the field of civil rights. He actively campaigned, though unsuccessfully, for a federal antilynching law, and he demanded that the restaurant in the House of Representatives be opened to federal employees of all races. At the same time, DePriest was an outspoken opponent of communism, which he considered completely inconsistent with American values. Finally, DePriest repeatedly denounced the conviction of the Scottsboro* defendants. In 1934, DePriest ran for reelection against black Democrat Arthur W. Mitchell. It was a bad year for Republican congressmen, and DePriest did not escape the electoral slaughter. Mitchell defeated him, and DePriest returned to the real estate development business. He died on May 12, 1951.

SUGGESTED READINGS: Maurine Christopher, *America's Black Congressmen*, 1971; Harold F. Gosnell, *Negro Politicians: The Rise of Negro Politics in Chicago*, 1967; *New York Times*, May 13, 1951.

DEWSON, MARY WILLIAMS. Mary Dewson, a major female figure in the Democratic Party during the 1930s, was born in Quincy, Massachusetts, on February 18, 1874. Her parents were active suffragettes, campaigning for the right of women to vote, and Dewson was politicized as a child. In 1897, she graduated from Wellesley College and took a position as an economist with the Women's Educational and Industrial Union. She switched careers in 1900, becoming superintendent of the Massachusetts Girls' Parole Department. During those years in Boston, Dewson became a close friend to Florence Kelley and joined the National Consumers' League (NCL) campaign for a national minimum wage. Her experiences with the NCL made Dewson a liberal Democrat interested in social welfare legislation.

During World War I, Dewson worked in Europe for the American Red Cross, helping international refugees trapped on the continent when the war broke out. When the war ended, Dewson returned to the United States and went to work in New York for the National Consumers' League. In 1925, she became president of the Consumers' League of New York, where she earned a national reputation for her advocacy of women's rights, national health insurance, a national minimum wage, and federal old-age pension programs. Her profile earned her the attention of prominent Democrats, and Dewson became a close friend of Eleanor Roosevelt,* wife of Governor Franklin D. Roosevelt* of New York. Dewson played a key role in organizing women's groups within the Democratic Party.

When Franklin D. Roosevelt won the presidential election of 1932,* Dewson inherited real political power. In 1933 she was named head of the women's division of the Democratic National Committee. As political momentum accelerated for Social Security legislation, Dewson's expertise positioned her for a key role. In 1934, Roosevelt named her to the Committee on Economic Security,* which was charged with studying and then drafting Social Security legislation. When the Social Security Act of 1935* was passed, Roosevelt credited Dewson for making a major contribution to the law. She was appointed a member of the Social Security Board in 1937. Poor health, however, forced her resignation in 1938. Mary Dewson retired that year and died on October 24, 1962.

SUGGESTED READINGS: *New York Times*, October 25, 1962; Susan Ware, *Beyond Suffrage: Women in the New Deal*, 1981; Susan Ware, *Partner and I: Molly Dewson, Feminism, and New Deal Politics*, 1987.

DICK TRACY. The fictional character of Dick Tracy was the genius of cartoonist Chester Gould and was serialized in hundreds of newspapers throughout the country during the years of the Great Depression. With courage and cunning, Tracy foiled criminals and protected the metropolis from ruthless criminals. The most important characters were detective Dick Tracy, his sidekick Pat Patton, girlfriend Tess Trueheart, and such villains as Flattop. In 1934, NBC brought the comic strip to radio, and it remained on the air until 1948, switching back and forth at one time or another from NBC to CBS, the Mutual Network, the Blue Network, and ABC.

SUGGESTED READINGS: Michael Benton, *The Comic Book in America*, 1989; John Dunning, *On the Air: The Encyclopedia of Old-Time Radio*, 1998; Will Jacobs and Gerard Jones, *The Comic Book Heroes*, 1985.

DIDRICKSON, MILDRED "BABE" (ZAHARIAS). Mildred "Babe" Didrickson was born in Port Arthur, Texas, on June 26, 1914. A gifted athlete who dominated every sport she entered, Didrickson came to national attention at the 1932 Olympic Games in Los Angeles, where she won gold medals in the women's javelin and the 80-meter hurdles. In 1935, she took up golf. Although she had been born with extraordinary athleticism, she added a devoted work ethic to her natural talent. Often hitting more than 1,000 golf balls a day, she soon became one of the top women golfers in the world. In 1940, Didrickson won the Western Open and the Texas Open, and by 1945 she owned every amateur title. After winning the British Amateur Championship in 1947, she turned professional. Didrickson won the World Championship in 1948, 1949, 1950, and 1951 and the National Championship in 1948 and 1950. In 1954, she took the U.S. Open by twelve strokes. More than any other athlete in the history of the United States, Babe Didrickson elevated women's sports. She died on September 27, 1956.

SUGGESTED READINGS: Susan Cayleff, *Babe: The Life and Legend of Babe Didrickson Zaharias*, 1995; *New York Times*, September 28, 1956.

DIFFERENTIAL ANALYZER. In 1930 scientists at the Massachusetts Institute of Technology, led by electrical engineering professor Vannevar Bush, set to work to build what they called a "differential analyzer," a forerunner of the modern computer. Within a year, they had a working model. The differential analyzer served as a transition between mechanical adding machines and electronic calculators. The machine consisted of hundreds of rotating steel rods that covered several hundred square feet of a laboratory. Operators armed with screwdrivers and hammers had to set the machine up before each run, but once it was ready, the analyzer could solve complex differential equations with as many as eighteen variables. By the time of World War II, Bush's electromechanical machine had been replaced by electronic technology. Historians of technology, however, look back upon Vannever Bush's differential analyzer as the "birth of the computer age."

SUGGESTED READING: Stan Augarten, *Bit by Bit: An Annotative History of Computers*, 1984.

DILLINGER, JOHN. John Dillinger was born on a farm outside of Mooresville, Indiana, in 1903. The Dillingers were a quiet farming family, but John was a rebellious son who had no intention of spending his life behind a mule, scraping out a living working twelve-hour days. He wanted money the easy way and even as a teenager began having trouble with the law. In 1924 he received a nine-year prison sentence for mugging and robbing a sixty-five-year-old neighbor in Mooresville. Dillinger was released on May 22, 1933, after serving his sentence.

He wasted no time in returning to crime, but in the political atmosphere of the Great Depression, where banks and authority figures were held in such disdain, he soon became a pop culture icon. Dillinger and his gang robbed banks in Indiana, Illinois, Michigan, and Iowa, and when they needed weapons, they frequently raided police stations. In October 1933, they raided a prison in Michigan City, Indiana, took a cache of weapons and ammunition, and freed ten prisoners. He was captured in March of 1934 and jailed under heavy guard in Crown Point, Indiana, but he carved a piece of wood into the shape of a gun, painted it black with shoe polish, and then escaped from the jail after threatening the guards. He stole a getaway car with two hostages, and once out of town he gave the hostages $4 for "carfare" and apologized for inconveniencing and frightening them.

Dillinger's exploits converted him into a bandit-hero, at least in terms of the decade's pop culture. He robbed banks in an era when bank failures had robbed Americans of hundreds of millions of dollars, and he flaunted his disregard for the police. To disguise himself, he grew a mustache, had plastic surgery, and removed his fingerprints with acid treatments of his fingertips. He even had a Robin Hood streak, occasionally giving some of his money away to the poor. The Federal Bureau of Investigation (FBI) put together a 765-man task force under the direction of Agent Melvin Purvis to capture Dillinger, and the Chicago police department organized a 50-man squad of sharpshooters.

The police got their break on July 22, 1934. Dillinger's lover, Anna Sage, was a Romanian national afraid of being deported, so she made a deal with the FBI, agreeing to set a trap for the killer in return for permanent residence. She informed the FBI that on the evening of July 22, Dillinger would be attending the Biograph Theater in downtown Chicago to watch the film *Manhattan Melodrama*. The federal agents were waiting outside the theater after the film, and when fifteen of them approached Dillinger, he pulled out a handgun. They opened fire on him, and he died within a few minutes.

News of Dillinger's death hit the wire services and became headlines across the country. The funeral home that handled his body treated him like a head of state, opening the casket for public viewing, and Chicagoans lined up by the thousands to catch a glimpse of the corpse. Millions of Americans actually mourned his death. "They got him before Christmas," remarked one man sadly. "I was hoping they wouldn't. I thought he'd come through like he said. He seemed like an honest guy."

SUGGESTED READING: *New York Times*, July 23–24, 1934.

DIONNE QUINTUPLETS. On May 28, 1934, Oliva Dionne gave birth to the world's first surviving quintuplets—Emilie, Yvonne, Cecile, Marie, and Annette. Her husband Elzire was a poor worker, and they were already the parents of nine children. The births captured the world's imagination, and newspapers made headlines of the quintuplets everywhere. In return for a pittance, the Dionnes signed away marketing rights to the quints, who were then used to commercially promote everything from automobiles to breakfast cereal. After one year, the publicity campaign soon degenerated into rank exploitation of the quintuplets, and the Canadian government, to put a stop to it, seized custody of the babies. The government converted a building across the street from the Dionnes and housed the children there under the care of nurses and social workers. Oliva and Elzire enjoyed limited visitation rights. It was not until 1944 that the government returned custody of the quints to their own parents.

SUGGESTED READINGS: James Brough, *"We Were Five": The Dionne Quintuplets*, 1965; *New York Times*, May 29–31, 1934.

DOS PASSOS, JOHN. John Dos Passos, one of the country's leading novelists and literary critics during the 1920s and 1930s, was born in Chicago, Illinois, on January 14, 1896. In 1916, he graduated from Harvard with all of the romantic illusions of the era, but World War I soon revolutionized his politics. The sheer brutality of the war and loss of tens of millions of lives stunned Dos Passos, leaving him depressed and without faith, completely convinced that human nature was inherently mean and brutal, and his first novels reflected that pessimism. In *One Man's Initiation* (1919) and *Three Soldiers* (1921) he argued for the absolute absurdity of war and how World War I had completely destroyed liberal illusions.

American culture during the 1920s only reinforced Dos Passos's pessimism. The rise of a consumer culture disgusted Dos Passos. The idea of an entire society existing only to make money and purchase commodities seemed pathetically empty to him, and having the federal government dominated by big business further alienated him. He worked diligently to prevent the execution of Nicola Sacco and Bartolomeo Vanzetti, who had been convicted of murder during a robbery in Braintree, Massachusetts, because he felt they were the victims of ethnic and political persecution. After their executions in 1927, Dos Passos began work on his famous literary trilogy: *The 42nd Parallel* (1930), *1919* (1932), and *The Big Money* (1936). In the novels, Dos Passos held up to ridicule the materialism, violence, and paranoia in American culture and society.

For John Dos Passos, the onset of the Great Depression proved his critique. A society devoted to consumerism found itself mired in an economic decline of unprecedented proportions. Massive unemployment, poverty, and pessimism had bankrupted the consumer culture, at least in Dos Passos's mind. For a time he became a socialist convinced that turning the economy over to the federal government was the only answer to the Great Depression. His second trilogy—*Adventures of a Young Man* (1939), *Number One* (1943), and *The Grand Design* (1948)—reflected that. Eventually, Dos Passos abandoned his belief in socialism. He became too skeptical of human nature to believe that government could rationally restructure society. Instead, he spent his last years as a confirmed Jeffersonian liberal. Dos Passos died on September 28, 1970.

SUGGESTED READINGS: Virginia Spencer Carr, *Dos Passos: A Life*, 1984; Townsend Ludington, *John Dos Passos: A Twentieth Century Odyssey*, 1980.

DOUGLAS, LEWIS WILLIAM. Lewis Douglas was born in Bisbee, Arizona, on July 2, 1894. In 1916 he graduated from Amherst College and then pursued graduate work at Massachusetts Institute of Technology in 1916 and 1917. Between 1923 and 1925 Douglas served as a Democrat in the Arizona state legislature, where he earned a reputation as a fiscal conservative. He won a seat in Congress in 1926, and in 1933, newly inaugurated President Franklin D. Roosevelt* named him director of the budget. Douglas would soon find himself on the wrong side of New Deal* policy. He believed that the federal government should balance the budget, cut spending, and pursue sound money policies. Instead, the New Deal took the country down the road to deficit spending and inflationary monetary policies. Douglas's only accomplishment was the Economy Act of 1933.* Douglas subsequently advised against New Deal spending programs, and in September 1933, when Roosevelt took the country off the gold standard,* Douglas labeled the event "the end of western civilization." Douglas remained with the administration until August 30, 1934, when he resigned. Before his death on March 7, 1974, Douglas served as vice-president of the American Cyanamid Company, vice-chancellor of McGill University (1937–1940), president of Mutual Life Insurance Company of New York (1940–1947), and U.S. ambassador to Great Britain (1947–1950).

SUGGESTED READINGS: *New York Times*, March 8, 1974; James E. Sargent, "FDR and Lewis Douglas: Budget Balancing and the Early New Deal," *Prologue*, 6 (1974), 33–44.

DOUGLAS, WILLIAM ORVILLE. William O. Douglas was born in Maine, Minnesota, on October 16, 1898. Raised in desperate poverty and a childhood victim of polio, Douglas never lost his sympathy for poor people and the underdog. He was raised in Yakima, Washington, graduated from Whitman College in 1920, and then earned a law degree at Columbia University in 1923, where his intellect impressed the faculty. Douglas worked on Wall Street for two years, but his already well-developed suspicions of big business only deepened there. After a brief teaching stint at Columbia Law School, Douglas in 1929 joined the law faculty at Yale. He soon developed a national reputation for his expertise in finance law. In 1936, President Franklin D. Roosevelt* appointed Douglas to the board of the Securities and Exchange Commission* (SEC), and one year later, Douglas became head of the SEC. On the SEC, Douglas's commitment to corporate regulation, progressive taxation, and antitrust action became obvious.

In 1939, President Roosevelt named Douglas to fill the vacancy on the Supreme Court caused by the death of Louis Brandeis.* An unabashed liberal, Douglas backed the rights of states to regulate their own economies and the right of the federal government to assume extraordinary powers during national emergencies. He quickly became part of the liberal majority on the Court. In the 1950s and 1960s, Douglas was an advocate of individual civil rights, civil liberties, antitrust action, and the rights of labor unions. He remained on the Supreme Court for thirty-seven years, resigning for health reasons in November 1975. Douglas died on January 19, 1980.

SUGGESTED READINGS: James C. Duram, *Justice William O. Douglas*, 1981; *New York Times*, January 20–21, 1980.

"DRY." During the early years of the Great Depression, the term "dry" was used to describe those who supported the Eighteenth Amendment to the Constitution, which had implemented Prohibition. It was also used to refer to restaurants and night clubs that adhered to the law. Individuals and businesses that skirted the law and served and consumed alcohol were known as "wets."

SUGGESTED READING: Norman H. Clark, *Deliver Us from Evil: An Interpretation of American Prohibition*, 1976.

DUBINSKY, DAVID. David Dubinsky, one of the great labor leaders in American history, was born David Dobnievski on February 22, 1892, in Brest-Litovsk, Russia. He followed his father into a career as a baker in Lodz, and he became active in labor union politics. Russian police arrested him as a labor radical and forced him to endure exile in Siberia. He escaped and in 1911 emigrated to the United States. Dubinsky found a job making women's clothing, and in 1919 he was elected vice-president of a local of the International Ladies' Garment Workers' Union (ILGWU). In 1922 he became vice-president of the national ILGWU. He was elected ILGWU president in 1932. Because of the provisions of the National Industrial Recovery Act of 1933, which protected labor's right to engage in collective bargaining, the ILGWU quickly sustained enormous increases in membership, from 40,000 in 1932 to 200,000 in 1935. Along with John L. Lewis,* Dubinsky formed the Committee for Industrial Organization later renamed the Congress of Industrial Organizations* (CIO), but he opposed making the CIO a permanent organization. The ILGWU then rejoined the American Federation of Labor.* In 1936, with Adolf Berle,* he organized the American Labor Party,* which had a very liberal political agenda but still endorsed Franklin D. Roosevelt's* reelection. Dubinsky remained at the helm of the ILGWU until his death on September 17, 1982.

SUGGESTED READINGS: Max D. Danish, *The World of David Dubinsky*, 1957; *New York Times*, September 18–20, 1982; Joseph M. Rowe, Jr., "David Dubinsky," in James S. Olson, ed., *Historical Dictionary of the New Deal*, 1985.

DUST BOWL. The term "Dust Bowl" became prominent in the mid-1930s to describe the huge dust storms blowing out of the Midwest. During World War I and the 1920s, when the economy boomed, farmers dramatically increased the number of acres in production, plowing up huge amounts of soil that for tens of thousands of years had been held in place by prairie grasses. When a drought hit the Great Plains in the 1930s, the exposed soil dried out and winds lifted clouds of dirt into the skies. More than 150,000 square miles of farmland in the Midwest were affected—especially in Kansas, Colorado, Oklahoma, Texas, and New Mexico.

The huge dust storms blackened the skies, dirtied homes, and exacerbated respiratory diseases. Farmers could not plant crops, and small-town economies throughout the affected areas suffered. In 1935, the dust storms, which tended to blow from west to east, darkened the skies of Baltimore, Washington, D.C., and Philadelphia. Tens of thousands of families pulled up stakes and hit the road, many of them making their way to California in a trek that John Steinbeck* immortalized in his novel *The Grapes of Wrath*.

SUGGESTED READING: Charles Shindo, *Dust Bowl Migrants in the American Imagination*, 1997.

E

EARHART, AMELIA. Although flying around the world had become almost commonplace by 1937, aviatrix Amelia Earhart decided to do what had not been done before—circumnavigate the globe by air along an equatorial route. In 1932, she had become the first woman to complete a solo flight across the Atlantic, and when an electrical storm damaged her airplane, she managed an emergency landing in Ireland. Earhart was undaunted, enjoying the challenge and the risks of long-distance flight, and she had become famous in the United States.

On June 1, 1937, Earhart climbed into the cockpit of a twin engine Lockheed Electra in Los Angeles. Her navigator was Fred Noonan. They flew first to Puerto Rico and stopped for refueling, and then they headed south, skirting the northern coast of South America before heading east across the Atlantic Ocean, northern Africa, India, and Southeast Asia. On June 28, 1937, Earhart reached Australia and then landed in New Guinea one day later. On July 2, Earhart and Noonan took off again, planning a 2,556-mile flight across the Pacific to tiny Howland Island, which had built a small airstrip just for the occasion of her landing.

They never made it to Howland, disappearing somewhere over the Pacific and never being seen or heard from again. The fate of Earhart became one of the great mysteries of twentieth-century aviation. Speculation has headed in a number of directions, from the fact that she simply ran out of fuel and ditched in the Pacific to the rumor that she was working for naval intelligence and was captured by the Japanese, who imprisoned her on Saipan. But no firm conclusions have ever been reached about the outcome of Amelia Earhart's last flight.

SUGGESTED READING: Susan Butler, *East to the Dawn: The Story of Amelia Earhart*, 1997.

THE EASY ACES. *The Easy Aces* was a popular radio comedy of the 1930s. It revolved around the relationship between Goodman Ace and his wife Jane Ace and her penchant for malapropisms. It debuted on KMBC Radio in Kansas

City in 1931, and CBS Radio picked it up and went national with it in 1931. The pain reliever Anacin was its longtime sponsor. *The Easy Aces* remained on the air, moving back and forth from CBS to NBC, until 1948.

SUGGESTED READING: John Dunning, *On the Air: The Encyclopedia of Old-Time Radio*, 1998.

ECCLES, MARRINER STODDARD. Marriner S. Eccles was born in Logan, Utah, on September 9, 1890. His family was wealthy, with their money rooted in lumber, sugar, railroads, food processing, cattle, and mining. After a three-year tour as a Mormon missionary in Scotland, Eccles returned to manage the family businesses, which he built into a multimillion-dollar enterprise. In 1929, he took the family into the banking business when he founded the First Security Corporation. Up until the onset of the Great Depression, Eccles had maintained a traditionally conservative Republican approach to questions of political economy.

By 1933, Eccles was convinced that the real cause of the Great Depression was underconsumption and that the federal government needed to stimulate the economy through deficit spending if necessary. In that sense, Eccles anticipated some of the economic views of English economist John Maynard Keynes.* In October 1933 he came to Washington, D.C., as an economic adviser to the Roosevelt administration. He continually urged more spending programs upon the Roosevelt administration as a means of reducing the suffering of the unemployed and to boost consumer purchasing power and revive the economy. In June 1934, Eccles was appointed to head the Federal Reserve Board.*

He presided there when the Banking Act of 1935* invested the Federal Reserve Board in Washington, D.C., with enhanced power. The legislation gave the Federal Reserve's open market operations more direct authority over monetary policy. Eccles became a leading member of the group of New Deal* advisers urging President Franklin D. Roosevelt* to stimulate the economy through relaxed monetary policies, deficit spending, and tax cuts. It was not until the recession of 1937–1938,* however, that Eccles's ideas finally prevailed. Eccles remained at the helm of the Federal Reserve Board until 1948. He spent three more years as a member of the board before returning to the family business. Eccles died on December 18, 1977.

SUGGESTED READINGS: Marriner S. Eccles, *Beckoning Frontiers*, 1951; Sidney Hyman, *Marriner S. Eccles*, 1976; Patrick D. Reagan, "Marriner Stoddard Eccles," in James S. Olson, ed., *Historical Dictionary of the New Deal*, 1985.

ECONOMY ACT OF 1933. When President Franklin D. Roosevelt* assumed office in March 1933, he faced a range of suggestions from Democrats about how to handle the depression. Many conservative Democrats were as committed as President Herbert Hoover* had been to fiscal caution and urged a balanced budget and cuts in federal spending. Their logic was that such policies would restore business confidence and lead to increases in business investment and industrial production. The Economy Act was designed to satisfy these conservatives. Signed by Roosevelt on March 20, 1933, the Economy Act cut $100 million from the federal budget by reducing government salaries and veterans' allowances and cutting departmental spending budgets. Eventually, the Economy Act saved a total of $243 million. Of course, at the same time, Congress was passing a series of relief and recovery measures that drove the federal budget through the roof and rendered the Economy Act meaningless in terms of the total economy.

SUGGESTED READING: James E. Sargent, "FDR and Lewis Douglas: Budget Balancing and the Early New Deal," *Prologue*, 6 (1974), 33–44.

***EDWARDS V. PEOPLE OF THE STATE OF CALIFORNIA* (1941).** During the 1930s, many California residents resented the influx of poor people from Texas, Oklahoma, Arkansas, and Missouri, and the state legislature made it a misdemeanor to assist indigent people in immigrating to California. The case of *Edwards v. People of the State of California* tested the constitutionality of the law. The U.S. Supreme Court decided the case on November 24, 1941, ruling against the state law because it placed "an unconstitutional burden on interstate commerce." Justice William O. Douglas* added that U.S. citizenship guaranteed the right of an individual to move freely from state to state.

SUGGESTED READINGS: Joseph M. Rowe, Jr., "*Edwards v. People of the State of California*," in James S. Olson, ed., *Historical Dictionary of the New Deal*, 1985; *Supreme Court Reporter*, 62 (1941), 164–71.

EDWARD VIII. On December 11, 1936, King Edward VIII of Great Britain delivered a radio address that was listened to around the world. He had fallen in love with Ms. Wallis Warfield Simpson, an American divorcee. He wanted to marry her, but since she was a commoner, marriage would force him to abdicate the British throne. The issue posed a political crisis in Great Britain, where Parliament and the royal family tried to dissuade him. But in the United States, it was better than the best of the romance novels. When the king decided to give up the throne to marry his American lover, Americans hailed the decision.

SUGGESTED READING: Philip Ziegler, *King Edward VIII*, 1991.

ELECTION OF 1930. The congressional elections of 1930 provided voters with their first opportunity, since the stock market crash* in September and October of 1929, to express sentiments about the policies of the Herbert Hoover* administration. They were, to put it mildly, very frustrated. Hoover had won the presidential election of 1928 by a landslide, and his coattails had proven quite long. Republicans took a 56 to 39 lead in the Senate, while the GOP (Grand Old Party) controlled the House of Representatives by a margin of 267 to 168. Democrats had been reduced to an inconsequential minority. But with unemployment exceeding 5 million people by September 1930, and banks failing in large numbers, Republicans had no chance of maintaining such dominance.

During the campaign, Democratic candidates pilloried Hoover for doing nothing to ameliorate the disastrous effects of the depression, and they tried to lump all Republican candidates together with Hoover in a guilt-by-association strategy. For their part, most Republican candidates tried to distance themselves from the president, and he became a virtual persona non grata on the campaign circuit. When the votes were finally counted, the GOP took a real hit. The Republican majority in the Senate slipped to 48 to 47, and when the lone Farmer-Laborite sided with the Democrats, the Senate had become a dead heat, with Republican Vice-President Alben Barkley casting the tie-breaking vote. In the House, the Republican majority was reduced to a razor-thin 218 to 216. And then, before Congress went into session in March 1931, fourteen House seats were vacated by death and resignation. Once special elections had been held, with Hoover growing more unpopular, the Democrats took control of the House of Representatives by a 219 to 214 margin.

For the GOP, the proverbial political handwriting was on the wall. Unless something was done to stimulate the economy before the presidential election of 1932,* Republicans were threatened with the loss of the White House, both houses of Congress, and a majority of state governorships. Also, Democrats had a sure-fire winner in Franklin D. Roosevelt,* governor of New York, who had won reelection by a landslide in 1930. Glib and charismatic, Roosevelt had all of Al Smith's* assets in being popular in New York, the Northeast, and the Midwest, as well as with urban machine politicians, without Smith's liability of being a Roman Catholic. Roosevelt's solid Episcopalian credentials would all but return the Deep South to the Democratic fold after its apostasy in the election of 1928.

SUGGESTED READINGS: *New York Times*, November 4–7, 1930, and March 3–6, 1931; Arthur M. Schlesinger, Jr., ed., *History of American Presidential Elections, 1788–1968*, 1977; Jordan A. Schwarz, *The Interregnum of Despair: Hoover, Congress, and the Depression*, 1970.

ELECTION OF 1932. By the time that the elections of 1932 rolled around, Republicans were in desperate political circumstances. The national unemployment rate had reached an unprecedented 25 percent, corporate profits had collapsed, industrial production had cratered, and the money markets were in a state of meltdown, with banks, savings banks, building and loan associations, and credit unions failing by the thousands. Public confidence in the economy and in the Herbert Hoover* administration had all but evaporated. The Republican Party nominated President Hoover for a second term, but Republican insiders had few illusions. Governor Franklin D. Roosevelt* of New York had won the Democratic nomination and then had electrified the Democratic convention in Chicago by appearing in person to accept the nomination. He delivered a rousing acceptance speech in which he promised a New Deal for the American people. The campaign had its slogan—"New Deal"*—and a campaign song—"Happy Days Are Here Again."* He then picked veteran Democratic congressman John Nance Garner* of Texas as his running mate. FDR and the Democrats were certain to win the election.

Whatever slim chance Hoover had of retaining the White House was dashed completely when the president mishandled the so-called Bonus Army.* In 1932, thousands of unemployed World War I veterans had marched on Washington, D.C., demanding early payment of their military pensions. They had served their country during its time of crisis and now wanted their country to assist them. But Hoover was not about to accede to their demands. Instead, he ordered General Douglas MacArthur to evict the veterans from their campgrounds at Anacostia Flats. MacArthur treated the veterans like an invading enemy, dispersing them with sword, rifle, and tear gas. The press had a fieldday with the event, splattering photos of bloodied veterans on the front pages of newspapers throughout the country. Hoover appeared even more insensitive and uncaring.

During the campaign, Roosevelt and the Democrats were long on rhetoric and short on specifics. They condemned Hoover for doing too little, too late, to stimulate the economy, but they did not spell out just how they would have behaved differently. Not that specifics really mattered. Few Americans kept track of election details, but they did suspect that Roosevelt would probably act more boldly than Hoover had and would probably employ the resources of the federal government in more substantial ways. Roosevelt used the radio to great advantage, sounding warm, comfortable, and congenial, his natural charisma radiating confidence. Hoover, on the other hand, appeared and sounded cold, uncomfortable, and pessimistic.

The election outcome was worse than even the most pessimistic Republican strategists could have imagined. In the general election, Roosevelt shattered all records when he won 22,809,638 popular votes to Hoover's 15,758,901. FDR's margin of victory in the electoral college was 472 to 59. The Democratic majority in the House of Representatives jumped from 219 to 214 to a huge 313 to 117. In the Senate, Democrats now outnumbered Republicans by 62 to 36. The victory was the most stunning and complete in American history.

SUGGESTED READINGS: *New York Times*, November 2–8, 1932; Richard Oulahan, *The Man Who . . . : The Story of the Democratic Convention of 1932*, 1971; Elliot Rosen, *Hoover, Roosevelt, and the Brains Trust: From Depression to New Deal*, 1977.

ELECTION OF 1932 (GERMANY). The 1930 elections proved to be a watershed in the history of modern Germany.* Until then, Adolf Hitler and his

Nazi Party had been confined to the political fringe, an extremist group that had little appeal beyond a small number of ultra German nationalists. But the onset of the Great Depression in 1929 jump-started the Nazi Party. As the German economy plummeted, along with prices and employment, fear and resentment among blue-collar and middle-class workers escalated, and Hitler's message— that the German *Volk*, or people, were a super race because of their Aryan roots and that Jews were the cause of the country's misery—gained a widespread following. Hitler preached racial superiority and national patriotism. He denounced democracy as an illusion and communism as the epitome of evil. When the votes were counted, the National Socialist Party, or Socialists, won 6.5 million votes and 107 of 577 seats in the Reichstag. Adolf Hitler, once considered a minor, if loud, nuisance in German politics, had become a force to be reckoned with.

SUGGESTED READING: Hans Mommsen, *The Rise and Fall of Weimar Democracy*, 1996.

ELECTION OF 1934. In the congressional elections of 1934, President Franklin D. Roosevelt* and the Democrats defied conventional logic. After their landslide victory in the presidential and congressional elections of 1932,* most pundits expected Republicans to rebound and regain some of the ground they had lost in Congress. But few people could gauge just how popular Franklin D. Roosevelt had become and just how relieved most Americans were that the worst of the Great Depression seemed behind them. In most off-year elections, the party in power in the White House and Congress lost a substantial number of seats, and the Democrats seemed to have many to lose. After the election of 1932, their majority in the House of Representatives was 310 to 117 Republicans and 5 Farmer-Laborites and in the Senate a total of 60 Democrats to 35 Republicans and 1 Farmer-Laborite.

But a unique combination of the Great Depression and its severe unemployment, Republican failure to address it successfully between 1929 and 1933, and the virtual whirlwind of federal government activity under the New Deal* had rendered FDR and the Democrats unbeatable. Roosevelt's "relief, recovery, and reform" programs appealed to the general public, who wanted to make sure that he kept his congressional majorities. When the votes were counted, the Democrats had unbelievably extended their reach in Congress. They ended up with 319 seats in the House, compared to 103 for the Republicans and 10 for the Farmer-Laborites. The Democratic majority in the Senate ended up at 60 to 36. Governorships were even more lopsided. After the elections of 1934, Democrats controlled forty-one governor's mansions, compared to only seven for the Republicans. Journalist William Allen White captured the significance of the moment when he wrote, "Franklin D. Roosevelt has been all but crowned by the people."

SUGGESTED READINGS: William F. Leuchtenburg, *Franklin D. Roosevelt and the New Deal, 1932–1940*, 1963; James T. Patterson, *Congressional Conservatism in the New Deal*, 1967.

ELECTION OF 1936. In the presidential and congressional elections of 1936, Republicans hoped to make a test case of Franklin D. Roosevelt* and the New Deal.* Some Republicans even hoped to regain control of the White House and Congress, but those hopes proved to be a pipedream. They nominated Governor Alf Landon* of Kansas as their presidential candidate, and because of a poll run by *The Literary Digest*,* they actually expected to win. *The Literary Digest* pollsters had called prospective voters by telephone and asked them how they were going to vote. A majority chose Landon, and the magazine predicted defeat for Roosevelt. The problem, of course, was that many Americans, especially poor Democrats, did not have telephones, so the poll was not the least bit scientific. The Republicans criticized the New Deal for its deficit spending and massive bureaucracy, predicted that Social Security would break the treasury, and warned that another Franklin D. Roosevelt administration would lead to the demise of free enterprise capitalism.

But most Americans were not listening. They credited FDR and the New Deal with easing the trauma of the Great Depression and putting people back to work, even though much of the work consisted of government relief jobs. Democrats warned voters that a vote for Alf Landon was a vote for Herbert Hoover* and the laissez-faire apathy of the superrich.

The real wild card of the 1936 election was the third-party campaign of William Lemke* of the Union Party.* The Union Party consisted of an unstable, anti-Roosevelt coalition of the followers of assassinated Senator Huey Long,* Roman Catholic priest Father Charles Coughlin,* old-age pension advocate Francis Townsend,* and William Lemke* of the Non-Partisan League. But the Union Party posed no real threat to FDR and the New Deal. Lemke's anti-Catholic, pro–Ku Klux Klan rhetoric drove Coughlin and his Catholic following from the ticket, and Lemke's suggestion that a paramilitary group be formed to storm Washington, D.C., and seize control of the federal government endeared him to few people.

When the votes were counted in November 1936, FDR won handily. He took 27,752,869 popular votes to Landon's 16,67,665 and Lemke's 882,479. The electoral college was even more lopsided, with Roosevelt getting 523 to Landon's 8. The Democrats even extended their congressional majorities. The Senate ended up with 76 Democrats, 16 Republicans, and 4 Farmer-Laborites. In the House of Representatives, the Democrats had 331 seats to 89 for the Republicans and 13 combined for the Socialists, Progressives, and Farmer-Laborites.

SUGGESTED READINGS: David H. Bennett, *Demagogues in the Depression: American Radicals and the Union Party, 1932–1936*, 1969; Edwin S. Davis, "The Election

of 1936," in James S. Olson, ed., *Historical Dictionary of the New Deal*, 1985; Howard
F. Gosnell, *Champion Campaigner: Franklin Roosevelt*, 1952.

ELECTION OF 1938. Franklin D. Roosevelt* and the Democrats enjoyed a
string of victories in the elections of 1930,* 1932,* 1934,* and 1936,* but in
the congressional elections of 1938, the New Deal* came up short. The recession
of 1937–1938* had produced new waves of layoffs, and the unemployment rate
spiked up again after several years of steady decline. In the farm belt, wheat
and corn prices fell in the face of record harvests. Many Americans worried that
the economy was slipping back into the Great Depression. Complicating President Roosevelt's political problem in 1938 was the public reaction to his court-
packing scheme* of 1937, when he had tried to expand the size of the Supreme
Court and "pack" it with liberal justices who would uphold New Deal legislation. Although most Americans disagreed with the Supreme Court's assault on
the New Deal, they were uncomfortable with Roosevelt's attempt to tamper with
the Court. It seemed to violate the constitutional principle of separation of powers. Feuding between the American Federation of Labor* and new Congress of
Industrial Organizations* also weakened the Democratic Party's cause in 1938
because labor could not deliver the votes they had come to rely upon. Unfounded
rumors that Harry Hopkins* and the Works Progress Administration* were corrupt and using government jobs to build a powerful political machine only complicated matters.

The president's political strategy in 1938 also backfired on him. He had grown
extremely frustrated with conservative Democrats, especially southerners, who
all too frequently joined hands with northern Republicans in blocking New Deal
initiatives. The president misjudged how protective Americans could be of local
prerogatives, and he personally entered a number of primary races to campaign
against certain conservative Democrats. He particularly wanted to unseat people
like Senator Ellison "Cotton Ed" Smith* of South Carolina, Senator Guy Gillette
of Iowa, Senator Walter George* of Georgia, Senator Millard Tydings* of Maryland, and Congressman John J. O'Connor* of New York.

Journalists dubbed FDR's intervention the "Purge of 1938," but his personal
campaigning proved to be counterproductive. John J. O'Connor was the only
Roosevelt enemy to lose the election, and most Americans felt the president had
gone too far. Southern Democrats were particularly irritated with the president's
actions. Resentment with Roosevelt lingered into the fall elections. Republicans
gained seventy-five seats in the House of Representatives, seven in the Senate,
and thirteen governorships. The conservative coalition in Congress of southern
Democrats and northern Republicans had grown much stronger.

SUGGESTED READING: James T. Patterson, *Congressional Conservatism in the New
Deal*, 1967.

ELECTION OF 1940. In 1940, a coalition of anti-Roosevelt Democrats, Wall
Street investors, and anti–New Deal* journalists began pushing utility magnate

Wendell Willkie's* candidacy for the Republican presidential nomination. He won the nomination on the sixth ballot at the Republican National Convention, and he selected Senator Charles McNary of Oregon as his running mate. Willkie built his campaign around a theme that accused President Franklin D. Roosevelt* of vastly expanding the federal bureaucracy without ever really solving the depression and with letting the country's military defenses lapse into a state of unreadiness.

The Republicans also tried to make the most out of the fact that President Roosevelt was seeking a third term in the White House, something George Washington had eschewed and no other president had even attempted. But Franklin D. Roosevelt had become for all intents and purposes a father figure to tens of millions of Americans, and with the world drifting again into war, voters were not inclined to change course.

The criticisms of the New Deal were certainly justified, but the Willkie-McNary ticket could not deal with the deteriorating international situation. The outbreak of World War II in Europe in 1939 had led to increased purchases of war goods in the United States, and millions of new jobs were being created. Most Americans could see the Great Depression slipping into the past. At the same time, Americans became loathe to switch leaders when war seemed on the horizon. When the votes were counted, FDR defeated Willkie 27,307,819 to 22,321,018, with 499 electoral votes to Willkie's 82. In Congress, the Democrats gained seven seats in the House of Representatives, while Republicans upped their Senate total by five seats.

SUGGESTED READINGS: Mary Earhart Dillon, *Wendell Willkie, 1892–1944*, 1952; Herbert S. Parmet and Marie B. Hecht, *Never Again: A President Runs for a Third Term*, 1968.

ELECTRIC HOME AND FARM AUTHORITY. A key mission of the Tennessee Valley Authority* was to generate electricity for sale to the public, but many Americans in the region were too poor to be able to afford to purchase the electrical appliances that would make their lives better. In 1933, the Electric Home and Farm Authority (EHFA) was established as a subsidiary of the Reconstruction Finance Corporation* to convince appliance manufacturers and retail dealers to make the equipment affordable to poorer consumers. The EHFA did so by purchasing installment contracts from retailers and finance companies. By 1939 the EHFA had purchased more than 100,000 of those contracts. With such a secondary market available for the contracts, retailers were more willing to finance appliance purchases. Sales went up, and so did production of appliances and electricity consumption.

SUGGESTED READINGS: James S. Olson, *Saving Capitalism: The Reconstruction Finance Corporation and the New Deal, 1933–1940*, 1988; Ronald C. Tobay, *Technology as Freedom: The New Deal and the Electrical Modernization of America*, 1996.

EMERGENCY BANKING ACT OF 1933. On March 4, 1933, when President Franklin D. Roosevelt* took the oath of office, the money markets were in a state of meltdown and banks were closing by the thousands. Roosevelt realized that only a dramatic gesture and credible federal intervention could prevent the complete collapse of the economy. On March 6, 1933, the president signed a proclamation declaring a moratorium on all banking operations in the United States. The bank holiday* closed every bank in the United States. On Thursday, March 9, 1933, Roosevelt convened Congress in special session to address the problem. He submitted a bill to them that had been partially drafted during the last days of the Hoover administration and to which Roosevelt's advisers added several provisions. Congress and the general public were desperate for action, and the Emergency Banking Act passed within a matter of hours.

Title I of the law legalized Roosevelt's extraordinary action of declaring a bank holiday. Title II authorized the office of the comptroller of the currency to name a conservator to subordinate certain depositor and stockholder interests so that those banks could then be legally reorganized. Title III permitted the Reconstruction Finance Corporation* (RFC) to invest in the preferred stock or capital notes of banks and trust companies. Such a provision, the administration believed, would provide banks with long-term capital and relieve them of short-term debt repayments to the RFC. Title IV permitted the Federal Reserve Banks to discount previously ineligible assets and to issue new Federal Reserve notes on the basis of those assets as a means of ending the currency shortages in certain regions of the country. Title V provided $2 million to implement the legislation. The Emergency Banking Act then provided the legal initiative for the reconstruction of the banking system during the rest of the decade.

SUGGESTED READINGS: James S. Olson, *Herbert Hoover and the Reconstruction Finance Corporation, 1931–1933*, 1977; James S. Olson, *Saving Capitalism: The Reconstruction Finance Corporation and the New Deal, 1933–1940*, 1988.

EMERGENCY FARM MORTGAGE ACT OF 1933. During the prosperous years of World War I, when European demand for American farm products drove up commodity prices, millions of farmers went heavily into debt to purchase the land and machinery needed to increase production. In most cases, they mortgaged their land. But after World War I, when European agricultural production revived and demand for American commodities fell, prices collapsed and many farmers felt hard-pressed to pay their debts. Bank foreclosures on farms became commonplace. Matters only got worse after the stock market crash.*

On April 3, 1933, President Franklin D. Roosevelt* asked Congress to pass legislation allowing for the readjustment of mortgage principal, reduction of contracted interest rates, and a lengthening of amortization schedules to give farmers more time to pay off their mortgages. Congress responded by passing an amendment to the Agricultural Adjustment Act* that authorized Federal Land Banks to issue up to $2 billion in 4 percent, tax-exempt bonds guaranteed by the federal government. Proceeds from the bond sales would be used to refinance the mortgages. The law imposed a loan ceiling of $50,000 per farmer and $25,000 per individual. Loans issued at 4.5 percent could not exceed 50 percent of the appraised value of the land, and farmers could make interest-only payments for the first five years. The law also authorized the RFC to supply $200 million to the Federal Farm Loan commissioner to be used to help farmers redeem property lost through foreclosure after July 1, 1931. The Emergency Farm Mortgage Act of 1933 dramatically reduced the frequency of farm foreclosures.

SUGGESTED READING: *Congressional Digest*, 12 (1933), 156–57.

EMERGENCY RAILROAD TRANSPORTATION ACT OF 1933. During the late nineteenth and early twentieth centuries, most American railroads took upon themselves long-term debts in order to finance construction. But they badly overbuilt, laying more miles of track than the economy could absorb. Competition for freight became cutthroat, and freight revenues declined. Early in the 1900s, the advent of the internal combustion engine and the appearance of the trucking industry brought even more competition. But because of their debt structures, the railroads had fixed payments on long-term bonds that had to be paid. The onset of the Great Depression only exacerbated railroad financial problems. By 1933, the American railroad industry teetered on collapse. Decades of overbuilding, duplication of services, and onerous debts left many railroads unable to meet their short-term or even long-term obligations. It was also a critical problem for the financial system because so many banks and other financial institutions had purchased long-term railroad bonds. If the roads went bankrupt, bank assets would decline even further.

The Emergency Railroad Transportation Act was designed to restore financial stability to the industry. It created a federal coordinator of transportation to divide the nation's railroad network into three subgroups: eastern, southern, and western. Each group would then establish a coordinating committee of railroad managers, who would then eliminate duplication, promote cost-saving joint use of tracks and terminals, and encourage financial reorganization to cut fixed costs. The federal coordinator had the administrative power to force recalcitrant managers to cooperate, although all decisions could be appealed to the Interstate Commerce Commission (ICC).

President Franklin D. Roosevelt* appointed Joseph B. Eastman as federal coordinator, but he could achieve very little in his position. At every turn, he encountered pitched opposition. Railroad managers resisted consolidation attempts because they feared the loss of corporate independence. Railroad labor unions opposed consolidation because it would cut costs and jobs. Many communities opposed consolidation because they feared losing railroad service. Finally, large, powerful industries shipping freight by railroad feared that consolidation would lead to higher freight rates. What saved the railroads from financial collapse during the 1930s were billions of dollars in loans from the Reconstruction Finance Corporation.*

SUGGESTED READINGS: Ari Hoogenboom and Olive Hoogenboom, *A History of the ICC: From Panacea to Palliative*, 1976; James S. Olson, *Herbert Hoover and the Reconstruction Finance Corporation, 1931–1933*, 1977; James S. Olson, *Saving Capitalism: The Reconstruction Finance Corporation and the New Deal, 1933–1940*, 1988.

EMERGENCY RELIEF AND CONSTRUCTION ACT OF 1932. When the economy slipped into the Great Depression in 1929 and 1930, President Herbert Hoover* was slow to implement any significant federal efforts to provide relief to the unemployed. He feared that federal relief would become a dole that would undermine the American character. But as the depression worsened in 1931 and 1932, Hoover had no choice. With the presidential election of 1932* approaching, political reality dictated some type of federal relief effort. The Emergency Relief and Construction Act, Hoover's answer to the problem, was passed in July 1932. The legislation was actually quite modest, too modest to address the massive unemployment problem. The bill authorized the Reconstruction Finance Corporation* to issue up to $1.5 billion in bonds to state and local governments, with the money targeted at self-amortizing public construction projects, such as toll roads, toll bridges, hydroelectric power projects, water systems, and sewage systems. The RFC also received authorization to loan up to $300 million to state and local government relief commissions for emergency distribution to the poor and the unemployed.

In the end, the money proved to be too little, too late. The public works construction projects had a long developmental lead time, and none of the money was spent during Hoover's administration. Also, the $300 million in relief loans was pitifully inadequate. Local relief commissions could have easily distributed $3 billion to the worthy poor. The Emergency Relief and Construction Act of 1932 eventually only reinforced the public impression of President Hoover as a stingy, heartless leader and all but doomed his chances for reelection.

SUGGESTED READING: James S. Olson, *Herbert Hoover and the Reconstruction Finance Corporation, 1931–1933*, 1977.

EMPIRE STATE BUILDING. At its time, the Empire State Building was one of the world's greatest architectural achievements. Conceived in the early 1920s with the American economy booming, it was designed to take advantage of exploding real estate prices in Manhattan. Many critics predicted that it would never earn a sufficient return on its investment. Construction was finally completed in 1931, and the building, with its television antennae, reached a height of 1,250 feet, by far the tallest building in the world. Its art deco style also attracted enormous attention. Journalists soon dubbed it the "Eighth Wonder of the World," and the 1933 film *King Kong*,* with the giant ape scaling its heights, gave the building even more caché. And the real estate critics were proved wrong. The Empire State Building soon became one of the most prestigious business addresses in the world, and the edifice was one of New York City's hottest tourist attractions.

SUGGESTED READING: John Jauranac, *The Empire State Building: The Making of a Landmark*, 1995.

EPSTEIN, ABRAHAM. Abraham Epstein, one of the country's most influential critics and advocates of Social Security, was born in Russia on April 20, 1872, and immigrated to the United States in 1910. He settled in Pittsburgh, where he attended the University of Pittsburgh. After graduating in 1917, Epstein accepted a position as researcher director for the Pennsylvania Commission on Old-Age Pensions. He worked indefatigably for a national Social Security program, and in 1927, he played a leading role in the establishment of the American Association for Old Age Security. In 1933, with the election of Franklin D. Roosevelt* and the Democrats, he changed the name of the organization to the American Association for Social Security. He also played a key role as a consultant to the Committee on Economic Security,* which drafted the Social Security Act of 1935.*

But Epstein also became Social Security's most articulate critic. He had long believed that any national system of Social Security should be financed by government appropriations and not by special Social Security taxes, which Epstein considered regressive and discriminatory against the poor. But when enacted, the Social Security system received its revenues from payroll taxes by employers and employees. For the rest of his life, Epstein campaigned, unsuccessfully as it turned out, for financing reform. Even today, Social Security is financed from payroll taxes. Abraham Epstein died on May 5, 1942.

SUGGESTED READING: Roy Lubove, *The Struggle for Social Security, 1900–1935*, 1968.

ETHIOPIA. Many historians look to Ethiopia as the opening salvo of World War II in the Mediterranean. In 1896, Italy* had suffered an embarrassing military defeat in Ethiopia, and dictator Benito Mussolini wanted revenge. He also wanted to promote his own standing vis-à-vis fellow fascist Adolf Hitler, who had recently announced his decision to rearm Germany.* Mussolini sent out diplomatic teasers to Great Britain and France, to see if they would openly oppose an Italian invasion of Ethiopia, and when they for the most part kept their silence, he decided to proceed with the invasion.

Mussolini began massing troops in Eritrea, an Italian colony that bordered on Ethiopia. In October 1935, Italian tanks crossed the Ethiopian-Eritrean frontier and attacked. Emperor Haile Selassie of Ethiopia tried to resist, but his horse-born cavalry troops were no match for Mussolini's tanks and poisonous gases. By May 1936, Italy's control of Ethiopia was complete.

The invasion stimulated an outburst of patriotic support for Mussolini in Italy, but it was a diplomatic disaster for Italy. The League of Nations condemned the invasion and imposed trade sanctions on Italy, but other major powers all but ignored them. Opposition to the invasion was intense in France and Great Britain, and those two countries vigorously condemned the invasion. Their outrage inadvertently drove Mussolini into closer relations with Adolf Hitler and Germany.

SUGGESTED READING: MacGregor Knox, *Mussolini Unleashed 1939–1941: Politics and Strategy in Fascist Italy's Last War*, 1982.

EVANS, WALKER. Walker Evans was born in 1903 in St. Louis, Missouri. The child of a wealthy family, Evans enjoyed private education and attended Williams College. He then studied art and literature in Paris, where he acquired an interest in photography, which eventually became his passion. In the 1930s, he joined the Farm Security Administration's* program to chronicle the suffering of poor people caught in an economic depression. He worked with such leading lights in American photography as Roy Stryker, Dorothea Lange,* Carl Mydans, and Arthur Rothstein, and they took more than 75,000 photographs. Evans worked in the slums of New York City; the coal mines of Ohio, West Virginia, and Pennsylvania; and the hard scrabble world of tenant farmers in the Southeast.

Evans is best remembered for his partnership with writer James Agee. He left the Farm Security Administration temporarily in 1938 and traveled in Alabama with Agee. They lived for two months with the families of sharecroppers Bud Fields, Frank Tengle, and Floyd Burroughs. Agee and Evans also traveled throughout Alabama, Georgia, and Mississippi. Their book *Let Us Now Praise Famous Men*, which revealed the lives of poor sharecoppers, became an American classic. Evans went on to become a contributing photographic editor at *Time* and then *Fortune*. From 1965 until his death in April 1975, Evans was a professor of design at Yale.

SUGGESTED READINGS: James R. Mellow, *Walker Evans*, 1999; John Szarkowski, *Walker Evans*, 1971; Barbara M. Tyson, "Walker Evans," in James S. Olson, ed., *Historical Dictionary of the New Deal*, 1985.

EXPORT-IMPORT BANK. Early in the New Deal,* President Franklin D. Roosevelt* decided to stimulate foreign trade and American exports in order to stimulate an economic recovery. The Reciprocal Trade Agreements Act of 1934* was designed to lower global tariff rates, and the Export-Import Bank was intended to provide loans to companies wishing to expand overseas operations. In February 1934, as part of extending diplomatic recognition to the Soviet Union,* Roosevelt established the Export-Import Bank as a subsidiary of the Reconstruction Finance Corporation.* In March 1934, when Cuba requested U.S. assistance to purchase and mint silver coins, the president established the Second Export-Import Bank to handle the transactions. Roosevelt soon expanded the Second Export-Import Bank's operations to include trade with other nations. The original Export-Import Bank remained confined to trade with the Soviet Union. The Second Export-Import made many direct loans, primarily for the export of railway and heavy equipment, and created a secondary market for commercial banks financing companies in the export business. By 1937, the bank had made $37 million worth of loans, a paltry amount given its grandiose goals. After 1937 its operations greatly expanded because it made loans directly to foreign governments. By 1940, the bank was more of a diplomatic than an economic institution.

SUGGESTED READINGS: James S. Olson, *Herbert Hoover and the Reconstruction Finance Corporation, 1931–1933*, 1977; James S. Olson, *Saving Capitalism: The Reconstruction Finance Corporation and the New Deal, 1933–1940*, 1988.

F

FAIR EMPLOYMENT PRACTICES COMMITTEE. In 1941, as the economy continued its shift toward increased defense spending, African American leaders expressed increasing concern about employment discrimination against black workers. A. Philip Randolph, head of the Brotherhood of Sleeping Car Porters, emerged as a black spokesman on the issue, especially after he threatened to stage a march on Washington, D.C., to protest racial discrimination. President Franklin D. Roosevelt* wanted to avoid such a march, which he was convinced would distract Americans from "more important" New Deal* issues and make the United States look bad abroad. After meeting with Randolph and other black leaders, Roosevelt asked New York City Mayor Fiorello La Guardia* to head a commission to study the issue, and La Guardia soon called for a presidential executive order banning such discrimination. Roosevelt agreed, and on June 25, 1941, by executive order, he established the Fair Employment Practices Committee (FEPC). The FEPC proved to be more symbolic than real. Roosevelt could not give the FEPC any real power or money for fear of alienating southern Democrats, who controlled most congressional committees. So the FEPC held hearings and made proposals but had no powers of enforcement.

SUGGESTED READINGS: John Kirby, *Black Americans in the Roosevelt Era: Liberalism and Race*, 1980; Ruth P. Morgan, *The President and Civil Rights*, 1970; Dan K. Utley, "Fair Employment Practices Committee," in James S. Olson, ed., *Historical Dictionary of the New Deal*, 1985.

FAIR LABOR STANDARDS ACT OF 1938. In 1935, when the Supreme Court in its *Schechter** decision declared unconstitutional the National Industrial Recovery Act of 1933 (NIRA), it also overturned the only significant federal labor standards laws on the books. The NIRA had mandated minimum wage and maximum hours standards and had declared yellow-dog contracts illegal, and when the law was declared unconstitutional, labor leaders began to lobby for new legislation. The Walsh-Healey Public Contracts Act of 1936* mandated

minimum wage and maximum hours for all federal contractors (requiring over-
time for work in excess of eight hours a day or forty hours a week), but comprehensive legislation did not emerge until 1938. The Fair Labor Standards Act
became law on June 25, 1938.

The legislation established a wage and hour division in the Department of
Labor to enforce its provisions. For all workers engaged in interstate commerce
or producing goods destined for interstate shipment, the law mandated a minimum wage of twenty-five cents an hour for 1938 and thirty cents an hour for
1939. The minimum wage would rise to forty cents an hour in 1946. The law
also set the maximum workweek at forty-four hours for 1938 and forty hours
for 1939 and after. It outlawed child labor and defined a child worker as anyone
under the age of sixteen. More than 13 million workers fell under the jurisdiction
of the Fair Labor Standards Act of 1938; the most conspicuous workers excluded
were agricultural laborers, intrastate retail employees, seamen, street railway
operators, and fishermen.

SUGGESTED READINGS: Paul H. Douglas and Joseph Hackman, "The Fair Labor
Standards Act of 1938 II," *Political Science Quarterly*, LIV (1939), 29–55; David Milton,
The Politics of U.S. Labor: From the Great Depression to the New Deal, 1980.

FANNIE MAE. See **FEDERAL NATIONAL MORTGAGE ASSOCIA-
TION**.

FARLEY, JAMES ALOYSIUS. James Farley was born in Grassy Point, New
York, on May 30, 1888. His father was a brick manufacturer and active in local
Democratic Party politics. As a child, Farley, too, worked in local Democratic
campaigns. He moved to New York City after graduating from high school,
studied bookkeeping, and went to work for the United Gypsum Company. In
1912, he was elected as town clerk for Stony Point, New York, which launched
his lifetime career in politics. He became close friends with Al Smith,* and in
1918, when Smith won the governorship of New York, Farley was appointed
port warden of New York. Farley served a term in the state legislature (1923–
1925), and he built his own successful construction business. Farley became
secretary of the New York State Democratic Committee in 1928 and helped
direct Franklin D. Roosevelt's* successful campaign for the governorship. In
1930, Farley became chair of the New York State Democratic Committee, and
in that post he directed FDR's successful reelection campaign.

Blessed with an uncanny gift for inside politics, Farley played a key role in
FDR's run for the presidency in 1932, and in 1933, Farley became postmaster
general in the New Deal* cabinet. He also served as chairman of the Democratic
National Committee. Farley managed FDR's successful reelection campaign in
1936. The Farley-FDR relationship, however, then soured. Farley opposed the
court-packing scheme* of 1937 and opposed the president's campaign against
Democratic conservatives in the so-called Purge of 1938. He also opposed

FDR's bid for a third term in 1940, primarily because Farley himself wanted to run for the White House. Farley resigned from the cabinet and from the Democratic National Committee. He remained active in politics for the rest of his life and died on June 9, 1976.

SUGGESTED READINGS: John T. Casey, *Farley and Tomorrow*, 1937; *New York Times*, June 10, 1976.

FARM CREDIT ACT OF 1933. The collapse of the nation's money markets in 1933 placed severe strains on the farming economy and on tens of millions of farmers, who carried heavy debt burdens. Commodity prices dropped, farm income declined, mortgage foreclosures reached epidemic proportions, and farmers experienced difficulty securing normal production loans from cautious rural bankers. In June 1933, Congress passed the Farm Credit Act to help relieve the crisis. The legislation authorized the establishment of local credit institutions for farmers to ease their working capital and marketing problems. It also provided legislative authorization for the president's March 1933 executive order creating the Farm Credit Administration.*

SUGGESTED READINGS: W. Gifford Hoag, *The Farm Credit System: A History of Financial Self-Help*, 1976; W. N. Stokes, Jr., *Credit to Farmers. The Story of the Federal Intermediate Credit Banks and Production Credit Associations*, 1973.

FARM CREDIT ADMINISTRATION. A dramatically expanded role for the federal government in agricultural affairs was central to the New Deal,* and in March 1933, by executive order, President Franklin D. Roosevelt* established the Farm Credit Administration (FCA) to coordinate the activities of the Federal Farm Board, the Federal Farm Loan Board, Federal Land Banks, Federal Intermediate Credit Banks, Reconstruction Finance Corporation* regional agricultural corporations, and Department of Agriculture farm loans. The president named Henry Morgenthau* as the first governor of the Farm Credit Administration. By early 1935, the FCA had refinanced more than 20 percent of the farm loans in the United States, rescuing millions of farmers from the threat of foreclosure. Also, Congress passed the Crop Loan Act in February 1934, which authorized the FCA to make direct production and harvest loans to farmers. In January 1934, Congress passed the Farm Mortgage Refinancing Act, which established the Federal Farm Mortgage Corporation with $2 billion to refinance farm debts. By the end of 1940, FCA loans totaled $6.87 billion.

SUGGESTED READINGS: W. Gifford Hoag, *The Farm Credit System: A History of Financial Self-Help*, 1976; W. N. Stokes, Jr., *Credit to Farmers. The Story of the Federal Intermediate Credit Banks and Production Credit Associations*, 1973.

FARM MORTGAGE MORATORIUM ACT OF 1935. See **FEDERAL FARM BANKRUPTCY ACT OF 1934**.

FARM MORTGAGE REFINANCING ACT OF 1934. See **FARM CREDIT ADMINISTRATION**.

FARM SECURITY ADMINISTRATION. During the mid-1930s, the activities of the Southern Tenant Farmers' Union* publicized the plight of poor sharecroppers and farm laborers. In January 1937, President Franklin D. Roosevelt* established the Special Committee on Farm Tenancy to study the problem, and several months later the committee recommended a comprehensive federal program of landownership, rehabilitation, and the use of farm cooperatives by poor farmers. Late in 1937, Secretary of Agriculture Henry Wallace, Jr.,* established the Farm Security Administration (FSA) to implement some of those objectives and to assume control over the activities of the Resettlement Administration.* The FSA also supervised the provisions of the Bankhead-Jones Farm Tenancy Act of 1937,* which authorized low-interest loans to tenants, farm laborers, and sharecroppers to purchase their own land. Will W. Alexander was appointed head of the FSA.

The Farm Security Administration invited the wrath of large commercial farmers, especially in the South, who feared losing their source of cheap labor. The FSA's resettlement programs helped only 15,000 farm families to relocate. Its loan programs supplied $300 million to help farmers purchase their own farms. Large commercial farmers hated the FSA's ninety-five camps for migrant laborers, which housed 75,000 people. The existence of the camps made migrant farmworkers more likely to demand higher wages from growers. The American Farm Bureau Federation* called for the dissolution of the Farm Security Administration, and the American Medical Association hated the FSA's health cooperatives. Conservatives in Congress accused the FSA of trying to redistribute wealth in the United States. Beginning in 1941, Congress steadily slashed the FSA budget, and in 1946 the Farmers Home Administration assumed its duties.

SUGGESTED READINGS: Sidney Baldwin, *Politics and Poverty: The Rise and Decline of the Farm Security Administration*, 1967; David Conrad, *The Forgotten Farmers: The Story of Sharecroppers in the New Deal*, 1965.

FAULKNER, WILLIAM. William Faulkner was born in New Albany, Mississippi, in 1897 and raised in neighboring Oxford, home of the University of Mississippi. Southern culture, with all of its virtues and vices, has seeped into Faulkner's intellect, but he eventually focused on the vices and how the dark impulses of human nature had warped the southern psyche. Slavery, racial violence, and class warfare, Faulkner had concluded, had imbued southern life and shaped southern history.

During the 1920s, Faulkner lived in New Orleans, where he came under the influence of novelist Sherwood Anderson. He soon moved out of Anderson's shadow. Faulkner's first novel was *Soldier's Pay* and was published in 1926. He followed with *Sartoris* (1929), *The Sound and the Fury* (1929), *As I Lay Dying* (1930), *Sanctuary* (1931), *Light in August* (1932), *Absalom! Absalom!* (1936), *The Hamlet* (1940), *Intruder in the Dust* (1948), and *Requiem for a Nun* (1951). Faulkner won the Nobel Prize for Literature in 1950. He died on July 6, 1962.

SUGGESTED READINGS: Joseph Leo Blotner, *Faulkner: A Biography*, 1991; Frederick J. Hoffman, *The 1920s: American Writing in the Postwar Decade*, 1949; Martin Seymour-Smith, *Who's Who in the Twentieth Century*, 1976.

FEDERAL ANTI-LYNCHING BILL. During the 1910s and 1920s, as lynchings of blacks in the South increased, the National Association for the Advancement of Colored People* (NAACP) made passage of a federal antilynching bill one of its priorities. It had all but become impossible to prosecute lynching in the South because white grand juries would not indict and white petit juries would not convict. Being able to prosecute accused lynchers under federal law, the NAACP believed, would make it easier to serve the demands of justice and discourage future lynching. Sixty blacks were lynched between 1930 and 1934, and the NAACP drafted the legislation. Senators Robert Wagner* of New York and Edward Costigan sponsored the bill in the Senate, but President Franklin D. Roosevelt,* for fear of alienating powerful southern Democratic congressmen, did not push it. Accusing the bill of being "anti-labor," "anti-states' rights," and "anti-South," such southern senators as James Byrnes of South Carolina, Josiah Bailey* of North Carolina, and Hugo Black* of Alabama filibustered the bill to death. The bill was brought up several more times to equally dismal results and finally shelved permanently in February 1938.

SUGGESTED READINGS: John Kirby, *Black Americans in the Roosevelt Era: Liberalism and Race*, 1980; Harvard Sitkoff, *A New Deal for Blacks: The Emergence of Civil Rights as a National Issue*, vol. I. *The Depression Decade*, 1978; Stewart E. Tolnay and E. M. Beck, *A Festival of Violence: An Analysis of Southern Lynchings, 1882–1930*, 1995.

FEDERAL ANTI-PRICE DISCRIMINATION ACT OF 1936. A great advantage large chain stores had over smaller retailers was an ability to purchase in bulk, at low costs, from wholesalers and manufacturers. The retail prices large chain stores charged were often lower than the wholesale prices small businessmen and wholesalers had to charge to cover margins and make a profit. Under the codes of the National Recovery Administration,* independent retailers and wholesalers had enjoyed protection from chain store buying power, but the

*Schechter** decision in 1935, which overturned the National Industrial Recovery Act, dislodged those protections.

Senator Joseph Robinson* of Arkansas and Congressman Wright Patman of Texas decided to push legislation that would restore those protections and give them statutory authority. Congress responded, and on June 20, 1936, President Franklin D. Roosevelt* signed the Federal Anti-Price Discrimination Act. The law prohibited price discrimination by manufacturers in favor of large chain stores. Discounts, rebates, and high selling allowances were also prohibited. Under the legislation, the Federal Trade Commission was empowered to investigate and abolish all forms of price discrimination that had the effect of reducing competition.

SUGGESTED READING: *New York Times*, June 21, 1936.

FEDERAL ART PROJECT. As part of the Works Progress Administration's* mission to relieve unemployment, the Franklin D. Roosevelt* administration established the Federal Art Project to provide work for unemployed artists. Holger Cahill was named director of the program. Because the Federal Art Project was decentralized and tried to accommodate itself to local tastes, it was an immediate hit. At its peak in March 1936, the Federal Art Project employed more than 6,000 people, who produced paintings, mosaics, and sculptures, taught art classes, and conducted art research, the most important of which was the Index of American Design. The Index of American Design completed more than 20,000 reproductions of American art, paintings, sculptures, handicrafts, and folk art. As part of its art education projects, the Federal Art Project also established hundreds of community art centers and staged hundreds of exhibitions. The Federal Art Project continued well into World War II before it was terminated.

SUGGESTED READINGS: Richard D. McKinzie, *The New Deal for Artists*, 1973; Barbara Melosh, *Engendering Culture: Manhood and Womanhood in New Deal Public Art and Theater*, 1991.

FEDERAL BUREAU OF INVESTIGATION. See HOOVER, J. EDGAR.

FEDERAL COMMUNICATIONS COMMISSION. To deal with the problems of rapid technological change in the communications industry and lack of service to rural areas, Congress passed the Communications Act, which became law on June 19, 1934. The legislation established the Federal Communications Commission (FCC) to replace the Federal Radio Commission and to assume the communications responsibilities of the Interstate Commerce Commission, the post office, and the Department of Commerce. The FCC received jurisdiction to regulate all radio, telegraph, wire, or cable communications in interstate commerce. The FCC had authority to regulate the rates charged in the communications industry. It was a daunting assignment, because at the time the United States had 800 commercial and educational broadcast stations and 51,000 private broadcast facilities.

SUGGESTED READINGS: Erik Barnouw, *The Golden Web: A History of Broadcasting in the United States, 1933 to 1953*, 1968; Charles Darby, "Federal Communications Commission," in James S. Olson, ed., *Historical Dictionary of the New Deal*, 1985.

FEDERAL CROP INSURANCE ACT OF 1938. Well back into the 1890s, farm advocates had proposed the idea of federal crop insurance to protect farmers from natural disasters. Widespread drought during the 1930s increased demands for some federal insurance program. Severe drought in 1936 prompted both presidential candidates—President Franklin D. Roosevelt* for the Democrats and Alf Landon* for the Republicans—to endorse the idea. Roosevelt established the President's Committee on Crop Insurance to study the issue, which early in 1937 recommended crop insurance for wheat. Senator James Pope of Idaho then introduced legislation into Congress, which was passed as Title V of the Agricultural Adjustment Act of 1938.* The legislation established a Federal Crop Insurance Corporation (FCIC), with capital of $100 million, in the Department of Agriculture. Congress also provided $6 million in annual operating costs. It provided insurance of 50 to 75 percent of the losses on wheat crops. By 1941 more than 371,392 farmers were participating in the program. In 1941, President Franklin D. Roosevelt signed legislation adding cotton to the program.

SUGGESTED READING: Randall A. Kramer, "Federal Crop Insurance, 1938–1942," *Agricultural History*, 57 (1983), 181–200.

FEDERAL DANCE PROJECT. As part of the Works Progress Administration's* effort to relieve unemployment, the Roosevelt administration established the Federal Theatre Project to provide work for unemployed professional actors, dancers, and theater technicians. Hallie Flanaghan became the first director of the Federal Theatre Project (FTP), but feuding erupted immediately between dancers and theater types in the FTP, and in March 1936, an independent Federal Dance Project (FDP) was established with Don Becque as director. Even then, internecine warfare characterized the FDP, especially between modern dancers and ballet enthusiasts. And when the FDP offered free dance classes to Americans, private dance teachers erupted in protest, worried that the Federal Dance Project would destroy their businesses. Late in the 1930s, conservatives accused the Federal Dance Project of being too liberal. Although the FDP put on hundreds of dance productions throughout the country, it became a victim of political infighting and external political hostility. The Emergency Relief Appropriation Act of 1939 cut funding to the Federal Dance Project.

SUGGESTED READINGS: Patty L. Haselbrath, "Federal Dance Project," in James S. Olson, ed., *Historical Dictionary of the New Deal*, 1985; Richard Kraus, *History of the Dance*, 1969.

FEDERAL DEPOSIT INSURANCE CORPORATION. Between 1921 and 1933, more than 9,000 banks failed in the United States, creating a monetary crisis of unprecedented proportions. During the presidency of Herbert Hoover,* Congressman Henry Steagall* of Alabama proposed creation of a federal corporation that would insure individual bank accounts. Steagall's logic was simple: If individual depositors knew that they would be able to get their money from a troubled bank or from the federal government, they would be less likely to make a "run" on the bank. During such runs, panic-stricken depositors demanded their money in cash, forcing banks to liquidate their assets, which only further eroded bank capital reserves. But President Hoover opposed such an expansion of federal authority, and private bankers were almost unanimous in their opposition.

But the virtual meltdown of the financial markets in 1932–1933, the bank holiday,* and the Emergency Banking Act of 1933* created a powerful political momentum in favor of bank deposit insurance. Early into the New Deal,* Steagall's proposal was included in the Banking Act of 1933,* which President Franklin D. Roosevelt* signed on June 16, 1933. It provided for creation of a Federal Deposit Insurance Corporation (FDIC). All national banks had to join the FDIC, and state banks wanting to join had to agree to join the Federal Reserve System as well. The insurance program went into effect on January 1, 1934, insuring bank deposits up to a maximum of $5,000. By the end of 1935, more than 14,400 banks had joined the FDIC, and bank failures that year totaled only thirty-two. The FDIC proved to be one of the most enduring and successful of the New Deal agencies, ending the era of depositor panic, epidemics of bank failures, and catastrophic fluctuations in the money supply.

SUGGESTED READINGS: Helen M. Burns, *The American Banking Community and New Deal Banking Reforms: 1933–1935*, 1974; James S. Olson, *Herbert Hoover and the Reconstruction Finance Corporation, 1931–1933*, 1977; James S. Olson, *Saving Capitalism: The Reconstruction Finance Corporation and the New Deal, 1933–1940*, 1988.

FEDERAL EMERGENCY RELIEF ACT OF 1933. See **FEDERAL EMERGENCY RELIEF ADMINISTRATION**.

FEDERAL EMERGENCY RELIEF ADMINISTRATION. When Franklin D. Roosevelt* took office in March 1933, more than 25 percent of Americans were unemployed, and the need for government relief and work relief was enormous. In July 1932, Congress had passed the Emergency Relief and Construction Act,* which among other things provided $300 million in loans to states for relief programs. The money was exhausted in a few months. Social workers and such leading politicians as Senators Robert Wagner* of New York, Edward Costigan of Colorado, and Robert La Follette* of Wisconsin demanded new federal appropriations, and on May 12, 1933, Congress responded with the Federal Emergency Relief Act, creating the Federal Emergency Relief Administration (FERA) and endowing it with $500 million in grants, not loans, to the states. President Franklin D. Roosevelt appointed Harry Hopkins* to head the FERA. The president charged Hopkins to put the money to work as quickly as possible, even if it meant ignoring local Democratic politicians who wanted to use the money as patronage. The FERA focused on small work projects—such as sidewalks, curbs, bridges, and parks—that could be implemented without expensive, time-consuming engineering and architectural planning. Eventually, the FERA completed 235,000 projects and employed nearly 2.5 million workers. The FERA was extremely popular among working-class people and helped cement FDR's reputation among the poor.

SUGGESTED READINGS: J. Christopher Schnell, "Federal Emergency Relief Administration," in James S. Olson, ed., *Historical Dictionary of the New Deal*, 1985; Charles Searle, *Minister of Relief*, 1963.

FEDERAL FARM BANKRUPTCY ACT OF 1934. The Federal Farm Bankruptcy Act of 1934, also known as the Frazier-Lemke Farm Bankruptcy Act, was designed to assist those farmers whose debts so exceeded the value of their property that their financial outlook was hopeless. Congressman William Lemke* of North Dakota sponsored legislation that was supported by the National Farmers' Holiday Association and the Non-Partisan League. The law allowed a debt-ridden farmer to declare bankruptcy; federal courts would then scale down a farmer's debts until they were roughly equal to the value of his or her property. Once the farmer succeeded in retiring his debts at the scaled-down figure, he would gain permanent title to the property. The law allowed farmers to repurchase their properties at the newly appraised value. They were charged 1 percent annual interest and had six years to pay the debt off. If creditors opposed such an arrangement, the farmer could retain possession of the property for five years with no foreclosure occurring.

Creditors, especially rural bankers, bitterly opposed the Federal Farm Bankruptcy Act of 1934 and sued in federal courts. The case of *Louisville Joint Stock Land Bank v. Radford* represented creditor interests, and in 1935 the U.S. Supreme Court declared the law unconstitutional because it denied creditors due process of law. William Lemke returned quickly with new legislation that Congress soon passed—the Farm Mortgage Moratorium Act of 1935, also known as the Frazier-Lemke Act of 1935. The law provided for a three-year moratorium on foreclosures against farmers who had defaulted on their debt payments.

SUGGESTED READING: Edward B. Blackorby, *Prairie Rebel. The Public Life of William Lemke*, 1963.

FEDERAL FARM MORTGAGE CORPORATION. See **FARM CREDIT ADMINISTRATION**.

FEDERAL HOME LOAN BANK ACT OF 1932. By early 1932, the nation's money markets were in an advanced state of meltdown. A liquidity crisis tied up tens of billions of dollars, and most financial institutions had grown quite cautious about lending. In fact, the economy was caught in a credit crisis. Economic confidence was at an all-time low and unemployment at an all-time high. President Herbert Hoover* was anxious to find new ways to stimulate the economy. The Federal Home Loan Bank Act of 1932 was one of his initiatives to do so. The president signed the bill into law on July 22, 1932. It established a five-person Home Loan Bank Board and a system of government banks empowered to discount home mortgages. Each Federal Home Loan Bank received $125 million in capital to discount the home mortgages issued by building and loan associations, savings banks, and insurance companies. As the logic of the legislation went, financial institutions would be more willing to make home mortgage loans if they knew they could get cash for the mortgages from the federal government. Hoover was convinced the Federal Home Loan Banks would help liquefy the money markets and stimulate a revival in the home construction industry.

What Hoover did not anticipate, however, was the reality of the liquidity trap. Interest rates were at all-time lows, but the number of credit-worthy borrowers applying for loans and the number of financial institutions willing to put their capital at risk were at an all-time low. Home construction throughout 1932 continued to decline, as did the number of new mortgages issued. Any hopes the president had of reviving the construction industry before the presidential election of 1932* were dashed.

SUGGESTED READINGS: David Burner, *Herbert Hoover: A Public Life*, 1979; James S. Olson, *Herbert Hoover and the Reconstruction Finance Corporation, 1931–1933*, 1977; Gail Radner, *Modern Housing for America: Policy Struggles in the New Deal Era*, 1996.

FEDERAL HOUSING ADMINISTRATION. In 1933, nearly one-third of all unemployed men in the United States were construction workers, and President Franklin D. Roosevelt* and the New Deal* became committed to reviving the home construction market. He appointed the President's Emergency Commission on Housing to study the issue, and among the commission's recommendations was the establishment of a Federal Housing Administration (FHA) to insure bank housing loans, for home repair or new construction, made to middle-income families. The commission felt that if banks and savings and loans had guarantees that the federal government would purchase any delinquent loans they made, they would be more willing to extend credit and revive the construction industry. In June 1934 Congress passed the National Housing Act,* which provided for establishment of the FHA. The measure attracted considerable opposition from building and loan associations. The law also established a Federal Savings and Loan Insurance Corporation* to insure deposits in building and loan and savings and loan associations. Between 1934 and 1940, the FHA provided credit to 1,544,217 homeowners to repair or modernize their houses. The FHA also helped finance construction of nearly 500,000 new homes. By 1940, FHA loans totaled nearly $4.1 billion.

SUGGESTED READINGS: Gertrude S. Fish, *The Story of Housing*, 1979; Gail Radner, *Modern Housing for America: Policy Struggles in the New Deal Era*, 1996; Jane A. Rosenberg, "Federal Housing Administration," in James S. Olson, ed., *Historical Dictionary of the New Deal*, 1985.

FEDERAL LOAN AGENCY. The Reorganization Act of 1939* required a consolidation of many of the federal government's lending agencies, and the Federal Loan Agency (FLA) was established to become the umbrella agency. Jesse Jones,* leader of the Reconstruction Finance Corporation,* was named head of the FLA. The Federal Loan Agency then supervised the activities of the Reconstruction Finance Corporation, the Export-Import Bank,* the Federal Housing Administration,* the Disaster Loan Corporation, the Home Owners' Loan Corporation,* the RFC Mortgage Company, the Federal National Mortgage Association,* and the Electric Home and Farm Authority.*

SUGGESTED READING: James S. Olson, *Saving Capitalism: The Reconstruction Finance Corporation and the New Deal, 1933–1940*, 1988.

FEDERAL MUSIC PROJECT. The Federal Music Project (FMP) was one of the Works Progress Administration's* programs for unemployed artists and professionals. By 1933, the unemployment rate among professional musicians exceeded 65 percent, primarily because music and entertainment were perceived as luxuries, not necessities. The FMP had two missions: educational and performance. FMP teachers directed bands, choruses, and orchestras and conducted classes in vocal and instrumental music. They also directed amateur community productions and local singing groups. On the performance side, the FMP staged public performances in schools, hospitals, nursing homes, parks, community centers, settlement houses, prisons, and orphanages. The FMP also produced radio programs. The FMP employed 15,000 musicians at its peak, and by March 1940, they had conducted 1.5 million music classes with 17.7 million students. Its performance groups had put on more than 14,000 performances to a combined audience of 159 million people, not including more than 14,000 radio broadcasts.

SUGGESTED READING: Virginia F. Haughton, "The Federal Music Project," in James S. Olson, ed., *Historical Dictionary of the New Deal*, 1985.

FEDERAL NATIONAL MORTGAGE ASSOCIATION. Because of the desperate condition of the money markets throughout much of the 1930s, many lending institutions were reluctant to make new housing loans. It was a critical issue because approximately one-third of all unemployed Americans had previously worked in the construction industry. In 1938, at the request of President Franklin D. Roosevelt,* Jesse Jones,* head of the Reconstruction Finance Corporation* (RFC), established the Federal National Mortgage Association (FNMA) as an RFC subsidiary. FNMA, or "Fannie Mae," as it came to be known, was authorized to purchase home mortgages from lending institutions so that banks, building and loan associations, and savings banks would no longer be so reluctant to make housing loans. By 1947, the FNMA had purchased 66,966 home mortgages worth nearly $218 million.

SUGGESTED READINGS: James S. Olson, *Saving Capitalism: The Reconstruction Finance Corporation and the New Deal, 1933–1940*, 1988; Gail Radner, *Modern Housing for America: Policy Struggles in the New Deal Era*, 1996.

FEDERAL ONE. The term "Federal One" was used within the Works Progress Administration* (WPA) to describe Federal Project No. 1, which includes the WPA's professional and artistic programs—the Federal Writers' Project,* the Federal Theatre Project,* the Federal Music Project,* the Federal Dance Project,* and the Historical Records Survey.

SUGGESTED READING: William F. McDonald, *Federal Relief Administration and the Arts*, 1969.

FEDERAL RESERVE BOARD. Economic historians today credit Federal Reserve Board policies with aggravating the speculative boom of the 1920s and contributing to the stock market crash* of 1929. Federal Reserve officials found themselves caught on the horns of two dilemmas. First, they erroneously believed that in the wake of World War I, European nations would not be able to stimulate their damaged economies until they could return to the gold standard,* but at the time, the strength of the American economy and its positive trade balance attracted gold away from Europe and to the United States. Only a credit rate differential between New York and London, with interests low in New York and high in London, could attract cash reserves to Europe. That reality made it difficult to inhibit the speculative stock market boom in the United States. If the Federal Reserve Board raised interest rates in the United States to discourage the stock market, it would only stimulate the flow of more gold from Europe to America. On the other hand, an easy money policy that reduced domestic interest rates would please foreign leaders but only stimulate the stock market. Either choice left Federal Reserve officials with potential consequences they did not want to face.

The second dilemma revolved around how to discourage securities speculation without at the same time inhibiting legitimate business expansion. High interest rates might stem the Wall Street tide but also make it more difficult for legitimate businessmen to acquire needed capital. Low interest rates would please businessmen but stimulate securities speculation. Throughout the 1920s, because of such impossible choices, Federal Reserve Board officials pursued contradictory and dilatory policies.

What the Federal Reserve Board decided was to peg discount rates at high levels while at the same time purchasing larger volumes of banker acceptances. They erroneously concluded that the funds banks received for the sale of the acceptances would only be used for legitimate business needs and not for speculation. They assumed that the method of increasing the money supply determined the uses to which the funds would be put; they failed to appreciate that the purchase of acceptances would increase the volume of excess reserves that could then be invested into the securities markets. The board actually expected that its high discount rates would discourage speculation, while its purchases of bankers' acceptances would stimulate a credit expansion and business growth. It was a pipe dream. With the fresh infusion of Federal Reserve funds, bankers increased their reserve balances and reduced their Federal Reserve Bank indebtedness, which negated the impact of the discount rate.

In the end, Federal Reserve policies attracted more money into the stock markets. Many corporations diverted surplus funds into the securities markets, which only drove prices higher. At the time, the Federal Reserve Board did not assume responsibility for managing the flow and destination of nonbank investment funds, and that oversight would prove critical to the speculative boom and to the ultimate crash of the stock market in 1929.

SUGGESTED READINGS: Lester V. Chandler, *American Monetary Policy, 1928–1941*, 1971; Elmus R. Wicker, *Federal Reserve Monetary Policy, 1917–1933*, 1966.

FEDERAL SAVINGS AND LOAN INSURANCE CORPORATION. In 1934, the National Housing Act* established the Federal Savings and Loan Insurance Corporation (FSLIC) to do for building and loan associations what the Federal Deposit Insurance Corporation* had done for banks. By insuring deposits, the FSLIC helped prevent runs on building and loan associations by panic-stricken depositors. The FSLIC insured deposits up to $5,000, and participating building and loan associations had to pay a small annual premium and allow FSLIC examiners to periodically audit their books. By 1940 a total of 2,189 building and loan associations had joined the FSLIC, and bankruptcies among those institutions all but stopped. During the 1930s, the FSLIC had to pay off depositors in only seven failed institutions.

SUGGESTED READINGS: *Monthly Labor Review*, 39 (1934), 369–70; James S. Olson, *Saving Capitalism: The Reconstruction Finance Corporation and the New Deal,*

1933–1940, 1988; Gail Radner, *Modern Housing for America: Policy Struggles in the New Deal Era*, 1996.

FEDERAL SECURITY AGENCY. The Reorganization Act of 1939* was designed to consolidate and streamline the federal government, and among other things, it established the Federal Security Agency as an umbrella agency to supervise the following agencies: the Social Security Board, the Public Health Service, the U.S. Office of Education, the National Youth Administration,* the Civilian Conservation Corps,* the Food and Drug Administration, the Columbia Institution for the Deaf, the Federal Advisory Board for Vocational Education, the Freedmen's Hospital, St. Elizabeth's Hospital, Howard University, and the U.S. Employment Service.

SUGGESTED READING: *Congressional Digest*, 21 (1942), 101.

FEDERAL SURPLUS RELIEF CORPORATION. One of the real ironies of the Great Depression was the existence of huge agricultural surpluses, along with tens of millions of poor, unemployed people, many of whom did not have enough to eat. To deal with that irony, President Franklin D. Roosevelt* had the Agricultural Adjustment Administration* in October 1933 establish the Federal Surplus Relief Corporation (FSRC). The FSRC was designed to collect surplus agricultural production and distribute the commodities to New Deal* relief agencies, which would then get the food in the hands of the poor. Harry Hopkins,* head of the Federal Emergency Relief Administration,* was named president of the FSRC. The problem, of course, was that perishable commodities often did not survive bureaucratic complexities. The FSRC did see to the distribution of such commodities as pork, butter, flour, syrup, and cotton, but it did prove inefficient and unable to fulfill the vision of its creators. When its programs were discontinued in November 1935, the FSRC's significance was more symbolic than real, but it did at least convey an image that the federal government was trying to deal with a chronic problem.

SUGGESTED READINGS: C. Roger Lambert, "Want and Plenty: The Federal Surplus Relief Corporation and the AAA," *Agricultural History*, 46 (1972), 390–400; Irving M. May, Jr., "Federal Surplus Relief Corporation," in James S. Olson, ed., *Historical Dictionary of the New Deal*, 1985.

FEDERAL THEATRE PROJECT. As part of its diverse programs to assist the unemployed, the Works Progress Administration* tried to put unemployed artists and professionals to work. The Federal Theatre Project (FTP) was designed to assist unemployed actors, directors, playwrights, and theater technicians. By the end of 1935, with headquarters in New York City, the FTP had hired 3,500 people and established five distinct units, which included the Living Newspaper, the Popular Price Theatre, the Experimental Theatre, the Negro Theatre, and the Tryout Theatre, as well as a classical repertory theater, a unit for poetic drama, a vaudeville unit that performed in Yiddish, an Anglo-Jewish theater, a children's unit, and a one-act play group. The FTP was headed by Hallie Flanagan. During the years of its existence, FTP groups played to a total audience of several million people. But it also found itself in constant political trouble, primarily because many conservatives perceived its plays as too liberal and too socially conscious. In 1939, Congressman Martin Dies and the House Committee to Investigate Un-American Activities Committee targeted the Federal Theatre Project, and Congress severely cut its funding.

SUGGESTED READING: William F. McDonald, *Federal Relief Administration and the Arts*, 1969.

FEDERAL WORKS AGENCY. The Federal Works Agency (FWA) was created by the Reorganization Act of 1939* to consolidate and coordinate all of the federal government's relief and work relief agencies. The FWA assumed control of the Works Progress Administration,* the Public Works Administration,* the Bureau of Public Roads, and the U.S. Housing Agency. Congress abolished the Federal Works Agency in 1949 and transferred its responsibilities to the General Services Administration.

SUGGESTED READING: *American City*, 54 (1939), 5.

FEDERAL WRITERS' PROJECT. The Federal Writers' Project (FWP) was one of the Works Progress Administration's* programs for unemployed professionals and artists. It primarily hired lawyers, teachers, social workers, librarians, journalists, and ministers, putting them to work as researchers and writers. Henry Alsberg was appointed head of the FWP. FWP writers wrote local history, travel guides, nature studies, ethnographies, and black studies. Eventually, the FWP spent more than $27 million and produced hundreds of books and monographs, including 378 books that were commercially published. The FWP's most memorable product was the American Guide Series, a state-by-state and city-by-city description of regional America as it existed in the mid-1930s. The books, one for each state as well as Puerto Rico, Alaska, and Hawaii, received almost universal praise. Late in the 1930s, however, like the Federal Theatre Project* and the Federal Music Project,* the FWP encountered serious criticism from conservative Republicans who believed the program was too liberal politically. Congress became more and more stingy with funds, and on June 30, 1943, the Federal Writers' Project went out of business.

SUGGESTED READINGS: Jerry Mangione, *The Dream and the Deal: The Federal Writers' Project 1935–1943*, 1972; Monty Naom Penkower, *The Federal Writers Project: A Study in Government Patronage of the Arts*, 1977.

FIBBER McGEE AND MOLLY. *Fibber McGee and Molly* was one of the best-loved and enduring radio programs in American history. It premiered on the Blue Network on April 16, 1935. It soon shifted to NBC Radio, where it remained until its last broadcast on September 6, 1959. It starred Jim Jordan as Fibber McGee, a hopelessly unrealistic but gentle blowhard who dreams implausible dreams, tells tall tales, and frustrates his long-suffering wife Molly, played by Marian Jordan. Fibber's high-pitched squeaky voice fit a whining character perfectly, and the shows revolved around life in the McGee home. The Jordans were veterans of vaudeville who had scratched their way up the entertainment ladder, and *Fibber McGee and Molly* made them household names. By the early 1940s, *Fibber McGee and Molly* regularly held a ratings position in the top five, and such signature comments as Molly's "heavenly days" became phrases in the language of American popular culture.

SUGGESTED READING: John Dunning, *On the Air: The Encyclopedia of Old-Time Radio*, 1998.

FINANCE COMMITTEE OF WOMEN. The Finance Committee of Women, organized in 1936 by conservative Republicans, was led by Grace H. Brosseau, who was convinced that Franklin D. Roosevelt* and the New Deal* were leading the country down the road to socialism and perhaps even communism. In the elections of 1936* and 1940,* respectively, the Finance Committee of Women endorsed the presidential candidacies of Republicans Alf Landon* and Wendell Willkie.*

SUGGESTED READING: George Wolfskill and John A. Hudson, *All But the People. Franklin D. Roosevelt and His Critics, 1933–1939*, 1969.

THE FIRE CHIEF. *The Fire Chief* was radio's first nationally broadcast comedy program. It premiered on April 26, 1932, starring Ed Wynn, with Texaco Oil Company as its sponsor. Wynn employed satire, pranks, and double entendres, and he pioneered the comedic technique of breaking into commercials with jokes. By 1932, *The Fire Chief* had a weekly audience of more than 30 million people. It remained on the air until 1935, when competing programs starring Jack Benny* and Eddie Cantor* eclipsed it.

SUGGESTED READING: John Dunning, *Tune in Yesterday: The Ultimate Encyclopedia of Old-Time Radio, 1925–1976*, 1976.

FIRESIDE CHATS. The term "fireside chats" referred to the informal radio talks Franklin D. Roosevelt* delivered during his governorship of New York (1929–1933) and his presidency. On March 12, 1933, just eight days into his administration, FDR delivered his first radio address, a soothing discussion of the banking crisis* and his reassurances that all would be well. He had an innate ability to address millions of people as if he were talking to a single family. More than 17 million families tuned into the address, and many historians believed that with that radio address FDR cemented his enduring political relationship with the American public. On June 24, 1933, before another FDR radio address, Harry C. Butcher of CBS Radio advertised the program as a "fireside chat." He eventually delivered twenty-eight fireside chats. In doing so, Roosevelt gave birth to the age of media politics.

SUGGESTED READINGS: Waldo W. Braden and Ernest Brandenburg, "Roosevelt's Fireside Chats," *Speech Monographs*, 22 (1955), 290–302; Bernard K. Duffy, "Fireside Chats," in James S. Olson, ed., *Historical Dictionary of the New Deal*, 1985.

FIRST HUNDRED DAYS. See "HUNDRED DAYS."

FIRST NEW DEAL. Historians have used the term "First New Deal" to describe the legislation passed by Congress in 1933 and 1934 to deal with the Great Depression. The key concerns of the First New Deal were relief and recovery and a commitment to using the federal government to coordinate diverse interest groups to boost production and employment. The First New Deal had no faith in the ability of the market economy to allocate resources and dictate production and prices and envisioned the federal government playing a new role in national economic planning. The First New Deal included the National Recovery Administration* (NRA), the Agricultural Adjustment Administration* (AAA), the Tennessee Valley Authority,* the Civilian Conservation Corps,* the Federal Emergency Relief Administration,* and the Civil Works Administration.*

But the First New Deal began to disintegrate late in 1934 and early in 1935. It became obvious to most Americans that large corporations had seized control of the National Recovery Administration and that the Agricultural Adjustment Administration had been captured by large commercial farmers. In 1935 and 1936, the Supreme Court declared the NRA and AAA unconstitutional. At this point, the First New Deal began to give way to what became known as the "Second New Deal,"* an emphasis on social reform, antitrust, and Keynesian economics.

SUGGESTED READINGS: Raymond Moley and Elliot Rosen, *The First New Deal*, 1966; James E. Sargent, *Roosevelt and the Hundred Days: Struggle for the Early New Deal*, 1981.

FISCHER, IRVING. Irving Fischer was one of the Great Depression's most popular and most misguided economists. He was born on February 27, 1867, in Saugerties, New York. Fischer earned his undergraduate and doctoral degrees at Yale, where he specialized in mathematical economics. In 1890, he joined the Yale faculty and published widely on bimetallism, prices, capital, and interest rates. At the same time, he became a health food fanatic, an advocate of the League of Nations, and a prohibitionist. His 1928 book *The Money Illusion* enjoyed wide popularity.

But Fischer's popularity and his personal fortune were wiped out with the stock market crash* of 1929. He also lost much of his reputation as one of the country's leading economists. Things only became worse for him. In 1930, his book *The Stock Market Crash and After* predicted that the nation's economic downturn would be shorter and superficial. When those predictions went unfulfilled, Fischer began touting currency manipulation as the way out of the Great Depression. He urged President Franklin D. Roosevelt* to scuttle the gold standard* to try to restore currency values to 1926 levels. Fischer had come to agree with silver advocates that bimetallism would end the depression. The president's ill-fated gold-buying program of 1933–1934 tried to manipulate prices and stem deflation by buying and selling gold. Of course, the scheme was poorly conceived and of no effect.

Fischer eventually became one of the New Deal's* most vociferous critics, blaming Franklin Roosevelt for leading the country down the road to socialism and big government. In the process, his own stature among economists fell steadily, particularly as Keynesian economics gained more and more acceptance. Irving Fischer died on April 29, 1947.

SUGGESTED READINGS: Irving Fischer, Jr., *My Father Irving Fischer*, 1956; *New York Times*, April 30, 1947.

FISSION. See NUCLEAR FISSION.

FLETCHER-RAYBURN BILL. See SECURITIES ACT OF 1933.

FOOD, DRUG, AND COSMETIC ACT OF 1938. Historians consider the Food, Drug, and Cosmetic Act of 1938 to be the last legislative achievement of the New Deal.* Consumer advocates had long been calling for a strengthening of the Pure Food and Drug Act of 1906, and major pharmaceutical companies joined the chorus in the 1930s because of the proliferation of inconsistent regulatory legislation at the state level. In October 1937, the push for new legislation accelerated when more than 100 Americans died after taking the drug sulfanilamide to treat venereal disease and strep infections. The drug was produced by S. E. Massengill Company, a manufacturer of veterinary medicines. Senator Royal Copeland of New York and Congressman Clarence Lea of California sponsored the Food, Drug, and Cosmetic Act, which President Franklin D. Roosevelt* signed into law on June 25, 1938. The law greatly expanded on the 1906 legislation, giving the Food and Drug Administration (FDA) the power of injunction to seize commodities and impose criminal sanctions on drug manufacturers guilty of mislabeling products or making unsubstantiated claims of drug effectiveness. The law also required food manufacturers to list ingredients on visible labels and to adhere to government standards on the quality and fill of containers. The FDA could also inspect factories to ensure compliance.

SUGGESTED READING: Charles O. Jackson, *Food and Drug Legislation in the New Deal*, 1970.

FORD, HENRY. Henry Ford is widely regarded today as America's most innovative and influential industrialist, the individual who all but defined the Industrial Revolution and single-handedly revolutionized modern social life. A poorly educated and often poorly informed man, he was a brilliant tinkerer, a mechanic who enjoyed taking things apart and discovering better ways of putting them back together. Ford was born near Dearborn, Michigan, on July 30, 1863. Ford attended school in Greenfield, Michigan, but dropped out in 1879 to apprentice himself as a machinist. A mechanical genius, he made money on the side as a traveling farm machinery repairman. Between 1884 and 1887, he managed a small sawmill operation and then returned to Detroit as chief engineer for the Edison Illuminating Company.

By that time, however, Ford had already decided that an automobile driven by an internal combustion engine was the future of American transportation, and he began building one himself. His great love was the gasoline engine. In 1896 he had completed a prototype automobile. Ford left Edison Illuminating and worked for a while with the Detroit Automobile Company, during which time he built his first racing car, which he dubbed the "999." In 1903, Ford went into business for himself, establishing the Ford Motor Company to manufacture automobiles.

Ford's great achievement was making an affordable automobile. "I will build a motor car for the great multitude," he promised. "It will be large enough for the family but small enough for the individual to run and care for. It will be constructed of the best materials, by the best men to be hired, after the simplest designs that modern engineering can devise." And this car "will be so low in price that no man making a good salary will be unable to own one." True to his words, Ford at his River Rouge factory produced in 1909 the Model T, or as it was dubbed, the Tin Lizzie—a simply designed and easily maintained vehicle that sold for $950. As Ford's volume went up, his prices came down; the Model T sold for $700 in 1911, $500 in 1914, $335 in 1920, and $290 in 1924. By 1925 a Ford factory turned out a Model T every ten seconds, and Fords sold almost as fast.

In 1919, 10 percent of families owned a car; by 1927, 82.8 percent did. By 1929, the industry employed 7 percent of all manufacturing workers and paid 9 percent of manufacturing wages. Related industries boomed since automobile plants needed steel, oil, glass, rubber, paint, leather, and other products. Drivers needed gasoline and better roads. On the outskirts of almost any town, other businesses mushroomed around the automobile—gas stations, body and mechanic shops, motels, used car dealers, and finance companies. Providing Americans with the option of relocating outside downtown areas, automobiles prompted a boom in suburban home construction.

What Ford began was nothing short of a revolution; as revolutionary was his belief that wages should be increased and hours reduced so that workers could buy and enjoy new cars. He paid some of his laborers $5 a day, shortened the workday from nine to eight hours, and adopted the five-day week. The idea of the "weekend"—time for working families, in Ford's words, to "enjoy the blessings of pleasure in God's great open spaces"—was novel. Toward the end of his life, Ford summarized his philosophy: "One day someone brought to us a slogan which read: 'Buy a Ford and Save the Difference.' I crossed out the 'save' and inserted 'spend'—'Buy a Ford and Spend the Difference.' It is the wiser thing to do." Certainly for Ford himself, it made good business sense: By 1925 he personally earned $264,000 a day. And eventually other businessmen adopted the concept that higher wages and leisure time stimulated economic growth. Ford served as president of Ford Motor Company until 1919, when his son Edsel assumed leadership of the company. During the 1920s, Ford devoted his time to political and philanthropic concerns. He was active in the world peace movement, which would have established him as somewhat of a liberal, but at the same time, he was a rabid anti-Semite, convinced that Jews were in control of international banking and politics.

But whatever Ford had done to endear himself to the American people, especially American workers, during the 1910s and 1920s vanished during the 1930s. High unemployment in the 1930s energized the labor movement, as did the New Deal's* pro-labor legislation. Labor leaders became especially committed to organizing unskilled workers in such mass production industries as steel, mining, rubber, and automobiles. Ford came to see the New Deal and the Congress of Industrial Organizations* as advance agents of a socialist and perhaps even a communist conspiracy to take over the country. In 1937, when the United Automobile Workers (UAW) implemented its "sit-down strike" policy, Ford reacted bitterly, refusing to sign a labor contract and employing his own armed goons to crush the strike. He did not give in to UAW demands until 1941, when the onset of World War II was producing huge government orders. He recognized the UAW, and the strike ended, but Ford's reputation as an enlightened labor leader was dead. When Edsel Ford died in 1943, Henry Ford once again took over management of Ford Motor Company and remained in that post until his death on April 7, 1947.

SUGGESTED READINGS: Peter Collier, *The Fords: An American Epic*, 1986; Robert Lacey, *Ford: The Men and the Machine*, 1986; Allan Nevins, *Ford*, 1954.

FOSTER, WILLIAM ZEBULON. William Z. Foster was born on February 25, 1881, in Taunton, Massachusetts. He was raised in Philadelphia amidst immigrant poverty. After leaving school he worked at a number of jobs, including paperboy, sailor, lumberjack, fruit picker, and sweeper, and he decided that the plight of working people was the same everywhere. Foster came to believe that only through labor union organization could workers secure a fair share of opportunity in America. In 1909 he joined the Industrial Workers of the World, and he spent World War I organizing for the American Federation of Labor.* By the end of the war, Foster had become convinced that capitalism was the enemy of working people. Early in the 1920s, he joined the Communist Party, and he was the party's presidential nominee in 1924, 1928, and 1932. In the election of 1932,* he criticized Herbert Hoover* and the Republicans and Franklin D. Roosevelt* and the Democrats as "different sides of the same capitalist coin." Foster managed only 102,785 votes in the election. He remained at the helm of the American Communist Party until 1945, when Earl Browder* took over. Foster died in Moscow on September 1, 1961.

SUGGESTED READING: *New York Times*, September 2, 1961.

"FOUR HORSEMEN." During the years of the New Deal,* journalists pejoratively used the term "Four Horsemen" to refer to the U.S. Supreme Court's most conservative justices. Those four men included James McReynolds,* Pierce Butler, George Sutherland,* and Willis Van Devanter.* In such decisions as *Railroad Retirement Board et al. v. Alton Railroad Company et al.* (1935),* *Schechter Poultry Corporation v. United States* (1935),* *United States v. Butler** (1936), and *Morehead v. New York ex rel. Tipaldo* (1936), the Supreme Court overturned the central institutions of the New Deal and precipitated President Franklin D. Roosevelt's* decision to reform and reorganize the federal judiciary through his so-called court-packing scheme.* Congress did not act on the proposal, but retirements and deaths of the "Four Horsemen" later in the 1930s allowed the president to nominate a more liberal majority.

SUGGESTED READING: William E. Leuchtenburg, *The Supreme Court Reborn: The Constitutional Revolution in the Age of Roosevelt*, 1995.

FOX, WILLIAM. William Fox, one of the leading lights in the American film industry during the 1920s and 1930s, was born in Tulchva, Hungary, on January 1, 1879. When he was still a baby, his family emigrated and settled in New York City, where Fox attended the public schools. Although he labored for several years in the garment district, Fox was fascinated with photography and the emerging technology of motion pictures, and in 1904, with all of his savings, he purchased a nickelodeon theater in Brooklyn. The future proved successful, and Fox kept purchasing more nickelodeons. By 1910, Fox owned fourteen of the theaters, and he began purchasing vaudeville theaters in New York. He also changed the billing, using movies for half of the programming. Attendance surged, and Fox began expanding the size of his theaters.

In 1912, Fox decided to vertically integrate his booming business. To compete with Thomas Edison's General Film Company, which distributed films, Fox formed the Greater New York Film Rental Company. In 1915, he established the Fox Film Corporation to make movies. The company's first film—*Carmen*—starred Theda Bara. With filmmaking capabilities, distribution facilities, and theaters, Fox had a business empire. In 1919 Fox moved his production facilities to Hollywood, California, where good weather allowed for year-round filmmaking. The Fox Studio became a leader in the film industry, producing hundreds of movies during the 1920s and 1930s, and Fox continued to acquire more theaters as well.

During the 1930s, in spite of the Great Depression, Americans attended movies in record numbers. For Fox, the depression was an economic disaster. He had highly leveraged his assets to purchase so many movie theaters, and although their value totaled $300 million, Fox was vulnerable to an economic downturn. The stock market crash* was a financial disaster for him. In 1933, Fox declared bankruptcy, and the Twentieth Century Film Corporation bought its assets two years later, creating the Twentieth Century–Fox Film Corporation. In 1941, Fox spent some time in prison after being convicted of attempting to bribe a bankruptcy court judge. Fox died on May 8, 1952.

SUGGESTED READINGS: Glendon Allvine, *The Greatest Fox of Them All*, 1969; *New York Times*, May 9, 1952; Upton Sinclair, *Upton Sinclair Presents William Fox*, 1933; Robert Sklar, *Movie Made America*, 1975.

FRANKENSTEIN. In 1931, Hollywood brought Mary Shelley's nineteenth-century novel *Frankenstein* to the screen. Starring Boris Karloff in a role originally turned down by Bela Lugosi, *Frankenstein* revolved around mad dreams of the grave-digging Dr. Frankenstein, who fashioned a monster out of the body parts of human corpses. Makeup artists turned Karloff into the stiff monster, whom theater audiences found thoroughly believable. Many film historians look back to *Frankenstein* as the formal birth of the horror film genre, and it is still highly regarded for the quality of its directing and performances. During a depression era when Americans wanted badly to escape their problems, *Frankenstein* became a box-office favorite.

SUGGESTED READING: Donald F. Glut, *The Frankenstein Legend: A Tribute to Mary Shelley and Boris Karloff*, 1973.

FRANKFURTER, FELIX. Felix Frankfurter was born in Vienna, Austria, on November 15, 1882. When he was twelve years old, his family immigrated to the United States. An intellectual prodigy as a child, he learned English quickly and attended the City College of New York, where he won rave reviews from professors. Frankfurter went on to graduate first in his class at the Harvard Law School. After leaving Harvard, Frankfurter became an assistant to the district attorney for the southern district of New York, where his progressive instincts, learned from the writings of Louis Brandeis,* led him to ferret out corporate wrongdoing. In 1913 Frankfurter joined the faculty of the Harvard Law School, and except for a stint during World War I as President Woodrow Wilson's labor troubleshooter, he remained at Harvard until 1939. By that time he was considered one of the top legal minds in the world and the man who had all but invented the field of administrative law. Finally, at Harvard, Frankfurter led the way as a pioneer of the belief that law school professors existed not just to pass on tradition to students but to teach them to engage in pragmatic evaluations of public policy.

During the 1930s, Frankfurter exerted great influence on public policy, primarily because of the hundreds of former students he supplied to President Franklin D. Roosevelt* and the New Deal* agencies. At Harvard, Frankfurter consistently attracted the best students, and he imbued them with his belief that enlightened government agencies could ameliorate society's most serious economic and social problems. He was also a behind-the-scenes adviser to President Roosevelt; indeed, he was one of FDR's must trusted advisers.

In 1939, the president appointed Frankfurter as a justice of the U.S. Supreme Court. Throughout much of the 1930s, the Supreme Court had struck down state and federal legislation aimed at stimulating the economy and eliminating the worst corporate abuses. Frankfurter became part of the new liberal majority on the Court, which was committed to the notion of judicial restraint—that judges should not intervene to thwart the desires of state legislatures and Congress, since those bodies best represented the will of the majority. Frankfurter was also convinced that good public policy represented a compromise or balancing of interest groups and that federal judges should not be in the business of overthrowing what thoughtful legislators had achieved. Laissez-faire, he believed, was an outmoded philosophy irrelevant in modern society. Between 1939 and 1945, Frankfurter remained one of FDR's most influential advisers, which some critics found inconsistent with the constitutional doctrine of separation of powers. Felix Frankfurter remained on the Supreme Court until his retirement in 1962. By that time legal historians recognized him as one of the most influential justices in U.S. history. Frankfurter died on February 21, 1965.

SUGGESTED READINGS: Leonard Baker, *Brandeis and Frankfurter: A Dual Biography*, 1984; Bruce Allen Murphy, *The Brandeis/Frankfurter Connection*, 1982; Michael E. Parrish, *Felix Frankfurter and His Times: The Reform Years*, 1982; Mark Silverman, *Constitutional Faiths: Felix Frankfurter, Hugo Black, and the Process of Judicial Decision Making*, 1984.

FRAZIER, LYNN JOSEPH. Lynn Frazier was born outside Medford, Minnesota, on December 21, 1874. He was raised on a homestead tract in Pembina County, Dakota Territory. In 1901, Frazier graduated from the University of North Dakota and then farmed for several years. But the plight of midwestern farmers pushed Frazier into politics, and he became active in the Non-Partisan League. In 1916, on the Non-Partisan League ticket, Frazier was elected governor of North Dakota. He was reelected in 1918 and 1920, but his progressive credentials were inconsistent with the new mood of the country, and in 1921 North Dakota voters recalled him. Frazier joined the Republican Party and was elected to the U.S. Senate in 1922. He proved himself to be an isolationist in foreign policy, opposing U.S. membership in the League of Nations or participation in the World Court, but a progressive in domestic affairs, endorsing the presidential candidacy of third-party nominee Robert M. La Follette* in 1924. Frazier was reelected to the Senate in 1928 and 1934. Because of his intense foreign policy isolationism, Frazier failed to secure renomination in the election of 1940. He lost the primary to William Langer. Frazier then returned to farming and died on January 11, 1947.

SUGGESTED READING: *New York Times*, January 12, 1947.

G

GABLE, CLARK. Clark William Gable was born in Cadiz, Ohio, on February 1, 1901. After leaving school, Gable tried his hand at a number of jobs, but he developed a passion for the theater. He moved to Hollywood in the 1920s, worked as a stage hand, and had a number of bit parts. With the help of Lionel Barrymore,* he signed a contract with MGM in 1931 and remained with the studio for the next twenty-three years. Gable's first film was *Painted Desert* (1931). During the rest of the decade, he became a certifiable box-office moneymaker playing a rugged, handsome man's man in literally dozens of films. Gable won an Academy Award for his comedic performance in *It Happened One Night** (1934), and he received Academy Award nominations for *Mutiny on the Bounty* (1935) and *Gone With the Wind** (1939). Before his death on November 16, 1960, Gable had made eight-three films and had become the dean of Hollywood male leads.

SUGGESTED READING: *New York Times*, November 17–18, 1960.

GANG BUSTERS. *Gang Busters* was a popular radio program of the 1930s. It was a weekly anthology of crime dramatizations and remained on the air from 1935 until 1957, with such sponsors as Chevrolet, Tide detergent, Wrigley's gum, and Colgate-Palmolive. It was known for its sound effects—car wrecks, gunfire, broken glass, shouting, and fighting. The program exploited an almost obsessive public interest in criminal celebrities like John Dillinger* and Pretty Boy Floyd and the FBI "G-men" who pursued them. Its bias, of course, was pro police.

SUGGESTED READING: John Dunning, *On the Air: The Encyclopedia of Old-Time Radio*, 1998.

GARBO, GRETA. Greta Garbo was born Greta Lovisa Gustafsson on September 18, 1905, in Stockholm, Sweden. She attended the Royal Dramatic Theater

School in Stockholm and paid her way with bit parts in a dozen or so European films. In 1925 she immigrated to the United States and settled in Hollywood, where she signed a contract with Metro-Goldwyn-Mayer studio. When the era of talking films began in the late 1920s, studio executives were extremely worried about whether Garbo could make the transition from the silent era. She was the world's sexual icon, but a host of other silent screen stars, because of foreign accents or light-sounding voices, did not succeed in the era of talking films. But Garbo also had mystery and a smoldering sexuality going for her. Still, there were doubts and concerns. She overcame them. During the next fifteen years, she developed an on-screen persona that captivated, and often titillated, moviegoers. Garbo appeared again and again on screen as a powerful, modern woman who flaunted her sexuality and made rational choices about her life. Her on-screen sexual encounters seemed to transcend moral constraints, and in such films as *The Temptress* (1926), *Love* (1927), *The Divine Woman* (1928), *The Kiss* (1929), *Anna Christie** (1930), *Romance* (1930), *Susan Lenox* (1931), and *Mati Hari* (1932), she developed a devoted following, especially in Europe. On March 14, 1930, Garbo's film *Anna Christie*, an adaptation of Eugene O'Neill's hit play, had premiered in New York, and she proved terrific, playing the role of a Swedish-born American prostitute plying her trade on the waterfront. Garbo flaunted convention, rejected gender restrictions, and spoke her mind.

But she proved too exotic for American audiences, who eventually abandoned her. In 1941, she starred in the film *The Two-Faced Woman*, but critics panned her performance, and Garbo took their barbs to heart. She left Hollywood, returned to Europe, and avoided the public limelight for the rest of her life, living almost as a hermit, at least as far as a celebrity could. Greta Garbo died on April 15, 1990.

SUGGESTED READING: Alexander Walker, *Greta Garbo: A Portrait*, 1980.

GARNER, JOHN NANCE. John Nance Garner, a leading Democratic politician during the early twentieth century, was born in Red River County, Texas, on November 22, 1868. In 1890, after reading law privately, he won admission to the Texas bar and began his own practice. In 1898 he won a seat as a Democrat in the state legislature, and in 1901, he won a seat in Congress. Garner held that post for the next thirty years, diligently meeting his constituents' needs and becoming one of the most powerful politicians in Washington, D.C. He was especially influential in the Democratic Party, and in 1931, he was elected Speaker of the House. In the presidential election of 1932,* Garner ran as a favorite son candidate from Texas, but he could not forestall the candidacy of Governor Franklin D. Roosevelt* (FDR) of New York. Roosevelt had a difficult time, however, securing the two-thirds majority of delegates required for the nomination, and when Garner released his delegates to FDR, the New York governor sewed up the nomination. In return, Roosevelt picked Garner as his vice-presidential candidate. They handily defeated President Herbert Hoover* in the general election.

But Garner hated the vice-presidency, comparing it to a "bucket of warm spit." It was largely a ceremonial office without power, and for man who had wielded tremendous power for three decades, the job was intolerable. He completed two terms as vice-president and in 1940 temporarily challenged FDR's run for a third term, but the president was too powerful, and Garner retired to his home in Uvalde, Texas. John Nance Garner died on November 7, 1967.

SUGGESTED READINGS: Ovie C. Fisher, *Cactus Jack*, 1978; Bascom N. Timmons, *Garner of Texas*, 1948.

THE GAY DIVORCEE. *The Gay Divorcee* premiered in New York City on November 15, 1934, and introduced to American movie audiences the dance team of Fred Astaire* and Ginger Rogers. Fred Astaire played Guy Holden, an American dancer pursuing Mimi, played by Ginger Rogers. A light comedy with glittering dance scenes and romantic music, *The Gay Divorcee* was one of 1934's most popular films, distracting Americans from the miseries of the Great Depression. For a few hours, they could huddle in a darkened theater and watch Fred Astaire and Ginger Rogers twinkle, as if the world had no problems at all.

SUGGESTED READINGS: Fred Astaire, *Steps in Time*, 1967; Stanley Grewn and Burt Goldblatt, *Starring Fred Astaire*, 1973; *New York Times*, November 16, 1934.

GEHRIG, HENRY LOUIS. Lou Gehrig, the great hitter for the New York Yankees, was born in New York City on June 19, 1903. His parents were German immigrants. A gifted athlete, Gehrig earned a baseball scholarship to Columbia and then signed with the Yankees. He ended up batting third in the lineup, before Babe Ruth, and he came to epitomize all that Ruth was not. A humble, family man not given to theatrics or flamboyance, Gehrig earned the nickname "Iron Horse" because he played in 2,130 consecutive games, a record not broken until 1998 when Cal Ripken of the Baltimore Orioles surpassed it. During the years of the Great Depression in America, Gehrig became an icon of durability, stability, and reliability. His career came to an end in 1939 when he was diagnosed with amyotrophic lateral sclerosis (ALS), a terminal, degenerative disease that now bears his name. At the time, Gehrig's career statistics included 493 home runs, 1,991 runs batted in, and a lifetime batting average of .340. On July 4, 1939, the Yankees held Lou Gehrig Appreciation Day at Yankee Stadium. Some 61,808 fans gathered there, and a radio audience in the tens of millions tuned in to hear Gehrig proclaim, "Today I consider myself the luckiest man on the face of the earth." Lou Gehrig died of ALS on June 2, 1941.

SUGGESTED READINGS: Martin Appel and Burt Goldblatt, *Baseball's Best: The Hall of Fame Gallery*, 1980; Eleanor Gehrig, *My Luke and I*, 1976; *New York Times*, June 3, 1941.

GENETICS. During the 1930s, enormous progress was made in the development of evolutionary genetics, and the pioneer in the discipline was Columbia University scientist Theodosius Dobzhansky. In 1937, his book *Genetics and the Origin of Species* fused Mendelian genetics with Darwinian evolution. Unlike most evolutionary biologists, who believed that the principle of natural selection functioned steadily over eons of time, Dobzhansky postulated natural selection through genetic adaptation. Genetic variability, he argued, explained the successful survival of some species, and the narrower the range of a species' genetic resources, the less likelihood of long-term survival. Dobzhansky called his theory "synthetic evolution," and it became a core principle of modern genetics and biology.

SUGGESTED READING: Theodosius Dobzhansky, *Genetics and the Origin of Species*, 1937.

GENEVA CONFERENCE OF 1932. Throughout the 1920s, world leaders tried to address the issue of disarmament and arms reduction, and a number of prominent international conferences revolved around the issues, including the Washington Naval Conference of 1921–1922, the Geneva Arms Convention of 1925, the Geneva Naval Conference of 1927, and the London Naval Conference of 1930. On February 2, 1932, a general disarmament conference was held in Geneva, Switzerland. The United States offered a proposal for elimination of offensive weapons, and when that failed, the American delegates came back with a proposal for a 30 percent reduction in offensive weapons. But that proposal too was stillborn. Subsequent follow-up meetings were held in February 1933, June 1933, and October 1933, but no agreements could be reached.

Diplomatic historians look back upon the Geneva Conference as the world's last try at arms reductions before the momentum leading to World War II began to accelerate. The Great Depression had put a premium on government spending, and military buildup seemed one way of stimulating the economy. Adolf Hitler had taken Germany* out of the League of Nations before the October 1933 conference. In April 1934 the arms reductions talks in Geneva were permanently suspended.

SUGGESTED READING: L. Ethan Ellis, *Republican Foreign Policy, 1921–1933*, 1968.

GEORGE, WALTER FRANKLIN. Walter George, a political nemesis to Franklin D. Roosevelt* during the 1930s, was born near Preston, Georgia, on January 29, 1878. His parents were poor tenant farmers, but George was ambitious and intelligent, and he earned undergraduate and law degrees from Mercer University in 1900 and 1901, respectively. George practiced law in Vienna, Georgia, and between 1907 and 1912 served as solicitor general for the Cordele judicial court. In 1912, he was appointed to the state supreme court, and in 1922 the governor of Georgia appointed George to fill the U.S. Senate seat vacated by the death of Thomas E. Watson. George won reelection in 1926 and again in 1932.

Although George generally supported President Franklin D. Roosevelt* and the New Deal* during 1933 and 1934, he broke ranks in 1935 when he became disturbed about such legislation as the National Labor Relations Act,* the Wealth Tax Act,* and the Public Utility Holding Company Act.* George had close personal and political ties to the Georgia Power Company. He fought the court-packing scheme* of 1937 and the Reorganization Act of 1939* as bald-faced attempts by Roosevelt to impose dictatorial control over the country. In the Democratic election primaries of 1938, Roosevelt openly sided with George's opponent—Lawrence Camp—but such presidential meddling irked Georgia voters, and they reelected George handily. Walter George was subsequently reelected in 1944 and 1950. He died on August 4, 1957.

SUGGESTED READINGS: *New York Times,* August 5, 1957; James T. Patterson, *Congressional Conservatism and the New Deal,* 1967.

GERMAN-SOVIET NON-AGGRESSION PACT. On August 23, 1939, Germany* and the Soviet Union* stunned the world by signing the Non-Aggression Pact, an agreement not to launch hostile military action against one another. The two countries had been mortal enemies ever since the Bolshevik Revolution, with their two dictators—Adolf Hitler and Joseph Stalin—equally hostile to one another. But both also had reasons for the agreement, or at least for the secret protocols it contained. Germany resented the loss of much of Prussia to Poland* in the Treaty of Versailles, as the Soviet Union resented the loss of its own Congress Poland region at Versailles. Both countries wanted to regain lost territory. The secret protocol permitted, during a period of "territorial and political transformation," Germany to occupy the eastern third of Poland and the Soviet Union to occupy the eastern two-thirds of Poland.

But each also wanted much more than that. The Soviet Union wanted its two-thirds of eastern Poland to stand as a buffer zone between western Russia and Germany in the event of a German invasion. And Adolf Hitler wanted a staging area in western Poland for an eventual German invasion of the Soviet Union. In September 1939, when Germany invaded and conquered Poland, the secret protocols were implemented. Hitler extended control over the eastern two-thirds of Poland to the Soviet Union, and in June 1941, he used western Poland as the launching point for Operation Barbarossa, the invasion of the Soviet Union.

SUGGESTED READING: Allan Bullock, *Hitler and Stalin,* 1992.

GERMANY. Although Adolf Hitler possessed a mesmerizing and charismatic personality, his Nazi Party operated on the fringe of German politics until 1929, when the onset of the Great Depression sent the economy, and the spirits of the German people, tumbling. Hitler's racist theories—that ethnic Germans constituted a superior "Aryan" race and that Jews were the source of all the world's miseries—resonated among the destitute German middle and working classes. In the election of 1930, the Nazi Party won more than 6.5 million votes and 107 seats in the country's 577-seat national legislature. Adolf Hitler, once regarded as a raving lunatic, had become a major political force.

With the economic effects of the depression deepening, political alienation in Germany deepened as well, and in the process, Adolf Hitler's Nazi Party made giant leaps in popularity. His ultranationalist message, combined with maniacal rhetorical assaults on Jews as the root of all evil, appealed to German voters. In the April 1931 elections, the Nazi Party won control of the governments of four states, and Hitler polled 37 percent of the vote, second only to President Paul von Hindenburg. In the Reichstag, the Nazis, or National Socialists, won 230 seats and became Germany's most powerful political party. During the next year, Hitler continued his political maneuvering, and in 1933 he was named chancellor of Germany.

From the time of his appointment as chancellor, Hitler wasted little time in establishing dictatorial control over the country. He continued to rant about the need to cleanse Germany of its political demons—communists—and its ethnic enemies—Jews—and the message proved popular. Hoping to give the Nazi Party a majority in the Reichstag legislature, he ordered new elections for March 5, 1933. He unleashed Nazi Storm Troopers on political opponents and drowned German voters in Nazi propaganda from state-owned radio stations. On the night of February 27, 1933, the Reichstag burned to the ground, an event many historians believe Hitler orchestrated in order to impose martial law. Hitler blamed the fire on communists and suspended civil liberties. Although the Nazis won only 44 percent of the vote on March 5, Hitler managed to form a majority coalition government with the Nationalist Party, a small patriotic group. He then pushed the Enabling Act through the legislature, which gave him authority to establish a dictatorship.

The new dictator quickly promoted a series of odious measures—dissolving all state and local governments, abolishing all political parties except the Nazis, purging the civil service of Jewish employees, boycotting Jewish-owned businesses, arresting tens of thousands of people as enemies of the state, burning books, and establishing Dachau, the first concentration camp. In October 1933, Hitler withdrew Germany from the League of Nations, announcing at the same time that the world would no longer be able to treat Germany as a "second-class citizen."

Hitler spent most of 1934 consolidating his political power and preparing for the conquest of Europe, a goal that had already formed up in his mind but that was known to few other people. European conquest depended upon support from the German military, which was quite suspicious of Hitler, not only because of his treatment of former general and president Paul von Hindenburg but because of the excesses of the SA—Hitler's Storm Troopers—who terrorized the political landscape. The fact that SA leaders wanted to secure control of the German army only further alienated military leaders.

On June 29, 1935—remembered by historians as the "Night of the Long Knives"—Hitler resolved the issue. With the assistance of Hermann Goering and SS leader Heinrich Himmler, Hitler purged the SA, arresting SA head Ernst Rohm and 400 others, including Nazis with liberal sympathies and monarchists, and had them all executed. In one stroke, Hitler had eliminated ultraconservatives and liberals, and in doing so, he reassured German generals and industrialists that the Nazi movement would protect business interests. When President Hindenburg died in August 1934, Hitler organized a voter plebiscite to approve him as chancellor, president, and commander in chief of the military. Voters approved the arrangement by a 90 percent majority.

In 1935, Hitler's lust for military conquest first revealed itself. In January 1935, German voters in the Saar, a coal-rich region that France had controlled since the end of World War I, chose to return to Germany. He then announced his decision to rearm Germany, institute a draft, and rebuild the once-vaunted German army. The League of Nations denounced the decision, but protests fell on deaf ears. Hitler could have cared less what the League of Nations thought of his actions.

The Nazi dictator was also ready to fulfill the vision he first elucidated in *Mein Kampf*. He intended to bring all of the German-speaking people of Europe into the Third Reich, regardless of where they lived. German-speaking people could be found in the Alsace-Lorraine region of France, the Sudetenland in western Czechoslovakia,* Austria,* and western Poland.* Hitler also claimed that Germany needed *Lebensraum*, or "living space," which also justified German territorial expansion. Finally, Hitler insisted that ethnic Germans were regularly discriminated against in Czechoslovakia by the Slavic majority. In 1938, at the Munich Conference, France and Great Britain acquiesced in Hitler's decision to occupy the Sudetenland. Czechoslovakia protested the move, but British Prime Minister Neville Chamberlain insisted that the agreement guaranteed "peace in our time."

It did not, of course. Later in the year, Hitler seized control of Austria in the so-called *Anschluss* and conquered the rest of Czechslovakia. He then turned his sights on Poland, invading on September 1, 1939, and conquering the country in a matter of days. Historians cite September 1, 1939, as the beginning of World War II because France and Great Britain, allied by treaty with Poland, declared war on Germany. Then in the spring of 1940, Hitler turned west and conquered Belgium, Denmark, the Netherlands, Norway, and France in rapid order.

SUGGESTED READING: Klaus P. Fischer, *Nazi Germany: A New History*, 1995.

GERSHWIN, GEORGE. George Gershwin was born in Brooklyn, New York, on September 26, 1898. He became interested in music—piano and cello—when he was twelve years old and studied with local teachers, but his brilliance was not manifest until a few years later, when he began displaying a gift for composition, creativity, and musical versatility. He began writing music for vaudeville and Broadway, combining styles ranging from classical to jazz. When he was twenty he wrote the musical comedy *La Lucille*, and from 1920 to 1925, he wrote the music for *Scandals* on Broadway. During the 1920s, when one critic said he was to music what F. Scott Fitzgerald was to prose, Gershwin wrote *Our Nell* (1922), *Sweet Little Devil* (1923), *Lady Be Good* (1924), *Primrose* (1924), *Tip Toes* (1925), *Song of the Flame* (1925), *Oh, Kay!* (1926), *Strike Up the Band* (1927), *Funny Face* (1927), *Shake Your Feet* (1927), *Rosalie* (1928), *Treasure Girl* (1928), *Show Girl* (1929), *Girl Crazy* (1930), *Of Thee I Sing* (1931), *Pardon My English* (1932), and *Let 'Em Eat Cake* (1933). In the 1930s, Gershwin became the recognized master of the modern light opera, and such compositions as *Rhapsody in Blue* (1924), *Porgy and Bess** (1935), and *An American in Paris* (1928) became classics. At the height of his talent, Gershwin was struck down by a brain tumor. He died on July 10, 1937.

SUGGESTED READING: Edward Yablonski, *Gershwin*, 1987.

GIANNINI, AMADEO PETER. Amadeo Peter Giannini was born in San Jose, California, on May 6, 1870, to an immigrant Italian family. When he was thirteen years old, he quit school to work in the family's fresh produce business. The business prospered, and in 1901, at the age of thirty-one, Giannini retired. His father died the next year, and family members asked Giannini to manage the estate, which included substantial holdings in the Columbus Savings and Loan Society. During his business career, Giannini had noticed the difficulty small businessmen had in locating working capital, and he set out to cultivate that market, even urging the company's directors to make loans to people who could not put up collateral. The directors were unwilling to assume such risks, and in 1904 Giannini organized the Bank of Italy. With $300,000 in capital, Giannini developed a clientele that consisted largely of Italian merchants, workers, and small businessmen. He proved to be fabulously successful, and by 1918 the Bank of Italy had twenty-four branch offices in addition to its main office in San Francisco. In 1927, the Bank of Italy was renamed the Bank of America, destined to become one of the world's premier financial institutions.

During the years of the Great Depression, Giannini was one of the few prominent bankers and financiers in the United States to support the Democratic Party. He openly criticized Republican tax policies during the 1920s as discriminatory against poor people, and he actively supported President Franklin D. Roosevelt's* New Deal* policies during the 1930s. When A. P. Giannini died on June 3, 1949, the Bank of America was one of the largest in the country.

SUGGESTED READINGS: Marquis James and Bessie R. James, *Biography of a Bank: The Story of the Bank of America, NT & SA*, 1954; *New York Times*, June 4, 1949.

GLASS, CARTER. Carter Glass was born on January 4, 1858, in Lynchburg, Virginia. His father was a local newspaper editor, and Glass ended up working for a number of years as a printer's apprentice, reporter, and writer for the *Lynchburg Daily News*. Between 1881 and 1901, Glass worked as clerk for the Lynchburg City Council, and from 1899 to 1903, he spent two terms in the state senate. In 1902, Glass was elected as a Democrat to the House of Representatives, and he eventually won reelection eight times, serving until 1918. He earned a reputation for expertise in banking and was known as the "father" of the Federal Reserve System for drafting and sponsoring the Federal Reserve Act of 1913. Glass resigned from Congress in 1918 to serve as secretary of the treasury under President Woodrow Wilson. When Senator Thomas S. Martin of Virginia died in 1920, Glass was appointed to fill the vacancy. He was eventually reelected in 1924, 1930, 1936, and 1942, becoming one of the most powerful politicians in the country.

As head of the Senate Banking and Currency Committee and later the Senate Appropriations Committee, Glass enjoyed a virtual veto power over all banking legislation. He protected the Federal Reserve System as if it were his private domain. Although he was a conservative states' rights Democrat and quite uncomfortable with the centralizing tendencies of President Franklin D. Roosevelt's* New Deal,* Glass nevertheless cooperated with the Roosevelt administration in securing the Emergency Banking Act of 1933.* He held out for a while on the Banking Act of 1933* because he was uncomfortable with its deposit insurance program but eventually came around to the idea and supported the legislation. Glass was similarly uncomfortable with the centralizing tendencies of the Banking Act of 1935,* but again Roosevelt convinced him to let the legislation make its way through Congress. Glass simply could not make the transition from Wilsonian progressivism to New Deal liberalism, and he was a thorn in President Roosevelt's side. Only his extraordinary power in Congress kept the president from scuttling their political relationship altogether. Carter Glass died on May 28, 1946.

SUGGESTED READINGS: Norman Beasley, *Carter Glass: A Biography*, 1939; *New York Times*, May 29–30, 1946; James T. Patterson, *Congressional Conservatism and the New Deal*, 1967.

GLASS-STEAGALL BANKING ACT OF 1933. See BANKING ACT OF 1933.

"GOD BLESS AMERICA." "God Bless America," which eventually became the unofficial national anthem of the United States, was written by Irving Berlin.* On Armistice Day in November 1938, diva Kate Smith* performed it on her popular program on CBS Radio. As the world slipped into war during the late 1930s and the United States was steadily drawn into the conflict, a burst of patriotism swept throughout the country, and "God Bless America" enjoyed extraordinary popularity. Berlin was so taken with Smith's performance of the song that for years he would let nobody else perform it.

SUGGESTED READING: Philip Furia, *Irving Berlin: A Life in Song*, 1998.

THE GOLDBERGS. During the early 1930s, *The Goldbergs* was one of the most listened to shows on radio. Sponsored by Pepsodent toothpaste, the show premiered on NBC in 1931. It was a nightly serialized comedy about a Jewish family living in New York City. The accents, jokes, and humor were ethnically rich, and *The Goldbergs* remained on the air until 1945.

SUGGESTED READING: John Dunning, *Tune in Yesterday: The Ultimate Encyclopedia of Old-Time Radio, 1925–1976*, 1976.

GOLD-BUYING PROGRAM. See **GOLD RESERVE ACT OF 1934**.

GOLD CLAUSE CASES. On February 18, 1935, by a narrow 5 to 4 vote, the U.S. Supreme Court decided four cases known as the "Gold Clause Cases"— *Norman v. Baltimore & Ohio Railroad Company, United States et al. v. Bankers' Trust Company, Nortz v. United States*, and *Perry v. United States*. All four cases revolved around Congress's decision in 1933 to nullify the clauses in public and private contracts requiring debt repayments in gold. At the time, President Franklin D. Roosevelt* and the New Deal* were trying to prevent the drain and ultimate exhaustion of the country's gold reserves, and by suspending redemption in gold of U.S. government bonds, the government conserved national gold reserves. Bondholders, however, argued that Congress had violated legal contracts in passing such legislation and in doing so had violated Fifth Amendment rights to due process and private property.

When the cases reached the Supreme Court, a bitter debate ensued behind the Court's closed doors. In the end, the Supreme Court upheld the New Deal's abrogation of gold clauses in contracts on the grounds that the federal government in general and Congress in particular exercised primary control over the monetary system. Although admitting that the legislation impaired existing contracts, the Court argued that congressional authority over monetary policy justified the action.

SUGGESTED READING: James S. Olson, *Saving Capitalism: The Reconstruction Finance Corporation and the New Deal, 1933–1940*, 1988.

GOLD RESERVE ACT OF 1934. A great concern to the Franklin D. Roosevelt* administration and to the business community during the early years of the Great Depression was the deflationary spiral in prices. Deflation made it difficult for businessmen to plan ahead and therefore reluctant to invest capital in their enterprises. At the same time, Roosevelt faced pressure from western farmers and western mining interests to inflate the currency. Convinced that adherence to the gold standard* only made deflation more intense, Roosevelt formally abandoned the gold standard on April 19, 1933. Several months later, the president implemented a gold-buying program to satisfy the demands of economists like Irving Fischer* and George Warren* who believed in the so-called commodity dollar. Their notion was that if the federal government bought gold at steadily rising prices, the value of the dollar would go down and prices would rise. In the process, the United States would also capture a larger share of world trade. Business confidence would rise, as would production and employment. From October 1933 to January 1934, Roosevelt met daily with economic advisers to set the price at which the government would purchase gold. To keep speculators off balance, they set the price above the world price for gold and changed it each day.

But the scheme made no economic sense. The price of commodities was not directly connected to the relative price of gold versus the dollar, and the administration's daily manipulation of gold prices only added chaos to the money markets. Also, farm prices continued to fall. In January 1934, President Roosevelt decided to abandon the scheme, and on January 30, he signed the Gold Reserve Act, which empowered him to fix the price of gold in the United States. The next day, he set the price of gold at $35 an ounce, which fixed the value of the dollar at 59 percent of its pre-1933 level. Wall Street could not have been happier, but inflationists out west kept up the pressure to inflate the currency. Their demands soon led to the Silver Purchase Act of 1934.*

SUGGESTED READING: James S. Olson, *Saving Capitalism: The Reconstruction Finance Corporation and the New Deal, 1933–1940,* 1988.

GOLD STANDARD. For centuries, the world's developed economies had taken pride in the fact that their currencies were backed by gold. The "gold standard," political leaders and economists were convinced, was a prerequisite to price stability and confidence in the world's money markets. But the onset of the Great Depression undermined the gold standard. Panic-stricken bank depositors and investors, worried about bankruptcies in financial institutions and imploding security prices, launched a "flight to gold," or hard currency, which they believed had inherent value. But in London, Paris, New York, Berlin, and Vienna, there was not enough gold to fill the demand. In 1931, the bankruptcy of Austria's* largest bank, the Credit Anstalt,* triggered a run for cash that led Great Britain to abandon the gold standard. In April 1933, President Franklin D. Roosevelt* took the United States off the gold standard, refusing any longer to convert paper currency into gold. Roosevelt's decision was extremely unpopular among America's richest investors, leading to the so-called Gold Clause Cases.*

SUGGESTED READING: James S. Olson, *Saving Capitalism: The Reconstruction Finance Corporation and the New Deal, 1933–1940,* 1988.

GONE WITH THE WIND. Margaret Mitchell's epic novel *Gone With the Wind* took America by storm in the 1930s, becoming a runaway bestseller, in spite of, or perhaps because of, its 1,037-page length. The book sold 1.4 million copies in its first year of release. *Gone With the Wind* perfectly reflected the prevailing historiography of the Civil War and Reconstruction as it existed in the 1930s. The South was portrayed as a land of plantation cavaliers and their corsetted ladies, who lived a superior lifestyle to the capitalist, competitive, greedy morays of the North. Slavery was presented as a benign, paternalistic institution presided over by gentile white plantation owners who treated their slaves as if they were their own children. The slaves were universally happy people, childlike and innocent and perfectly content with their lot in life. In fact, according to Margaret Mitchell's point of view, slavery was as natural as summer heat in the South, since blacks were incapable of caring for themselves. The Civil War was a clear case of an aggressive North, out to destroy an innocent South, employing superior economic resources and terrorism to achieve victory. Finally, Reconstruction was no more than an era in which greedy Northerners came south to exploit their military victory.

In the film version, which was directed by Victor Fleming and premiered in December 1939, Clark Gable* played Rhett Butler, a dashing but amoral gun runner and financier willing to make a dollar selling weapons and supplies to either side. Vivian Leigh starred as Scarlett O'Hara, the conniving Southern belle who never found happiness with men. Leslie Howard was Ashley Wilkes, a southern gentleman, and Olivia de Havilland played Melanie Hamilton, a long-suffering, salt-of-the-earth, Southern woman of extraordinary patience and strength. *Gone With the Wind* was a three-hour-forty-five-minute melodrama that barely escaped degenerating into a long soap opera. At the box office, it was a huge success, dwarfing the attendance figures of any other film in Hollywood history. In subsequent years, including 1998, MGM periodically rereleased *Gone With the Wind*, and the film continued to be a box-office winner.

During the years of the Great Depression, Americans went to the movies more often than any other time in U.S. history. In darkened theaters, they could forget about the miseries outside and transport themselves to a different time. In *Gone With the Wind*, they returned to a mythical South that had never really existed, and in doing so they found a comfort, albeit a temporary one, that did not exist in the depressing reality of the 1930s.

SUGGESTED READING: *New York Times,* December 20, 1939.

THE GOOD EARTH. *The Good Earth* was the title of Pearl S. Buck's best-selling novel of 1931. The novel revolved around Wang Lung, a Chinese peasant, and his family. Industrious and resourceful, as well as stoical and peaceful, the Wang Lung family became, throughout the industrial world at least, the stereotypical Chinese peasant because of the novel. Pearl Buck, born to Chinese parents in China but raised in West Virginia, was accused by some critics of creating a false image of Chinese society, but readers could not get enough of the trilogy. Hollywood made a film out of the novel starring Paul Muni. One reason *The Good Earth* resonated so well with readers was Japan's* 1931 invasion of Manchuria.* While newspapers carried stories of the "rape of Manchuria," readers of *The Good Earth* in Great Britain and the United States sympathized with the Chinese peasants and came to view Japan as a ruthless aggressor. Pearl Buck's *The Good Earth* helped shape the anti-Japanese opinions that developed in the United States during the 1930s. In 1938, she was awarded the Nobel Prize for Literature.

SUGGESTED READING: Pearl S. Buck, *The Good Earth*, 1931.

GOOD NEIGHBOR POLICY. During the first two decades of the twentieth century, the United States aggressively asserted its economic and military power in the Western Hemisphere. To build the Panama Canal, President Theodore Roosevelt had actually fomented revolution in the region, and in the Roosevelt Corollary of 1904 he asserted the right of the United States to interfere in the internal affairs of hemispheric countries in order to forestall European intervention. President Woodrow Wilson's and William Howard Taft's "Dollar Diplomacy" promoted American corporate interests abroad, and in Latin America and the Caribbean, that often involved military occupation. Eventually, those policies resulted in the deployment of American troops to Mexico, Haiti, Nicaragua, and the Dominican Republic.

Politicians in Latin America grew tired of the intervention, arguing that the United States had no respect for their sovereignty. During the Calvin Coolidge administration, a process of disengagement began. U.S. soldiers were removed from the Dominican Republic in 1924. The president also dispatched Dwight Morrow as ambassador to Mexico, and Morrow settled a number of outstanding issues between the two countries, particularly getting Mexico to recognize the property rights of American oil companies doing business south of the border. For many historians, Morrow's negotiations marked the beginning of the "Good Neighbor Policy," in which the United States tried more diligently to negotiate in good faith with hemispheric partners and respect their national sovereignties.

The policy continued under the administrations of Herbert Hoover* and Franklin D. Roosevelt.* Hoover removed U.S. troops from Haiti in 1932 and Nicaragua in 1933. He also approved the Clark Memorandum to the Monroe Doctrine. Undersecretary of State J. Reuben Clark drafted the document, which repudiated the right of the United States to interfere in Latin America's internal affairs. The Good Neighbor Policy, however, reached its fulfillment at the 1933 Seventh International Conference of American States, which met in Montevideo, Uruguay. Cordell Hull,* the new secretary of state, attended the conference and announced officially that "no state has the right to intervene in the internal or external affairs of another." Latin Americans hailed the policy shift. In March 1934, President Franklin Roosevelt then officially repudiated the Platt Amendment, which had long given the United States the right to interfere in the internal affairs of Cuba. When World War II erupted in 1940, the decision of so many Latin American countries to join the Allies can be largely attributed to the effects of the Good Neighbor Policy.

SUGGESTED READINGS: Alexander DeConde, *Herbert Hoover's Latin American Policy*, 1951; E. O. Guerrant, *Roosevelt's Good Neighbor Policy*, 1950; Dexter Perkins, *A History of the Monroe Doctrine*, 1955.

GRAND ILLUSION. Grand Illusion was Jean Renoir's masterpiece film of 1937. The film starred Erich von Stroheim, Pierre Fresnay, and Jean Gabin. A devout pacifist, Renoir wanted the film to stand in sharp contrast to European politics, which seemed to be drifting once again toward war. The film revolves around French prisoners of war and their German guards in a World War I prison camp. In Renoir's world, the lines dividing religions, nationalities, politics, and economic classes blur under close examination, but they manage nonetheless to overwhelm the essential brotherhood of man. Critics in the United States, France, and Great Britain hailed *Grand Illusion* as the greatest antiwar film ever made, and President Franklin D. Roosevelt* urged "every democratic person [to] see the film." The reaction was quite different in Germany.* Nazi Minister of Information Joseph Goebbels declared it "public cinematographic enemy number one," and Hitler banned it in Germany and Austria.* Mussolini banned it in Italy.* The film eventually left a bittersweet taste in Renoir. "I made a picture," he said, "in which I tried to express all my deep feelings for the cause of peace. The film was very successful. Three years later the war broke out. That is the only answer I can find."

SUGGESTED READING: Christopher Faulkner, *The Social Cinema of Jean Renoir*, 1986.

GRAND SLAM. The term "grand slam" emerged from baseball in the early 1900s to describe a bases-loaded home run that scored four runs. In 1938, however, sports journalists applied the term to tennis to describe Don Budge's victories that year in the Australian Open, the French Open, the British Open (Wimbledon), and the U.S. Open. Budge had pioneered the use of the backhand stroke as an offensive weapon, while other tennis players simply used it defensively to volley. Budge earned the "Grand Slam" in 1938 as an amateur. He turned professional in 1939 and was a dominant figure in tennis throughout the 1940s and 1950s. In 1930, golfer Bobby Jones gave the term new meaning when he won, in a single year, the four most prestigious tournaments in golf— the U.S. Open, the U.S. Amateur, the British Open, and the British Amateur.

SUGGESTED READING: Bobby Jones, *Secrets of the Master: The Best of Bobby Jones*, 1996.

THE GRAPES OF WRATH. In 1939, Viking Press published John Steinbeck's* *The Grapes of Wrath.* The novel traces the plight of the Joads, a farm family from southern Oklahoma who lose their land to the banks during the Great Depression. After seeing the family foreclosed and auctioned, the Joads head west to California with tens of thousands of other "Okies,"* where the "promised land" turns out to be a life of misery and exploitation as migrant farmworkers. The novel was didactic and expressed a powerful left-wing perspective, in which capitalism is the culprit forcing poverty and suffering on poor people and the federal government an agent in their redemption. Literary historians characterize *The Grapes of Wrath* as a "proletarian novel." The novel remained on the bestseller lists for more than a year.

Steinbeck's novel was made into a film of the same name in 1940. Nunnelly Johnson wrote the script and John Ford directed it, with Henry Fonda starring as Tom Joad, Jane Darwell as Ma Joad, John Carradine as Casy, Charley Grapewin as Granpa, and Russell Simpson as Pa Joad. Writing for the *New York Times*, reviewer Frank Nugent said that the film "is just about as good as any picture has a right to be; if it were any better, we just couldn't believe our eyes."

SUGGESTED READING: *New York Times*, January 25, 1940.

GREAT CRASH. Historians use the term "Great Crash" to describe the collapse of the stock market that began in October 1929. During the 1920s, the securities markets had witnessed unprecedented growth. A speculative mania swept throughout the country, particularly between 1925 and 1929. The *New York Times* stock index had risen from 65 in 1921 to 134 at the end of 1924. It went up to 180 at the end of 1926, 245 in 1927, 331 in 1928, and 449 in August 1929. The markets declined modestly in September, but few traders or investors seemed concerned. Panic appeared, however, on Wednesday, October 23, when the index dropped from 415 to 384. The next day, remembered by historians as "Black Thursday,"* a total of 12,894,650 shares were traded, and the index fell to 372. During the weekend, major banks, investment companies, and brokerage houses tried to organize a buying campaign, channeling millions into the markets.

But on "Black Monday" (October 28),* the panic resumed and quickly became a route. The *New York Times* index went into a free fall, dropping 49 points that day on 9,250,000 traded shares. The next day—"Black Tuesday"*— a record 16,400,000 shares were traded, and the index fell another 43 points. The decline did not stop until mid-November, when the index stood at 221, less than half of what it had been back in August. The stock market did not bottom out until July 1932, with the index at 58. Although economic historians do not look back on the Great Crash of 1929 as the sole cause of the Great Depression, they identify it as an important contributing factor because it helped freeze up the money markets and led to even more severe liquidity problems.

SUGGESTED READINGS: John Kenneth Galbraith, *The Great Crash 1929*, 1955; Robert Sobel, *The Great Bull Market: Wall Street in the 1920s*, 1968.

GREEN, WILLIAM. William Green, one of the country's most influential labor leaders during the 1930s, was born on March 3, 1873, in Coshocton, Ohio. Like his father and grandfather before him, Green went to work in the coal mines, but he also found a home in union politics and learned that he had a gift for it. He rose steadily through the ranks of the United Mine Workers (UMW) and in 1906 became president of the UMW's Ohio chapter. In 1910, Green won a seat in the state legislature, where he played a key role in securing passage of the first workmen's compensation law. In 1922, Green was elected secretary-treasurer of the national UMW. He served there for ten years and simultaneously filled a seat on the executive council of the American Federation of Labor* (AFL). When Samuel Gompers died in 1924, Green was a natural choice to replace him.

   Throughout the 1920s, Green promoted AFL interests, pushed for federal fair labor standards legislation and Social Security, and lobbied for federal legislation to end labor injunctions and yellow-dog contracts. In 1932, he helped Senator George Norris* and Congressman Fiorello La Guardia* draft the Norris–La Guardia Labor Relations Act,* which outlawed yellow-dog contracts. Green was also a bitter anticommunist who was convinced that communist infiltration of unions would destroy the American labor movement. He also tried to avoid unnecessary confrontation with management as a way of building confidence. During the years of the New Deal,* Green threw the resources of the AFL behind the National Industrial Recovery Act of 1933, the National Labor Relations Act of 1935,* and the Social Security Act of 1935.* Although labor historians credit Samuel Gompers with giving birth to the AFL and leading it through its most dangerous years, it was William Green who made the AFL part of the American political and economic establishment. Green died on November 21, 1952.

SUGGESTED READINGS: Max D. Danish, *William Green*, 1952; Melvyn Dubofsky and Warren Van Tine, *John L. Lewis: A Biography*, 1977; *New York Times*, November 22, 1952; Philip Taft, *The A.F. of L. from the Death of Gompers to the Merger*, 1959.

GROSJEAN V. AMERICAN PRESS CO. (1936). During the 1930s, Senator Huey Long* of Louisiana posed a regional political threat to President Franklin D. Roosevelt* and the New Deal.* He held an iron grip on state politics and did anything and everything necessary to crush his political opposition. In 1934, the state legislature imposed a heavy tax on all newspapers with a circulation of more than 20,000 copies per week. Only thirteen of the state's 163 newspapers had such a circulation, and twelve of them opposed the Long administration. Several of the opposition newspapers sued, claiming that the tax was not a legitimate exercise of state taxing power in order to generate revenue but an attempt to suppress freedom of the press by punishing political opposition. On February 10, 1936, by a unanimous vote, the U.S. Supreme Court agreed, overthrowing the tax as a violation of the First Amendment to the Constitution. The Court did uphold, however, that newspapers were still subject to nondiscriminatory economic regulation.

SUGGESTED READING: 297 U.S. 233 (1936).

GUERNICA. Guernica, the provincial capital of Basque country in northern Spain and a holy site to the Basque people, was immortalized in Pablo Picasso's painting of the same name. With the outbreak of the Spanish Civil War,* fascist and Nationalist leader Francisco Franco sought out and secured the military support of Germany* and Italy,* where Adolf Hitler and Benito Mussolini hoped to develop a fascist state and ally in western Europe. They pledged to Franco their military support and never hesitated to use it. In April 1937, Hitler used the Spanish Civil War to test his increasingly powerful military machine. German bombers laid waste to the city of Guernica, destroying 70 percent of its buildings, strafing peasants in their fields and in the market, and slaughtering more than 1,000 people. The attack demonstrated just how bloodthirsty and pathological Hitler could be.

Pablo Picasso, certifiably the most famous artist in the world, was horrified by the atrocity, and when he was asked to produce a painting for Spain's pavilion at the Paris World's Fair, he produced *Guernica*, a cubist portrayal of the Nazi air attack. In a world increasingly alarmed about Nazi aggression, Guernica became a sensation, a graphic, unrelenting portrait of the horror of war. After the fair, the painting was shipped to the Museum of Modern Art in New York. Picasso refused to allow it to be displayed in Spain until Franco was gone and democracy restored to the country. That did not take place for another forty-three years. In 1981, *Guernica* was returned to Spain and made the feature exhibit in Madrid's Prado Museum. The painting remains today a graphic, moving portrait of how modern warfare destroys innocence and the innocent.

SUGGESTED READING: Eberhard Fisch, *Guernica by Picasso: A Study of the Picture and Its Contents*, 1988.

GUFFEY-SNYDER BITUMINOUS COAL STABILIZATION ACT OF 1935. See "LITTLE NRA."

GUFFEY-VINSON BITUMINOUS COAL ACT OF 1937. See "LITTLE NRA."

GUY LOMBARDO BAND. The Guy Lombardo Band was perhaps the most popular big band of the 1930s. Guy Lombardo came to the United States from Canada in 1924, formed his band, and played radio spots in Cleveland and Chicago, gradually becoming more popular. He came to New York City in 1928 and played out of the Roosevelt Hotel. He did his first network broadcast on December 25, 1928, for CBS Radio, and he remained on the air throughout the decade, playing alternatively for the CBS, NBC, Blue/ABC, and Mutual networks.

SUGGESTED READINGS: Albert McCarthy, *The Dance Band Era*, 1971; George T. Simon, *The Big Bands*, 1967.

H

HANSEN, ALVIN. Alvin Hansen was born in Viborg, South Dakota, on August 23, 1887. His parents were Danish immigrants. In 1910, Hansen graduated from Yankton College, worked in the public schools for several years, and then pursued a doctorate in economics at the University of Wisconsin, where John R. Commons served as his mentor. Hansen then had professorships at the University of Wisconsin, Brown University, and the University of Minnesota. His book *Business Cycle Theory* was published in 1927. Hansen moved to Harvard University in 1937, where he soon became known as the "American Keynes" because of convictions that the federal government, through spending and taxation policies, could manipulate production, employment, and prices in the economy. Hansen urged the Franklin D. Roosevelt* administration to use deficit spending as a means of lifting the country out of the Great Depression. In short, government spending needed to replace declining private investment and declining consumer purchasing power. In May 1939, Hansen testified before the Temporary National Economic Committee* and made his case. Although the Roosevelt administration proved quite slow in moving toward Keynes,* Hansen's was nevertheless one of the most important voices in eventually enthroning Keynes as the theoretical leader in U.S. public policy during the 1950s, 1960s, and 1970s. Hansen retired from Harvard in 1958. He died on June 6, 1975.

SUGGESTED READINGS: J. Ronnie Davis, *The New Economics and the Old Economists*, 1971; Robert Lekachman, *The Age of Keynes*, 1966; Patrick D. Reagan, "Alvin Hansen," in James S. Olson, ed., *Historical Dictionary of the New Deal*, 1985; Theodore Rosenof, *Economics in the Long Run: New Deal Theorists and Their Legacies, 1933–1993*, 1997.

"HAPPY DAYS ARE HERE AGAIN." The song "Happy Days Are Here Again" was first heard in *Forever Rainbows*, a 1929 MGM musical film. Composer Milton Alger wrote the sing, and Jack Yellen supplied the lyrics. In 1932, "Happy Days Are Here Again" was played as Democratic presidential candidate

Franklin D. Roosevelt's* theme song at the 1932 Democratic National Convention in Chicago. Wherever Roosevelt appeared during the campaign, the song was played to greet him and to bid him adieu, and it was also played as theme songs in the subsequent presidential campaigns of Harry Truman, John F. Kennedy, and Jimmy Carter.

SUGGESTED READINGS: Bernard K. Duffy, "Happy Days Are Here Again," in James S. Olson, ed., *Historical Dictionary of the New Deal*, 1985; David Ewen, ed., *American Popular Songs*, 1966.

HARLOW, JEAN. Jean Harlow was born as Harlean Carpenter on March 3, 1911, in Kansas City, Missouri. She was raised by her mother in Hollywood, California. In 1928, she signed on with central casting and took the name of Jean Harlow. She appeared as an extra in a number of films but got her first big break in 1929 when Howard Hughes picked her to star in his film *Hell's Angels* (1930). Her platinum-blonde hair and sultry sexuality rocketed Harlow to instant stardom. In rapid succession, Harlow starred in *Iron Man* (1931), *The Secret Six* (1931), *The Public Enemy* (1931), *Goldie* (1931), *The Beast in the City* (1932), *Red-Headed Woman* (1932), *Hold Your Man* (1933), *Bombshell* (1933), and many others. Harlow became a sexual icon during the 1930s. But her life was cut short by a serious infection that resulted in uremic poisoning, and she died on June 7, 1937.

SUGGESTED READING: Michael Conahy, *The Films of Jean Harlow*, 1965.

HATCH ACTS. Throughout the 1930s, Republicans often criticized President Franklin D. Roosevelt* for padding the employment rolls of federal relief agencies in order to boost his own election campaigns, and those charges became particularly acute in the late 1930s over the activities of the Works Progress Administration.* The Hatch Acts were designed to limit the opportunities for political corruption in government agencies. The Hatch Act of 1939 prohibited civil service employees from holding any elected public office and, except for voting, participating in elections. The Hatch Act of 1940 extended these provisions to state and local government employees whose salaries were paid, even partially, by the federal government. Only in districts where government employees constituted the majority of voters were exceptions made.

SUGGESTED READING: Duane Windsor, "The Hatch Acts," in James S. Olson, ed., *Historical Dictionary of the New Deal*, 1985.

HAUPTMANN, BRUNO RICHARD. Bruno Richard Hauptmann, one of the most notorious and controversial figures of the 1930s, was born in Germany* in 1899. During World War I, he served in the German army. When he mustered out, he began work as a carpenter but was soon arrested on a series of burglary charges. He was in prison between 1920 and 1923, and within weeks of his parole, he was arrested again. To avoid prosecution, he emigrated to the United States. In 1934, Hauptmann was arrested for the kidnapping and murder of Charles A. Lindbergh, Jr., the infant son of world-famous aviator Charles Lindbergh* and Anne Morrow Lindbergh. The case caught the imagination of the entire country, and solving it became a high priority for J. Edgar Hoover* and the Federal Bureau of Investigation (FBI). Because of his criminal record in Germany, the FBI had tracked Hauptmann since his arrival in the United States, and circumstantial evidence linked him to the crime. A jury convicted Hauptmann and sentenced him to death.

But Hauptmann and his wife insisted that he was innocent of the crime, and it was true that Hoover had withheld some evidence that might have led to Hauptmann's acquittal. Governor Harold Hoffmann of New Jersey told Hauptmann he would commute his sentence to life in prison in exchange for a confession, but Hauptmann refused. On April 3, 1936, Bruno Hauptmann died in New Jersey's electric chair. Debate over Hauptmann's guilt or innocence continues today.

SUGGESTED READING: Jim Fisher, *The Lindbergh Case*, 1987.

HAWLEY-SMOOT TARIFF OF 1930. During the 1920s, strong protectionist sentiments infected Republican Party leaders, who were convinced that keeping foreign goods out of American markets would stimulate American manufacturing and insulate American jobs from competition. But economic theorists argue that protectionism in the long run stunts economic growth, and that would prove all too true. During the 1920s, American exports far exceeded American imports, and when foreign countries retaliated against high U.S. tariffs by passing high tariffs of their own, the United States found itself losing valuable export markets. Two tariffs in particular brought about the decline: the Fordner-McCumber Tariff Act of 1921 and the Hawley-Smoot Tariff of 1930.

President Herbert Hoover,* when he came into office in March 1929, was unusual among Republicans because he wanted tariff reform and understood economic theory. But as the legislation made its way through Congress, the "logrolling" effect took over, in which individual congressmen added tariff after tariff to those products needing protection within their own district. Congressman Willis C. Hawley of Oregon, a tariff reformer, shepherded it through the House, but Senator Reed Smoot of Utah, an avowed protectionist, was in charge of the bill in the Senate. When it finally passed, the Hawley-Smoot Tariff raised tariffs on raw materials between 50 and 100 percent and upped ad valorem rates from 33 to 40 percent. President Hoover criticized the measure but eventually signed it into law.

The Hawley-Smoot Tariff received universal criticism from economists and international trade experts who knew that it would reduce exports and imports, increase prices, subsidize wasteful and inefficient production, and generate retaliatory tariffs from other countries. That is exactly what happened, and economic historians today identify the Hawley-Smoot Tariff as one of the causes of the Great Depression. Just as the stock market was collapsing, international trade went into a tailspin, forcing American manufacturing enterprises to lay off workers. Between 1929 and 1933, the total annual volume of world trade fell from nearly $35 billion to less than $12 billion, exacerbating what was already a serious worldwide depression.

SUGGESTED READINGS: David Burner, *Herbert Hoover: A Public Life*, 1979; Martin L. Fausold, *The Presidency of Herbert C. Hoover*, 1985.

HEARST, WILLIAM RANDOLPH. William Randolph Hearst, perhaps the most powerful journalist in U.S. history, was born on April 29, 1863, in San Francisco, California. He studied at Harvard, inherited $5 million from his mother, and in 1895 purchased the *New York Journal*. Hearst pioneered sensationalism in mass circulation journalism, emphasizing the salacious and sleeze because it sold papers. Along with Joseph Pulitzer of the *New York World*, Hearst became the father of what historians call "yellow journalism." Over the years, Hearst used his success in New York to expand throughout the country, and he eventually included in his stable of newspapers the *San Francisco Examiner, Los Angeles Examiner, Los Angeles Herald and Express, Chicago Herald-American, Boston American, Boston Record, New-York Journal American, Baltimore News-Post, New York Mirror, Pittsburgh Sun-Telegram, Detroit Times*, and the *Milwaukee Sentinel*. By the mid-1920s, Hearst owned ninety newspapers, three radio stations, and several magazines, including *Good Housekeeping* and *Harper's Bazaar*.

As a media giant, Hearst had enormous influence on public opinion, and during the Great Depression, he was an outspoken, vociferous opponent of Franklin D. Roosevelt* and the New Deal.* Roosevelt, he was convinced, was leading the country down the road to communism, and Hearst condemned most of the New Deal's initiatives. In the presidential election of 1936,* he threw the weight of his entire newspaper chain behind the candidacy of Republican Alf Landon,* but Roosevelt's overwhelming victory soured Hearst on politics, and he subsequently took a lower profile. He was simply too conservative and out of touch with the feelings and ideas of most Americans. Hearst died on August 14, 1951.

SUGGESTED READINGS: Rodney P. Carlisle, *Hearst and the New Deal: The Progressive as Reactionary*, 1982; *New York Times*, August 15, 1951; William A. Swanberg, *Hearst: Citizen Hearst*, 1961.

HELICOPTER. In 1936, Germany* tested the first successful helicopter—a twin rotor Focke-Achgelis Fa-61, but it was Igor Sikorsky who developed the modern prototype. A Russian-born engineer, Sikorsky was living near Stratford,

Connecticut, and in September 1939 his VS-300 helicopter prototype became airborne for several seconds. Sikorsky's helicopter incorporated most of the elements of a modern helicopter—a main horizontal rotor and a smaller vertical rotor installed at the tail. The two rotors allowed a pilot to rise, hover, and move forward with balance and control. Sikorsky completed his first production model in 1942. An aging Wilbur Wright, upon seeing the craft, told Sikorsky, "I designed one just like this back in 1906, but I never thought it would work. Congratulations."

SUGGESTED READING: Charles Gablehouse, *Helicopters and Autogiros: A Chronicle of Rotating-Wing Aircraft*, 1967.

HELVERING V. DAVIS **(1937).** The case of *Helvering v. Davis* was one of the first to indicate that the conservative majority on the U.S. Supreme Court was beginning to disintegrate. In 1935 and 1936, the Supreme Court had overthrown the National Recovery Administration* and the Agricultural Adjustment Administration,* two linchpins of the New Deal,* and in response, President Franklin D. Roosevelt* had launched his ill-conceived attempt to "pack" the Supreme Court. But in *Helvering v. Davis*, Justice Owen Roberts,* once part of the conservative majority, switched sides, indicating a drift for the Court toward more liberal decisions.

The case revolved around the constitutionality of the Social Security Act of 1935.* Opponents sued, arguing that old-age pensions were properly the domain of state governments, not Congress, and that, therefore, the legislation violated the Tenth Amendment to the Constitution. The Court disagreed and on May 24, 1937, by a 7 to 2 vote, upheld the constitutionality of the Social Security Act. The justices claimed that the Great Depression had posed a national crisis far beyond the ability of forty-eight state legislatures to address independently.

SUGGESTED READING: 301 U.S. 619 (1937).

HENDERSON, LEON. Leon Henderson was born on May 26, 1895, in Millville, New Jersey, and educated at Swarthmore and the University of Pennsylvania. A gifted economist, Henderson taught at the Wharton School of the University of Pennsylvania and then at the Carnegie Institute of Technology. Between 1925 and 1934 he served as director of consumer credit for the Russell Sage Foundation. He was working there when he became director of research and planning at the National Recovery Administration* (NRA). When the NRA was declared unconstitutional, Henderson went to work for the Senate Committee on Manufactures. He then worked for a time for the Democratic National Committee and then for Harry Hopkins* in the Works Progress Administration.* Inside the Roosevelt administration, Henderson joined people like Lauchlin Currie,* Marriner Eccles,* William Douglas,* and Harry Hopkins, who had converted to Keynesian economics and called for the federal government to spend the country out of the depression. As executive secretary of the Temporary National Economic Committee* in 1938–1939, Henderson also called on the federal government to engage in antitrust activities in order to maintain a competitive economy. Between 1939 and 1941, Henderson served on the board of the Securities and Exchange Commission.* During World War II, he worked for the Office of Price Administration and then the War Production Board. After the war, Henderson was president of the International Hudson Corporation. He died on October 19, 1986.

SUGGESTED READING: Theodore Rosenof, *Economics in the Long Run: New Deal Theorists and Their Legacies, 1933–1993*, 1997.

HICKOK, LORENA. Lorena Hickok was born on March 7, 1893, in East Troy, Wisconsin. Just a few years out of high school, she went to work as a reporter for the Associated Press, specializing in politics and election campaigns. During the 1932 presidential campaign, she became acquainted with Eleanor Roosevelt,* and their ensuing friendship lasted for the rest of their lives. When Franklin D. Roosevelt* was inaugurated in March 1933, Hickok left the Associated Press and went to work for the administration, traveling widely throughout the country, serving as the eyes and ears of the New Deal.* She regularly reported back to Harry Hopkins* on how New Deal legislation was being implemented and how the public was reacting to government initiatives. Hickok's reports were read by the most powerful people in the Roosevelt administration, including the president, and gave her tremendous influence. Her gifted prose described the suffering of poor, unemployed people throughout the country and led to increased federal relief and welfare efforts. Hickok left Washington, D.C., in 1936 and worked for several years in public relations, but in 1940 she returned to Washington, D.C., lived in the White House with the Roosevelts, and worked for the Democratic National Committee. She returned to private life in 1945 and spent the rest of her life writing. Included in her later work are *The Story of Franklin D. Roosevelt* (1959), *The Story of Eleanor Roosevelt* (1959), and *Reluctant First Lady* (1962). Hickok died on May 1, 1968.

SUGGESTED READINGS: Doris Faber, *The Life of Lorena Hickok*, 1980; Richard Lowitt and Maurine Beasley, *One Third of a Nation: Lorena Hickok Reports on the Great Depression*, 1983.

HILLMAN, SIDNEY. Sidney Hillman was born in Zagare, Lithuania, on March 23, 1887. He attended Slobodka Rabbinical Seminary in Lithuania before emigrating to the United States and settling in Chicago. He went to work as a cutter for Hart, Schaffner, and Marx and became active in labor union politics, particularly campaigning for a ten-hour workday. In 1910, Hillman played a key role in negotiating an agreement to end a strike of working women at the Marx factory, and the results were so favorable to the workers that Hillman's political profile rose substantially. He joined the Amalgamated Clothing Workers' Union and became its president in 1914. During the 1930s, he worked diligently in support of Franklin D. Roosevelt* and the New Deal* and became a leading figure in the formation of the Congress of Industrial Organizations* (CIO). He served as vice-president of the CIO from 1935 to 1940. He was also a founder of the American Labor Party* and Labor's Non-Partisan League,* both of which backed FDR. Hillman died on July 10, 1946.

SUGGESTED READING: Matthew Josephson, *Sidney Hillman, Statesman of American Labor*, 1952.

HINDENBURG. The *Hindenburg* was the world greatest dirigible, or "zeppelin," during the 1930s. A dirigible was a "blimp," or a lighter-than-air aircraft. Constructed of a light steel frame and a cloth cover, the *Hindenburg* was inflated with hydrogen, a highly flammable gas. It was a German airship that regularly made transatlantic flights. On May 6, 1937, the *Hindenburg* became part of history while trying to dock at the U.S. naval base in Lakehurst, New Jersey. First launched in 1936, the *Hindenburg* was considered a luxury airship and had already made ten round trips between Europe and the United States. But just before docking, the *Hindenburg* went up in flames when atmospheric electricity ignited a hydrogen gas leak in the *Hindenburg* shell. The floating palace became an instant inferno. Herb Morrison, a reporter from a Chicago radio station, was at the naval station to report on the *Hindenburg*'s arrival, and his live broadcast of the disaster would go down as one of the most memorable in radio history. Remarkably, only thirty-six of the ninety-seven passengers died in the crash.

SUGGESTED READINGS: Harold G. Duck, *The Golden Age of the Great Passenger Airships, Graf Zeppelin and Hindenburg*, 1985; *New York Times*, May 7–8, 1937.

HOLIDAY, BILLIE. Billie Holiday began making jazz history in January 1937 when she joined forces with tenor saxophonist Lester Young and recorded "This Year's Kisses." She had a haunting, bittersweet voice and revealed all of the pain she had experienced in her life. She was born on April 7, 1915, in Baltimore, Maryland. Her family moved to New York City in 1928. Holiday spent her early years living in virtual servitude and then supporting herself as a prostitute. She also battled a heroin addiction much of her adult life. Her first recording came in 1933 when she was only eighteen years old. Band leader Benny Goodman had been impressed with her and recorded her. In 1936, Holiday joined Count Basie's band, and for years her magical voice and his innovative music became the heart and soul of jazz. She also became an icon of the independent black woman. But in the end, Holiday could not overcome the heroin addiction that finally killed her on July 17, 1959.

SUGGESTED READING: Donald Clarke, *Wishing on the Moon: The Life and Times of Billie Holiday*, 1994.

HOME BUILDING AND LOAN ASSOCIATION V. BLAISDELL

(1934). The case of *Home Building and Loan Association v. Blaisdell* revolved around whether or not a state legislature had the right to interfere in the economy in order to ameliorate some of the effects of the Great Depression. In order to provide relief to poverty-stricken farmers and home owners, the Minnesota legislature suspended mortgage clauses providing for foreclosures in the event of nonpayment. John H. Blaisdell took advantage of the law and adopted a postponed repayment plan. The directors of Home Building and Loan Association, which owned the mortgage, sued, claiming that the Minnesota legislation, by voiding a legal contract, violated Article I of the Constitution and the due process clause of the Fourteenth Amendment. On June 8, 1934, by a 5 to 4 vote, the Court upheld the legislation, arguing that during times of national emergency, government could tamper with the contract clause of the Constitution in order to meet the needs of the majority of the country's citizens.

SUGGESTED READING: 290 U.S. 398 (1934).

HOME OWNERS' LOAN ACT OF 1934. See HOME OWNERS' LOAN CORPORATION.

HOME OWNERS' LOAN CORPORATION. Because of the collapse of the economy and the disintegration of the banking system in 1932–1933, millions of home owners faced the loss of their homes through foreclosure. By 1933, a total of 41 percent of all home mortgages, worth more than $20 billion, were in default. Not only did home owners face the loss of their houses, but thousands of lending institutions confronted serious erosions of their capital. To deal with the problem, Senator Joseph Robinson* of Arkansas sponsored the Home Owners' Refinancing Act, which President Franklin D. Roosevelt* signed on June 13, 1933. A Home Owners' Loan Corporation (HOLC) was established with $200 million in capital from the Reconstruction Finance Corporation.* The HOLC was authorized to issue up to $2 billion in its own bonds, and that amount was increased to $3 billion in June 1934 and $4.75 billion in May 1935. The Home Owners' Loan Act of April 1934 then provided federal guarantees of the principal and interest on HOLC bonds.

The law allowed investors or home owners to trade up to $14,000 in HOLC bonds for mortgages and their conversion into a single new mortgage. In addition, the HOLC could make cash advances for payment of taxes and repairs up to 50 percent of the value of the home. The HOLC also had the authority to redeem properties lost by foreclosure after January 1, 1930. Mortgagees had to repay the HOLC at 5 percent interest over a period of fifteen years. By 1936, after it had stopped accepting loan applications, the HOLC had made 992,531 loans for a total of more than $3 billion. The HOLC went out of business in 1951 after it had collected its outstanding debts.

SUGGESTED READINGS: *Congressional Digest*, 15 (1937), 107–8; Gail Radner, *Modern Housing for America: Policy Struggles in the New Deal Era*, 1996.

HOME OWNERS' REFINANCING ACT OF 1933. See **HOME OWNERS' LOAN CORPORATION**.

HOOVER, HERBERT CLARK. Herbert Hoover was born in West Branch, Iowa, on August 10, 1974, to a Quaker family. He had a particularly difficult childhood. Orphaned as a small child, he spent years moving back and forth between distant relatives. Finally, he ended up with an uncle in Oregon, where Hoover for the first time enjoyed a stable home and family life. He proved to be an intelligent, ambitious, and resilient adolescent, and in 1895 he graduated from Stanford University with a degree in mining and metallurgical engineering. Times were hard in 1895. The effects of the depression of 1893 still lingered in the economy, and he took whatever work he could get in the mines.

To his employers, Hoover's talents were obvious, and once the depression ended, he became extraordinarily successful, working around the world between 1895 and 1913 and amassing a personal fortune. Hoover's international reputation began when World War I broke out in Europe. Hoover happened to be in Europe on business at the time, and he immediately began organizing the effort to get stranded Americans back to the United States. He spent a great deal of his own money on the project and raised millions more from private sources. Later in the war, Hoover established the Commission for the Relief of Belgium to provide food and clothing for Belgians caught in the German occupation. He eventually saw that millions of tons of food were shipped to the Low Countries. By the time he returned to the United States in 1917, he had earned reputations as a brilliant administrator and as a great humanitarian.

Hoover then began his political career. President Woodrow Wilson appointed him to head up the U.S. Food Administration, a federal agency designed to increase food production and ration food and fiber use so the needs of the soldiers in Europe could be met. He was highly successful, and between 1918 and 1921, he served as head of the American Relief Association, which generated relief supplies for war-damaged regions of Europe and the Soviet Union.*

In 1921, newly elected President Warren G. Harding named Hoover to his cabinet as secretary of commerce. Historians today acknowledge Hoover as one of the most successful secretaries of commerce in American history. Hoover promoted what he called the "associative state," in which the federal government encouraged the development of organized interest groups—trade associations, labor unions, farm cooperatives, and marketing groups—which he believed would increase rational competition and improve professional standards in the economy. Such groups, he believed, would increase productivity in the economy through research, planning, and efficiency. Hoover served as secretary of commerce from 1921 to 1929 in the cabinets of Warren G. Harding and Calvin Coolidge.

In 1928, as the Republican Party nominee, Hoover easily defeated Democratic candidate Al Smith* for president. It was an auspicious beginning for a presidential administration full of great promise, and at his inaugural, Hoover promised "two chickens in every pot and a car in every garage," as well as an end to poverty in America. But seven months later, the stock market crashed and the economy nosedived into the most severe depression in U.S. history. With the economy went Hoover's reputation as a humanitarian and a brilliant administrator. Afraid of creating a huge federal bureaucracy, he postponed establishing government relief programs, and his name soon became synonymous with wealth, apathy, and arrogance.

Actually, Hoover had not relied on laissez-faire indifference and market forces to correct the economy. At first he tried to marshal private, voluntary resources to stimulate the economy and provide relief to the unemployed and to use the federal government to coordinate the effort. When those initiatives failed, he tried other programs, including the Agricultural Marketing Act of 1929, the Reconstruction Finance Corporation* Act of 1932, the Emergency Relief and Construction Act of 1932,* and the Federal Home Loan Bank Act of 1932.*

But nothing worked. Hoover was still wedded to classical economic notions and believed that massive infusions of credit into the economy would automatically lead to increases in consumer purchasing power, production, and employment. But the Great Depression had its roots not in credit shortages but in a lack of consumer purchasing power, and Hoover never realized that. The economy got steadily worse during his administration, with the unemployment rate hitting 25 percent by the end of 1932. When Hoover ran for reelection in November 1932, he did not have a chance of victory. The man whose name had become synonymous with poverty, homelessness, and hunger—"Hoovervilles," "Hoover blankets," and "Hoover hogs"—lost to Franklin D. Roosevelt* by the greatest margin in American history.

Hoover retired to private life and during the 1930s offered a mild critique of the New Deal.* He worried that the unprecedented expansion in the size and power of the federal government would, in the long term, damage the American economy and American society. He came out of retirement late in the 1940s to preside over a government commission designed to streamline the operation of the federal government. For the rest of his life, Hoover served as an elder statesman of the Republican Party. He died on October 20, 1964.

SUGGESTED READINGS: David Burner, *Herbert Hoover: A Public Life*, 1979; James S. Olson, *Herbert Hoover and the Reconstruction Finance Corporation, 1931–1933*, 1977.

HOOVER, J. EDGAR. J. Edgar Hoover, the most well known and perhaps notorious law enforcement official in American history, was born on January 1,

1895, in Washington, D.C. In 1916 he graduated from George Washington University and then earned a law degree there one year later. He took a job with the Justice Department and spent the rest of his life there. In 1919, Attorney General A. Mitchell Palmer named him his special assistant, and Hoover soon found himself the heart and soul of the Red Scare, investigating political radicals of every stripe. He became assistant director of the Bureau of Investigation in 1921, working under the direction of William J. Burns, and in 1924, Hoover was appointed to head the newly organized Federal Bureau of Investigation (FBI). Hoover spent the rest of his life as director of the FBI. A confirmed bachelor, the FBI was all the family Hoover ever needed.

During the 1930s, Hoover became the most well-known civil servant in the country, primarily because his FBI "G-men" went after gangsters like John Dillinger,* Bonnie and Clyde,* "Baby Face" Nelson, and "Pretty Boy" Floyd. Later in the decade and throughout World War II, the FBI targeted Nazis for scrutiny, and during the late 1940s and 1950s, Hoover turned his attention to the issue of communist subversion in the United States. Because of widespread public support and the fact that he had investigated and kept files on every prominent person in the United States, Hoover became one of the most powerful people in the country. He died on May 2, 1972.

SUGGESTED READINGS: Kenneth O'Reilly, "A New Deal for the FBI: The Roosevelt Administration, Crime Control, and National Security," *Journal of American History*, 69 (1982), 638–58; Richard G. Powers, *Secrecy and Power: The Life of J. Edgar Hoover*, 1987.

HOOVER BLANKET. During the years of the Great Depression, President Herbert Hoover's* name became synonymous with poverty and suffering in the United States. The collapse of the economy, widespread unemployment, and the president's own political ineptitude all contributed to new lexicon. Americans began referring to newspapers as "Hoover blankets" because so many homeless Americans covered themselves with newspapers at night in order to keep warm. Park benches became known as "Hoover homes" because so many homeless Americans slept on them at night. Garbage dumps and landfills were dubbed "Hoovervilles" because so many hungry people scavanged them for food. In Arkansas, Texas, Louisiana, and Mississippi, armadillos became known as "Hoover hogs" because so many hungry people had resorted to eating them.

SUGGESTED READINGS: David Burner, *Herbert Hoover: A Public Life*, 1979; James S. Olson, *Herbert Hoover and the Reconstruction Finance Corporation, 1931–1933*, 1977.

HOOVER DAM. The greatest challenge facing economic development in the western states has always been water allocation, but in the 1920s, great progress was made in establishing a formula for water use on the Colorado River watershed. The leading figure in working out the agreement between Utah, Arizona, Colorado, and Nevada was Secretary of Commerce Herbert Hoover.* Congress passed the Boulder Canyon Project Act on December 21, 1928. The linchpin of the water allocation program was construction of a dam on the Colorado River at Boulder Canyon, twenty-five miles southeast of the city of Las Vegas.

It took three years for the engineering and architectural plans to be formulated, and construction began in 1931. Construction consumed six years, but when the dam was finished, it was considered the world's great engineering achievement. It stood 726 feet high and 1,244 feet long. Because of Herbert Hoover's role in the Colorado River project, the dam was dedicated in his honor. Hoover Dam remains today one of the world's most spectacular engineering feats.

SUGGESTED READINGS: Andrew J. Dunar and Dennis McBride, *Building Hoover Dam: An Oral History of the Great Depression*, 1993; Norris Hundley, *Water for the West*, 1974.

HOOVER HOG. See **HOOVER BLANKET**.

HOOVER HOME. See **HOOVER BLANKET**.

HOOVER MORATORIUM. Blaming Germany* for the devastation of World War I, the Allied Powers at the Versailles Conference of 1919 decided to punish their former adversary. The Treaty of Versailles saddled Germany with a $56 billion reparations bill for the cost of the war. It was a catastrophically bad decision, for it destabilized the German economy and weakened the rest of Europe as well. By 1924, when it had become obvious that Germany would never be able to pay the bill, the Allied Powers in the Dawes Plan reduced the debt. The Young Plan of 1929 reduced the total reparations debt to $8 billion. Even that, however, was impossibly high once the world's economy entered the Great Depression.

By 1931, with the world's money markets facing collapse, handling the international reparations issue became critical. The French did not want to forgive the German debt until the United States had forgiven the Allied war debt. In May 1931, the central bank of Austria* declared bankruptcy, creating a worldwide liquidity crisis. President Herbert Hoover* then acted. On June 20, 1931, he proposed a twelve-month moratorium on all Allied war debts payments and on German reparations payments. France accepted the plan in July 1931, and the moratorium was imposed. Then, at the Lausanne Conference of 1932,* the Allied Powers reduced German reparations to $1 billion. The complete collapse of the U.S. banking system in 1933 and the rise of Adolf Hitler to power in Germany in 1933–1934 all but ended the debt-reparations issue.

SUGGESTED READINGS: Edward W. Bennett, *Germany and the Diplomacy of the Financial Crisis*, 1962; Bernard V. Burke, "American Economic Diplomacy and the

Weimar Republic," *Mid-America*, 54 (October 1972), 211–33; Benjamin Rhodes, "Herbert Hoover and the War Debts, 1919–1933," *Prologue*, 6 (Summer 1974), 150–80.

HOOVERVILLE. See HOOVER BLANKET.

HOPE, BOB. Born in England on May 29, 1903, as Leslie Townes Hope, Bob Hope immigrated to the United States in 1907 with his family. His father was a stonemason and his mother an actress who had performed on the stage in Wales. She taught the boy to sing and gave him his lifelong interest in show business. To avoid being ridiculed by schoolmates, the young Hope changed his name to "Bob." During the 1920s, he worked the vaudeville circuit in New York and Chicago, singing and performing in black face, and in 1932 he got his first big break, winning a vocal part in the Broadway musical *Ballyhoo of 1932*. In 1933 he played Huckleberry Haines in Jerome Kern's production of *Roberta*, and in 1936 he appeared with Fannie Brice in Ziegfeld's *Follies* and in Cole Porter's *Red, Hot, and Blue*.

Hope achieved his status as a national celebrity in 1935 when *The Bob Hope Comedy Show* debuted on the Blue Network. The show switched to CBS at the end of the year and remained there until September 1936, when the Blue Network resigned Hope. Late in 1937 Hope returned to NBC, where his radio show occupied prime time for the next decade. His comedic banter, one-liners, and zany antics won the hearts, and the ears, of millions of Americans, and he became one of the decade's most popular radio personalities. Beginning in 1938, Hope also began starring in Hollywood film hits. The radio show had launched Hope to stardom and to recognition as the twentieth century's most enduring entertainer. During World War II, the Korean War, and the Vietnam War, Hope's annual Christmas tours to U.S. military bases abroad also made him one of America's most beloved figures.

SUGGESTED READINGS: Bob Hope, *Don't Shoot: It's Only Me*, 1990; Joe Morella, Edward Z. Epstein, and Eleanor Clark, *The Amazing Career of Bob Hope*, 1973.

HOPKINS, HARRY LLOYD. Harry Lloyd Hopkins was born in Sioux City, Iowa, on August 17, 1890. He graduated from Grinnel College in 1911 and began a career in social work. In New York City, Hopkins worked for Christadora House, a settlement house, and for the Association for Improving the Condition of the Poor. In both positions, he acquired a lifelong sympathy for the problem of urban poverty and a commitment to ameliorating its effects through governmental activism. Hopkins became active in local Democratic Party politics, and in 1931 Governor Franklin D. Roosevelt* of New York appointed him deputy director of the state's Temporary Emergency Relief Administration, a state agency designed to assist the unemployed. Hopkins became a close personal friend and influential adviser to Governor Roosevelt, and in 1933, when FDR became president of the United States, Hopkins went to Washington, D.C.,

with him to head up a succession of federal government relief agencies—Federal
Emergency Relief Administration* (1933), Civil Works Administration* (1933–
1934), and the Works Progress Administration* (1935–1938). Hopkins served
in Roosevelt's cabinet as secretary of commerce from 1983 to 1940. Although
Republicans often criticized Hopkins's administration of federal relief programs,
he was a dutiful civil servant who emphasized work relief over the dole.

Much of the criticism Republicans directed at Hopkins came from his conversion to Keynesian economics. Using the power of the federal government,
through government spending and taxation policies, to stimulate an ailing economy seemed perfectly logical to Hopkins. It also seemed perfectly logical to use
such powers for political reasons—to make sure that the economy was in as
good shape as possible during election years. Although such reasoning has become commonplace in recent years, among Republicans as well as Democrats,
it was an innovative public policy initiative in the late 1930s and early 1940s
and earned Hopkins the wrath of political enemies.

During World War II, Hopkins had an office in the White House, where he
worked as a special adviser to the president on foreign and domestic affairs. He
often served as FDR's personal emissary to foreign leaders, troubleshooting
serious problems, and attending all of the major conferences between Allied
leaders. Passionately committed to a world at peace and to the right of every
individual to a decent standard of living, Harry Hopkins is today considered to
be a founding father of the modern federal government and an architect of the
New Deal.* Hopkins died on January 19, 1946.

SUGGESTED READINGS: Charles F. Searle, *Minister of Relief: Harry Hopkins and
the Depression*, 1963; David Kennedy, *Freedom from Fear: The American People in
Depression and War, 1929–1945*, 2000; *New York Times*, January 30–31, 1946.

HOWE, LOUIS McHENRY. Louis Howe was born in Indianapolis, Indiana,
on January 14, 1871. He was raised in Saratoga Springs, New York. He attended
Yale and then went to work for the *New York Herald* in Albany, New York,
where he became an insider in state politics. In 1911 he met state senator Franklin D. Roosevelt* and came away extremely impressed. Roosevelt had Howe
manage his 1912 reelection campaign, and when FDR won a major victory,
Howe became his political confidant. In 1913, Howe became secretary to Roosevelt, who had been appointed assistant secretary of the navy. When Roosevelt
ran and lost for vice-president in 1920, Howe was by his side, and when FDR
later came down with polio, Howe encouraged him not to surrender to his
paralysis but to come back strong. Howe continued to serve as secretary to FDR
when Roosevelt won the governorship of New York and then came to the White
House in 1933. Although Howe continued to advise Roosevelt, health problems
limited his activities, and he died on April 18, 1936.

SUGGESTED READINGS: Alfred B. Rollins, *Roosevelt and Howe*, 1962; Lela Stiles,
The Man behind Roosevelt: The Story of Louis McHenry Howe, 1954.

HOW TO WIN FRIENDS AND INFLUENCE PEOPLE. In 1936, Dale
Carnegie published his book *How to Win Friends and Influence People*, a book
that explained his success in overcoming the rural poverty of his native-born
Missouri to become a successful syndicated columnist, lecturer, and radio star.
Carnegie's book touted the benefits of positive thinking, treating people with
respect, and using everything possible to one's advantage, including any physical handicap capable of generating sympathy. The book struck a responsive
chord during the years of the 1930s, becoming a runaway bestseller. Historians
look back upon the book as a symbol of the American character. Although the
country was mired in the worst economic depression of its history, most people
still looked on the present and the future with confidence and hope.

SUGGESTED READING: Dale Carnegie, *How to Win Friends and Influence People*,
1936.

HUGHES, CHARLES EVANS. Charles Evans Hughes was born in Glen
Falls, New York, on April 11, 1862. His father, a Methodist minister, immigrated to the United States from Wales, and his mother descended from a Dutch
family with deep roots in upstate New York. An intellectual child prodigy with
a photographic memory, Charles Hughes attended Brown University and then
graduated from the Columbia Law School. He practiced corporate law for several years and then accepted a position on the law faculty at Cornell. After
several years at Cornell, Hughes returned to private practice in New York City.
He also became active in Republican Party politics, and in 1906, he was elected
governor of New York. As governor, Hughes earned a reputation as a progressive reformer who was comfortable with government regulation of economic
activity. In 1910, President William Howard Taft appointed Hughes to the U.S.
Supreme Court. Hughes remained an associate justice for five years, stepping
down in 1916 to accept the Republican nomination for president. In the election
of 1916, however, President Woodrow Wilson defeated Hughes, who then returned to private law practice.

In 1921, Hughes became secretary of state under President Warren Harding
and then under President Calvin Coolidge. A confirmed internationalist, he
played a key role in negotiating the Washington Treaty of 1921, which reduced
naval weapons, the Five Power Pact, and the Nine Power Act, and he worked,
unsuccessfully, for U.S. membership in the League of Nations and the World
Court. In 1930, President Herbert Hoover* appointed Hughes as chief justice of
the U.S. Supreme Court.

It was a difficult time to be chief justice because of the vast expansion of
federal authority inherent in New Deal* legislation, but Hughes was not a doc-
trinaire ideologue. In cases of racial discrimination, such as the Scottsboro case,*
he denounced the denial of individual liberties to blacks. In matters of economic
regulation, Hughes was often a sway vote between liberals and conservative
justices. In the *Schechter** case, for example, he voted to outlaw the National

Recovery Administration* because he considered it a too broad increase in federal power, but on the other hand, he upheld regulatory powers in *West Coast Hotel v. Parrish* (1937).* Many conservatives, however, held Hughes responsible for the liberal course the Supreme Court took after President Franklin D. Roosevelt* launched his ill-fated court-packing scheme* in 1937. Hughes retired from the Court in 1941 and died in Cape Cod, Massachusetts, on August 27, 1948.

SUGGESTED READINGS: Samuel Hughes, *Charles Evans Hughes and the Supreme Court*, 1951; Merlo Pussey, *Charles Evans Hughes*, 1951.

HULL, CORDELL. Cordell Hull, the longtime secretary of state under President Franklin D. Roosevelt,* was born in Overton County, Tennessee, on October 2, 1871. In 1891 he graduated from the Cumberland University Law School and then began practicing law. Between 1893 and 1897 he served as a Democrat in the state legislature and then returned to his law practice. In 1903 he was appointed to the 5th Judicial Circuit of Tennessee. Hull served there until 1907 when he was elected to the House of Representatives. Except for 1921 and 1922, Hull served in Congress until his election to the U.S. Senate in 1931. During his years in Congress, Hull earned a reputation as a leading progressive Democrat. President Franklin D. Roosevelt appointed him secretary of state in 1933. A firm believer in tariff reduction as one way to help rebuild the world economy and stimulate production, Hull engineered the Reciprocal Trade Agreements Act of 1934,* which became his major achievement of the depression years. He was also a key figure in implementing the Good Neighbor Policy* with Latin America. Hull remained at the State Department until 1944, when he retired. He died on July 23, 1955.

SUGGESTED READINGS: John S. Leiby, "Cordell Hull," in James S. Olson, ed., *Historical Dictionary of the New Deal*, 1985; Julius W. Pratt, *Cordell Hull, 1933–1944*, 1964.

"HUNDRED DAYS." The term "Hundred Days" came to be used to describe the special session of the 73rd Congress that launched the New Deal.* Between March 9 and June 16, 1933, Congress passed more major legislation than at any other time in U.S. history. Included in the "Hundred Days" were the Emergency Banking Act,* the Economy Act,* the Civilian Conservation Corps* Reforestation Relief Act, the Federal Emergency Relief Act, the Agricultural Adjustment Act,* the Tennessee Valley Authority,* the Securities Act,* the National Employment System Act, the Home Owners' Refinancing Act, the Banking Act,* the Farm Credit Act,* the Emergency Railroad Transportation Act,* and the National Industrial Recovery Act. Historians today regard the "Hundred Days" as the most dramatic period in the history of American public policy.

SUGGESTED READING: James E. Sargent, *Roosevelt and the Hundred Days: Struggle for the Early New Deal*, 1981.

I

ICKES, HAROLD LECLAIR. Harold Ickes was born in Frankstown, Pennsylvania, on March 15, 1874. In 1897 he graduated from the University of Chicago and went to work as a reporter for the *Chicago Tribune* and the *Chicago Record*. An independent Republican with progressive views, Ickes endorsed Theodore Roosevelt and the Bull Moose Party in the presidential election of 1912. Although he came back to the Republican fold in 1916 and endorsed Charles Evans Hughes,* he defected again in 1920 and endorsed the Democratic ticket of James Cox and Franklin D. Roosevelt.* In Chicago during the 1920s, Ickes was active in the local chapter of the National Association for the Advancement of Colored People* (NAACP) and became an advocate of civil rights. Ickes was also active in the conservation movement.

In 1933 President-elect Franklin D. Roosevelt named Ickes secretary of the interior in his cabinet, and several months later, he asked Ickes also to head up the Public Works Administration* (PWA). As head of the PWA and Department of the Interior, Ickes consistently promoted conservation, national economic planning, and civil rights. Ickes worked studiously to make sure that blacks got a fair share of jobs in the administration, public works construction jobs, and relief money. He was responsible for the establishment of the "black cabinet"* to advise the Roosevelt administration on minority affairs. Throughout the 1930s, Harold Ickes was one of the most influential men in the country. He did not leave the Department of the Interior until 1946. Ickes died on February 3, 1952.

SUGGESTED READINGS: Linda J. Lear, *Harold L. Ickes: The Aggressive Progressive, 1874–1933*, 1981; *New York Times*, February 4–5, 1952; T. H. Watkins, *The Righteous Pilgrim: The Life and Times of Harold L. Ickes*, 1990.

INDIAN NEW DEAL. See **INDIAN REORGANIZATON ACT OF 1934**.

INDIAN REORGANIZATION ACT OF 1934. Also named the Wheeler-Howard Act because it was sponsored in Congress by Senator Burton K.

Wheeler* of Montana and Representative Edgar Howard of Nebraska, the Indian Reorganization Act became law on June 18, 1934. The law turned the tide on eighty years of federal assimilationist policy concerning Indians by repealing the allotment provisions of the Dawes Act of 1887 and provided $2 million annually to buy land back for Native Americans. It also provided a $10 million revolving credit fund to loan money to tribal corporations and appropriated $250,000 a year to provide tribal entities with legal assistance. The Indian Reorganization Act also contained affirmative action provisions giving Indians preference for civil service jobs in the Bureau of Indian Affairs. Two years later, in 1936, the Alaska Reorganization Act provided similar assistance to Alaskan natives, and the Oklahoma Indian Welfare Act did so for Indian peoples of Oklahoma. The law gave Indian tribes the right to approve or reject the legislation. In the end, roughly 181 tribes with 129,750 people approved it and seventy-seven tribes with 86,235 people rejected it. Although the legislation of the Indian New Deal was controversial and did not achieve all that Commissioner of Indian Affairs John Collier* wanted, it nevertheless ended allotment, increased the tribal land base, and provided tribal governments with more legal authority.

SUGGESTED READINGS: Kenneth R. Philp, *John Collier's Crusade for Indian Reform, 1920–1954*, 1977; Graham D. Taylor, *The New Deal and American Indian Tribalism: The Administration of the Indian Reorganization Act, 1934–1945*, 1980.

INSULL, SAMUEL. Samuel Insull, whose name would become synonymous with the hubris of American financiers during the 1920s and 1930s, was born on November 11, 1859, in London, England. He received a fine private education and in 1879 became secretary to Colonel George E. Gourard, Thomas Edison's representative in Europe. Gourard was working to expand the electric utility industry on the continent. Edison was impressed with Insull's work, and in 1881, he brought Insull to the United States as his secretary. In 1892, Insull was named president of Chicago Edison.

He soon went independent and constructed an unparalleled public utility empire. During the speculative mania of the 1920s, he was able to sell stock in holding companies. Through the deft use of corporation combinations and holding companies, Insull eventually created a network of five separate corporate systems consisting of 150 subsidiaries, 4.5 million customers, and $2.5 billion in assets. Atop the empire were two companies—Insull Utility Investments, Inc., and Corporation Securities Company of Chicago.

But the Insull empire had a fatal weakness. Revenue from the operating companies paid the dividends for all of the stacked-up holding companies, and any interruption in operating company profits would bring down the holding companies. When the stock market crashed in 1929, Insull's worst nightmares were realized. By December 1931, Insull Utility Investments was bankrupt, and the rest of his companies had failed by December 1932. To avoid prosecution for fraud, Insull fled to Europe. As journalists covered the case and as the Great Depression worsened, Insull became a national bogeyman, an icon for the economic misery affecting the country. Public outrage over his criminal excesses led to the Banking Act of 1933,* the Corporate Bankruptcy Act, the Wagner-Connery Act, and the Public Utility Holding Company Act.* Insull was eventually indicted, but a jury acquitted him of embezzlement and mail fraud. He died in France on July 16, 1938.

SUGGESTED READING: Forrest McDonald, *Insull*, 1962.

INVESTMENT ADVISERS ACT OF 1940. The Investment Advisers Act of 1940 was designed to continue to clean up the securities industry. It required all individuals and companies planning to make money from the sale of securities to register with the Securities and Exchange Commission.* Unregistered people were forbidden to use the federal mail, interstate commerce, and national securities exchanges to promote securities sales. The legislation was a follow-up to the Securities Act of 1933,* the Securities Exchange Act of 1934, the Public Utility Holding Company Act of 1935,* and the Chandler Act of 1938.*

SUGGESTED READINGS: *New York Times*, August 2, 9, and 24, 1940.

INVESTMENT COMPANY ACT OF 1940. During the late 1930s, after the revelations of the Pecora Committee* and such federal regulatory legislation as the Securities Act of 1933,* the Securities Exchange Act of 1934, and the Public Utility Holding Company Act of 1935,* the securities industry decided to adopt some self-policing policies. The Investment Bankers Association (IBA) worked to standardize industry-wide practices and eliminate corruption and fraud. The IBA and the Securities and Exchange Commission* (SEC) jointly drafted the law that became known as the Investment Company Act of 1940. It prohibited "self-dealing" between companies and their affiliates, enforced proportion of independent directorships, and outlawed changes in investment policies without the consent of stockholders. All investment trust companies had to register with the SEC and provide full information to stockholders, and the SEC was empowered to oversee their operations.

SUGGESTED READINGS: *New York Times*, August 2, 9, and 24, 1940.

ITALY. In 1924, Benito Mussolini and the fascists assumed control of the Italian government, and for the next twenty years, Italy's fortunes were in their hands. Anxious to return Italy to its former glory on the world stage, Mussolini decided to expand Italy's empire in North Africa by conquering Ethiopia.* Late in 1935, to the consternation of most world leaders, Italian forces invaded Ethiopia. The Ethiopians were no match for the Italian army, but the image of Italian tanks running over Ethiopian soldiers equipped with spears did little to enhance

Mussolini's reputation. The dictator also decided to throw in his foreign policy lot with that of Adolf Hitler. In 1937, Italy joined the Anti-Comintern Pact of Germany* and Japan* and left the League of Nations. The decision became known as the "Rome-Berlin-Tokyo Axis." When Hitler invaded Poland* on September 1, 1939, and Great Britain and France declared war, Benito Mussolini and Italy found themselves in the middle of the global conflict.

SUGGESTED READING: C. J. Lowe, *Italian Foreign Policy, 1870–1940*, 1975.

IT HAPPENED ONE NIGHT. The 1934 film *It Happened One Night* was one of the most popular films of the decade. MGM, hoping to put an uppity Clark Gable* in his place, loaned the star out to lowly Columbia Pictures for the film. But Gable turned the tables on MGM. A zany comedy directed by Frank Capra, *It Happened One Night* costarred Claudette Colbert,* and Gable and Colbert had an on-screen sparkle, which enhanced the comedy and gave the film real sex appeal. It featured Clark Gable as Peter Warne and Claudette Colbert as Ellie Andrew. Andrew hits the road in order to escape the oppressive control of her newspaperman father Alexander (Walter Connolly), who has trapped her in an arranged marriage. In the process, she finds herself sitting next to Warne on a long-distance ride from Miami to New York. They end up doing some hitchhiking and enduring tourist camps, but in the process they fall in love. *It Happened One Night* launched Gable and Colbert to super stardom in Hollywood. *It Happened One Night* was a runaway hit that won five Academy Awards. In its most memorable scene, Gable removed his shirt to expose a bare chest. Within weeks, undershirt sales in the United States had plummeted.

SUGGESTED READING: *New York Times*, February 23, 1934.

J

JAMES TRUE ASSOCIATES. James True Associates was one of many anti–New Deal,* anti-Semitic lobbying organizations during the 1930s. James True, leader of the group, believed that President Franklin D. Roosevelt* was heading up a Jewish conspiracy to seize control of the United States. He even talked of the need to "kill kikes." James True Associates disappeared soon after the onset of World War II.

SUGGESTED READING: George Wolfskill and John A. Hudson, *All But the People. Franklin D. Roosevelt and His Critics, 1933–1939,* 1969.

JAPAN. When Japan invaded Manchuria in 1931, World War II officially began, at leasts in the minds of some historians. Chronically short of the natural resources needed to run a modern industrial economy and military machine, and badly dependent on Western powers for those resources, Japan's leaders embarked on a radical political course. To secure its own, permanent supplies of coal, iron ore, rubber, and oil, Japan decided on a course of conquest and to establish the "Greatest East Asia Co-Prosperity Sphere." By conquering vital areas of East Asia, Japan could augment its resource base and liberate itself from dependence on the Western powers. In addition to needing a secure source of natural resources, Japanese leaders also needed the ability to import rice. Japan's annual production of rice often fell short of demand, and to meet consumer needs, the grain needed to be imported. China was a natural supplier.

Manchuria became Japan's first target. Rich in coal and iron ore, and under the control of a corrupt, politically emaciated Chinese government, Manchuria became the first stepping stone in Japan's road to Asian dominance. In 1931, Japanese troops invaded Manchuria. Although Western leaders protested the invasion, they did nothing to stop it or to push it back. In February 1933, on the grounds that China's army posed a military threat to the new Japanese-backed Manchukuo government in Manchuria, Japan expanded its invasion, heading into Jehol Province, barely 100 miles from China's capital at Beijing. The United States, France, and Great Britain protested the invasion, and in response, Japan withdrew from the League of Nations.

The decade of the 1930s was a time of political turmoil in Japan, with military leaders gradually eclipsing civilian politicians in dominance, and in February 1936, the Japanese army conspired to assassinate four members of Prime Minister Keisuke Okada's cabinet. The Okada government fell, to be replaced by that of Koki Hirota, who was a puppet of the Japanese army. Hirota vastly escalated the military budget and used government revenues to underwrite the heavy industries necessary to support an expanded defense industry.

In July 1937, Japanese leaders decided to complete the conquest of China. Using the disappearance of a Japanese soldier outside Beijing as a pretext, Japan launched an offensive against Beijing, soon coming to control a wide swath of Chinese territory stretching from Beijing west to the Gulf of Chihli. Then turning south, Japanese troops overran Shanghai in October 1937. By December, the Japanese army had occupied Nanjing, forcing the relocation of Chiang Kai-shek's government to the city of Chongqing in Sichuan Province. Japanese soldiers perpetrated what historians remember as the "Rape of Nanjing," the wholesale slaughter of hundreds of thousands of Chinese civilians and the leveling of 70 percent of the city. By the end of 1939, Japanese forces had added Wuhan, the industrial heartland of China, to its list of conquests.

At that point, the Japanese invasion of China stalled. With troops so deep into the Chinese interior, Japanese generals had logistical problems keeping them supplied. Chiang Kai-shek and Mao Zedong, head of the Chinese Communist Party, then declared a cease fire in their own civil war and concentrated their forces in a guerrilla war against Japanese troops. Chinese engineers also dynamited the dykes on the Yellow River, flooding much of southern China and killing tens of thousands of Chinese peasants but also vastly reducing the mobility of the Japanese army. The southern advance of Japanese forces came to a halt.

Japan then bided its time, waiting for events in Europe to dictate its future. Events did. German victories over France, Belgium, The Netherlands, Denmark, and Norway in the spring of 1940, and the war against Great Britain, left Europe's Southeast Asian colonies ripe for conquest. To gain access to French rubber plantations in Indochina, Japan invaded northern Vietnam in 1940 and then moved into southern Vietnam in 1941. After attacking Pearl Harbor in December 1941, Japan set its sights on British Malaya, the Dutch East Indies, and the American Philippines, all of which had been conquered before the summer of 1942. With the fall of Malaya and the Dutch East Indies, Japan had control of the petroleum resources of Royal Dutch Shell and British Petroleum.

SUGGESTED READING: Jonathan Utley, *Going to War with Japan, 1937–1941*, 1985.

JOBLESS PARTY. The Jobless Party was established in St. Louis in 1932 by Father James R. Cox, a Roman Catholic priest. In the presidential election of 1932,* the Jobless Party nominated Cox for president and called for nationalization of the banks, government seizure of private wealth and fortunes, and a massive public works construction project program by the federal government. Cox won less than 1,000 votes in the election.

SUGGESTED READING: Edward L. Schapsmeier and Frederick H. Schapsmeier, *Political Parties and Civil Action Groups*, 1981.

JOHNSON, HUGH SAMUEL. Hugh Samuel Johnson, who headed the National Recovery Administration* (NRA) during the 1930s, was born in Ft. Scott, Kansas, on August 5, 1882. He was raised in Oklahoma's Cherokee Strip, and after earning a degree from Northwestern Teachers' College in Oklahoma in 1901, he went on to the U.S. Military Academy, where he graduated in 1903. Johnson pursued a military career, rising in rank to brigadier general by 1918, and in 1916 he finished a law degree from the University of California. He was a logistical genius, and during World War I, he served on the War Industries Board, where he became a close confidant of Bernard Baruch,* a leading figure in the Democratic Party. During the 1920s, Johnson served as vice-president and then as chairman of the board of the Moline Plow Company. In 1933, President Franklin D. Roosevelt* picked Johnson to head up the NRA.

Blessed with the personality of a pit bull, Johnson made friends with difficulty and enemies with ease. He led a heavy-handed crusade to get major industries to sign up to cooperate with the National Recovery Administration's production codes, and he personally designed the "Blue Eagle,"* which became the NRA's logo. During the spring and summer of 1933, Johnson succeeded in securing the approval and cooperation of the cotton textile, shipbuilding, electrical, wool textile, garment, oil, steel, lumber, and automobile industries. In September 1933, Johnson reached the peak of his popularity because it appeared that the NRA was poised to lead the country out of the depression.

But the NRA was soon mired in controversy. Southern Democrats criticized the NRA for the huge federal bureaucracy it seemed to be generating, while progressives considered it a government agency that encouraged monopolies. Union leaders criticized Johnson because the NRA did little to enforce the minimum wage and maximum hours standards of the National Industrial Recovery Act of 1933. Some economists also argued that rather than stimulating an economic recovery the NRA was prolonging the depression by trying to secure reductions in industrial production. Finally, the National Recovery Review Board, a federal commission headed by famous attorney Clarence Darrow* and designed to evaluate the effectiveness of the NRA, concluded that the NRA had become the pawn of big business. Johnson resigned in October 1934. In subsequent years, as a columnist for the Scripps-Howard newspaper chain, Johnson became quite critical of Roosevelt and the New Deal.* He died on April 15, 1942.

SUGGESTED READINGS: *New York Times*, April 16, 1942; George Wolfskill and John A. Hudson, *All But the People. Franklin D. Roosevelt and His Critics, 1933–1939*, 1969.

JOHNSON-O'MALLEY ACT OF 1934. The Johnson-O'Malley Act is considered by historians to be part of the so-called Indian New Deal of the 1930s. It authorized the secretary of the interior to enter into contracts with states and territories to channel money to Indian medical, educational, agricultural, and social welfare projects. All too often in the past, federal money given to school districts for the education of Indian children simply went into some general fund and was used for general expenditures and not targeted at Indian students. Those problems continued even after the law was passed because of racism on the part of local communities, non-Indian students, and school district officials. Still, the Johnson-O'Malley Act was a step in the right direction.

SUGGESTED READING: Margaret Szasz, *Education and the American Indian: The Road to Self-Determination since 1928*, 1977.

JOLSON, AL. Al Jolson was born as Asa Yoelson, in Srednike, Russia, on May 26, 1886. The Yoelsons immigrated to the United States when Asa was a still a child, and they settled in New York, where Asa soon began singing and dancing on vaudeville. His Jewish parents discouraged such a career, but Asa persisted. As a teenager he became popular with Broadway audiences by singing in black face, and he was a hit in 1913 in *Honeymoon Express*. His song "Mammy"—sentimental and sincere—became his trademark, and he adopted "Al Jolson" as his stage name. In 1927, he starred in the country's first commercially successful sound film, *The Jazz Singer*. He followed that up with the hit films *The Singing Fool* (1928) and *Mammy* (1930). During the 1930s, in a string of film and radio performances, Al Jolson became one of the most recognizable voices and faces in the country. But he was also desperately unhappy, in constant need of attention and adulation, an affliction that became the source of frequent bouts of depression. Al Jolson died in San Francisco, on October 23, 1950.

SUGGESTED READINGS: Michael Freedland, *Al Jolson*, 1972; *New York Times*, October 24, 1950.

JONES, JESSE HOLMAN. Jesse Jones, next to President Franklin D. Roosevelt* the most powerful man in Washington, D.C., during the 1930s, was born in Robertson County, Tennessee, on April 22, 1874. The family moved to Dallas, Texas, and in 1891 Jones graduated from Hill's Business College. He went to work in his uncle's lumber business and then branched out on his own, moving to Houston and becoming deeply involved in lumber, construction, real estate, oil and gas, and banking. By the early 1920s, he was one of the most successful real estate developers in the country and owned dozens of major

Houston properties. He helped found what became the Texas Commerce Bank, the *Houston Chronicle* newspaper, and Exxon. While he made a personal fortune, Jones was also a leading light in Houston politics and in the state Democratic Party. Between 1913 and 1917, he served as chairman of the Houston Harbor Board, which built the Houston ship channel, and during World War I, he played a key role in American Red Cross activities. He also became a close personal friend of President Woodrow Wilson. In 1928, Jones succeeded in bringing the Democratic National Convention to Houston.

When the banking system disintegrated in 1932, President Herbert Hoover* named Jesse Jones to the board of directors of the Reconstruction Finance Corporation* (RFC), a federal agency designed to liquefy the money markets by loaning money to troubled banks so they would not have to close. In 1933, President Franklin D. Roosevelt named Jones to head up the RFC, where Jones remained until 1945. The RFC became the most powerful government agency in American history, becoming known as the "Fourth Branch of Government," and as head of the RFC, Jones presided over a government credit empire that, at one time or another, included or funded the Federal Emergency Relief Administration,* the Home Owners' Loan Corporation,* the Farm Credit Administration,* the Federal Home Loan Bank Board, the Regional Agricultural Credit Corporations, the Federal Housing Administration,* the Rural Electrification Administration,* the Resettlement Administration,* the Federal National Mortgage Association,* the Electric Home and Farm Authority,* the Disaster Loan Corporation, the Commodity Credit Corporation,* and the Export-Import Bank.* In 1939, President Roosevelt added the Federal Loan Agency* to Jones's New Deal* empire. By 1940, the RFC and its subsidiaries had loaned more than $10 billion to tens of thousands of American banks, building and loan associations, industrial banks, municipal savings banks, credit unions, railroads, insurance companies, and private businesses. Jones's responsibilities then grew geometrically during World War II, when the Reconstruction Finance Corporation assumed responsibility for funding the expansion of the wartime economy. By 1945 the total volume of RFC loans exceeded $50 billion. Jones returned to private life in 1945 and devoted his energies to his personal business empire and to philanthropy through the Jesse Jones Foundation. He continued to be active in national and state Democratic Party politics. Jesse Jones died on June 1, 1956.

SUGGESTED READINGS: Jesse Jones, *Fifty Billion Dollars*, 1951; James S. Olson, *Herbert Hoover and the Reconstruction Finance Corporation, 1931–1933*, 1977; James S. Olson; *Saving Capitalism: The Reconstruction Finance Corporation and the New Deal, 1933–1940*, 1988.

JONES-CONNALLY FARM RELIEF ACT OF 1934. After the severe drought of 1933–1934 on the Great Plains, ranchers began demanding some assistance from the federal government, and Secretary of Agriculture Henry

Wallace* invited representatives from the Southwestern Cattle Raisers Association, the American National Livestock Association, the Texas and Southwestern Cattle Raisers, and the Panhandle Livestock Association to meet in Denver, Colorado, to address the problem. Marvin Jones of Texas, chairman of the House Agriculture Committee, attended the meeting as well. As a result of the meeting, cattle became defined as a basic commodity for the Agricultural Adjustment Administration,* and Marvin Jones, along with Senator Tom Connally, introduced legislation to Congress. After an intense lobbying process, the Jones-Connally Farm Relief Act of 1934 was passed. It made cattle a basic commodity, appropriated $200 million to assist ranchers in cutting production in order to raise beef prices, provided funds for the elimination of brucellosis among cattle, and awarded basic commodity status to barley, rye, peanuts, flax, and grain sorghum.

SUGGESTED READING: Irvin M. May, Jr., "Jones-Connally Farm Relief Act of 1934," in James S. Olson, *Historical Dictionary of the New Deal*, 1985; Irvin M. May, Jr., *Marvin Jones: The Pubic Life of an Agrarian Advocate*, 1980; John T. Schlebecker, *Cattle Raising on the Plains, 1900–1961*, 1963.

JONES-COSTIGAN SUGAR ACT OF 1934. Sugar producers, like most other farmers in the United States, had the challenge of overproduction and falling prices to deal with, and the Jones-Costigan Sugar Act of 1934 was designed to help them. The legislation defined sugar cane and sugar beets as basic commodities, making them eligible for inclusion in the program of the Agricultural Adjustment Administration,* and allowed for benefit payments to be paid from a processing tax on sugar. Sugar cane producers in Hawaii and Puerto Rico opposed the measure, but it passed handily in Congress because of the backing of two powerful congressmen—Representative Marvin Jones of Texas and Senator Edward Costigan of Colorado.

SUGGESTED READINGS: Irvin M. May, Jr., "Jones-Connally Farm Relief Act of 1934," in James S. Olson, *Historical Dictionary of the New Deal*, 1985; Irvin M. May, Jr., *Marvin Jones: The Pubic Life of an Agrarian Advocate*, 1980.

K

KERR-SMITH TOBACCO CONTROL ACT OF 1934. The Agricultural Adjustment Act of 1933* was designed to address the problem of falling commodity prices by getting American farmers to reduce the number of acres planted each year. The Agricultural Adjustment Administration* (AAA) paid farmers for the number of acres held out of production. The AAA's goal was to bring the annual production of flue-cured tobacco to 500 million pounds. Individual farmers agreed to reduce acreage and production by 30 percent of their previous three-year average. In return, each farmer received a rental payment of $17.50 per acre and an annual payment of 12 percent of the selling price of his tobacco. Farmers were not compelled to participate.

AAA economists soon became worried, however, that those farmers not participating might increase their own production so much as to defeat the entire purpose of New Deal* economic policy. The Kerr-Smith Tobacco Control Act of 1934 made participation virtually compulsory. It imposed a tax of 25 to 33 percent on the sale price of all tobacco and then awarded tax-exempt certificates in that amount to participating farmers. In 1935 tobacco production in the United States was 557 million pounds, and the average price of flue-cured tobacco went up to 27.3 cents per pound, making the program a modest success.

SUGGESTED READING: Anthony J. Badger, *Prosperity Road: The New Deal, Tobacco, and North Carolina*, 1980.

KEYNES, JOHN MAYNARD. John Maynard Keynes, arguably one of the most influential figures of the twentieth century, was born in Cambridge, England, in 1883. A brilliant student at Eton and King's College, Cambridge, he studied economics and after graduation became a civil servant with the India Office. After just two years, he returned to Cambridge and wrote *Indian Currency and Finance* (1913). Considered an intellectual triumph, the book earned Keynes the editorship of the prestigious *Economic Journal*. In 1918, he was involved as a deputy to the chancellor of the exchequer for the Supreme Economic Council in the Versailles negotiations to end World War I. He considered the final treaty, because of its punitive reparations package for Germany,* an economic disaster, and in protest he wrote *The Economic Consequences of the Peace* (1918), a book that gave him an international reputation.

During the 1920s Keynes became wealthy, not because of his faculty position at Cambridge but because of successful speculation in international currencies. He hated the world's preoccupation with gold, currency, and money supply and argued so in two books: *Tract on Monetary Reform* (1923) and *Treatise on Money* (1930). But it was his 1936 book *The General Theory of Employment, Interest, and Money* that turned the world of economic theory upside down. He rejected the ideas of classical economic theory that in the long run an economy will balance itself; instead, he argued that in a modern industrial economy declines could go on indefinitely, since declines in employment, production, and purchasing could be mutually reinforcing. Unlike classical economists, who wanted to wait for an economy to rejuvenate itself, Keynes called on government to use its own spending and taxation policies to supplement temporarily private investment, income, and spending. Deficit spending—issuing government bonds to well-to-do investors—and then spending the proceeds on unemployment relief and public works construction would stimulate the economy and lift the country out of the depression.

During the 1930s, Keynes wrote several letters to President Franklin D. Roosevelt,* and a number of prominent New Deal* figures, such as Marriner Eccles* and Leon Keyserling,* converted to "Keynesian economics." Roosevelt moved slowly in the direction of Keynes, but it was not until World War II, when massive government spending lifted the country out of the Great Depression, that his theories were demonstrated conclusively. John Maynard Keynes died on April 21, 1946.

SUGGESTED READINGS: Robert Lekachman, *The Age of Keynes*, 1966; *New York Times*, April 22, 1946; Theodore Rosenof, *Economics in the Long Run: New Deal Theorists and Their Legacies, 1933–1993*, 1997.

KEYSERLING, LEON. Leon Keyserling was born in 1908 in Charleston, South Carolina. In 1928 he graduated from Columbia University and in 1931 received a law degree from Harvard. At Columbia he had become a favorite student of Rexford Tugwell,* and in 1933, Tugwell brought him to Washington, D.C., to work for the Agricultural Adjustment Administration.* Soon, however, Keyserling had joined the staff of Senator Robert Wagner* of New York, where he advocated increased government relief and welfare spending to stimulate purchasing power in the economy. Keyserling was among the earliest New Deal* policymakers to promote federal government deficit spending as a way out of the Great Depression. Keyserling played a key role in drafting such major New Deal legislation as the National Industrial Recovery Act of 1933, the Home Owners' Refinancing Act of 1933, the National Housing Act of 1934,* the

National Labor Relations Act of 1935,* and the Wagner-Steagall Housing Act
of 1937.* Keyserling went on to serve as a member of the Council of Economic
Advisers in the Harry Truman administration. After a prolific career at Columbia
University, Keyserling died on December 13, 1988.

SUGGESTED READINGS: Katie Loucheim, ed., *The Making of the New Deal. The
Insiders Speak*, 1983; Theodore Rosenof, *Economics in the Long Run: New Deal Theorists and Their Legacies, 1933–1993*, 1997.

KHAKI SHIRTS. Although most of the so-called Bonus Marchers left Washington, D.C., in the summer of 1932, a small contingent remained behind under
the leadership of Art J. Smith. They labeled themselves the Khaki Shirts and
called for payment of veterans bonuses, abolition of Congress, expansion of the
money supply through silver currency, and large increases in the defense budget.
The Khaki Shirts were also militantly anti-Semitic. Smith staged demonstrations
in several cities in 1933, but when a rally in New York ended in a riot that
killed one person and wounded twenty-four others, Smith was arrested and sentenced to prison. The Khaki Shirts then disintegrated.

SUGGESTED READING: George Wolfskill and John A. Hudson, *All But the People.
Franklin D. Roosevelt and His Critics, 1933–1939*, 1969.

KING KONG. The film *King Kong* premiered in New York on March 11,
1933, and was a huge hit among moviegoers, especially New Yorkers, who got
to watch a giant ape climb the Empire State Building* and do battle with incoming aircraft. Based on Sir Arthur Conan Doyle's novel *The Lost World*, the
film revolved around the discovery of a fifty-foot gorilla living on a Pacific
island. To make money, the discoverers trap the beast and bring it to Manhattan,
where it escapes and wreaks havoc in the city. The film was noted for its state-
of-the-art special effects and for the humanlike personality the ape enjoyed. In
the end, of course, civilization kills King Kong. Actually, military aircraft
machine-gun the giant ape while he is atop the Empire State Building. Audiences
sensed the death of innocence as well, not unlike what World War I and the
Great Depression had done to America. *King Kong* was one of the most popular
films of the decade.

SUGGESTED READING: *New York Times*, March 12, 1933.

KNIGHTS OF THE WHITE CAMELIA. The Knights of the White Camelia
was a fascist political organization of the 1930s. It was headed by George Deatherage and employed a swastika as its emblem. Deatherage regularly accused
Franklin D. Roosevelt* and his "Jew Deal" of promoting a takeover of America
by Jews and blacks. Of course, the more Deatherage adopted the ideas of Adolf
Hitler in the 1930s, the less influence he had.

SUGGESTED READING: George Wolfskill and John A. Hudson, *All But the People. Franklin D. Roosevelt and His Critics, 1933–1939*, 1969.

KRISTALLNACHT. Kristallnacht, or Night of the Crystal, took place in Germany* on the evening of November 9, 1938. The anti-Semitic rampage was triggered by the murder in Paris, France, of Ernst von Rath, a German diplomat, by Herschel Grynszpan, a Polish Jew. Adolf Hitler used the event as an opportunity to launch a pogrom throughout Germany against Jews. Mobs led by SS men, Nazi Storm Troopers, and Hitler Youth moved into Jewish neighborhoods, burning synagogues, breaking store windows (hence the name Crystal Night), and terrorizing Jews on the streets. When it was over, ninety-one Jews had been murdered, 200 synagogues destroyed, and 30,000 Jews arrested and sent off to newly opened concentration camps. Some historians remember Kristallnacht as the opening salvo in the Holocaust.

SUGGESTED READINGS: *New York Times*, November 11–12, 1938.

L

LABOR'S NON-PARTISAN LEAGUE. Between 1933 and 1936, because of such legislation as the National Industrial Recovery Act of 1933 and the National Labor Relations Act of 1935,* President Franklin D. Roosevelt* had secured the absolute and complete support of organized labor. To boost Roosevelt's chances of reelection in 1936, such prominent union leaders as John L. Lewis* and Sidney Hillman* established Labor's Non-Partisan League to marshal American Federation of Labor* and Congress of Industrial Organizations* support for the president. Union members donated more than $1 million to the campaign through the League, and the League also helped found the American Labor Party* in New York to give socialists a vehicle for voting for FDR. Roosevelt's margin of victory was an unprecedented 61 percent of the popular vote, and Labor's Non-Partisan League took much of the credit. In 1940, however, the League all but disintegrated with John L. Lewis's defection and decision to endorse Wendell Willkie* for president.

SUGGESTED READING: Irving Bernstein, *Turbulent Years: A History of the American Worker, 1933–1941*, 1970.

LA FOLLETTE, ROBERT MARION, JR. Robert M. La Follette, Jr., was born in Madison, Wisconsin, on February 6, 1895. His father, Robert La Follette, was renowned for his progressive politics and served as a congressman, governor, and U.S. senator. The younger La Follette attended the University of Wisconsin but never graduated, quitting college and accepting a job as a clerk in his father's U.S. Senate office. When his father died in 1924, Robert La Follette, Jr., was appointed to fill the office, and he remained in office until 1946. Although he was a Republican, La Follette became an outspoken critic of President Herbert Hoover* and his conservative policies. He wanted the president to implement public works construction and federal relief to ease the suffering of the unemployed, and he argued for national economic planning. He soon became known as one of the Senate's most liberal members, in spite of his Republican credentials. After Franklin D. Roosevelt's* election in 1932, La Follette consistently urged the president to the left, criticizing him for not moving far enough or fast enough in boosting consumer purchasing power, protecting collective bargaining rights for labor unions, and implementing more progressive taxation. Passionate and committed in his politics, La Follette was also subject to depression, a disorder that plagued him for much of his life. When he failed to secure reelection in 1946, La Follette went into a severe depression that consumed his last years. He committed suicide on February 24, 1953.

SUGGESTED READINGS: Jerold S. Auerbach, *Labor and Liberty: The La Follette Committee and the New Deal*, 1966; Patrick J. Maney, *"Young Bob" La Follette: A Biography of Robert M. La Follette, Jr., 1895–1953*, 1978; *New York Times*, February 24–25, 1953.

LA GUARDIA, FIORELLO HENRY. Fiorello La Guardia was born in New York City on December 11, 1882. He lived for a time in Arizona and worked as a journalist for the Phoenix *Morning Gazette*, and he then worked as a war correspondent for the St. Louis *Post-Dispatch* during the Spanish American War. Blessed with unusual linguistic gifts, La Guardia became fluent in seven languages, and between 1907 and 1910, while earning a law degree at New York University, he worked for the federal government interviewing immigrants at Ellis Island. A progressive Republican who hated Tammany Hall corruption, La Guardia served as deputy attorney general of New York from 1915 to 1917, the year he won election to Congress. He resigned in 1918 to join the army air corps during World War I. After the war, he was reelected to Congress and served until 1933. His most significant accomplishment in Congress was the Norris–La Guardia Labor Relations Act of 1932,* which protected labor unions from antistrike judicial court orders.

In 1933, La Guardia became mayor of New York, and in that position he forged a close relationship with President Franklin D. Roosevelt* and the New Deal.* He always worked to acquire more federal relief, public works construction, and welfare money for the city. La Guardia was convinced that such federal agencies as the Civil Works Administration,* the Public Works Administration,* the Works Progress Administration,* and the Federal Emergency Relief Administration* had saved American cities from revolution and anarchy during the depression. La Guardia died on September 20, 1947.

SUGGESTED READINGS: Barbara Blumberg, *The New Deal and the Unemployed: The View from New York City*, 1979; *New York Times*, September 21, 1947.

LANDON, ALFRED MOSSMAN. Alfred M. "Alf" Landon was born in West Middlesex, Pennsylvania, on September 9, 1887. After graduating from the University of Kansas, Landon pursued successful careers in banking, petroleum, and the law. He also became active in state Republican Party politics, earning a reputation as a progressive. He was elected governor of Kansas in 1932, defying the overwhelming, nationwide Democratic victories that year. In 1936, Landon was a natural for the Republican presidential nomination. He campaigned on a platform opposing deficit spending, bloated federal budgets, and large federal bureaucracies, but Americans were not listening. Franklin D. Roosevelt* was the hero of most voters, and he won reelection in a landslide. Landon carried only two states and eight electoral votes. He remained a marginally influential figure in Republican Party politics but spent most of his time attending to his business interests. Landon died on October 12, 1987.

SUGGESTED READINGS: Donald R. McCoy, *Landon of Kansas*, 1966; Francis W. Schruben, *Kansas in Turmoil, 1930–1936*, 1969.

LANGE, DOROTHEA. Dorothea Lange was born in Hoboken, New Jersey, on May 26, 1895. Although she graduated from the New York Training School for Teachers, she had no intention of going into public education. Instead, she moved to San Francisco and opened her own photography studio. Her business did well, catering to the city's wealthiest families, but the onset of the Great Depression sharpened Lange's social conscience. The gap between the living conditions of her wealthy clients and the city's poorest residents seemed scandalously wide to Lange. She decided to use photography to expose poverty in America. Her exhibitions proved to be political and commercial excesses, and Lange attracted the attention of Eleanor Roosevelt.* Between 1936 and 1938, as the official photographer of the Resettlement Administration* and then the Farm Security Administration,* she traveled widely throughout the country, exposing the poverty of midwestern farm families, southern tenant farmers, and urban ghetto families. Lange's photographs were published widely in books, newspapers, and magazines and appeared in dozens of exhibitions. In 1939 she published a collection of the photographs as *An American Exodus: A Record of Human Erosion*. During World War II, she worked as a photographer for the War Relocation Authority and for the Office of War Information. She retired after the war and died on October 11, 1965.

SUGGESTED READINGS: Therese T. Heyman, *Celebrating a Collection: The Work of Dorothea Lange*, 1978; Milton Meltzer, *Dorothea Lange: A Photographer's Life*, 1978; Karin B. Ohrn, *Dorothea Lange and the Documentary Tradition*, 1980.

LAUSANNE CONFERENCE OF 1932. During the 1920s, the nastiest issue in international finance was the question of German reparations payments and Allied repayments of their World War I debts to the United States. The Dawes Plan of 1924 and the Young Plan of 1929 had all reduced German reparations, but the United States insisted that the Allied nations forgive Germany* its reparations without the United States forgiving the Allied debts. The European countries, especially France, tied the two issues together. They would not cancel reparations until the United States canceled the Allied debts. The Lausanne Conference of 1932 met simultaneously with the World Disarmament Conference,* and delegates agreed to reduce German reparations to $715 million (they had once stood at $56 billion). But back in the United States, Congress refused to go along. Americans expected the Allied nations to pay off their American loans in full. The issue surfaced in the presidential election, and neither President Herbert Hoover* nor Democratic candidate Franklin D. Roosevelt* would seriously address it. All the Allied nations except Finland defaulted on their debts in 1932 and 1933, and Germany did not make any more reparations payments.

SUGGESTED READINGS: Robert Ferrell, *American Diplomacy in the Great Depression*, 1957; Joan Hoff Wilson, *American Business and Foreign Policy, 1920–1933*, 1971.

LEAGUE FOR INDEPENDENT POLITICAL ACTION. In 1929 John Dewey, the legendary progressive educator, founded the League for Independent Political Action (LIPA). Cofounders included journalist Oswald Garrison Villard and Paul H. Douglas, an economist at the University of Chicago. LIPA members found both the Democratic and Republican Parties too conservative and hoped to promote more liberal and socialist values in the United States, especially the need for national economic planning, expanded social welfare programs, and nationalization of key industries. In 1932, LIPA endorsed socialist Norman Thomas* for president and managed to get two of its candidates elected to Congress. But LIPA did not manage to survive the New Deal,* which pushed the Democratic Party considerably to the left. After FDR's reelection in 1936, the LIPA disintegrated.

SUGGESTED READING: Donald R. McCoy, *Angry Voices: Left-of-Center Politics in the New Deal Era*, 1958.

LEMKE, WILLIAM. William Lemke was born on August 13, 1878, in Albany, Minnesota, but he was raised in the Dakota Territory where the family acquired a large farm. In 1898, Lemke graduated from the University of North Dakota. Three years later, he earned a law degree at Yale. Lemke then practiced law in North Dakota and published a monthly magazine—*The Common Good*. As an attorney for the Non-Partisan League, Lemke developed progressive Republican values and an interest in the plight of farmers. He promoted government regulation of railroads, public utilities, banks, and insurance companies. Lemke won a seat in Congress in the election of 1932, and he was reelected in 1934, 1936, and 1938. Lemke's major accomplishment in Congress was the Federal Farm Bankruptcy Act of 1934,* also known as the Frazier-Lemke Farm Bankruptcy Act, which brought mortgage relief to troubled farm families.

In 1935, when President Franklin D. Roosevelt* and the New Deal* opposed

Lemke's inflationary monetary proposals, Lemke became one of the administration's most bitter critics. In the presidential election of 1936,* Lemke threw in his lot with Huey Long,* Francis Townsend,* and Father Charles Coughlin* and their Union Party,* but they secured less than a million votes in the election. In 1940, Lemke lost a bid for a seat in the U.S. Senate. He died on May 30, 1950.

SUGGESTED READING: Edward C. Blackorby, *Prairie Rebel: The Public Life of William Lemke*, 1963.

LEWIS, JOHN LLEWELLYN. John L. Lewis, the most prominent labor leader of the 1930s, was born on February 12, 1880, in Lucas, Iowa. Lewis's father was a coal miner, and the younger Lewis pursued the career. As a young man he worked in a variety of coal, lead, and silver mines in the western states, and he became active in union politics. In 1909, Lewis was elected president of the Panama, Illinois, chapter of the United Mine Workers (UMW), and his profile in the national UMW rose steadily. He was smart, tenacious, and tough. Between 1909 and 1920, he served as the UMW's chief statistician, business manager of the *United Mine Workers Journal*, and national vice-president of the union. In 1920, Lewis was elected national UMW president.

His initial thirteen years at the helm of the UMW were difficult for the union. Management hostility toward the union during the 1920s caused membership declines, and when the Great Depression hit in 1929, membership slipped even more. Between 1920 and 1933, UMW membership dropped from more than 500,000 workers to less than 75,000. The mining industry was characterized by overproduction, falling prices, massive unemployment, and declining wages for those miners who managed to keep their jobs. Although opposition to Lewis's leadership emerged in the union, he was ruthless in crushing rivals and maintaining his control.

When Franklin D. Roosevelt* and the Democrats came into power in 1933, Lewis suddenly enjoyed access to the seat of power in the United States, and he used that access to promote the labor movement. Lewis promised Roosevelt millions of votes if the New Deal* would finally underwrite labor's major demands, and Roosevelt agreed. Lewis supported the National Industrial Recovery Act of 1933 and the National Labor Relations Act of 1935,* and as a result of the laws, Lewis soon had more than 90 percent of miners in the UMW.

Lewis also had a vision for labor that extended beyond the United Mine Workers. The UMW was an affiliate of the American Federation of Labor,* which confined its membership to skilled workers in the major craft unions. Lewis was convinced that mass production workers needed to be organized into unions as well, and in 1935 he helped establish the Committee for Industrial Organization (CIO). Lewis was elected president of the CIO in 1936 and changed its name to the Congress of Industrial Organizations.* His own party membership was Republican, but in the election of 1936* he endorsed Franklin

D. Roosevelt, contributed $500,000 to the president's campaign, and marshaled the CIO's organization behind the reelection bid. Lewis eventually soured on Roosevelt and returned to the Republican Party. John L. Lewis died on June 11, 1969.

SUGGESTED READINGS: Melvin Dubofsky and Warren van Tine, *John L. Lewis: A Biography*, 1977; Charles K. McFarland, *Roosevelt, Lewis, and the New Deal, 1933–1940*, 1970; *New York Times*, June 12–13, 1969.

LIBERTY PARTY. In 1932, Frank E. Webb founded the Liberty Party to promote socialist solutions to the Great Depression. At the party's national convention, former Populist leader and author of *Coin's Financial School* William Harvey was nominated for president. Harvey proposed massive relief and public works construction by the federal government as well as nationalization of all major industries. The Liberty Party managed to get on the ticket in nine states but only secured 53,425 votes in the presidential election. The party then disintegrated.

SUGGESTED READING: Donald R. McCoy, *Angry Voices: Left-of-Center Politics in the New Deal Era*, 1958.

LINDBERGH, CHARLES. Charles Lindbergh, who during his lifetime was one of the most famous people in the world, was born in Detroit, Michigan, on February 4, 1902. He was raised in Little Falls, Minnesota. His father, an avowed isolationist, served several terms in Congress. Lindbergh completed two years at the University of Wisconsin, but academic life bored him. He was more interested in airplanes, and in 1922, he left school to go barnstorming. At the time, pilots were trying to set distance and speed records, and Lindbergh got the idea of making the world's first solo transatlantic flight. Lindbergh became the most famous person in the world on May 20, 1927, when he landed his plane—*The Spirit of St. Louis*—outside Paris after a flight from New York. Lindbergh became a certifiable hero and celebrity, a man who had committed an act of great individual courage in an age of urbanization, modernization, industrialization, and bureaucratization.

But Lindbergh's fame, which had at first given him great satisfaction, turned into a nightmare. In 1930 he married Anne Morrow, daughter of prominent banker and diplomat Dwight Morrow, and they soon had a baby boy. But in 1932, their baby was kidnapped and murdered, and police soon arrested Bruno Hauptmann.* Many consider it the trial of the century. The atmosphere of the trial more resembled a circus than a judicial proceeding. Although the evidence against him was circumstantial, and he vigorously claimed to be innocent, a jury convicted him and he was executed.

The Lindberghs never recovered emotionally from the death of their son and the trial. From 1935 to 1939, they lived in seclusion in Europe, but as the

continent drifted toward war, Lindbergh returned home and resurrected the isolationist ideas of his father. He became the most visible member of the America
First Committee, and in 1941, he was accused of being anti-Semitic for arguing
that Jews were trying to bring the United States into World War II. Lindbergh
changed his stance, however, after Japan's* attack on Pearl Harbor. With the
end of the war, Lindbergh became director of Pan American Airways and became a well-known environmentalist. Charles Lindbergh died on August 26,
1974.

SUGGESTED READINGS: Wayne S. Cole, *Charles A. Lindbergh and the Battle
against American Intervention in World War II*, 1974; Jim Fisher, *The Lindbergh Case*,
1987.

LINDBERGH KIDNAPPING. In 1925, when he flew solo across the Atlantic
from the United States to Paris, France, Charles Lindbergh* became a certifiable
hero, the most popular man in the world. It was a role he never really escaped,
and his fame ended up inspiring a family tragedy. On the night of March 1,
1932, Lindbergh's infant son was kidnapped from the family home in rural New
Jersey. The kidnapper carried a homemade wooden ladder onto the Lindbergh
property, leaned it up against the second-story house, entered Charles Lindbergh,
Jr.'s bedroom, and abducted the baby. The kidnapper left the ladder behind. He
left a crudely written ransom note in broken English, indicating perhaps that the
culprit was an immigrant. But the instructions in the note were vague and im-
precise.

    J. Edgar Hoover* and the Federal Bureau of Investigation (FBI) entered the
investigation, but leads were few and far between, although the number of false
leads, generated by letters and telephone calls from a public unable to separate
rumor from fact, consumed thousands of FBI man-hours. Finally, a phone caller
with a German accent revealed information about the case that only an FBI
agent, a New Jersey detective, or the kidnapper himself would know. A meeting
was arranged at a nearby cemetery, where the caller received a $50,000 ransom
in return for revealing that the baby was on Martha's Vineyard in Massachusetts.
An exhaustive search, however, failed to turn up the baby.

    In May 1932, however, a truck driver found the baby's corpse on the side of
a road close to the Lindbergh mansion. FBI agents concluded that the baby had
probably died the very night of the kidnapping from a blunt trauma to the head.
Perhaps he had fallen from the second story during the kidnapping. The trail of
the killer then went cold.

    But in 1934 the FBI came up with a new suspect—Bruno Richard Haupt-
mann*—a German immigrant, who at a New Jersey gas station had spent a $10
bill that police were able to track, through its serial number, back to the cemetery
exchange. With a search warrant, FBI agents found another $30,000 of the cash
in Hauptmann's home. They also discovered lumber in his home that matched
the lumber of the ladder used in the kidnapping.

Bruno Hauptmann was indicted for the murder and put on trial, and historians looking back on the event question whether he really received a fair trial. Hauptmann insisted again and again on his innocence, but he was convicted and sentenced to death. Hauptmann was executed in 1936. Most scholars who have reviewed the case, however, wonder if the real kidnapper and killer remained at large.

SUGGESTED READING: Jim Fisher, *The Lindbergh Case*, 1987.

THE LITERARY DIGEST. *The Literary Digest* was a weekly magazine established by Isaac K. Funk and Adam Wagnalls in 1890. By the late 1920s, circulation exceeded 1.5 million copies. It began running informal political polls with the election of 1920, and its first national, presidential poll was published in 1924. Using automobile registration information, magazine subscription lists, and telephone directories, the editors polled prospective voters. The polls proved quite popular, securing newspaper coverage and increased subscriptions. But in the election of 1936,* *The Literary Digest* poll predicted a victory for Republican nominee Alf Landon.* When President Franklin D. Roosevelt* was elected by a landslide, the magazine lost credibility. Its polling methodology, of course, was flawed. Most people who voted for Roosevelt did not own automobiles or telephones. In February 1938, *The Literary Digest* suspended publication.

SUGGESTED READINGS: Virginia F. Haughton, *"The Literary Digest,"* in James S. Olson, ed., *Historical Dictionary of the New Deal*, 1985; Theodore Peterson, *Magazines in the Twentieth Century*, 1964.

"LITTLE NEW DEAL." Journalists used the term "Little New Deal" to describe state governments in the 1930s that established vigorous work relief and construction works programs to relieve the suffering of the unemployed. Some of the so-called Little New Deals also included unemployment insurance, workmen's compensation, union rights, and bans on child labor. The most prominent of the Little New Deals developed under the leadership of Governor George Earl of Pennsylvania, Governor Herbert Lehman of New York, Governor Frank Murphy of Michigan, Governor Robert La Follette* of Wisconsin, and Governor Culbert Olson* of California.

SUGGESTED READING: James T. Patterson, *The New Deal in the States: Federalism in Transition*, 1969.

"LITTLE NRA." In 1935, the Supreme Court declared the National Industrial Recovery Act (NIRA) unconstitutional, destroying the National Recovery Administration,* which was the linchpin of the New Deal's* program to revive the economy. Outraged about the Supreme Court's action, the Roosevelt administration passed a series of laws designed to salvage as much of the NRA as possible. The Guffey-Snyder Bituminous Coal Stabilization Act of 1935 guaranteed labor's right to collective bargaining, established standard wage and hour scales, created a bituminous coal commission to control coal production and to set coal prices, and closed marginally profitable mines. When the Supreme Court declared the Guffey-Snyder Bituminous Coal Stabilization Act unconstitutional, the Guffey-Vinson Bituminous Coal Act of 1937 restored the wages and hours provisions. The Connally Act of 1935 outlawed the shipment in interstate commerce of so-called hot oil—oil produced in excess of production quotas. To protect small retailers, the Robinson-Patman Act of 1936 prohibited manufacturers from giving discounts or rebates to large-volume buyers. The Walsh-Healey Public Contracts Act of 1936* required minimum wage and maximum hours standards in all federal contracts. Finally, the Miller-Tydings Act of 1937* amended the Sherman Antitrust Act of 1890 to allow for the passage of "fair trade" laws.

SUGGESTED READING: William E. Leuchtenburg, *Franklin D. Roosevelt and the New Deal, 1932–1940*, 1963.

LITTLE ORPHAN ANNIE. Created and written by Harold Gray, "Little Orphan Annie" was one of the most popular comic strips of the 1920s and 1930s, and in April 1930, when it came to radio, it proved to be equally popular in that medium. It became a forerunner of the children's serial format—an ongoing plot that changed only slightly from week to week. *Little Orphan Annie* remained on the radio until 1943. The comic strip survived into the 1980s and was made into the hit Broadway musical *Annie*.

SUGGESTED READINGS: Michael Benton, *The Comic Book in America*, 1989; John Dunning, *Tune in Yesterday: The Ultimate Encyclopedia of Old-Time Radio, 1925–1976*, 1976; Will Jacobs and Gerard Jones, *The Comic Book Heroes*, 1985.

LONDON ECONOMIC CONFERENCE OF 1933. Because of the collapse of international money markets in 1931 and 1932, world leaders decided to convene an international economic conference in London in 1933. The goal of the conference was for the major powers—the United States, France, and Great Britain—to stabilize their currencies. Nothing came of the meetings, primarily because the Europeans were unwilling to tolerate President Franklin D. Roosevelt's* plan to inflate the currency through the gold-buying scheme and remonetization of silver. The Europeans hated inflationary ideas and wanted the United States to return to the gold standard.* The meetings in June and July 1933 were undermined by Roosevelt's unwillingness to abandon his inflation schemes.

SUGGESTED READING: James R. Moore, "Sources of New Deal Economic Policy: The International Dimension," *Journal of American History*, 61 (1974), 728–44.

LONDON NAVAL CONFERENCE OF 1930. In 1930, delegations from the United States, Great Britain, France, Italy,* and Japan* met in London to address the issue of naval arms limitations. With the world economy slipping into depression, the major naval powers did not want to keep making large investments in naval construction, and they also believed that arms limitations would reduce tensions around the world. Secretary of State Henry L. Stimson* led the American delegation. The negotiations soon erupted in acrimony. The Italian delegation refused to stay at the conference because of enmity with France, and France then insisted that new anti-German security measures be implemented. The United States and Great Britain wanted to look forward, not back to World War I, and refused to go along with France. France withdrew from the conference, leaving only Japan, Great Britain, and the United States. The final settlement was quite modest, extending the moratorium on capital ship construction until 1936, altering slightly the 5:5:3 tonnage arrangement reached at the Washington Naval Conference of 1921. The new ratio of capital ships for the United States, Great Britain, and Japan was 10:10:7, which gave Japan a modestly higher cruiser ratio. Japan also received submarine parity with the United States and Great Britain. The U.S. Senate ratified the treaty changes on July 21, 1930.

SUGGESTED READINGS: L. Ethan Ellis, *Republican Foreign Policy, 1921–1933*, 1968; Robert H. Ferrell, *American Diplomacy in the Great Depression: Hoover-Stimson Foreign Policy, 1929–1933*, 1957.

THE LONE RANGER. *The Lone Ranger* was one of radio's most popular and long-running series. It was first broadcast locally over WXYZ Radio in Detroit in 1933, and additional stations soon signed on to the program. Those stations—which included WGN in Chicago, WOR in New York, and WLW in Cincinnati—soon merged into the Mutual Radio Network and used *The Lone Ranger* as its foundation program. Beginning in 1944, ABC picked up *The Lone Ranger*, and they continued broadcasting it until 1956. The lead character in *The Lone Ranger* was a Texas Ranger who had survived an ambush, donned a mask, and along with his Indian sidekick Tonto and his horse Silver rode the range fighting for truth and justice. The show was a huge success in the 1930s, and promotional appearances of the "masked man" and his horse drew thousands of spectators. The opening signature of each program—"a fiery horse with the speed of light, a cloud of dust and a hearty Hi-Yo, Silver! The Lone Ranger!"—became the most well-known phrase in America. The Lone Ranger himself was known for being the ultimate do-gooder, and parents tuned in not only to enjoy western drama but to have values taught to their children. The last episode of *The Lone Ranger* was broadcast on May 25, 1956.

SUGGESTED READING: David Rothel, *Who Was That Masked Man? The Story of the Lone Ranger*, 1976.

LONG, HUEY PIERCE. Huey P. Long was born near Winnfield, Winn Parish, Louisiana, on August 30, 1893. Long's family had a streak of populism that ran deep, with equally hostile feelings for the ruling, upper classes, especially big banks, utility companies, and railroads. Long passed the Louisiana bar exam after studying briefly at the University of Oklahoma Law School and the Tulane University Law School. He then opened a law practice in Winnfield.

But Long had bigger dreams than being a small-town southern attorney. In 1918 he was elected state railroad commissioner, and he was reelected in 1924. He also launched an attack on Standard Oil Company and found that anti–big business rhetoric resonated well with Louisiana's poor, rural farmers. He was elected governor of Louisiana in 1928 and proceeded to create a powerful political machine that dominated the entire state. Long made sure that poor people had public works construction jobs and that rural children attended improved public schools, and in 1930, voters put him in the U.S. Senate. As a U.S. senator, Long began calling for a redistribution of national wealth and then criticized the Franklin D. Roosevelt* administration for being too conservative.

In 1934, Long established the Share Our Wealth Society, which essentially became a national political vehicle for Long. He called for a living minimum wage for all families to be paid for by high taxes on the rich and the well-to-do. In November 1935, Long announced his intention of seeking the Democratic presidential nomination in 1936. Although his chances of unseating Franklin D. Roosevelt were next to none, FDR nevertheless took Long's threat seriously, especially when Long agreed to run as the presidential candidate of the new Union Party.* Roosevelt did not have to worry. On September 8, 1936, Long was assassinated.

SUGGESTED READING: T. Harry Williams, *Huey Long*, 1969.

LORENTZ, PARE. Pare Lorentz, the New Deal's* great filmmaker, was born in Clarkburg, West Virginia, in 1905. He began working as a freelance journalist and film critic in West Virginia, but after moving to New York, he acquired a national reputation, writing regularly for *Harper's* and *Fortune*. In 1930, his first book was published—*Censored: The Private Life of Movies*—and in 1934 he wrote a second book—*The Roosevelt Year: 1933*. Lorentz was an unabashed fan of Franklin D. Roosevelt* and the New Deal, and in 1935, he went to work for the Resettlement Administration* as a filmmaker. He teamed up with Hollywood director King Vidor and photographer Dorothea Lange,* and the result was *The Plow That Broke the Plains*, a brilliant description of Great Plains ecology and the impact of dust storms, overgrazing, overplanting, and migrant poverty. The film premiered in May 1936 and was a critical success. Lorentz followed that up with *The River*, an equally compelling portrait of flooding, soil erosion, and poverty in the Mississippi River Valley. Roosevelt was so impressed with *The River* that he established the U.S. Film Service to make more documentaries. Lorentz's third film in his Great Depression trilogy was *The*

Fight for Life, a documentary on infant mortality and poverty. During and after World War II, Lorentz made documentaries for the War Department. He died on March 4, 1992.

SUGGESTED READING: Robert L. Snyder, *Pare Lorentz and the Documentary Film*, 1968.

LOUIS, JOE. Joe Louis, nicknamed the "Brown Bomber" by adoring sports journalists, was born in Lexington, Kentucky, on May 13, 1914. His family moved to New York when Louis was still a boy, and he became interested in boxing. Unusually quick for a heavyweight, he rose quickly through the ranks. His road to the heavyweight championship, however, collided with a "German roadblock" in 1936 when he lost a twelve-round decision to Max Schmeling. But in 1937, Louis won the heavyweight championship by knocking out James Braddock in an eight-round fight in Chicago. Schmeling then negotiated a re-match with Louis, and Germans anxiously awaited the fight. German Chancellor Adolf Hitler confidently predicted a Schmeling victory, since the Aryan German was racially superior to the dark-skinned Louis. Louis wanted to avenge his 1936 defeat. The fight played to worldwide radio audiences but proved to be no fight at all. During the first two minutes of the first round, Louis pummeled Schmeling with fifty body and head shots. Schmeling began to wobble and stagger and Louis went in for the kill. In Germany* Nazi censors cut off the broadcast even before the fight was finished, and then in newsreels, Nazi censors tried to splice in footage of the first Louis-Schmeling match. Louis was the first African American to hold the heavyweight championship since Jack London, who had won the belt in 1908.

Louis was a quiet but proud man who hated segregation. He would not sit in "black" sections of restaurants, train stations, and theaters. And during World War II, when he served in the army and put on exhibition fights throughout the country, Louis played an important role in desegregating military boxing, foot-ball, and baseball teams. In 1949, Louis retired undefeated from the ring. Bad debts, however, and a vanished fortune forced Louis back into the ring. On October 26, 1951, he entered the ring with Rocky Marciano, but Marciano knocked him out in the eighth round. Louis then spent much of the rest of his life working in Las Vegas. He died on April 12, 1981.

SUGGESTED READINGS: Joe Louis, *My Life Story*, 1946; Chris Mead, *Champion—Joe Louis: Black Hero in White America*, 1985.

LUX RADIO THEATER. *Lux Radio Theater* was the most popular dramatic series in American radio history. It premiered on the Blue Network on October 14, 1934, taking up an hour each Sunday evening. CBS picked up the show on July 29, 1935, and kept it on the air until September 14, 1954, when NBC optioned it. The last episode of *Lux Radio Theater* was broadcast on June 7,

1955. The show began as anthologies of Broadway plays, but as theater plots played out, the show shifted to movie themes, basing its weekly broadcasts on popular films. In 1936, Cecil B. DeMille, the famed Hollywood director, took over directorship of *Lux Radio Theater*, and its ratings skyrocketed. DeMille attracted Hollywood's best talent to the program, and the show attracted the attention only certifiable celebrities can attract. Clark Gable,* Marlene Dietrich, Gary Cooper, Frederic March, Robert Taylor, John Wayne, and a host of others appeared at DeMille's request. DeMille left the *Lux Radio Theater* in 1946, and although the show remained a ratings success, it no longer attracted the audiences it had once enjoyed. Also, the advent of television undermined audience interest in audio repeats of films.

SUGGESTED READING: John Dunning, *On the Air: The Encyclopedia of Old-Time Radio*, 1998.

M

MAJOR BOWES' ORIGINAL AMATEUR HOUR. The *Major Bowes' Original Amateur Hour* was a broadcasting phenomenon of the 1930s. In 1934, Major Edward Bowes brought the show to NBC Radio, where it staked out Sunday evening prime time. In 1936 it was renamed *The Original Amateur Hour*. Desperate to hit it big in depression America, literally hundreds of thousands of amateur acts applied for the chance of performing on the show, winning a prize, and perhaps being noticed by big-time producers. From 1936 to 1945, CBS broadcast the show, and then ABC did so from 1948 to 1952. Bowes was also known for a cruel streak, which often prompted him to ridicule acts he considered subpar. But the show was especially popular during the Great Depression, when listeners waited for an amateur act that would hit it big.

SUGGESTED READING: John Dunning, *On the Air: The Encyclopedia of Old-Time Radio*, 1998.

MANCHURIA. During the 1920s, Japanese leaders began giving serious thought to the strategic implications of being a natural resource–poor country. In order to sustain industrial development and the modern military needed to establish its hegemony in East Asia, Japanese politicians decided on a course of conquest. They imported rubber from French Indochina; oil from British Malaya, the United States, and the Dutch East Indies; and iron ore from Manchuria. Such economic dependence, they concluded, could easily translate into political and military subjugation. Only by securing their own political and military control of East Asia and Southeast Asia, they insisted, could Japan* avoid that reality.

Japan's first target was Manchuria, where abundant coal and iron ore deposits beckoned. Manchuria also seemed attractive because compared to much of the rest of eastern China* and Japan, population density was relatively low, and Japan might be able to relocate some of its own excess population there. In 1905, with the conclusion of their victory in the Russo-Japanese War, Japan secured treaty rights to control and, if necessary, militarily defend the South Manchurian Railway. Using those treaty rights as a pretext, Japan accused the Chinese of bombing a railroad depot at Mukden and launched an invasion of Manchuria. Many historians acknowledge the Japanese invasion of Manchuria as the beginning of World War II. After attacking and seizing the Chinese military barracks at Mukden, Japanese troops occupied the city and then headed north, taking other Manchurian cities and towns in rapid succession. No sooner had the dust of battle settled than a small army of Japanese engineers, railroad experts, and accountants descended on Manchuria and began arranging an accelerated extraction of coal and iron ore.

China filed diplomatic protests with Tokyo denouncing the invasion, demanding an immediate withdrawal and appealing to the League of Nations for support. But the League had little power and less will. France, Great Britain, and the United States denounced the invasion, but offered China only platitudes, not bullets or troops. In what historians remember as the Stimson Doctrine, named after Secretary of State Henry Stimson,* the United States refused to extend diplomatic recognition to the puppet Japanese government in Manchuria but also proved unwilling to do anything more to stem the invasion. On January 28, 1932, emboldened by the tepid response of Europe and the United States, the Japanese army attacked Shanghai, slaughtering thousands of people. Little more than a year later, using Manchuria as a staging area, the Japanese army moved into Jehol Province, putting them within only 100 miles of Beijing. When the United States, France, and Great Britain denounced the latest invasion, Japan withdrew from the League of Nations.

SUGGESTED READINGS: David Kennedy, *Freedom from Fear: The American People in Depression and War, 1929–1945*, 2000; Louise Young, *Japan's Total Empire: Manchuria and the Culture of Wartime Imperialism*, 1998.

MA PERKINS. *Ma Perkins* was a popular radio program of the 1930s. A classic soap opera that set the tone for that genre on radio and television, *Ma Perkins* debuted in 1933 at WLW in Cincinnati and went to the NBC Network in December. It was a fifteen-minute weekday broadcast. Plots revolved around the family of Ma Perkins, a matriarch who owned a small-town lumber yard in the fictitious midwestern town of Rushville Center. It remained on the air until 1960.

SUGGESTED READING: John Dunning, *On the Air: The Encyclopedia of Old-Time Radio*, 1998.

THE MARCH OF TIME. *The March of Time* was one of the most enduring shows of the radio era. A news documentary complete with dramatization and reenactments of world events, *The March of Time* debuted on CBS Radio on March 6, 1931. It eventually moved from CBS to the Blue Network and then to NBC and ABC and gave listeners, through its actors and its sound effects, the feel of a movie newsreel or even a live broadcast. Although domestic issues dominated, the program also handled some "foreign news." Late in the 1930s, the show began doing less dramatization and more straight news and evolved into a forerunner of the radio and television news shows of the 1950s and 1960s.

SUGGESTED READING: Raymond Fielding, *The March of Time, 1935–1951*, 1978.

THE MARIAN ANDERSON INCIDENT (1939). In 1939, after an enormously successful European tour, contralto Marian Anderson tried to rent Constitution Hall in Washington, D.C., to stage her American debut. But the Daughters of the American Revolution (DAR), a patriotic group of women who had descended from men who had served in the Continental Army, owned Constitution Hall, and they refused to rent it to Anderson because she was an African American. News of the DAR's decision triggered an enormous controversy. First Lady Eleanor Roosevelt* was especially outraged and publicly announced her resignation from the DAR. Secretary of the Interior Harold Ickes,* an outspoken civil rights advocate, gave Anderson permission to stage an outdoor concert on the steps of the Lincoln Memorial. On April 9, 1939, Anderson performed before an audience of 75,000 people. The incident played an important role in raising the civil rights conscience of the nation.

SUGGESTED READING: Allan Keiler, *Marian Anderson: A Singer's Journey*, 2000.

McREYNOLDS, JAMES CLARK. James McReynolds was born in Elkton, Kentucky, on February 3, 1862. In 1882, he graduated from Vanderbilt University, and two years later, he received a law degree from the University of Virginia. McReynolds practiced law in Nashville, Tennessee, and became active in local Democratic politics. Like most southern Democrats, he was conservative in his politics and a state's rightist in his political philosophy. In 1903, McReynolds became an assistant attorney general of the United States, serving under Attorney General Philander Knox. He specialized in antitrust cases and pursued them vigorously, even though he did have some concerns about the growing power of the federal government. In 1913, President Woodrow Wilson appointed McReynolds to his cabinet as attorney general. One year later, Wilson appointed McReynolds to the U.S. Supreme Court.

Although trust-busting during his years in the Department of Justice had given McReynolds a reputation as a progressive, he turned increasingly conservative over the years, and by the 1930s, he was one of the most cautious, conservative justices on the Supreme Court. His commitment to states' rights had only rigidified over the years, and the onset of the Great Depression did not change his point of view. He became part of the conservative majority on the Court—along with Charles Evans Hughes,* Owen Roberts,* George Sutherland,* Pierce Butler, and Willis Van Devanter*—that blocked so much early New Deal* legislation. In fact, McReynolds was by far the most conservative of the conservative justices.

McReynolds was angry when President Franklin D. Roosevelt* tried to implement the famous court-packing scheme* in 1937, but he was even more incensed when Charles Evans Hughes and Owen Roberts switched sides and began voting with the liberals. McReynolds considered them traitors and became increasingly isolated on the Court and in Washington, D.C. By the end of the 1930s, he had all but become a minority of one on the Supreme Court, wedded to a judicial philosophy that had become an anachronism. James McReynolds retired on February 1, 1941, and died on August 24, 1946.

SUGGESTED READINGS: Alpheus Thomas Mason, *The Supreme Court from Taft to Warren*, 1958; *New York Times*, August 26, 1946.

MELLON, ANDREW. Andrew Mellon was born on March 24, 1855, in Pittsburgh, Pennsylvania. After attending the Western University of Pennsylvania for a few years, he quit school to establish his own building supply and construction business. He joined his father's banking business in 1874 and became president of the firm in 1882. Mellon had an eye for opportunity and for the deal, and during the next three decades, he founded the Union Trust Company, the Gulf Oil Corporation, and the Aluminum Company of America. By 1921, when President Warren G. Harding named him secretary of the treasury, Mellon was one of the country's, and the world's, richest men.

His tenure as secretary of the treasury was controversial. Mellon believed that the big federal budgets and confiscatory income taxes of the World War I era had been necessary to the war effort, but he was also convinced that their extension into a peacetime economy would be disastrous. So Mellon worked diligently to cut federal spending, and during his tenure at the treasury, the federal government accumulated a total of $8 billion in budget surpluses. Mellon also believed that taxes should be cut on the rich, who would then invest their tax savings back into the economy. Congress passed tax cuts in 1921, 1924, 1926, 1928, and 1929.

But critics charged that Mellon had benefitted personally from the federal tax cuts, to the tune of $800,000. When the economy fell into depression in 1929 and 1930, Andrew Mellon became a symbol of all that was wrong with America—vast gaps between the rich and the poor and a federal government anxious to meet the needs of the rich while ignoring the suffering of the poor. Mellon resigned as secretary of the treasury in 1932 and was appointed U.S. ambassador to Great Britain. He died on August 26, 1937.

SUGGESTED READINGS: Martin L. Fausold, *The Presidency of Herbert C. Hoover*, 1985; Donald R. McCoy, *Calvin Coolidge: The Quiet President*, 1967; Harvey O'Conner,

Mellon's Millions, 1933; Eugene P. Trani and David L. Wilson, *The Presidency of Warren G. Harding*, 1977.

MILLER-TYDINGS ACT OF 1937. The Miller-Tydings Act of 1937 was one of the so-called Little NRA* laws passed in the wake of the Supreme Court's decision in the *Schechter** case declaring the National Industrial Recovery Act of 1933 unconstitutional. It amended the Sherman Antitrust Act of 1890 to allow the passage of fair trade laws. Manufacturers and retailers could establish a minimum resale price for their products without fear of antitrust action. The idea behind the legislation was to stem the deflationary tide that was cutting into corporate profits and having a chilling effect on corporate investment. With prices stabilized, so the logic of the Miller-Tydings Act went, business profits would rise, as would employment, production, and capital investment.

SUGGESTED READING: *Dictionary of American History*, 1976, II: 482–84.

MISSOURI EX REL. GAINES V. CANADA (1938). *Missouri ex rel. Gaines v. Canada* was a landmark in the civil rights movement. Lloyd L. Gaines was denied admission to the law school of the University of Missouri because he was an African American and Missouri had not integrated higher education. The National Association for the Advancement of Colored People* (NAACP) filed a lawsuit on behalf of Gaines. The Missouri Supreme Court upheld the denial of admission, so the NAACP moved the suit into the federal courts. It reached the U.S. Supreme Court in 1938. The Court rendered its decision by a 6 to 2 vote on November 9, 1938. The Court ordered Gaines admitted to the all-white law school, arguing that the decision had violated the equal protection clause of the Fourteenth Amendment. The Court also found that the state's offer to pay Gaines's tuition to an out-of-state law school similarly violated the Fourteenth Amendment. The *Missouri* case was one of the NAACP's first substantial civil rights victories at the federal level.

SUGGESTED READING: 305 U.S. 337 (1938).

MITCHELL, CHARLES EDWIN. Charles Mitchell was born on October 6, 1877, in Chelsea, Massachusetts. After graduating from Amherst College in 1899, he took a job with the Western Electric Company. In 1907, he was named president of the Trust Company of America in New York. Four years later, he founded Charles E. Mitchell & Company Investments, and in 1921, he was named president of the National City Bank. Under Mitchell's direction, the National City Bank became a powerhouse in the industry and a full participant in the securities speculation of the 1920s.

But when the stock market crashed in 1929, congressional investigators began taking a closer look at banking practices in the 1920s, and Mitchell came under close scrutiny. In 1932–1933, the Pecora Committee* exposed a series of shady loan deals and bank fraud at National City Bank, and Mitchell's reputation suffered as well. He was virtually demonized as a symbol of the causes of the Great Depression. In what was certainly a public relations disaster, Mitchell defended the bank's practices as an example of the rights of private property and liberty and urged laissez-faire on the federal government. Mitchell's public standing declined even more when Pecora revealed that he had speculated in the stock of National City. He resigned from the bank in 1933 and joined the investment banking firm of Blyth & Company. Mitchell died on December 14, 1955.

SUGGESTED READINGS: *New York Times*, December 15, 1955; Ferdinand Pecora, *Wall Street under Oath*, 1939; Giulio Pontrecorvo, "Investment Banking and Security Regulation in the Late 1920s," *Business History Review* (Summer 1958), 166–91; Earl Sparling, *Mystery Men of Wall Street*, 1930.

MODERN TIMES. In 1936, Charlie Chaplin produced, wrote, scored, directed, and starred in *Modern Times*, a satirical film that blamed the "Machine Age" for the plight of contemporary society. Chaplin once again played "The Little Tramp," a favorite character he had played in previous films, who is a disillusioned assembly line worker who eventually runs amok in the factory. He earns a jail sentence for his antics. The film was blunt in its socialistic perspective and reflected a widespread disillusionment with capitalism and its failure to prevent the Great Depression.

SUGGESTED READING: Charles Maland, *Chaplin and American Culture: The Evolution of a Star Image*, 1989.

MOLEY, RAYMOND. Raymond Moley was born on September 27, 1886, in Berea, Ohio. In 1906, he graduated from Baldwin-Wallace College with a degree in political science and became a school superintendent in Olmstead Falls, Ohio. He then taught high school in Cleveland for several years before earning a master's degree at Oberlin College. In 1918, while teaching at Case Western Reserve University, he received a Ph.D. in political science from Columbia University. After four years as director of the Cleveland Foundation, Moley became a professor at Columbia. A prolific writer, his publications included *Lessons in American Citizenship* (1918), *The State Movement for Efficiency and Economy* (1918), *Lessons in Democracy* (1919), and *Parties, Politics, and People* (1921).

During the presidential election campaign of 1932,* Moley became an adviser to Democratic candidate Franklin D. Roosevelt* as one of the so-called Brains Trust.* In fact, Moley emerged as the leader of the Brains Trust. After the inauguration of Franklin D. Roosevelt, Moley remained as a president's adviser and speech writer and an effective advocate for an expanded role of the federal government in dealing with the depression. He also served as editor in 1934–

1935 of *Today* magazine, which many considered to be a quasi-official organ of the New Deal.*

Later in the 1930s, however, Moley grew increasingly uncomfortable with the antibusiness drift of the New Deal. He criticized the Wealth Tax Act of 1935* and the president's court-packing scheme* in 1937. Moley so loathed the massive deficit spending of the late 1930s that he officially broke with the administration and joined the Republican Party. He endorsed Wendell Willkie* in the presidential election of 1940.* Moley continued to teach at Columbia and continued to write. His later books included *Twenty Seven Masters of Politics* (1949), *How to Keep Our Liberty* (1952), *Political Responsibility* (1958), and *The Republican Opportunity* (1962). Raymond Moley died on February 18, 1975.

SUGGESTED READINGS: Raymond Moley and Elliot A. Rosen, *The First New Deal*, 1966; *New York Times*, February 19, 1975; James E. Sargent, "Raymond Moley and the New Deal: An Appraisal," *Ball State University Forum*, 18 (1977), 62–72.

MORGAN, JOHN PIERPONT, JR. J. P. Morgan, Jr., was heir to one of America's greatest financial fortunes and a key figure in the investment banking community during the early twentieth century. He was born at Irvington-on-Hudson, New York, on September 7, 1867, and in 1889, he graduated from Harvard. Morgan spent two years in Boston with Jacob C. Rogers and Company, a banking firm, and in 1891, he moved to New York and joined his father's firm—Drexel, Morgan & Company. Between 1898 and 1905, he lived in London as a junior partner in J. P. Morgan and Company. When his father died in 1913, Morgan returned to New York as senior partner of J. P. Morgan and Company and within a few years was widely recognized as the world's best international banker.

The company especially prospered during the 1920s, when a huge market for new securities emerged. Morgan also became a specialist in financing government debt and recapitalizing government bonds and national debts. During his tenure, J. P. Morgan floated bond issues for dozens of countries, including Great Britain, France, Belgium, Italy,* Austria,* Cuba, Canada, and Germany.* He played a key role in the negotiations that led to the Dawes Plan of 1924 and the Young Plan of 1929, which reduced German reparations payments.

At first, Morgan praised the efforts of President Franklin D. Roosevelt* to stabilize the money markets, but he soon soured on the New Deal,* especially when the Banking Act of 1933* forced him to separate his investment banking operations from his commercial operations. J. P. Morgan and Company functioned thereafter as a commercial bank, and Morgan, Stanley & Company assumed control of the securities underwriting business. Morgan eventually came to see the New Deal as fundamentally an anti-American, antibusiness, pro-bureaucracy operation that stifled incentive and limited private property rights. Higher tax rates on the well-to-do cost Morgan money as well, which did nothing to endear the New Deal to him. During the late 1930s, Morgan went into semiretirement, and he died on March 13, 1943.

SUGGESTED READING: John D. Forbes, *J. P. Morgan, Jr., 1867–1932*, 1981.

MORGENTHAU, HENRY, JR. Henry Morgenthau, Jr., was born on May 11, 1891, in New York City. He came from a wealthy family that made its money in real estate. Morgenthau attended Phillips Exeter Academy and then studied architecture and agriculture at Cornell University. To try out his education, he purchased several hundred acres of land in Dutchess County, New York, where he met Franklin D. Roosevelt.* They became close friends and confidants, and the friendship grew even deeper during FDR's long convalescence from polio. Morgenthau began publishing the magazine *American Agriculturalist* in 1922, and he had a large readership in New York. During Roosevelt's campaign for the governorship of New York in 1928, Morgenthau worked as his driver, adviser, and advance man. When FDR won the governorship, Morgenthau served as New York's commissioner of conservation, where he supervised a $2 billion tree-planting program.

When Roosevelt was inaugurated president, he appointed Morgenthau as chairman of the Federal Farm Board, but early in 1934, after the death of William Woodin,* Morgenthau became secretary of the treasury. He remained at the post throughout the 1930s and World War II. Toward the end of the war, Morgenthau played a key role in establishment of the International Monetary Fund, which was designed to stabilize postwar global money markets. In July 1945, Morgenthau resigned from President Harry Truman's cabinet. Morgenthau spent the rest of his life active in Jewish affairs and in support of the state of Israel. He died on February 6, 1967.

SUGGESTED READINGS: John Morton Blum, *From the Morgenthau Diaries*, 3 vols., 1959–1967; *New York Times*, February 8, 1967.

MOSES, ANNA MARY ROBERTSON. Anna Mary Robertson Moses, a self-taught New Englander, became an overnight art sensation in the late 1930s. In 1939, a New York art critic on a trip to New England noticed in a local drugstore a series of paintings that were on display. He found them uniquely original, brilliant displays of rural New England scenes, and he purchased all fifteen of them. He then had them put on display at the Museum of Modern Art in New York City. The press quickly dubbed Anna Mary "Grandma Moses," since she was seventy-eight years old at the time.

SUGGESTED READING: Otto Kallir, *Grandma Moses*, 1975.

MOSES, GRANDMA. See **MOSES, ANNA MARY ROBERTSON.**

MOTOR CARRIER ACT OF 1935. By the mid-1930s, the nation's transportation industry was in disarray. Most railroads were suffering from heavy debt burdens and increased competition from trucks. At the same time, the trucking industry was suffering from declining freight rates, primarily from cutthroat competition. To settle the problem, Joseph Eastman of the Interstate Commerce Commission (ICC) wanted federal legislation to rationalize the industry. The Eastman bill became the Motor Carrier Act on August 9, 1935.

The Motor Carrier Act gave the ICC new authority over the trucking industry, particularly to control maximum and minimum rates, service, accounting, finances, organization, and management of common carriers. It was also authorized to issue permits to contract carriers. Throughout the decade, however, the Motor Carrier Act had little impact. Because freight rates kept falling, few complaints were received from shippers, and most truckers simply ignored ICC trucking regulations. With relative few employees and a limited budget, the ICC could not really enforce its regulations. Still, the Motor Carrier Act greatly expanded the power of the ICC, and after World War II, that new power was vigorously exercised.

SUGGESTED READING: Ari Hoogenboom and Olive Hoogenboom, *A History of the ICC: From Panacea to Palliative*, 1976.

MUKDEN INCIDENT OF 1931. Diplomatic historians look back on the Mukden incident of 1931 as the first salvo in World War II. In September 1931, when rebels destroyed a small section of the Southern Manchurian Railroad's track near Mukden, Manchuria,* Japan* blamed China.* Japan had a financial and strategic interest in the railroad and was looking for a pretext to invade the region, which was rich in coal and iron ore. Resource-poor Japan was ready to implement the Greater East Asia Co-Prosperity Sphere, a strategic initiative to secure control over regions in Asia where Japan would have guaranteed access to oil, coal, iron ore, and rubber. Japan invaded Manchuria, proclaimed the Manchukuo puppet government, and precipitated the Manchurian crisis of 1931. The United States reacted with the so-called Stimson Doctrine.

SUGGESTED READINGS: L. Ethan Ellis, *Republican Foreign Policy, 1921–1933*, 1968; Robert H. Ferrell, *American Diplomacy in the Great Depression: Hoover-Stimson Foreign Policy, 1929–1933*, 1957.

***MULFORD V. SMITH* (1939).** The case of *Mulford v. Smith* posed a direct challenge to the Agricultural Adjustment Act of 1938.* In the *United States v. Butler** case of 1936, the Supreme Court had declared unconstitutional the Agricultural Adjustment Act of 1933.* The New Deal* of President Franklin D. Roosevelt* remained determined, however, to ameliorate the economic plight of American farmers by imposing production quotas on farmers and paying them not to produce with taxes on processors. By a 7 to 2 vote, on April 17, 1939, the Supreme Court upheld the Agricultural Adjustment Act of 1938 and admitted that its 1936 decision in *Butler* had been a mistake. The Court readily admitted that the agricultural crisis was national in scope, well beyond the ability of state legislatures to solve, and that therefore Congress did enjoy jurisdiction.

SUGGESTED READING: 307 U.S. 38 (1939).

MUNICH. See **APPEASEMENT** and **CZECHOSLOVAKIA**.

MUNICIPAL BANKRUPTCY ACT OF 1934. Because of declining tax revenues during the years of the Great Depression, many towns and cities found themselves unable to make payments on their own outstanding bonds. The municipal bond market was in a state of shambles, and many bankers worried that defaults on those bonds would further damage the money markets. Urban mayors and the Investment Bankers Association demanded federal action, and Congress passed the Municipal Bankruptcy Act, which President Franklin D. Roosevelt* signed on May 24, 1934. The law allowed cities and towns, with the approval of 51 percent of the holders of outstanding obligations, to seek the assistance of federal courts in scaling down their debts. If the court found the plan equitable and 75 percent of the bondholders approved, the reorganization plan would go into effect. Because of the legislation, the municipal bond market recovered.

SUGGESTED READING: *New York Times*, May 25, 1934.

MUSCLE SHOALS. See **NORRIS, GEORGE WILLIAM**, and **TENNESSEE VALLEY AUTHORITY**.

N

**NATIONAL ASSOCIATION FOR THE ADVANCEMENT OF COL-
ORED PEOPLE.** During the 1930s and much of the twentieth century, the
National Association for the Advancement of Colored People (NAACP) was
the nation's premier civil rights organization. During the 1930s, under the leadership of Walter White,* the NAACP focused its energies on five distinct goals.
First, it provided financial support to the Southern Tenant Farmers' Union*
because so many southern blacks worked as farm tenants, laborers, and sharecroppers. Second, it pursued legal cases, such as that of the so-called Scottsboro*
boys, in order to protect black civil rights. Third, it worked, unsuccessfully as
it turned out, to secure a Federal Anti-Lynching Bill* to make it easier to prosecute southern whites who had lynched blacks. Fourth, the NAACP worked to
make sure that New Deal* relief agencies provided a fair number of jobs to
black workers and a wage equal to that of white workers. Finally, the NAACP
worked, with some success, to convince labor unions to organize black workers.
The unions of the Congress of Industrial Organizations* did so.

SUGGESTED READINGS: Robert H. Brisbane, *The Black Vanguard: Origins of the
Negro Social Revolution, 1900–1960*, 1970; John B. Kirby, *Black Americans in the Roosevelt Era: Liberals and Race*, 1980; Patricia Sullivan, *Days of Hope: Race and Diversity
in the New Deal Era*, 1996.

NATIONAL ASSOCIATION OF MANUFACTURERS. Established in
1895, the National Association of Manufacturers (NAM) was a trade association
representing major industrial corporations. By the 1920s, the NAM had become
an organ of big business and a vociferous opponent of collective bargaining and
union organization. The Great Depression cost the NAM dearly, reducing its
membership from 5,350 members in 1929 to 1,500 in 1933. In spite of those
losses, the National Association of Manufacturers became an inveterate opponent of the New Deal,* arguing that President Franklin D. Roosevelt* was lead-

ing the country down the road to socialism. The NAM openly opposed Roosevelt's candidacy in 1932, 1936, 1940, and 1944.

SUGGESTED READINGS: Albert K. Steigerwalt, *The National Association of Manufacturers*, 1964; Richard S. Tedlow, "The National Association of Manufacturers and Public Relations during the New Deal," *Business History Review*, 50 (1976), 25–35.

NATIONAL CANCER INSTITUTE ACT OF 1937. Sponsored by Senator Royal Copeland of New York, the National Cancer Institute Act of 1937 established the National Cancer Institute as a branch of the National Institutes of Health in Bethesda, Maryland. Its purpose was to conduct research into the causes, treatment, and prevention of cancer.

SUGGESTED READING: James Patterson, *The Dread Disease: Cancer and Modern American Culture*, 1987.

NATIONAL CREDIT CORPORATION. When Great Britain abandoned the gold standard* on September 21, 1931, the world's money markets went into a free fall. In the United States, panic-stricken depositors launched runs on their banks, trying to convert assets into cash, and the number of bank failures skyrocketed. President Herbert Hoover* intervened by convincing major bankers to establish the National Credit Corporation (NCC), a private company that would discount for cash the assets of troubled banks. Secretary of the Treasury Andrew Mellon* met in New York with prominent bankers, who endowed the NCC with $500 million in capital. But the NCC was soon overwhelmed by the staggering breadth and depth of the banking crisis.* The NCC ended up loaning money primarily to sound banks, not to weak banks, because it wanted the loans paid back. By December 1931, the NCC had loaned only $10 million. President Hoover then opted for a governmental solution, proposing to Congress the establishment of the Reconstruction Finance Corporation.*

SUGGESTED READINGS: James S. Olson, "The End of Voluntarism: Herbert Hoover and the National Credit Corporation," *Annals of Iowa*, 41 (Fall 1972), 1104–13; James S. Olson, *Herbert Hoover and the Reconstruction Finance Corporation, 1931–1933*, 1977.

NATIONAL EMPLOYMENT SYSTEM ACT OF 1933. See **WAGNER-PEYSER ACT OF 1933**.

NATIONAL FARMERS' HOLIDAY ASSOCIATION. See **RENO, MILO**.

NATIONAL FARMERS' UNION. During the 1930s, the National Farmers' Union (NFU) was a lobbying organization committed to representing the interests of the small family farm. The American Farm Bureau Federation* (AFBF) tended to represent large commercial farmers, so the National Farmers' Union often found itself at odds with the AFBF. Led by John A. Simpson,* the NFU at first opposed the drift of New Deal* farm policy because the Agricultural Adjustment Act of 1933* provided so many benefits to large commercial farmers and so few to small family farmers. But the NFU also praised such New Deal agencies as the Farm Credit Administration* and the Commodity Credit Corporation,* which eased the small farmers' burden. Later in the New Deal, when such federal agencies as the Resettlement Administration,* the Rural Electrification Administration,* and the Farm Security Administration* appeared, the NFU became wholeheartedly pro–New Deal. The NFU also worked to prevent the industrialization of American agriculture, which its leaders knew would favor the capital-rich large commercial farmers. The NFU dream of stopping technological advance and increasing farm size was, of course, a pipe dream. During the last sixty years, the family farm has gradually become an endangered species as large commercial operations have become increasingly common.

SUGGESTED READINGS: Thomas D. Isern, "The National Farmers' Union," in James S. Olson, ed., *Historical Dictionary of the New Deal*, 1985; William P. Tucker, "Populism Up-to-Date: The Story of the Farmers' Union," *Agricultural History*, 21 (1947), 198–208.

NATIONAL HOUSING ACT OF 1934. By 1933, the housing market in the United States was in a state of shambles. Because of the virtual collapse of the money markets, a host of financial institutions—banks, savings banks, building and loan associations, and insurance companies—were trapped in a liquidity crisis, unable and unwilling to extend credit to finance housing construction. At the same time, the unprecedented unemployment problem in the economy had badly eroded demand for new housing. To stimulate the housing industry, the Franklin D. Roosevelt* administration proposed and Congress passed the National Housing Act of 1934. Roosevelt signed the law on June 28, 1934. The legislation created the Federal Housing Administration* (FHA) to insure banks, mortgage companies, and building and loan associations against losses they sustained as a result of making home improvement and new construction loans. With the FHA willing to assume those losses, so the logic went, financial institutions would be more willing to make the loans. The Reconstruction Finance Corporation* supplied $200 million in capital to the FHA. An FHA home improvement loan could not exceed $2,000, nor could a new home loan exceed $12,000. No more than 20 percent of any institution's total loan portfolio could consist of FHA-guaranteed loans. Under the law, the FHA could create national mortgage associations to purchase first mortgages from banks and building and loan associations. Finally, the National Housing Act of 1934 increased to $3 billion the borrowing power of the Home Owners' Loan Corporation.*

SUGGESTED READINGS: Pearl Janet Davies, *Real Estate in American History*, 1958; *Monthly Labor Review*, 39 (1934), 369–70.

NATIONAL INDUSTRIAL RECOVERY ACT OF 1933. See NATIONAL RECOVERY ADMINISTRATION.

NATIONAL LABOR BOARD. See NATIONAL LABOR RELATIONS ACT OF 1935.

NATIONAL LABOR RELATIONS ACT OF 1935. The National Labor Relations Act of 1935 (Wagner-Connery Act), also known as the "Magna Carta of Labor in the United States," guaranteed the right of labor unions to engage in collective bargaining; required management to bargain in good faith with union representatives; prohibited management from engaging in such anti-union activities as espionage, blacklisting, yellow-dog contracts, strikebreaking, or wage discrimination against union members; prohibited management from interfering in the operations of company unions; required that the union elected by a majority of workers in free elections would be recognized as the sole bargaining agent for those workers; and established a new National Labor Relations Board (NLRB) to serve as a "Supreme Court" in adjudicating labor disputes with management. Unlike the earlier National Labor Board and the first National Labor Relations Board, the new NLRB enjoyed administrative and statutory authority to enforce its decisions. Not surprisingly, business groups argued that the measure was unconstitutional, but in *National Labor Relations Board v. Jones & Laughlin Steel Corporation* (1937),* the Supreme Court upheld the constitutionality of the law. Because of the National Labor Relations Act of 1935, union membership in the United States boomed, reaching more than 9 million people in 1940.

SUGGESTED READINGS: James A. Gross, *The Making of the N.L.R.B.: A Study in Economics, Politics and the Law*, 1974; Peter Irons, *The New Deal Lawyers*, 1982.

NATIONAL LABOR RELATIONS BOARD. The National Labor Relations Board was established by the National Labor Relations Act of 1935.* In August 1933 President Franklin D. Roosevelt* had established by executive order the National Labor Board (NLB) to mediate labor-management disputes in order to prevent economically disruptive labor union strikes. But the NLB had neither administrative nor statutory authority to enforce its will, and in June 1934, Roosevelt abolished it. With another executive order, he created the National Labor Relations Board (NLRB), but it did not have much more authority than the defunct NLB. With voluntarism and mediation not working, the Roosevelt administration decided to seek a National Labor Relations Board with administrative and statutory authority, and the National Labor Relations Act of 1935 did so.

The NLRB spent the first two years of its existence fending off hostile suits filed by members of the National Association of Manufacturers,* but in 1937, when the Supreme Court upheld the constitutionality of the National Labor Relations Act in the case of *National Labor Relations Board v. Jones & Laughlin Steel Corporation*,* the NLRB secured complete legitimacy and began hearing cases of violations of labor union rights. It still faced challenges, however, because the American Federation of Labor* resented the board's willingness to hear cases from rival Congress of Industrial Organizations* (CIO) unions and because many southern Democrats considered the NLRB a symbol of the leftward drift of the New Deal.* It was not until World War II that the NLRB became effective in protecting union rights.

SUGGESTED READINGS: James A. Gross, *The Making of the N.L.R.B.: A Study in Economics, Politics and the Law*, 1974; Peter Irons, *The New Deal Lawyers*, 1982.

NATIONAL LABOR RELATIONS BOARD (first). See **NATIONAL LABOR RELATIONS ACT OF 1935** and **NATIONAL LABOR RELATIONS BOARD**.

NATIONAL LABOR RELATIONS BOARD V. JONES & LAUGHLIN STEEL CORPORATION **(1937).** In 1935, Congress passed the National Labor Relations Act,* a key New Deal* measure that pleased labor unions by protecting the right of workers to organize unions and prohibiting employers from firing or dismissing employees because of their union membership. At the time, most corporate leaders considered the measure radical and dangerous, a violation of the Constitution, particularly the contract clause and the Fifth Amendment's protection of property rights. Lawyers for Jones & Laughlin Steel sued in federal courts, charging that the National Labor Relations Act—what union leaders considered the "Magna Carta of organized labor"—was unconstitutional.

The case wound its way through the federal courts, and the Supreme Court rendered its decision on April 12, 1937. Labor lawyers were pessimistic, since the Court had only recently upheld the notion that labor relations were inherently local, not national, matters and therefore beyond congressional jurisdiction. But Court observers were in for a surprise. By a narrow vote of 5 to 4, the Court upheld the constitutionality of the legislation. Four other cases, with similar issues at stake, were automatically resolved with the *Jones & Laughlin Steel* decision.

The *Jones & Laughlin Steel* decision was of great import for the Supreme Court. It came just as President Franklin D. Roosevelt* was launching his famous, or infamous, court-packing scheme.* Chief Justice Charles Evans

Hughes* and Justice Owen Roberts* sided with the Court's liberal minority to produce a narrow majority. In doing so, the justices emasculated much of the president's scheme to reorganize the federal judiciary and signaled that henceforth the Supreme Court would not interfere with Congress's right to regulate the economy.

SUGGESTED READING: 301 U.S. 1 (1937); James A. Gross, *The Making of the N.L.R.B.: A Study in Economics, Politics and the Law*, 1974; Peter Irons, *The New Deal Lawyers*, 1982; Joseph M. Rowe, Jr., "*National Labor Relations Board v. Jones & Laughlin Steel Corporation*," in James S. Olson, ed., *Historical Dictionary of the New Deal*, 1985.

NATIONAL PLANNING BOARD. See **NATIONAL RESOURCES PLANNING BOARD**.

NATIONAL PROGRESSIVES OF AMERICA. In 1938, Governor Philip La Follette of Wisconsin organized the National Progressives of America, a new political party. La Follette was convinced that both the Democratic Party and his own Republican Party were far too conservative for the country's good, and he hoped that the National Progressives of America would push political discourse in the United States toward the Left. The party's platform called for an isolationist foreign policy, strict government regulation of Wall Street investment firms, federal government ownership of all public utilities, and stricter federal control over the money markets. But the party proved to be a disaster. In the elections of 1938, all of its major candidates, including Governor La Follette himself, failed to secure reelection. The National Progressives of America then quickly disintegrated and disappeared.

SUGGESTED READING: Roger T. Johnson, *Robert M. La Follette, Jr., and the Decline of the Progressive Party in Wisconsin*, 1964.

NATIONAL RECOVERY ADMINISTRATION. Between 1929 and 1933, as the economy sank steadily into a deep depression, explanations of the country's plight abounded. One belief—proposed by such prominent businessmen as Bernard Baruch,* Gerard Swope, and Henry I. Harriman—argued that the depression had been caused by overproduction and too much competition in the industrial economy, which had brought about price deflation, layoffs, and profit declines. They wanted the federal government to eliminate destructive competition, encourage national economic planning, and improve business confidence. Some business leaders even called for the federal government to suspend the antitrust laws and impose industrial codes regulating production and prices. As their model, they remembered the War Industries Board of World War I, which had worked out cooperative arrangements between the federal government and major industries.

Such prominent labor leaders as John L. Lewis* of the United Mine Workers and Sidney Hillman* of the Amalgamated Clothing Workers supported such proposals. But union leaders also wanted the federal government to establish nationwide labor standards, including a minimum wage and maximum hours regulations for workers. Senator Hugo Black* of Alabama was pushing an idea of limiting the workweek to thirty hours so that jobs could be spread around. His legislation—known as the Black-Connery Bill—began moving through Congress late in 1932. Finally, Senator Robert Wagner* of New York was calling for a massive federal public works construction program to relieve unemployment. All of these disparate proposals came together in an omnibus bill passed by Congress and signed by President Franklin D. Roosevelt* on June 16, 1933.

The National Industrial Recovery Act (NIRA) consisted of several titles. Title I established the National Recovery Administration to implement a broad series of government rules to promote cooperative economic action, eliminate unfair trade practices, increase consumer purchasing power, expand production, reduce unemployment, stabilize prices, and conserve national resources. Businesses could enter into cooperative arrangements to achieve the purposes of the law, and the president could establish enforceable codes to implement them. Title I also established basic labor standards, provided for a minimum wage, outlawed yellow-dog contracts, and guaranteed the rights of workers to bargain collectively. Title II of the NIRA established the Public Works Administration* (PWA) and endowed the PWA with $3.3 billion to finance the construction of highways, dams, federal buildings, naval construction, and other projects.

President Franklin D. Roosevelt established the National Recovery Administration and named Hugh Johnson* as its director. During World War I, Johnson had served on the War Industries Board, and he believed in the NRA's mission. Johnson campaigned for the NRA as if it were a patriotic issue, urging businessmen to cooperate for the good of the country. Each business cooperating with the NRA could display the NRA emblem—a Blue Eagle*—in advertising literature or on store and factory windows, and Johnson urged buyers to boycott all non-NRA companies. Johnson eventually wrote codes governing codes, competition, and prices in 541 industries.

But within a matter of months, critics of every stripe were targeting the NRA. Labor leaders accused businessmen of noncompliance with the labor standards provisions of the National Industrial Recovery Act, while small businessmen complained that the NRA had been seized by big businessmen who were trying to squeeze small companies out of the market. Many consumer advocates and political leftists complained that the NRA was actually sanctioning monopolies and exploiting the law's suspension of antitrust action. Conservatives accused the NRA specifically and the federal government in general of exercising too much control over economic processes. Finally, many economists held the NRA responsible for the economic downturn of late 1933 and early 1934, arguing that the NRA was actually encouraging cuts in production in order to raise prices and that the cuts in production actually led to more layoffs and a degeneration in the unemployment problem. Under such intense, varied political criticism, public support for the NRA evaporated. Hugh Johnson's personal style did not help matters. The proverbial "bull in a china shop," Johnson managed to offend just about everybody, and in September 1934, Roosevelt eased him out of the NRA.

Actually, the NRA's days were numbered. On May 27, 1935, in the case of *Schechter Poultry Corporation v. United States*,* the U.S. Supreme Court declared the National Industrial Recovery Act to be unconstitutional. The code system, the justices said, was an illegal delegation of legislative power to the executive branch and an unconstitutional expansion of federal power over interstate commerce. The Roosevelt administration responded with the so-called Little NRA,* which attempted to preserve NRA activities in certain limited industries, but it had little effect. The original logic of the NIRA had been so badly flawed that its chances of bringing about a recovery were nil. In fact, many historians argue that the NRA actually made economic matters worse in the United States.

SUGGESTED READINGS: Bernard Bellush, *The Failure of the NRA*, 1975; Donald R. Brand, *Corporatism and the Rule of Law: A Study of the National Recovery Administration*, 1988; Ellis W. Hawley, "National Recovery Administration," in James S. Olson, ed., *Historical Dictionary of the New Deal*, 1985; Ellis W. Hawley, *The New Deal and the Problem of Monopoly: A Study in Economic Ambivalence*, 1966; Robert F. Himmelberg, *The Origins of the National Recovery Administration: Business, Government, and the Trade Association Issue, 1921–1933*, 1976; Leverett S. Lyon, ed., *The National Recovery Administration*, 1934.

NATIONAL RESOURCES BOARD. See **NATIONAL RESOURCES PLANNING BOARD**.

NATIONAL RESOURCES COMMITTEE. See **NATIONAL RESOURCES PLANNING BOARD**.

NATIONAL RESOURCES PLANNING BOARD. Under Title II of the National Industrial Recovery Act of 1933, President Franklin D. Roosevelt* established a National Planning Board to consider national economic planning as a way of stimulating the economy and ending the Great Depression. The idea behind the planning board was for experts to supply the White House and Congress with important data to be employed in establishing guidelines and legislation for land-use planning, water-use planning, demographics, mineral policy, energy policy, transportation policy, and technology. But in May 1935, when the Supreme Court declared the National Industrial Recovery Act unconstitutional, the National Planning Board, which had already been renamed the National Resources Board, lost its legislative mandate. It then became known as the National Resources Committee. In 1939 it was renamed again, this time being known as the National Resources Planning Board (NRPB).

But whatever its name, the NRPB became increasingly controversial during the 1930s. Conservative businessmen hated the very thought of national economic planning, seeing in it a loss of their own prerogatives and a subversion of market forces by the federal government. The fact that the NRPB by 1938 was a powerful advocate of Keynesian economics and deficit spending only attracted more criticism. In 1939, Roosevelt failed to get a provision for a permanent national planning board into the Reorganization Act.* Under fierce attack in Congress because of its liberal tendencies, the NRPB was dissolved in 1943.

SUGGESTED READINGS: Marion Clawson, *New Deal Planning: The National Resources Planning Board*, 1981; Patrick D. Reagan, "The National Resources Planning Board," in James S. Olson, ed., *Historical Dictionary of the New Deal*, 1985; Philip Warken, *A History of the National Resources Planning Board, 1933–1943*, 1979.

NATIONAL SMALL BUSINESS MEN'S ASSOCIATION. In 1938, Secretary of Commerce Daniel Roper* founded the National Small Business Men's Association. At the time, the New Deal* had grown increasingly concerned about the formation of business monopolies and a perceived inability of small businesses to remain competitive. In February 1938, the Department of Commerce then sponsored a special small business conference attended by more than 1,0000 small business men and women. As one outcome of the conference, Roper founded the National Small Business Men's Association to represent small business men and to lobby for federal legislation responsive to their needs. At the conference, President Franklin D. Roosevelt* also promised to expand the Reconstruction Finance Corporation's* small business loan program.

SUGGESTED READINGS: James J. Bean, *Beyond the Broker State: Federal Policies toward Small Business, 1936–1961*, 1996; Harmon Zeigler, *The Politics of Small Business*, 1961.

NATIONAL UNION FOR SOCIAL JUSTICE. See COUGHLIN, CHARLES EDWARD.

NATIONAL YOUTH ADMINISTRATION. In June 1935, Congress passed the bill and President Franklin D. Roosevelt* signed it, creating the National Youth Administration (NYA). The NYA was designed to address an unemployment problem among young people that exceeded 5 million people. The NYA was authorized to assist college students to continue their education through government work-study programs, and eventually more than 620,000 did so. The NYA also supplied part-time employment to 1,514,000 high school students and to 2,677,000 young people who had either dropped out of school or had just graduated. The NYA was led by Aubrey Williams.* To make sure that black youths were treated fairly, Williams created a division of Negro affairs in the NYA and named Mary McLeod Bethune* to head it. More than any other New Deal* agency, the NYA worked diligently to deal with the race issue in a fair and equitable manner. Eventually, completed NYA projects included the construction of 2,000 bridges, the paving of 1,500 miles of public roads, the completion of more than 6,000 public buildings, and the construction of 1,429 libraries and public schools.

SUGGESTED READINGS: Richard R. Reiman, "The National Youth Administration," in James S. Olson, ed., *Historical Dictionary of the New Deal*, 1985; Richard R. Reiman, *The New Deal & American Youth: Ideas & Ideals in a Depression Decade*, 1992; John A. Salmond, *A Southern Rebel: The Life and Times of Aubrey Willis Williams, 1890–1965*, 1983.

NEBBIA V. NEW YORK **(1934).** In 1933, the New York legislature passed the Milk Control Act, which allowed state regulatory authorities to fix milk prices, ostensibly to protect the poor from price gouging during the Great Depression. Leo Nebbia, a Rochester, New York, grocer, defied the law and sold milk above the fixed price. He was prosecuted and convicted for violating the Milk Control Act, and he sued. On March 5, 1934, the Supreme Court, by a 5 to 4 vote, upheld Nebbia's conviction on the grounds that state governments possessed the right to "adopt whatever economic policy may reasonably be deemed to promote public welfare, and to enforce that policy by legislation adapted to its purpose."

SUGGESTED READING: 291 U.S. 502 (1934).

NESCAFÉ. In 1938 Nestlé introduced "Nescafé," the world's first instant coffee. Using a process in which they crystallized ground coffee beans, Nestlé's scientists created a product that instantly turned into coffee when boiling water was added to it. Although consumers universally preferred the taste of brewed coffee, Nescafé was a retail success because of its convenience.

SUGGESTED READING: Gregory Dicum, *The Coffee Book*, 1999.

NEUTRALITY ACTS. During the years between World War I and II, U.S. foreign policy worked assiduously at avoiding overseas entanglements. Traditional U.S. isolationism had been reinforced by the bitterness and skepticism resulting from the outcome of the Treaty of Versailles. Early in the 1930s, when Senator Gerald Nye* of North Dakota accused U.S. arms manufacturers of leading the country into World War I in order to profit from munitions sales, public skepticism only deepened. As political developments in Europe deteriorated during the 1930s, many Americans were anxious to avoid involvement in any future conflicts. Congress responded to their sentiments with a series of "Neutrality Acts."

The first Neutrality Act came in 1935 after Italy* invaded Ethiopia.* It authorized the president, for a six-month period, to embargo all U.S. arms shipments to the belligerents and warned U.S. citizens that they traveled on the ships of belligerents "at their own risk." In the Neutrality Act of 1936, Congress extended the provision of the original neutrality law and prohibited American banks from making loans to belligerents. Two Neutrality Acts were passed in 1937. The first prohibited the sale of munitions to either side in the Spanish Civil War,* and the second prohibited U.S. citizens from sailing on the ships of nations at war. The logic of these laws was simple: The United States was less likely to be dragged into war if American companies did not sell war goods to belligerents, if American banks did not loan money to nations at war, and if American citizens did not sail on the ships of nations at war.

But by 1939, when Germany* invaded Poland* and triggered World War II, the American public's sympathies had shifted in favor of Great Britain and France, even though isolationism remained alive and well. Earlier neutrality legislation had prohibited American companies from supplying war goods to belligerents, but with the British and the French threatened by Nazi Germany, President Franklin D. Roosevelt* called Congress into special session to repeal the arms embargo. Debate raged in Congress for nearly six weeks before Congress followed Roosevelt's lead and greed to lift the embargo. The Neutrality Act of 1939 still proclaimed American neutrality, but American companies were now free to sell weapons and ammunition to Great Britain and France.

SUGGESTED READINGS: Wayne S. Cole, *Roosevelt and the Isolationists, 1932–1945*, 1983; L. Ethan Ellis, *Republican Foreign Policy, 1921–1933*, 1968; Robert H. Ferrell, *American Diplomacy in the Great Depression: Hoover-Stimson Foreign Policy, 1929–1933*, 1957.

NEW DEAL. The term "New Deal" has become politically synonymous among historians and public officials with the first two presidential administrations of Franklin D. Roosevelt* (1933–1941). Among political conservatives, the term "New Deal" has also become synonymous with big government and a bloated federal bureaucracy. The term was first heard in June 1932 when Governor Franklin D. Roosevelt of New York, working from a speech drafted by Samuel Rosenman, accepted the Democratic presidential nomination in Chicago and said, "I pledge you, I pledge myself, to a new deal for the American people. Let us all here assembled constitute ourselves prophets of a new order of competence and courage." Stuart Chase, a writer for *The New Republic*, picked up on the phrase and published a series of articles entitled "A New Deal for America." By mid-1933, the term was firmly esconced in American political culture as a synonym for the political and economic policies of Franklin D. Roosevelt.

SUGGESTED READING: Arthur M. Schlesinger, Jr., *The Age of Roosevelt*, vol. I, *The Crisis of the Old Order, 1919–1933*, 1957.

"NINE OLD MEN." During the early 1930s, the tradition-bound U.S. Supreme Court, through such decisions as *United States v. Butler** and *Schechter Poultry Corporation v. United States*,* gutted major efforts of President Franklin D. Roosevelt's* New Deal* to ameliorate some of the economic effects of the Great Depression. Tens of millions of Americans loathed the Supreme Court, and in 1935, journalists Drew Pearson and Robert Allen took advantage of that discontent by writing a book entitled *Nine Old Men*, referring to the nine justices of the Supreme Court. In the book, they charged the Court with being bound to dogma and tradition at a time when pragmatic approaches to the economy and to the law were necessary. The book helped inspire President Roosevelt's court-packing scheme* to reform and reorganize the federal bureaucracy.

SUGGESTED READING: Drew Pearson and Robert Allen, *Nine Old Men*, 1935.

NORBECK, PETER. Peter Norbeck was born on August 27, 1870, near Vermillion, South Dakota. He spent several years at the University of South Dakota and then worked in construction and the oil drilling industry. He also farmed for a while. In 1909 Norbeck won a seat in the state legislature as a Republican. He proved to be a natural at politics. Norbeck won election as lieutenant governor of South Dakota in 1914 and then as governor in 1916. He won a U.S. Senate seat in 1920 and soon emerged as a leader of the farm bloc, advocating federal legislation to ease the plight of American farmers during the 1920s. He backed the McNary-Haugen Bill and the Agricultural Marketing Act of 1929. Norbeck won reelection in 1926 and again in 1932.

The Great Depression posed a real political problem for Norbeck. As a Republican, he wanted to be loyal to the party, but the party was dominated by conservatives at a time when the country and the economy needed progressive legislation. When Franklin D. Roosevelt* was elected president in 1932, Norbeck soon found himself part of the coalition of liberal Republicans and Democrats that produced the New Deal.* Republican Party officials felt betrayed by Norbeck, but his political convictions demanded loyalty to the idea of federal government activism. In 1936, Norbeck endorsed the reelection campaign of the president, arguing that Republican nominee Alf Landon* was just too conservative. Republican officials were outraged, but they did not have time to read Norbeck out of the party. Norbeck died on December 20, 1936.

SUGGESTED READING: *New York Times*, December 21, 1936.

NORRIS, GEORGE WILLIAM. George Norris, a leading progressive Republican of the early twentieth century, was born in Sandusky County, Ohio, on July 11, 1861. After attending Baldwin University for two years, he earned a law degree at Northern Indiana Normal School and Business Institute, which later became Valparaiso University. After teaching school for two years, Norris moved to Nebraska and opened a law practice. The practice thrived, and Norris became active in local Republican Party politics. In 1890 Norris won election as prosecuting attorney for Furnas County, and in 1895, he became state judge for the 14th Judicial District. In 1902, Norris was elected to Congress, and he soon established his progressive credentials, pushing for lower tariffs, antitrust legislation, railroad regulation, and implementation of the initiative, referendum, and recall. In 1912, Norris was elected to the U.S. Senate, an office he would hold for the next thirty-two years.

During the 1920s, Norris became well known for his isolationist foreign policy and his reform-minded domestic agenda. Against the wishes of the Republican majority, he called for lower tariffs, the McNary-Haugen Bill for farmers, and construction of a comprehensive federal hydroelectric, flood control, and immigration project at Muscle Shoals, Alabama. Such a project, he was convinced, would benefit the people of the Tennessee River Valley. Although Norris pushed it through Congress, President Calvin Coolidge vetoed it. President Herbert Hoover* vetoed it in 1931. Norris also played a key role in what became known as the Norris–La Guardia Labor Relations Act of 1932,* which prohibited federal courts from issuing injunctions to suppress such ordinary collective bargaining practices as strikes, picketing, and boycotts.

Norris claimed to be a Republican, but the party's policies were so conservative that Norris began endorsing Democratic candidates. In the presidential elections of 1928, 1932,* and 1936,* he endorsed Al Smith* and Franklin D. Roosevelt,* respectively. During the years of the New Deal,* Norris became an enthusiastic supporter of the New Deal. Norris's beloved Muscle Shoals project became the Tennessee Valley Authority* in 1933, and Norris also backed FDR on such major laws as the Public Utility Holding Company Act of 1935,* the National Labor Relations Act of 1935,* the Wealth Tax Act of 1935,* and the Rural Electrification Act of 1936.

But over the years, Norris had become more Democrat than Republican, and he had consistently alienated major figures in the Republican Party, both in Nebraska and in Washington, D.C. In 1942, he failed in his bid for a sixth term. George Norris died on September 2, 1944.

SUGGESTED READINGS: Richard Lowitt, *George W. Norris: The Making of a Progressive, 1861–1912*, 1963; Richard Lowitt, *George W. Norris: The Persistence of a Progressive, 1913–1933*, 1971; Richard Lowitt, *George W. Norris: The Triumph of a Progressive, 1933–1944*, 1978.

NORRIS–LA GUARDIA LABOR RELATIONS ACT OF 1932. Ever since the 1880s, in labor-management disputes, management often sought and secured the support of the federal courts, which issued injunctions suppressing strikes, picketing, and boycotts by labor unions. Labor leaders began campaigning for legislation to prohibit federal courts from issuing such injunctions, but they had little success. Labor leaders also opposed the management tactic of securing from employees, as a condition of employment, a promise not to join a labor union. Union leaders termed such arrangements "yellow-dog contracts" and wanted them outlawed.

The onset of the Great Depression discredited business leaders among most Americans, and support for pro-union legislation gained strength. In 1932, Congressman Fiorello La Guardia* of New York and Senator George W. Norris* teamed up to sponsor legislation outlawing such injunctions and yellow-dog contracts. Congress passed the law in March 1932, and President Herbert Hoover* reluctantly signed it. Until various New Deal* laws were passed in 1933–1936, the Norris–La Guardia Labor Relations Act was the most significant piece of labor legislation in U.S. history.

SUGGESTED READINGS: C. O. Gregory and H. A. Katz, *Labor and the Law*, 1979; Richard Lowitt, *George W. Norris: The Persistence of a Progressive, 1913–1933*, 1971.

NORRIS V. ALABAMA **(1935).** The national controversy over the Scottsboro case* ricocheted through the federal court system. On April 1, 1935, the Supreme Court decided the fate of Clarence Norris, one of the Scottsboro defendants who had been retried in the wake of *Powell v. Alabama* (1932),* convicted again, and then sentenced to death. Norris's NAACP (National Association for the Advancement of Colored People*) attorneys argued that because Alabama had systematically excluded African Americans from the trial jury and from the grand jury that had returned the indictment, he had not received a fair trial as dictated by the Fifth, Sixth, and Fourteenth Amendments to the Constitution. By a unanimous vote, the Court overturned the conviction, agreeing that Norris had been denied his rights to due process.

SUGGESTED READING: 294 U.S. 587 (1935).

NUCLEAR FISSION. The most important scientific advance of the 1930s was the discovery of nuclear fission, or the ability to split an atom. Ever since the 1920s, physicists in France, Great Britain, Germany,* Italy,* and the United States had pursued the idea. When he received, with his wife Irene Joliot-Curie, the Nobel Prize of 1935 for the discovery of artificial radioactivity, Frederic Joliot-Curie announced, "Explosive nuclear chain reactions" would lead to "the liberation of enormous quantities of usable energy." At the University of Berlin, German physicists Otto Hahn, Fritz Strassmann, and Lise Meitner experimented by bombarding uranium atoms with neutrons. They fully expected the experiment to produce heavier elements like uranium, but they ended up with a lighter element they labeled "barium." What they soon learned was that the neutrons had split the uranium nucleus into two lighter elements whose total mass was less than that of the original uranium used in the experiment. The difference in the weight of the original uranium and the split by-products had been released in the form of energy. Lise Meitner coined the term "fission" to describe the splitting of the atom and the conversion of mass into energy. The Curies soon discovered that when the process of uranium fission began, it released additional neutrons that could then split other uranium atoms, creating a chain reaction that released enormous amounts of energy. That discovery would lead directly to the atomic bomb.

SUGGESTED READING: Richard Rhodes, *The Making of the Atomic Bomb*, 1986.

NUREMBERG LAWS. On September 15, 1935, Adolf Hitler proposed and the Reichstag rubber-stamped the Nuremberg Laws, which formally launched a legal pogrom of Jews that eventually evolved into the Holocaust. The legislation rescinded all civil liberties from Germany's* more than 600,000 Jewish citizens. The Law of the Reich Citizen and the Law for the Protection of German Blood and German Honor combined to strip Jews of their German citizenship; forbade them to vote, hold public office, and display the German flag; barred them from studying for law and medicine; outlawed marriage and sexual relations between Jews and non-Jews; and abrogated existing marriages between Jews and non-Jews. The law also defined Jews as any individual with more than one Jewish grandparent. The effect of the Nuremberg Laws was to deprive many Jews of their livelihoods and turn Jews into social pariahs, beginning the creation of a social and political atmosphere in which the Holocaust could occur.

SUGGESTED READING: Klaus P. Fischer, *Nazi Germany: A New History*, 1995.

NYE, GERALD PRENTICE. Gerald P. Nye was born on December 19, 1892, in Hortonville, Wisconsin. After graduating from high school, he worked as a journalist in Iowa and then North Dakota. In 1919 he purchased the *Fryburg Pioneer*, and in 1920, he bought the *Griggs County Sentinel-Courier*. Those newspaper venues gave Nye considerable political influence in the state, and when Senator Edwin F. Ladd died, the governor appointed Nye to fill the vacancy. He won the seat in his own right in 1926 and then earned a reputation as a progressive Republican. He criticized the Coolidge and then the Hoover administrations for being too conservative in the area of farm and unemployment relief.

But he soon became a thorn in the side of President Franklin D. Roosevelt* and the New Deal.* He believed that the original thrust of the New Deal was too bureaucratic and concentrated too much power in the federal government, and he also criticized the internationalist foreign policy of the Roosevelt administration. He also readily accepted conspiracy theories that the armaments industry had led the United States into World War I in order to profit from government defense contracts. He led a widely publicized Senate investigation of the theory in 1934 and secured enough publicity to force Congress to pass the Neutrality Acts* of 1935, 1936, and 1937. During the election of 1936,* Nye campaigned widely against Roosevelt's reelection. During the late 1930s, as Europe drifted toward war and U.S. foreign policy leaned increasingly toward Great Britain and France and against Germany,* Nye became even more vitriolic in his attacks on the Roosevelt administration. He had become the leading isolationist in the United States.

But when Japan* bombed Pearl Harbor in 1941 and the United States went to war, Nye suddenly found himself the leader of a shrinking minority. In the election of 1944, he lost by a landslide and retired from politics. Nye died on July 17, 1971.

SUGGESTED READINGS: John S. Leiby, "Gerald Prentice Nye," in James S. Olson, ed., *Historical Dictionary of the New Deal*, 1985; *New York Times*, July 18, 1971.

NYLONS. During World War I, when shortages of natural rubber threatened to compromise the war effort, scientists began searching for a synthetic substitute. In 1931, scientists at Du Pont Company came up with a neoprene, a synthetic rubber. With neoprene as a foundation, Du Pont scientists continued their search for a synthetic polymer, and in 1934, they came up with nylon, a synthetic fiber manufactured from coal, air, and water. Its chemical name was polyhexamethyleneadipamide, but the nickname "nylon" stuck. Hunting for a way to turn the invention into a commercially viable product, Du Pont scientists came up with nylon stockings, a product they introduced in 1939. Nylons were an immediate hit among women.

SUGGESTED READING: Susannah Handley, *Nylon: The Story of the Fashion Revolution*, 1999.

O

O'CONNOR, JOHN JOSEPH. John J. O'Connor, the powerful Democratic congressman from New York in the 1930s, was born in Raynham, Massachusetts, on November 23, 1885. He graduated from Brown in 1908 and from Harvard Law School in 1911, and after a brief stint practicing law in Massachusetts, O'Connor moved to New York City and became active in Tammany Hall politics. He served in the state legislature from 1920 until 1923, when he was appointed to fill the congressional seat vacated by the death of W. Bourke Cochran. A gifted political operative, O'Connor rose to become head of the House Rules Committee in 1934, and in that position he blocked some serious initiatives from President Franklin D. Roosevelt.* O'Connor was uncomfortable with deficit spending, the administration's sympathy with labor unions, and such "class-conscious" legislation as the Public Utility Holding Company Act of 1935* and the Wealth Tax Act of 1935.* Roosevelt grew so frustrated with O'Connor that in 1938 he personally campaigned against him in the Democratic Party primaries. Roosevelt allowed a team of government employees to work on his opponent's campaign. O'Connor lost the election and jumped to the Republican Party but lost in the general election. He then returned to the practice of law and died on January 26, 1960.

SUGGESTED READINGS: *New York Times*, January 27, 1960; James T. Patterson, *Congressional Conservatism and the New Deal*, 1967.

OKIES. The term "Okies" first appeared in California during the 1930s as an epithet to describe the tens of thousands of poor farmers who had lost their land in Texas, Arkansas, Missouri, and Oklahoma and had headed west to California hoping to find work, land, or both. The migration had actually started in the 1920s when the nation's farm economy went into depression, but it accelerated during the 1930s. Historians estimate that between 300,000 and 400,000 people left those four states for California, of whom perhaps 100,000 were actually from Oklahoma. Most of them drove out Route 66 in ramshackle trucks and automobiles carrying with them everything they owned. Many of them came to California based on highly exaggerated rumors of abundant jobs, but when they arrived, they were sorely disappointed. They often ended up unemployed in what became known as "ditch bank" settlements near irrigation ditches, in "Hoovervilles" near large city landfills, or in urban slums.

Native Californians resented the immigrants, who imposed increased demands on public schools, city shelters, and public hospitals and increased competition for limited jobs. And when Okie workers joined the United Cannery, Agricultural, Packing, and Allied Workers of America Union, resentment increased even more. Through such agencies as the Resettlement Administration* and the Farm Security Administration,* the federal government tried to assist the migrants, and their plight was immortalized in 1939 by John Steinbeck's* novel *The Grapes of Wrath** and by John Ford's 1940 film of the same name.

SUGGESTED READINGS: Thomas D. Isern, "Okies," in James S. Olson, ed., *Historical Dictionary of the New Deal*, 1985; Walter J. Stein, *California and the Dust Bowl Migration*, 1973.

OKLAHOMA INDIAN WELFARE ACT OF 1936. See INDIAN REORGANIZATION ACT OF 1934.

OLD-AGE REVOLVING PENSIONS, LTD. See TOWNSEND, FRANCIS EVERETT.

OLSON, CULBERT. Culbert Olson was born in Millard County, Utah, on November 7, 1876. He attended Brigham Young University and then became a reporter for the *Ogden Standard*. In 1897 Olson became secretary to his first cousin, Congressman William King of Utah. While living in Washington, D.C., Olson earned a law degree at Columbian University (today known as George Washington University). He then returned to Utah to practice law and became active in politics as a progressive Democrat. As a member of the state legislature in 1916, Olson called for collective bargaining rights for labor unions, unemployment compensation, and state regulation of public utilities, none of which Utah voters were prepared to implement.

In 1920, Olson moved his law practice to Los Angeles, California. He supported and worked for Franklin D. Roosevelt* in the presidential election campaign of 1932, and in 1934 he supported Upton Sinclair's* candidacy for the governorship of California. That year, Olson became chairman of the state Democratic Party. As a member of the state legislature, he submitted bills for a state income tax, higher inheritance taxes, and business franchise taxes. Olson ran successfully for governor of California in 1938 on a liberal platform that included federal financing of old-age pensions, urban public housing, state regulation of bank interest rates, consumer protection, and expanded state programs for treating the mentally ill. Olson served two terms as governor before being defeated in 1942. He died on April 13, 1962.

SUGGESTED READINGS: Lenna Allred, "Culbert Olson," in James S. Olson, ed., *Historical Dictionary of the New Deal*, 1985; Robert E. Burke, *Olson's New Deal for California*, 1953; *Los Angeles Times*, April 14, 1962.

OLSON, FLOYD BJORNSTJERNE. Floyd Olson was born on November 13, 1891, in Minneapolis, Minnesota. Afer graduating from the University of Minnesota, he earned a law degree at Northwestern in 1915. He practiced law in Hennepin County and from 1919 until 1930 served as county attorney. Olson made an unsuccessful bid for governorship of Minnesota in 1924, but he won the office in 1930 as the nominee of the Farmer-Labor Party. He supported Franklin D. Roosevelt* for president in 1932 and won reelection himself that year. Olson was credited with implementing a "Little New Deal"* in Minnesota that included unemployment relief, unemployment compensation, higher corporate income taxes, moratoriums on mortgage payments, and public ownership of utilities. In 1934, Olson turned more radical and proposed a socialist agenda that included government nationalization of mines and railroads and the eventual abolition of capitalism. Olson was reelected in 1934 but died of cancer on August 22, 1936.

SUGGESTED READINGS: Lenna Allred, "Floyd Bjornstjerne Olson," in James S. Olson, ed., *Historical Dictionary of the New Deal*, 1985; *New York Times*, August 23, 1936; James T. Patterson, *The New Deal in the States: Federalism in Transition*, 1969.

OLYMPIC GAMES (1936). In 1936, the Olympic games were held in Berlin, Germany,* with Chancellor Adolf Hitler hoping to use the athletic competition to demonstrate the clear superiority of the Germanic people, or as he called them, the "Aryan people." Leni Riefenstahl, filmmaker for the Third Reich, was directed to record the games for German posterity. But Hitler did not anticipate Jesse Owens, an African American whose athletic prowess became an international phenomenon. Owens won gold medals in the 100-meter dash, the 200-meter dash, the broad jump, and as the anchor of the 400-meter relay. His success so enraged Hitler that the chancellor refused to remain on the stand to give Owens his gold medals. Back home in the United States, white and black Americans heralded Owens's success, making him, along with heavyweight boxing champion Joe Louis,* one of the country's two most famous African Americans.

SUGGESTED READING: Duff Hart-Davis, *Hitler's Games: The 1936 Olympics*, 1986.

O'NEAL, EDWARD ASBURY. Edward Asbury O'Neal was born on October 26, 1875, outside of Florence, Alabama. In 1898 he graduated from Washington and Lee University and then returned to the family farm in Florence. He also became active in local farm politics. O'Neal became head of the Lauderdale County Farm Bureau in 1921 and vice-president of the Alabama Farm Bureau Federation in 1922. In 1924, he was elected vice-president of the American Farm Bureau Federation.* He became president of the national federation in 1931 and remained at that post until 1947. The American Farm Bureau Federation was the voice of large commercial farmers in the United States, and not surprisingly, O'Neal vigorously supported the Agricultural Adjustment Acts of 1933* and 1938,* backed the idea of the "ever-normal granary," and called for parity* for farmers. He also had little interest in the problems of small farmers and tenant farmers. In fact, O'Neal was primarily interested in making sure that large commercial farmers enjoyed a steady supply of cheap labor. He opposed the work of the Resettlement Administration* and the Farm Security Administration,* which he feared would raise the wage levels of farm laborers. What he tried but failed to achieve was congressional authorization of a National Farm Authority, which would have consolidated all federal farm programs and had them administered through the extension service. The proposal would have given the American Farm Bureau Federation virtual control of all federal farm policy. O'Neal died on February 26, 1958.

SUGGESTED READINGS: Christina M. Campbell, *The Farm Bureau and the New Deal: A Study of the Making of National Farm Policy, 1933–1940*, 1962; *New York Times*, February 27, 1958.

ONE MAN'S FAMILY. *One Man's Family* was a popular radio serial that premiered on NBC Radio on April 29, 1932. It was broadcast for fifteen minutes each weekday evening and revolved around the lives of the Barbour family of Sea Cliff, a San Francisco community. The program was the brainchild of Carlton E. Morse, who based it loosely on *The Forsyte Saga*. It starred J. Anthony Smythe as Henry Barbour and tracked his family from the time he was a young, ambitious middle-class business executive to his life as an elderly grandfather. The Barbour family had its ups and downs, full of disagreements and strife, but they also cared about each other, and listeners could identify with many of its themes. Children were born, grew up, left home, and started families of their own. In 1950, *One Man's Family* left CBS for NBC, where it remained until its last broadcast on May 8, 1959.

SUGGESTED READING: John Dunning, *On the Air: The Encyclopedia of Old-Time Radio*, 1998.

OUR TOWN. Thornton Wilder's *Our Town* premiered on Broadway in 1938. On the surface, it appeared to be a Rockwellian portrait of small-town American life, but it was highly innovative, theatrically and philosophically. Wilder did away with such standard theatrical conventions as stage sets, props, and even a clear narrative. Instead, he presented a bare stage and a running narrative offered by a stage manager sitting off to the side. *Our Town* examined life in Grover's Corner, New Hampshire, and followed their lives through three acts—Act I ("Daily Life"), Act II ("Love and Marriage"), and Act III ("Death"). Wilder juxtaposed joy and misery and quaintness and desolation in the lives of the people of Grover's Corner. The overriding theme of *Our Town* is existentialist, revealed in Wilder's statement about the untimely death of the play's heroine: "She dies, we die, they die." The universe, for Wilder, was numbingly indifferent to the fate of human beings, and the meaning of life, or its meaningless, must be judged against an existentialist backdrop.

Over the years, as the play was performed hundreds of times in hundreds of different venues, it often took on a bucolic tone, almost praising the virtues of small-town American life. The trend frustrated Wilder, who often complained that his play had been transformed into an ode to rural values, a portrait of "Quaint Hayseed Family Life." Nevertheless, historians recognize *Our Town* as a seminal event in the American theater.

SUGGESTED READING: Gilbert A. Harrison, *The Enthusiast: A Life of Thornton Wilder*, 1983.

OWENS, JESSE. See **OLYMPIC GAMES (1936)**.

P

PACT OF STEEL. The term "Pact of Steel" was coined by Italian dictator Benito Mussolini when he signed a formal military alliance with Adolf Hitler, linking together the fortunes of Germany* and Italy.* He had signed the Anti-Comintern Pact of 1937 with Germany, but it was more diplomatic entente than alliance. The Pact of Steel marked the real beginning of the so-called Axis Powers.

SUGGESTED READING: R. Lee Ready, *The Forgotten Axis: Germany's Partners and Foreign Volunteers in World War II*, 1987.

PANAMA REFINING COMPANY V. RYAN (1935). During the years of the Great Depression, price deflation afflicted the economy, wreaking havoc with corporate strategic planning and profit margins. Economists discussed at length what might be done to stem the deflation tide, and in the spring of 1933, during the famous "Hundred Days"* of the early New Deal,* Congress passed the National Industrial Recovery Act (NIRA), which created the National Recovery Administration* (NRA), a large federal bureaucracy, to help businesses cut production and, so the logic went, raise prices and profit margins. Republican conservatives, enraged at such an expansion of federal power, condemned the legislation in no uncertain terms.

The oil industry found itself in deep economic troubles. Oil-producing states, which could not muster up the strength to create a cartel and limit production, turned to the NRA for help. In an administrative order, the NRA prohibited the transport across state lines of so-called hot oil—oil produced in excess of state-mandated production quotas. One case contesting the constitutionality of the "hot oil" provisions of the NIRA was *Panama Refining Company v. Ryan*, which claimed the law defied the Constitution by violating the principle of separation of powers. The NIRA delegated essential legislative powers to the executive branch.

The case was argued before the U.S. Supreme Court on December 10–11, 1934, and decided on January 7, 1935. The conservative, tradition-bound Court voted 8 to 1 to overturn the "hot oil" provision of the NIRA, agreeing that it was an unconstitutional delegation of legislative powers to the president. The decision in *Panama Refining Company* boded ill for the rest of the New Deal's attempts to lift the country out of the Great Depression, and the Supreme Count soon confirmed those fears, declaring the entire National Industrial Recovery Act unconstitutional in the *Schechter Poultry Corporation v. United States** in 1935.

SUGGESTED READING: 293 U.S. 388 (1935).

PARITY. "Parity" is an economic concept that has been central to farm activism since the early twentieth century and to federal agricultural policy since the 1930s. The real issue surrounding parity was whether or not a farmer was getting a fair price for his commodities, that is, a price fairly connected to the labor invested in production. Government economists created a series of indexes designed to establish a ratio between the price, or gross income, from a commodity and an index of the prices of nonfarm commodities, which allowed for a measurement of farmer costs. Government policy during the New Deal* worked to restore farmer purchasing power by restoring the ratio between income and costs that had existed during the early 1900s.

SUGGESTED READINGS: Donald L. Chapman, "Parity," in James S. Olson, ed., *Historical Dictionary of the New Deal*, 1985; Gilbert C. Fite, *George N. Peek and the Fight for Farm Parity*, 1954.

PARKER, JOHN JOHNSTON. John J. Parker was born in Monroe, North Carolina, on November 20, 1885. A gifted North Carolina attorney, he was appointed in 1925 by President Calvin Coolidge to the Fourth Circuit of the U.S. Court of Appeals. In 1930, President Herbert Hoover* nominated him to replace Edward Sanford on the U.S. Supreme Court. The nomination sparked one of the most bitter confirmation struggles in U.S. history. During his tenure on the Fourth Circuit, Parker had upheld the legality of "yellow-dog contracts," which severely limited collective bargaining by workers and were anathema to labor unions. The American Federation of Labor* protested his confirmation. So did the National Association for the Advancement of Colored People* because of racist remarks Johnson had frequently made and because of his 1920 comment that blacks should not be allowed a place in the American political process. When the vote to confirm Johnson took place on May 7, 1930, the Senate voted against him by a margin of 41 to 39. Parker continued to serve on the Fourth Circuit until his death on March 17, 1958. Historians look back on his failure to secure confirmation as one of the first times in American history that organized interest groups successfully lobbied against a Supreme Court nominee.

SUGGESTED READING: *New York Times*, May 8, 1930.

PASSFIELD WHITE PAPER. At the negotiations in Versailles, France, to end World War I, President Woodrow Wilson of the United States made national self-determination a key element of his so-called Fourteen Points. As a result of the Treaty of Versailles, Palestine was awarded as a mandate to Great Britain. The Zionist movement, with power bases in the United States and Great Britain, was committed to the creation of a Jewish homeland in Palestine, and during the 1920s, Jews began immigrating to the region. The influx was so significant that the Arab residents of Palestine—the Palestinians—became concerned about the loss of their homeland. In 1930, the British government in Palestine launched an investigation of the Jewish immigration. As a result of the investigation, Palestine recommended restrictions on future Jewish immigration. In London, the British government responded with what became known as the Passfield White Paper, which limited Jewish immigration and imposed restrictions on the purchase of land by Jews.

The Passfield White Paper triggered a storm of protest on both sides of the Atlantic. Palestinian Jews rioted against the measures, and Zionist leaders in the United States and Great Britain condemned the decisions. Also, evangelical Protestants in the United States, who believed that biblical prophecy required the creation of a Jewish state in Palestine, also protested the decision. In the end, international political pressures proved so strong that Great Britain had to back down. The measures were repealed in 1931, which only antagonized Palestinian Arabs even more.

SUGGESTED READINGS: Yonathan Shapiro, *Leadership of the American Zionist Organization*, 1971; Melvin Urofsky, *American Zionism from Herzl to the Holocaust*, 1975.

PATMAN BONUS BILL OF 1935. See **BONUS ARMY**.

PAUL REVERES. The Paul Reveres was an anti-Roosevelt, antifascist, and anti–New Deal* organization founded in 1937 by Colonel Edwin Marshall Hadley. Its membership was small in number but loud in volume, and they disappeared as Adolf Hitler and European fascism grew more threatening in the late 1930s.

SUGGESTED READING: George Wolfskill and John A. Hudson, *All But the People. Franklin D. Roosevelt and His Critics, 1933–1939*, 1969.

PECORA COMMITTEE. The stock market crash* of 1929 and subsequent collapse of the nation's money markets precipitated concern in the United States about endemic fraud in the banking system. In 1933, Republican Senator Peter Norbeck* of North Dakota, chair of the Senate Banking and Currency Committee, engaged progressive Republican Ferdinand Pecora to head up an investigation of the nation's securities markets. The investigation, which came to be known as the Pecora Committee hearings, continued through 1933 and 1934. Pecora subpeoned Wall Street's major figures, including J. P. Morgan,* Richard Whitney,* Winthrop Aldrich, and Thomas W. Lamont. Pecora exposed the existence of widespread fraud in the securities markets, including rigged stock market pools, tax evasion, byzantine holding company networks, and outright criminal activity. The Pecora Committee's findings led directly to the Securities Exchange Act of 1934. President Franklin D. Roosevelt* then appointed Pecora as an original member of the Securities and Exchange Commission* board.

SUGGESTED READING: Michael Parrish, *Securities Regulation and the New Deal*, 1970.

PEEK, GEORGE NELSON. George N. Peek, a leading figure in American agriculture during the 1930s, was born on November 19, 1873, in Polo, Illinois. He was raised in Oregon, Illinois, attended Northwestern University, and then became a farm equipment salesman in Minneapolis, Minnesota, for Deere and Company. He rose steadily through the company, becoming general manager of John Deere Plow Company in Omaha, Nebraska, in 1901. Peek was a fine businessman, and in 1911, he was named vice-president of sales for Deere and Company. The first two decades of the twentieth century were generally quite good for farmers, and when World War I broke out, Peek was named to the War Industries Board, a powerful government agency charged with organizing the economy to maximize industrial and agricultural production. In 1918 and 1919 Peek headed up the federal government's Industrial Board, which was to ease the economy back into peacetime production; he then returned to Moline, Illinois, to serve as president of the Moline Plow Company.

When the American farm economy cratered during the 1920s, Peek emerged as an influential spokesman for farm interests. He developed a comprehensive program to rescue farmers that involved an activist federal government. He wanted the federal government to implement protective tariffs, marketing cooperatives, farm loans, and a domestic price support system. More specifically, he wanted the federal government to purchase farm surpluses at market prices and export them abroad, and if the domestic price was higher than the export price, the government would collect an equalization fee. In Congress, the proposal became the McNary-Haugen Bill. Peek left Moline Plow to lobby full-time for the legislation, and the bill passed once in 1927 and again in 1928, but on both occasions, President Calvin Coolidge vetoed it.

Disgusted with the Republican Party, Peek endorsed for president Democrats

Al Smith* in 1928 and Franklin D. Roosevelt* in 1932. In 1933, newly elected President Franklin D. Roosevelt placed Peek in charge of the Agricultural Adjustment Administration* (AAA), a government agency committed to dealing with the farm crisis by cutting production. Peek soon loathed the AAA, finding it to be a cumbersome bureaucratic arrangement that completely defied market realities. He remained committed to his own idea of solving the farm crisis—export marketing. Peek resigned from the AAA late in 1933 for a brief tenure as head of the Export-Import Bank.* In 1935 he retired to private relief and returned to the Republican Party. George Peek died on December 17, 1943.

SUGGESTED READINGS: Gilbert C. Fite, *George N. Peek and the Fight for Farm Parity,* 1954; *New York Times,* December 18, 1943.

PERKINS, FRANCES. Frances Perkins, next to Eleanor Roosevelt* the leading woman of the New Deal,* was born on April 10, 1880, in Boston, Massachusetts. In 1902, she graduated from Mount Holyoke College, planning a career as a teacher, but after five years in the classroom, Perkins moved to Chicago, Illinois, and became active in the settlement house movement. She worked for Jane Addams at Hull House and then moved to New York City, where she earned a master's degree at Columbia University. In 1910, Perkins was named secretary of the New York City Consumers' League.

The seminal event in Perkins's life occurred in 1911 with the Triangle Shirtwaist Fire. A total of 146 laborers, most of them women, died when the high-rise factory caught fire. Most of them died leaping from the burning upper floors. Working conditions at Triangle had always been bad, but the fire killed so many women because there were no fire escapes and because employers had locked doors from the outside. The fire redirected Perkins's energies into a crusade for women's safety in the workplace. In 1912 she became secretary to the New York Committee on Safety. That position gave Perkins an increasingly higher profile in New York State politics, and she came to the attention of state legislators Al Smith,* who later became governor, and Robert Wagner,* who went on to become a powerful and influential U.S. senator.

In 1919, Governor Al Smith appointed Perkins to the New York State Industrial Commission, which was responsible for enforcing state industrial legislation, and in 1926, she became chairman of the commission. In that position Perkins became close to Governor Franklin D. Roosevelt* of New York and his wife Eleanor. Eleanor was in charge of organizing Democratic Party activities for women in New York. In 1929, the governor named Perkins state industrial commissioner. She was serving in the position when Roosevelt was elected president of the United States. In 1933, the new president named Perkins to his cabinet as secretary of labor. As such, Perkins became the first woman in U.S. history to hold a cabinet post.

As secretary of labor, Perkins played a key role in such New Deal labor legislation as the National Industrial Recovery Act of 1933 and the National

Labor Relations Act of 1935.* She also headed the Committee on Economic Security,* a presidential board charged with studying the feasibility of Social Security legislation and drafting a bill. When the Social Security Act* was passed in 1935, Perkins was widely recognized for her contribution. She served as secretary of labor until 1945, then spent eight years as a member of the U.S. Civil Service Commission. Frances Perkins died on May 14, 1965.

SUGGESTED READINGS: George Martin, *Madame Secretary: Frances Perkins*, 1976; *New York Times*, May 15, 1965.

PITTMAN, KEY. Key Pittman was born in Vicksburg, Mississippi, on September 19, 1872. He was raised in Louisiana, attended Southwestern Presbyterian University in Tennessee, read law privately in Seattle, Washington, and was admitted to the bar. In 1897, after five years in Seattle, Pittman headed off to Alaska as part of the gold rush. He soon learned that he could make more money practicing mining law than panning for gold himself. When gold was discovered in Tonopah, Nevada, in 1901, Pittman relocated again. He was appointed as a Democrat to the U.S. Senate in 1912, and he was reelected in 1916, 1922, 1928, 1934, and 1940. During the 1930s, Pittman was a strong advocate of inflationary monetary schemes, not because he really believed in the theory of it but because he knew that government purchases and monetization of silver would keep silver miners working and mine owners making money. He backed the Silver Purchase Act of 1934.* As chairman of the Senate Foreign Relations Committee, Pittman supported isolationist policies. He died on November 10, 1940.

SUGGESTED READINGS: Fred Israel, *Nevada's Key Pittman*, 1963; *New York Times*, November 11, 1940.

POLAND. The modern nation of Poland was born at the Paris Peace Conference of 1919–1920, when the Allied Powers took territory from Germany,* Austria-Hungary, and Russia to create Poland. Poland had long before existed as a nation, but in the nineteenth century, particularly after the Napoleonic Wars and the emergence of Germany, Polish-speaking people found themselves divided. Polish nationalists in the nineteenth century had campaigned for reunification, and World War I finally gave them the opportunity. President Woodrow Wilson of the United States believed strongly in national self-determination, and since Germany and Austria-Hungary had ended up on the losing side of the war, they were subject to punishment. The fact that Russia had withdrawn from the war and then undergone the Bolshevik Revolution left them vulnerable, and to create Poland, the Treaty of Versailles unified the Polish-speaking regions of Europe under a new Polish government.

The Soviet Union* resented losing so much territory that it considered its own, and the rise of Adolf Hitler in Germany made the issue even more imperative. Premier Joseph Stalin wanted to get back his territory in Poland as a buffer against a German attack on the Soviet Union. In March 1939, Germany and the Soviet Union signed the Non-Aggression Pact, in which each agreed not to attack the other. The agreement, however, contained a secret protocol, which permitted, during a period of "territorial and political transformation," Germany to occupy the western third of Poland and the Soviet Union to occupy the eastern two-thirds of Poland. Ironically, Stalin now had his buffer zone against German attack, but Hitler now had his staging area for an attack on the Soviet Union.

On August 31, 1939, Hitler had a squad of SS troops, dressed in Polish military uniforms, stage a mock raid on a radio station just across the German-Polish border in Germany. He then used that as a justification for the invasion of Poland, claiming that Germany had no choice but to do so to protect its territorial sovereignty from Polish aggression. On September 1, 1939, German troops poured across the border, and on September 3, Poland and France declared war on Germany. World War II was under way. The German army employed its *panzer* tanks and infantry in what would soon become known as a *blitzkrieg* offensive. Poland surrendered on September 28, 1940. Faithful to the secret protocol of the Non-Aggression Act, Stalin ordered Soviet troops to occupy eastern Poland.

SUGGESTED READING: Norman Davies, *God's Playground: A Short History of Poland*, 1970.

PORGY AND BESS. On October 10, 1935, the musical *Porgy and Bess* opened on Broadway. George Gershwin* wrote the music, and his brother Ira and DuBose Heyward provided the libretto. The musical, soon dubbed an operetta, was based on Heyward's short story about Catfish Row, a black ghetto in Charleston, South Carolina. In what is today considered pure genius, Gershwin brought together jazz, rhythm and blues, gospel, opera, and popular music, exposing the richness of the black musical tradition. Although *Porgy and Bess* only had a run of sixteen weeks, musicologists consider it to be George Gershwin's masterpiece.

SUGGESTED READING: Edward Yablonski, *Gershwin*, 1987.

POWELL V. ALABAMA (1932). The case of the so-called Scottsboro boys* is among the most notorious in United States history. In March 1931, eleven African American young men were changed with the rape of two white women while riding on a freight train in Alabama. Even though they were indigent, legal counsel was not provided, and African Americans were excluded from the jury. The evidence against them was marginal at best. Eight were convicted and sentenced to death. The plight of the Scottsboro boys became a cause célèbre in the United States, and both the National Association for the Advancement of Colored People* and the Communist Party mounted appeals for them. The Alabama Supreme Court upheld seven of the convictions while reversing the conviction of the youngest defendant. The U.S. Supreme Court decided *Powell v. Alabama* on November 7, 1932. By a 7 to 2 vote, the justices reversed all eight convictions, arguing that the young men, lacking attorneys, had been denied their Fourteenth Amendment right to due process. Legal historians remember *Powell v. Alabama* as a landmark case in the right of defendants to enjoy legal counsel.

SUGGESTED READING: 287 U.S. 45 (1932).

PRESIDENT'S COMMITTEE ON ADMINISTRATIVE MANAGEMENT. See REORGANIZATION ACT OF 1939.

PRESIDENT'S COMMITTEE ON CROP INSURANCE. See FEDERAL CROP INSURANCE ACT OF 1938.

PRESIDENT'S EMERGENCY COMMISSION ON HOUSING. See FEDERAL HOUSING ADMINISTRATION.

PRESIDENT'S ORGANIZATION ON UNEMPLOYMENT RELIEF. As unemployment steadily grew worse in 1930, Democrats and liberal Republicans clamored for federal action to provide unemployment relief. President Herbert Hoover,* however, worried about the long-term implications of a large federal relief bureaucracy, and he opted for private initiatives. In 1930 he established the President's Emergency Committee for Employment (PECE) to coordinate the relief efforts of the federal government, business, labor unions, state and local governments, women's groups, and social welfare agencies. He appointed Arthur Woods to head the group. Woods quickly grew frustrated by PECE's inadequacies, and early in 1931, he urged the president to support a $375 million congressional appropriation to fund relief efforts. Hoover rejected the proposal out of hand. Woods then resigned from the organization. It had become clear to him that the unemployment problem was severe and getting worse and that the private sector did not have the resources or the will to address the problem in a serious way.

On August 13, 1931, PECE was absorbed by the new President's Organization on Unemployment Relief (POUR). Hoover put AT&T president Walter S. Gifford in charge of the government's unemployment relief effort. POUR deemphasized direct federal relief action in favor of private efforts, but time quickly proved that Arthur Woods's fears were being realized. The unemployment crisis dwarfed private resources. The nation's unemployment rate reached 15 percent in 1931 and 20 percent early in 1932. It was obvious that POUR's campaign was hopelessly inadequate, and President Hoover, with the presidential election of 1932* looming on the horizon, had to do something to provide real unemployment relief to retain any chance of reelection. In July 1932, POUR was eclipsed when Congress passed the Emergency Relief and Construction Act.*

SUGGESTED READINGS: David Burner, *Herbert Hoover: A Public Life*, 1979; Martin L. Fausold, *The Presidency of Herbert C. Hoover*, 1985; James S. Olson, *Herbert Hoover and the Reconstruction Finance Corporation, 1931–1933*, 1977.

PRIVATE LIVES. *Private Lives* is the title of playwright Noel Coward's savage critique of upper-crust British life. Coward wrote the play during a four-day stint battling the flu in a hotel in Shanghai, China,* and it opened in London on September 24, 1930. Coward played the male lead of Elyot, while Gertrude Lawrence played his ex-wife Amanda. They happen to be honeymooning at the same French hotel with new spouses. They engage in a series of nasty, acerbic dialogues with one another, exposing the vacuousness of their lives. *Private Lives* was a hit in London that crossed the Atlantic to become a hit on Broadway in 1931.

SUGGESTED READING: Sheridan Morley, *A Talent to Amuse: A Biography of Noel Coward*, 1985.

PROGRESSIVE NATIONAL COMMITTEE. The Progressive National Committee (PNC) was an organization of Democrats trying to attract the loyalty of progressive Republicans in the presidential election of 1936.* When Republican nominee Alf Landon* attacked the New Deal,* a coalition of progressive Republicans and New Deal Democrats met in Chicago in September 1936 and formed the PNC. Included in the group were John L. Lewis,* Adolf Berle,* Robert La Follette, Jr.,* Sidney Hillman,* Fiorello La Guardia,* George Norris,* and Frank P. Walsh. The PNC endorsed Franklin D. Roosevelt* for president and actively worked to bring that about.

SUGGESTED READING: Arthur M. Schlesinger, Jr., *The Age of Roosevelt*, vol. III, *The Politics of Upheaval, 1935–1936*, 1960.

THE PUBLIC ENEMY. *The Public Enemy*, a film released in 1931, launched the career of James Cagney.* Cagney played a vicious, amoral mob enforcer and hit man who possessed no scruples, no values, and no redeeming qualities. He robbed, assaulted, and killed with glee, enjoying the terror he inflicted on others and striking a similar terror on movie audiences. Critics took particular note of a scene when the frustrated mobster, tired of his girlfriend's incessant nagging, smashes a grapefruit in her face. In the end, of course, the gangster saw the evil of his ways, but only in his dying moments with his body filled with police bullets. *The Public Enemy* made James Cagney a certifiable international film superstar.

SUGGESTED READING: James Cagney, *Cagney on Cagney*, 1976.

PUBLIC UTILITY HOLDING COMPANY ACT OF 1935. During the 1920s, the public utility industry had behaved quite irresponsibly in making money by creating and issuing new securities for multiple holding companies stacked on top of a single operating company. The public utility holding company empire of Samuel Insull* had been especially egregious, and when the stock market fell in 1929, the multiple holding companies collapsed in value. Many New Dealers, especially those with a Brandesian faith in the obligation of the federal government to maintain a competitive economic environment through antitrust action, called for government regulation. President Franklin D. Roosevelt* had Benjamin Cohen* and Thomas Corcoran* draft the bill. Congressman Sam Rayburn* of Texas and Senator Burton K. Wheeler* sponsored the legislation in Congress. The bill contained the so-called death sentence clause that allowed the Securities and Exchange Commission* (SEC) to dissolve any public utility holding company that could not justify its own existence. In other words, a public utility holding company could not exist simply as a device for issuing new securities.

Not surprisingly, the public utility industry marshaled all of its resources in fighting the Public Utility Holding Company Act, also known as the Wheeler-Rayburn Bill. In the end, industry lobbyists managed to eliminate the "death sentence" clause. Roosevelt signed it into law on August 28, 1935. The law awarded the Federal Power Commission the authority to regulate interstate shipments of electrical power and extended similar authority over natural gas to the Federal Trade Commission. The law also eliminated all holding companies twice removed from their public utility operating companies. The law required all public utility holding companies to register with the SEC, which also enjoyed the power to supervise the financial activities of holding companies. The SEC also enjoyed the power to dissolve any holding company that could not justify its own existence after a five-year period. That power, however, was severely limited by the fact that the burden of proof rested on the SEC. By 1952, under the authority of the Public Utility Holding Company Act, the SEC had forced public utilities to divest themselves or to dissolve 753 affiliated holding companies with a total value of more than $10 billion.

SUGGESTED READING: Philip J. Funigiello, *Toward a National Power Policy: The New Deal and the Electric Utility Industry, 1933–1941*, 1973.

PUBLIC WORKS ADMINISTRATION. As far back as the depression of 1893, when Jacob Coxey led a march of unemployed men to Washington, D.C., to demand a federal public works program for unemployed workers, social welfare advocates have seen in government jobs programs a way to alleviate the suffering caused by downturns in the economy. During the 1920s, such progressive politicians as Senators Robert La Follette* of Wisconsin, Robert Wagner* of New York, and Edward P. Costigan of Colorado endorsed the idea, as did a well-received 1930 book by William T. Foster and Waddill Catchings—*The Long Range Planning of Public Works*. Foster and Catchings called for creation of a federal reserve fund for the construction of new highways, public buildings, and other projects. They argued that such a program would relieve the suffering of the unemployed and augment consumer purchasing power.

In July 1932, Congress passed the Emergency Relief and Construction Act* to provide unemployment relief, and among its provisions was authority for the Reconstruction Finance Corporation* (RFC) to establish a public works division to construct "self-liquidating" projects, such as water and sewage systems and toll roads and bridges, that would pay for themselves in a few years. When Franklin D. Roosevelt* was inaugurated, Congress passed the National Industrial Recovery Act of 1933, and Title II of the law created a Public Works Administration (PWA) to take over the RFC's work. The PWA had an appropriation of $3.3 billion. By 1940, the PWA had constructed more than 34,000 projects, including Grand Coulee Dam, Queens Midtown Tunnel, and the All American Canal.

SUGGESTED READINGS: James S. Olson, *Herbert Hoover and the Reconstruction Finance Corporation, 1931–1933*, 1977; James S. Olson, *Saving Capitalism: The Reconstruction Finance Corporation and the New Deal, 1933–1940*, 1988.

PURGE OF 1938. See **ELECTION OF 1938**.

R

RADICALS OF THE RIGHT. The political action group Radicals of the Right was formed in April 1933 by Seward Collins, who also published the *American Review*, a rabidly anti–Franklin D. Roosevelt,* anti–New Deal* journal. Accusing the New Deal of harboring "Communist tendencies," Collins tried to appeal to conservative intellectuals. He was also anti-Semitic and eventually became an intellectual fascist dedicated to monarchy, feudalism, unlimited property rights, and Christianity. During World War II, Radicals of the Right became an openly pro-Nazi group that soon disintegrated.

SUGGESTED READING: Arthur M. Schlesinger, Jr., *The Age of Roosevelt*, Vol. III, *The Politics of Upheaval 1935–1940*, 1960.

THE RADIO GUILD. During the 1920s, radio took America by storm, becoming the country's leading form of mass entertainment. *The Radio Guild*, which premiered on NBC in 1929, was radio's first national, hour-long dramatic program. It was essentially the first successful "soap opera" because it occupied late afternoon, weekday time slots when women listeners were busy with their household chores. *The Radio Guild* remained on the air for ten years.

SUGGESTED READING: John Dunning, *Tune in Yesterday: The Ultimate Encyclopedia of Old-Time Radio, 1925–1976*, 1976.

RAILROAD RETIREMENT ACT OF 1934. See *RAILROAD RETIREMENT BOARD ET AL. V. ALTON RAILROAD COMPANY ET AL.* (1935).

RAILROAD RETIREMENT ACT OF 1935. See *RAILROAD RETIREMENT BOARD ET AL. V. ALTON RAILROAD COMPANY ET AL.* (1935).

RAILROAD RETIREMENT ACT OF 1937. See *RAILROAD RETIREMENT BOARD ET AL. V. ALTON RAILROAD COMPANY ET AL.* (1935).

RAILROAD RETIREMENT BOARD ET AL. V. ALTON RAILROAD COMPANY ET AL. (1935).

In 1934, Congress passed the Railroad Retirement Act, which established a federal government retirement program for railroad workers. The law established a Railroad Retirement Board to administer the retirement program, whose pensions were financed by a 2 percent payroll tax on all railroad workers and a 4 percent tax on all railroad carriers. The law required 150,000 railroad workers to retire at age sixty-five. Many New Dealers hoped such a measure would make that many new jobs available to ease the country's unemployment problem.

But railway executives hated the measure, and the Association of Railway Executives filed a lawsuit in federal court. They labeled the law unconstitutional on the grounds that it violated their Fifth Amendment rights to private property. The case of *Railroad Retirement Board et al. v. Alton Railroad Company et al.* reached the Supreme Court in 1935. The Court declared the Railroad Retirement Act of 1934 unconstitutional, siding with the Association of Railway Executives. The justices claimed that mandatory pensions did not come under the commerce clause of the U.S. Constitution and therefore Congress did not have the power to enact such a law.

Congress almost immediately responded with the Railroad Retirement Act of 1935, also known as the Wagner-Crosser Railroad Retirement Act of 1935.* The replacement legislation exempted railroad employees from provisions of the Social Security Act of 1935* and financed railroad pensions by an excise tax of 3.5 percent on employee payrolls and an income tax of an equal amount on the carriers. But in June 1936, a federal district court declared the Railroad Retirement Act of 1935 unconstitutional.

Congress again reacted, though not so quickly. In 1937, a new Railroad Retirement Act became law. Before the law was passed, President Franklin D. Roosevelt* had asked the railway unions and railway executives to work out a compromise pension plan. The Railroad Retirement Act of 1937 represented that compromise. A companion bill—the Carriers' Taxing Act—financed the pension plan by income taxes levied on carriers and employees. The Association of Railway Executives did not contest the law.

SUGGESTED READINGS: "Railroad Retirement Act of 1937," *Monthly Labor Review*, 45 (1937), 377–79; "Railroads and Their Employees," *Monthly Labor Review*, 39 (1934), 352–55; *Supreme Court Reporter*, 55 (1935), 758–80.

RASKOB, JOHN JACOB. John Jacob Raskob, a leading figure in the Democratic Party during the 1920s and a controversial figure during the 1930s, was born on March 17, 1879, in Lockport, New York. After finishing school, Raskob went to work as a stenographer for the Worthington Pump Company, and he parlayed that into a job as secretary to Pierre S. Du Pont, president of a series of street railway companies in Ohio. Raskob's association with the Du Pont family launched him a very successful career as a businessman and industrialist.

Eventually, Raskob became treasurer, director, and vice-president of E. I. Du Pont de Nemours & Company. During his rise to power at Du Pont, Raskob was buying stock in General Motors, and the revolution in automobile production in the 1910s and 1920s made him a multimillionaire. He became chairman and director of finance at General Motors, and he played a leading role in restructuring the company and developing the installment plan method for consumers to purchase automobiles.

Raskob was also active in the Democratic Party, and in 1928 he became head of the Democratic National Committee. In that position, he had a central role in Franklin D. Roosevelt's* landslide victory in the 1932 presidential election. But the direction of the New Deal*—its massive increases in federal government budgets, deficit spending, and huge bureaucracies—soon alienated Raskob, and he became a critic of President Roosevelt. Raskob also hated the antibusiness flavor of New Deal rhetoric. He became a leading figure in the anti-Roosevelt, anti–New Deal American Liberty League.* Late in the 1930s, Raskob resigned from the Democratic Party. He died on October 15, 1950.

SUGGESTED READINGS: David Burner, *The Politics of Provincialism: The Democratic Party in Transition, 1918–1932*, 1968; *New York Times*, October 16, 1950.

RAYBURN, SAMUEL. Samuel Rayburn was born on January 6, 1882, on a small farm in Tennessee. When he was five years old, the Rayburn family moved to a small farm in Fallin County, Texas. A victim of stifling poverty as a child, in which he put in long hours picking cotton, Rayburn never lost his sympathies for poor people or his resentment for rich people, big government, and the corrupt politicians who exploited them. He particularly loathed railroads for their high freight rates and banks for the high interest rates. He also believed that the Republican Party symbolized evil—big businesses using the government to enrich themselves at the expense of poor people. Republicans had caused the Civil War, invaded and occupied his state after the war, and exploited it economically for decades. Sam Rayburn could have been called an ideological Democrat, and he would keep fighting the Civil War all of his life.

After graduating from East Texas Normal College, Rayburn taught school for two years, but in 1906 he won a seat in the state legislature. He was an unreconstructed Democratic populist, passionate in his commitment to the needs of poor farmers and absolutely incorruptible. In 1912 he was elected to Congress. By the time of the Great Depression, Rayburn was one of the most powerful people in Congress, and he threw his weight behind President Franklin D. Roosevelt* and the New Deal.* Rayburn came to consider FDR to be one of the great figures in U.S. history.

During the 1910s and 1920s, Rayburn had seen desperate, poor farmers invest and lose their life savings in worthless stock issues, and he enthusiastically backed and sponsored the Securities Act of 1933* and the Securities Exchange Act of 1934. He also sponsored the Public Utility Holding Company Act of

1935.* Rayburn considered the major public utilities to be hopelessly greedy, unwilling to provide service to the poorest of Americans and guilty of gouging the rest.

In 1940, Sam Rayburn became speaker of the House of Representatives, a post he held for the next seventeen years. Except for a marriage that lasted only three months, Rayburn had no family and all but made the House of Representatives his home. Known for hard work and absolute integrity, he is remembered by historians as one of the most effective congressmen in U.S. history. When he died on November 16, 1961, he had served forty-seven years in Congress.

SUGGESTED READINGS: D. B. Hardeman, *Rayburn: A Biography*, 1987; Booth Mooney, *Roosevelt and Rayburn: A Political Partnership*, 1971; *New York Times*, November 16–17, 1961.

RECESSION OF 1937–1938. By mid-1937, the unemployment rate had fallen dramatically from its highs in 1932, and the stock market had risen. Many New Deal* economists concluded that the end of the Great Depression was in sight, that the New Deal's recovery measures were finally yielding results. But what they did not realize was that a series of fiscal decisions by the Roosevelt administration and monetary decisions by the Federal Reserve Board* had undermined the prosperity. Out of a misguided fear of the possibility of inflation, the Federal Reserve Board in 1936 pursued tight money policies, doubling reserve requirements and putting a damper on the money markets. At the same time, Social Security taxes began to be collected without benefits yet being paid, which removed purchasing power from the economy. Declining federal spending on relief and work relief also cut purchasing power.

These policies combined to drive the economy into recession. Beginning in September 1937 and lasting until June 1938, the economy headed back into the depression. Industrial production and payrolls declined by a third, manufacturing employment by a quarter, and industrial stocks by more than half. The economic downturn precipitated a huge debate inside the Roosevelt administration, with conservatives like Jesse Jones,* Daniel Roper,* and Henry Morgenthau, Jr.,* calling for balanced budgets and probusiness policies, and such liberals as Leon Henderson,* Robert Jackson, Thomas Corcoran,* Benjamin Cohen,* Harold Ickes,* and Marriner Eccles* advocating deficit spending and antitrust action to stimulate the economy. In April 1938, President Franklin D. Roosevelt* announced that he was siding with the liberals. It was not until the spring of 1940, however, with war raging in Europe, that federal government spending finally pulled the economy out of the depression.

SUGGESTED READINGS: Dean May, *From New Deal to New Economics*, 1982; Patrick D. Reagan, "Recession of 1937–1938," in James S. Olson, ed., *Historical Dictionary of the New Deal*, 1985; Albert U. Romasco, *The Politics of Recovery: Roosevelt's New Deal*, 1983.

RECIPROCAL TRADE AGREEMENTS ACT OF 1934. During the 1920s, tariff policies in the United States and abroad restricted trade and stimulated declines in industrial production. In the United States, the Republican administrations of Warren G. Harding, Calvin Coolidge, and Herbert Hoover* pursued high tariff policies, symbolized by the Fordney-McCumber Tariff of 1921 and the Hawley-Smoot Tariff of 1930.* The Republican logic was simple: By keeping European industrial products out of U.S. markets, American manufacturing jobs would be protected. But the opposite happened. Europeans retaliated with high tariffs of their own, and the combined effect was to discourage economic activity.

By the early 1930s, it was obvious to many economists and Democrats that U.S. tariff policy had to be drastically revised downward if there was going to be any hope of stimulating the economy. Between 1929 and 1932 American exports had fallen by a third. Secretary of State Cordell Hull* led the fight for tariff reductions, which he believed would improve U.S. foreign relations and stimulate the economy. He proposed a bill that would authorize the State Department to negotiate bilateral tariff reductions with other countries. Congress passed the measure in June 1934, and President Franklin D. Roosevelt* signed it.

The Reciprocal Trade Agreements Act of 1934 authorized the president to negotiate bilateral tariff agreements with other nations without seeking congressional approval, as long as those tariffs did not raise or lower rates by more than 50 percent from the levels of the Hawley-Smoot Tariff. Congress renewed the legislation in 1937, 1940, 1943, and 1945, by which time a total of thirty-seven bilateral tariff reductions had been negotiated.

SUGGESTED READING: James C. Pearson, *The Reciprocal Trade Agreements Program: The Policy of the United States and Its Effectiveness*, 1942.

RECONSTRUCTION FINANCE CORPORATION. The Reconstruction Finance Corporation (RFC) was perhaps the most important federal agency of the Great Depression, although historians have tended to ignore it. The RFC had its beginnings in the collapse of the banking system early in the 1930s. Because of long-term problems with the banking system during the 1920s—more than 5,000 banks had failed during the decade—depositors had completely lost confidence, and their demands for deposits created a liquidity crisis in the economy. In October 1931, to keep banks from closing their doors or selling off their assets at panic-level prices, President Herbert Hoover* established the National Credit Corporation* (NCC), a private organization of major banks designed to loan money to troubled financial institutions. If depositors realized that banks could come up with the cash to redeem deposits, they would be less likely to launch runs on the banks.

The NCC, however, proved inadequate to the task. The weaknesses in the banking system in particular and the money markets in general proved to be deep and endemic, and to prevent bankruptcy throughout the entire system, President Hoover proposed and Congress created the Reconstruction Finance Corporation in January 1932. The RFC received an appropriation of $500 million and the right to issue its own bonds to raise another $2 billion. It could then loan that money to troubled banks, savings banks, industrial banks, insurance companies, credit unions, and building and loan associations. With the money, the president hoped, the banks would enjoy greater liquidity, depositors would be reassured, and bankers could increase their volume of commercial loans. With credit again flowing in the economy, Hoover presumed, industrial production and employment would increase too. The RFC could also make loans to railroads. During the previous two decades, banks had invested heavily in railroad bonds, but when automobiles and trucks cut into railroad freight revenues, many railroads found themselves in serious financial difficulties and defaulted on their bond payments, which seriously compromised the investment portfolios of thousands of financial institutions.

Hoover named prominent banker and Republican politician Charles Dawes* to head the RFC, and RFC loans did restore some stability, temporarily, to the money markets. Many liberal Democrats, however, pilloried the RFC because a substantial volume of its loans went to large commercial banks, big insurance companies, and high-profile railroads. They accused the RFC of bailing out the rich and powerful while the poor and the unemployed suffered without any federal assistance. The president insisted that the economy would not recover until the money markets recovered, and he was probably right, but it was a tough position to sell politically. When Charles Dawes quit the RFC in June 1932 and the RFC turned around and loaned $90 million to Dawes's troubled Central Republic Bank of Chicago, the Democrats howled in protest and talked scandal, and Hoover lost even more ground politically.

In response to the political criticism, Congress passed the Emergency Relief and Construction Act* in July 1932, which authorized the RFC to loan $300 million to state and local governments for unemployment relief and up $1.5 billion to the states for public works construction. The legislation was politically imperative since the unemployment rate had hit 25 percent.

Within a few months, however, virtually all of the RFC's programs were bankrupt. Late in December 1932 and in January and February 1933, the money markets collapsed, and it appeared that the entire banking system was about to go bankrupt, in spite of billions of dollars in RFC loans. Unemployment continued to rise, and the RFC relief funds proved pitifully inadequate. The $1.5 billion in public works construction money had little impact because the projects, many of them very complex, had not even gotten under way yet. The RFC had failed. Frightened depositors were hoarding currency in even greater volumes; bankers were accumulating large volumes of excess reserves at Federal Reserve Banks; and businessmen were laying off workers in record numbers. The RFC had failed because all of its loans had to be repaid, and borrowers were cautious about undertaking such obligations during hard times.

By February 1933, a series of banking panics were spreading throughout the country, and to deal with the crisis, the RFC would have literally needed billions more dollars to loan out. When President Hoover left office in March 1933, nearly all of the banks in the country had shut down, and the Reconstruction Finance Corporation, one of the largest federal agencies in U.S. history, had failed.

But the RFC was resurrected during the years of the New Deal.* For President Franklin D. Roosevelt,* the RFC became an all but ubiquitous agency, used for a variety of purposes. He named Houston banker Jesse Jones* to head the RFC. Under the authority of the Emergency Banking Act of 1933,* the RFC was authorized to purchase the preferred stock and capital notes of troubled banks. In the previous year, RFC loans had not helped that much because bankers had to pay them off on a short-term basis. But by buying preferred stock and only receiving annual dividends on the stock, the RFC essentially supplied banks with long-term capital, which allowed them to hold on to assets until values had recovered. By the mid-1930s, the RFC owned stock in more than 6,000 American banks. The RFC also created and supervised the work of such other New Deal agencies as the Commodity Credit Corporation,* the Federal National Mortgage Association,* the Disaster Loan Corporation, the Electric Home and Farm Authority,* the Export-Import Bank,* and the RFC Mortgage Company. Finally, the RFC was a funding agency for such New Deal agencies as the Works Progress Administration,* the Civil Works Administration,* and the Federal Emergency Relief Administration.* By 1940, the RFC had loaned more than $10 billion, making it by far the most powerful of the New Deal agencies.

SUGGESTED READINGS: James S. Olson, *Herbert Hoover and the Reconstruction Finance Corporation, 1931–1933*, 1977; James S. Olson, *Saving Capitalism: The Reconstruction Finance Corporation and the New Deal, 1933–1940*, 1988.

REED, STANLEY FORMAN. Stanley Reed was born in Minerva, Kentucky, on December 31, 1884. His small-town background in Mason County, Kentucky, did not limit Reed's intellectual vision. He graduated from Kentucky Wesleyan College and then headed east for a second bachelor's degree, this time at Yale. He spent a year at the University of Virginia Law School and then another year at Columbia, but he never graduated with a law degree. Nevertheless, he passed the Kentucky bar examination in 1910 and opened his own private practice in Mason County. He became very active in local Democratic Party politics and then served two terms in the state legislature before joining the army during World War I. After the war, he returned to private practice.

In 1929, President Herbert Hoover* appointed Reed as general counsel to the Federal Farm Board, and Reed soon earned a reputation as a peerless expert in administrative law and bureaucratic maneuvering. In 1932 Hoover named him general counsel to the Reconstruction Finance Corporation,* the country's most important government agency in the war on the Great Depression. In 1935,

President Franklin D. Roosevelt* appointed Reed to the office of solicitor general.

In that post, Reed argued before the U.S. Supreme Court the *Schechter Poultry Corporation v. United States** case in 1935 and the *United States v. Butler** case in 1936. He lost both cases, and in the process, the Supreme Court destroyed the National Industrial Recovery Act of 1933 and the Agricultural Adjustment Act of 1933,* the two linchpins of the New Deal.* An enraged President Roosevelt then decided to reorganize the federal judiciary in his ill-fated court-packing scheme.* The plan failed, but because of several retirements, the president was eventually able to replace the Court's conservative majority with liberals. Stanley Reed was one of them. He was appointed as a justice of the Supreme Court in 1938. He remained on the Court for the next nineteen years, becoming well known for his role as an economic liberal but a civil rights and civil liberties conservative. Stanley Reed retired from the Court in 1957 and died in Maysville, Kentucky, on April 2, 1980.

SUGGESTED READING: F. William O'Brien, *Justice Reed and the First Amendment*, 1958; *New York Times*, April 3, 1980.

RENO, MILO. Milo Reno was born near Agency, Iowa, on January 5, 1866. He attended William Penn College in Oskaloosa, Iowa, in order to study for the ministry, but he left school after losing interest in a ministerial career. Reno tried his hand at selling insurance and farm equipment, but the plight of midwestern farmers steadily consumed more of his attention, and in 1918, he joined the National Farmers' Union* (NFU). A popular, engaging individual, Reno became quite influential in the NFU, and he began speaking to larger and larger audiences, always insisting that farmers "deserved the cost of production plus a reasonable profit."

In 1932, Reno was elected president of the National Farmers' Holiday Association (NFHA), a group dedicated to holding crops off the market until farmers received fair prices for them. In August 1932, the NFHA took militant action by preventing milk and livestock trucks from delivering crops to market. The strike spread from Iowa to four other states, and in the process, Reno became a national figure. Reno called off the strike in March 1933 when President Franklin D. Roosevelt* was president, hoping that the new administration would address the farm problem. But the New Deal* soon disappointed Reno, who believed that the acreage reduction plans of the Agricultural Adjustment Administration* would only benefit large commercial farmers, not troubled family farmers. In September 1933, he tried to resurrect the strikes again, but few farmers were willing to listen to him anymore. The movement collapsed, and Reno retreated into obscurity. He died on May 5, 1936.

SUGGESTED READING: John L. Shover, *Cornbelt Rebellion; The Farmers' Holiday Association*, 1965; Ronald A. White, *Milo Reno: Farmers' Union Pioneer*, 1941.

REORGANIZATION ACT OF 1939. As governor of New York, Franklin D. Roosevelt* had earned a reputation as an advocate of government efficiency, but when he became president, the impact of the Great Depression put a premium on federal government activism and federal spending, both of which militated against Roosevelt's reputation as a conservative. In fact, two months into the New Deal,* both liberals and conservatives would have found it laughable to describe the president as a supporter of government reorganization, retrenchment, and efficiency. In the Economy Act of 1933,* the president had gained the authority to implement government reorganization schemes, but he could not act upon that authority because of the compelling need for government relief and recovery programs.

But in 1936 President Roosevelt began paying more attention to issues of efficiency and administrative management. He established the President's Committee on Administrative Management, under the leadership of Louis Brownlow, head of the public administration committee of the Social Science Research Council. In 1937 the committee produced its report—*Report of the President's Committee on Administrative Management*—which was delivered to Congress. After more than two years of congressional debate and maneuvering, Congress passed the Reorganization Act of 1939. Roosevelt signed it on April 3, 1939.

He began to implement the legislation three weeks later. The president submitted Reorganization Plan No. 1 to Congress, which created the Federal Security Agency,* the Federal Works Agency,* the Federal Loan Agency,* and an executive office of the president. The Federal Security Agency consolidated into one agency more than a dozen federal agencies, including the Social Security Board, the Public Health Service, the National Youth Administration,* the U.S. Office of Education, the Civilian Conservation Corps,* the Food and Drug Administration, and the U.S. Employment Service. The Federal Works Agency consolidated into one agency the Works Progress Administration,* the Public Works Administration,* the Bureau of Public Roads, and the U.S. Housing Agency. The Federal Loan Agency consolidated the Reconstruction Finance Corporation,* the Export-Import Bank,* the Federal Housing Administration,* the Home Owners' Loan Corporation,* the RFC Mortgage Company, the Disaster Loan Corporation, the Federal National Mortgage Association,* and the Electric Home and Farm Authority.*

SUGGESTED READINGS: Barry D. Karl, *Executive Reorganization and Reform in the New Deal: The Genesis of Administrative Management, 1900–1939*, 1963; Richard Polenberg, *Reorganizing Roosevelt's Government: The Controversy over Executive Reorganization, 1936–1939*, 1966; Duane Windsor, "Reorganization Act of 1939," in James S. Olson, *Historical Dictionary of the New Deal*, 1985.

RESETTLEMENT ADMINISTRATION. The great problem facing American agriculture during the 1920s and 1930s was overproduction. Commodity production exceeded demand in the United States, and mechanisms for marketing surpluses abroad with profitable margins were not available. Commodity prices and the purchasing power of farm families steadily declined between World War I and the early 1930s. As farm income declined, millions of farmers found themselves unable to meet mortgage payments and ended up losing their land in foreclosure proceedings. New Deal* farm policy addressed these two problems by trying to reduce production and to liquefy the credit markets.

The programs implemented under the Agricultural Adjustment Act of 1933,* the Soil Conservation and Domestic Allotment Act of 1935, the Bankhead Cotton Control Act,* the Warren Potato Control Act,* and the Agricultural Adjustment Act of 1938* all worked to reduce the number of acres in production, and farmers were compensated for the acreage removed. In some areas, especially the labor-intensive cotton fields of the South, the acreage reductions wreaked havoc with poor farm laborers and tenant farmers. While the large commercial landowners received government checks for their acreage reductions, farm laborers ended up with crops to pick and tenant farmers and sharecroppers found themselves without land to work. Displaced from the land and unable to find work in other sectors of the economy, they suffered a numbing poverty.

The rise of the Southern Tenant Farmers' Union* and its activities brought their plight to the attention of the public, and in 1935, President Franklin D. Roosevelt* established the Special Committee on Farm Tenancy to investigate their situation and to make recommendations. The Resettlement Administration grew out of the committee's recommendation that the federal government assume some responsibility for what New Deal farm policy had done to poor farm families, especially in the South. Of course, the larger commercial farmers resisted any such efforts because they feared losing access to a supply of cheap, easily exploitable labor. But Congress nevertheless responded and in 1935 created the Resettlement Administration and placed Rexford G. Tugwell* at its head.

The Resettlement Administration was the most class-conscious of New Deal agencies. Its mission was to upgrade the lives of the poorest of Americans, at the expense of wealthy commercial landowners, and of many black Americans, at the expense of wealthy whites. Tugwell initially wanted to resettle more than 500,000 poor families on their own land or in suburban developments; provide decent camps and sanitary living conditions for migratory farmworkers; and farm rehabilitation and land utilization projects to assist poor farmers who owned small amounts of land to maximize their assets. The Resettlement Administration even organized large collective farms in Casa Grande, Arizona; Lake Dick, Arkansas; Walker Country, Alabama; and New Madrid, Louisiana. The collective farms were complete with project managers, family cottages, medical cooperatives, and heavy farm machinery. Finally, the Resettlement Administration, through its Suburban Resettlement Division, worked to depopulate urban slums and tenant farm slums and build twenty-five new towns in suburban areas.

The Resettlement Administration never even came close to achieving its goals because it upset so many entrenched interest groups. Conservatives labeled these collective farms socialistic or communistic, and large commercial farmers resented the assistance given to poor tenant farmers, primarily because they feared it would raise their labor costs. The American Medical Association protested the medical cooperatives; real estate developers protested the new suburban towns; and labor unions complained that the federal government was assuming some of their functions.

Because of all the opposition, the Resettlement Administration's actual achievements were quite meager. Instead of relocating 500,000 families, the Resettlement Administration actually relocated only 4,441 families. Instead of twenty-five new towns, the Resettlement Administration built only three: Greenbelt, Maryland, near Washington, D.C.; Greendale, Wisconsin, near Milwaukee; and Green Hills, Ohio, near Cincinnati. In the end, the Farm Security Administration* absorbed the Resettlement Administration and its programs.

SUGGESTED READINGS: Sidney Baldwin, *Politics and Poverty: The Rise and Decline of the Farm Security Administration*, 1968; Donald H. Grubbs, *Cry from the Cotton: The Southern Tenant Farmers' Union and the New Deal*, 1971.

REVENUE ACT OF 1932. Because of declining industrial production and increasing unemployment during the early 1930s, federal government revenues dropped precipitously, leaving the Hoover administration with a deficit. For President Herbert Hoover,* the deficit only increased public skepticism about the health of the economy and made a recovery less likely. The only answer, the president was convinced, was a tax increase, which would balance the federal budget and restore confidence to the economy. Congress passed the Revenue Act of 1932, which raised the corporate income tax to 13.75 percent, the maximum surtax from 25 to 55 percent, and general tax rate schedules from 4 to 8 percent. President Hoover signed the bill on June 6, 1932.

In one way, the Revenue Act of 1932 marked a watershed in the history of public policy in the United States. The idea of raising taxes during an economic downturn, exactly what the Revenue Act of 1932 accomplished, would soon be discredited by the advent of Keynesian economics and the use of deficit spending to stimulate the economy. Never again would policymakers raise taxes during a recession.

SUGGESTED READING: Martin L. Fausold, *The Presidency of Herbert C. Hoover*, 1985.

RIN-TIN-TIN. *Rin-Tin-Tin* was one of radio's more popular dramatic, adventure programs during the early 1930s. It premiered on NBC in 1930 and remained on the air well into 1934. *Rin-Tin-Tin* featured a German shepherd dog who battled against Indians and desperadoes and helped rescue women and children from natural disasters.

SUGGESTED READING: John Dunning, *Tune in Yesterday: The Ultimate Encyclopedia of Old-Time Radio, 1925–1976*, 1976.

ROBERTS, OWEN JOSEPHUS. Owen J. Roberts was born in Germantown, Pennsylvania, on May 2, 1875. He attended the University of Pennsylvania for both his undergraduate and law degrees, where his intellectual brilliance became obvious to faculty and students alike. The law school hired him as a faculty member as soon as he graduated, and for the next twenty years, Roberts taught there and practiced privately as a trial attorney. Between 1903 and 1906, he served as first assistant district attorney of Philadelphia. He came to national attention, however, during the 1920s, when he was appointed special counsel to investigate the Teapot Dome and Elk Hills oil scandals, where Secretary of the Interior Albert Fall had accepted kickbacks from private oil companies by agreeing to open up federal naval oil reserves to development. Secretary of Commerce Herbert Hoover* took special note of Roberts's skills and legal acumen, and in May 1930, when he had become president, Hoover named Roberts to the U.S. Supreme Court.

When Roberts joined the Court, it was balanced between liberals and conservatives, and Roberts often found himself casting key votes. On the liberal side were Louis Brandeis,* Harlan F. Stone,* and Benjamin N. Cardozo,* while the conservative bloc consisted of justices Willis Van Devanter,* James McReynolds,* George Sutherland,* and Pierce Butler. Chief Justice Charles Evans Hughes,* like Roberts, occupied middle ground as well. Both Hughes and Roberts defied easy classification.

During the beginning of his tenure, Roberts tended to vote more conservatively, especially concerning early New Deal* legislation. He voted with the majority in declaring the National Industrial Recovery Act of 1933 and the Agricultural Adjustment Act of 1933* unconstitutional. Along with the other conservative justices, Roberts found himself under severe criticism from President Franklin D. Roosevelt* and other New Dealers, who accused the Supreme Court of allowing judicial tradition to obstruct attempts to ameliorate the suffering of the Great Depression. In 1937, Roosevelt tried to implement his court-packing scheme,* to expand the size of the Supreme Court to fifteen justices and then appoint a liberal majority. The plan was politically ill-advised and backfired, and Roosevelt took considerable heat for the proposal. But at the same time, Roberts switched sides and began voting, along with Chief Justice Hughes, with the liberals, giving them a narrow majority. Journalists began to identify Roberts as the justice who made "the switch in time to save nine," meaning the man who changed his point of view so that the Supreme Court, with nine justices, would remain intact.

Roberts remained on the Supreme Court until his retirement in 1945. During World War II, he headed the federal government's investigation into the Pearl Harbor disaster and concluded that there was no evidence that American officials knew in advance of the attack or had actually conspired. Owen Roberts died on May 17, 1955.

SUGGESTED READINGS: Charles A. Leonard, *A Search for a Judicial Philosophy: Mr. Justice Roberts and the Constitutional Revolution of 1937*, 1971; *New York Times*, May 18, 1955.

ROBINSON, JOSEPH TAYLOR. Joseph Robinson was born in Lonoke County, Arkansas, on August 26, 1872. He graduated from the University of Arkansas and then earned a law degree at the University of Virginia. In 1895, Robinson launched a private law practice in Lonoke County and won a seat as a Democrat in the state legislature. He served three terms before being elected to Congress, and after five terms there, Robinson was elected governor of Arkansas. He did not spend much time in the state capital because he was elected to the U.S. Senate in 1913. Robinson won reelection in 1918, 1924, 1930, and 1936. A confirmed internationalist, Robinson supported Woodrow Wilson's foreign policy during and after World War I, and he played a key role in restructuring German reparations by supporting the Dawes Plan of 1924 and the Young Plan of 1929.

Robinson became a leading figure in the Democratic Party in the 1920s, serving as party chairman throughout much of the decade and seeking the vice-presidency as Al Smith's* running mate in 1928. He was, to be sure, a conservative Democrat, and he called for balanced budgets and opposed federal government development of Muscle Shoals. Robinson also frequently warned about the dangers of a too-powerful federal government. With Franklin D. Roosevelt's* landslide victory in the election of 1932,* Democrats took over the U.S. Senate and selected Robinson as majority leader. Although Robinson worried about the drift of the New Deal and the power accruing to the federal government, he was a loyal Democrat and backed Roosevelt. Joseph Robinson died on July 14, 1937.

SUGGESTED READINGS: Neven E. Neal, "A Biography of Joseph T. Robinson," Ph.D. diss., University of Oklahoma, 1957; *New York Times*, July 15, 1937.

ROBINSON-PATMAN ACT OF 1936. See **"LITTLE NRA."**

ROGERS, GINGER. See **ASTAIRE, FREDERICK AUSTERLITZ.**

THE ROMANCE OF HELEN TRENT. *The Romance of Helen Trent* was radio's classic soap opera, a daytime broadcast that endured for twenty-seven years. It premiered on CBS on October 30, 1933, and remained on the air—7,222 broadcasts—until 1960. Helen Trent was the proverbial, virtuous heroine who never aged. She was impervious to impure thoughts and lived without guile.

Disaster often struck her, but she remained unintimidated and unflappable. The broadcast was fifteen minutes a day and attracted millions of listeners.

SUGGESTED READING: John Dunning, *On the Air: The Encyclopedia of Old-Time Radio*, 1998.

ROOSEVELT, ANNA ELEANOR. Eleanor Roosevelt, arguably the most influential woman of twentieth-century America, was born in New York City on October 11, 1884, to one of the country's most distinguished families. To put it mildly, she suffered in a dysfunctional family. Although the family put on a facade of strict Victorian morality and respectability, her father was a drunk and her mother a woman who withheld love and affection from her daughter. Eleanor was orphaned by the time she was ten years old. She attended the Allenswood School outside of London, where she managed to recover, or least begin to develop, her identity. In 1905, Eleanor married Franklin D. Roosevelt,* a distant cousin. They had five children and eventually forged one of the greatest political partnerships in U.S. history.

In 1913 the Roosevelts moved to Washington, D.C., when Franklin was appointed assistant secretary of the navy in the Woodrow Wilson administration. The normal routine of their marriage was shattered when Eleanor learned that her husband had had an affair with her social secretary. The affair was an emotional catastrophe for Eleanor, but it forced her to develop an independent identity, one quite distinct from that of her husband. Their marriage never again enjoyed any physical intimacy but survived because it suited the political objectives of both partners.

Franklin D. Roosevelt ran unsuccessfully for the vice-presidency in the election of 1920, but after his defeat, they returned to New York City, where Eleanor became active in the Women's Trade Union League and in Democratic politics, especially in the party's women's division. She actively campaigned for federal minimum wage and maximum hours legislation, outspokenly opposed child labor, and crusaded for the Sheppard-Towner Act, which provided modest government protections for working women. Eleanor also took a firm stand against the Equal Rights Amendment, which she believed would actually hurt working-class women by removing gender-based protective legislation. When her husband was elected governor of New York in 1928, Eleanor's political profile increased even more.

On March 4, 1933, Eleanor became First Lady when her husband was inaugurated president of the United States. Over the years, she became the liberal conscience of the New Deal,* serving as the country's most powerful lobbyist for civil rights, Social Security, unemployment relief, and labor standards legislation. She was outspoken in her opposition to lynching and in her support for a federal antilynching law. Her role was a critical one in the history of the New Deal, since her husband so often found himself trying to balance the demands of liberal Democrats in the Northeast and conservative Democrats in the South.

Because of Eleanor, legislation that might never have garnered the support of the president managed to do so.

After Franklin D. Roosevelt's death in 1945, Eleanor Roosevelt emerged as the most famous and influential woman in the world. She became the matron of the Democratic Party and an icon for liberals interested in civil rights and social welfare legislation. She also was an avowed internationalist who realized that the United States possessed a moral responsibility to use its economic and military power to promote education, civil rights, and social welfare around the world. Eleanor Roosevelt died on November 7, 1962.

SUGGESTED READINGS: Maureen Beasley, *The Eleanor Roosevelt Encyclopedia*, 2001; Blanche Weisen Cook, *Eleanor Roosevelt: 1884–1933*, 1992; Tamara R. Hareven, *Eleanor Roosevelt: An American Conscience*, 1968; Joseph P. Lash, *Eleanor and Franklin*, 1971; Joan Hoff Wilson and Marjorie Ligniman, eds., *Without Precedent: The Life and Career of Eleanor Roosevelt*, 1984.

ROOSEVELT, FRANKLIN DELANO. In most surveys of professional historians, Franklin D. Roosevelt joins the ranks of George Washington and Abraham Lincoln as one of America's three greatest presidents. Blessed with enormous political talent, he led the country through two crises—the Great Depression and World War II—and in the process earned the esteem of most Americans. To be sure, his New Deal* was anathema to most conservatives and big businessmen, but he provided middle-of-the-road leadership at a time when, because of the suffering caused by the Great Depression, he could have taken the country down the path to socialism. In that sense, Franklin D. Roosevelt can be credited with saving capitalism in the United States.

He was born in New York City on January 30, 1882, to a prominent, prosperous family. He was an only child and as such enjoyed and endured the close attention of an elderly, indulgent father and a doting mother who made his life her life. The wealth of the Roosevelt family reached back to the mercantile and shipping industries of the colonial period, and as such it was "old money," which gave Franklin a patrician outlook on life. He remembered growing up on the family estate at Hyde Park and "never really [being] told no about anything I really wanted." He grew up competitive but not really acquisitive, as if money had always been available and therefore not something to scramble after. In 1905 he married Eleanor Roosevelt,* a distant cousin, and they had five children.

Roosevelt had a gilt-edged education—at Groton, Harvard, and Columbia, where he earned a law degree. He practiced law privately but had no real passion for it. The money had no real interest to him, but he did have a sense of noblesse oblige that pushed him toward politics. Roosevelt had no ideology or any fixed political philosophy. He was generally conservative but certainly not dogmatic, and a real pragmatic streak governed his thinking about the world. Such values, or lack thereof, prepared him for a political world where compromise and the art of the possible governed reality.

In 1911, Roosevelt was elected to the state legislature on a platform that opposed the political corruption so endemic to Tammany Hall, the Democratic political machine in New York City. But he soon realized that opposing Tammany Hall might win him votes in upstate New York, but it would surely keep him from winning statewide office, since Tammany Hall controlled so much of the New York City vote. So Roosevelt made peace with Tammany Hall. In 1913, President Woodrow Wilson picked Roosevelt as assistant secretary of the navy, a post that brought Roosevelt and his family to Washington, D.C., where they resided for the next seven years. Roosevelt's stature in the Democratic Party grew steadily, and in 1920 he was nominated as James Cox's vice-presidential running mate. They lost in a landslide to Republican nominee Warren G. Harding.

The Roosevelts then returned to New York City, but in the summer of 1921, their lives changed dramatically. While vacationing at the family compound at Campobello, Roosevelt came down with a case of infantile paralysis, or polio, that attacked his legs and left him a paraplegic. Confined to a wheelchair, he retreated into a depression and farther into a private life. The depression proved to be short-lived. With the assistance of his wife Eleanor, he reevaluated his life and decided to return to politics. He became active in New York Democratic politics, and at the conventions of 1924 and 1928, he delivered the formal speeches nominating New York governor Al Smith* for president. In 1928, Al Smith lost to Herbert Hoover,* and Roosevelt won the New York governorship, becoming overnight the most prominent Democrat in the country.

Roosevelt's first term as governor of New York was a distinguished one. He emphasized conservation, state regulation of major public utilities, prison reform, and old-age pensions. When the economy fell into the Great Depression, New York became a model for unemployment relief, public works construction, and social welfare legislation. New York's Temporary Emergency Relief Administration* paved the way for much of the New Deal's* subsequent unemployment relief program. Roosevelt's administration in New York stood in stark contrast to President Herbert Hoover's administration in Washington, D.C., where procrastination, delay, and doubt characterized the approach to unemployment. Roosevelt won the Democratic nomination for president in 1932, and he immediately became the frontrunner, since Hoover's reputation with the American public had grown so dismal. In the election, Roosevelt enjoyed a landslide victory, and Democrats came to control Congress by huge margins.

Roosevelt immediately set about rewarding the political constituencies that had put him in office. He knew that President Hoover had been too slow to move on federal unemployment relief projects, leaving Americans with the distinct impression that he did not care about the suffering of the poor, and Roosevelt was committed to portraying exactly the opposite. He also knew that Americans expected him to do something to stimulate the economy and lift the economy out of the depression. Finally, Roosevelt realized that the federal government would have to undertake important initiatives to prevent future economic collapses. The early New Deal, therefore, soon became known for its commitment to "Relief, Recovery, and Reform."

Between March 9 and June 16, 1933, in what became known as the "Hundred Days,"* Congress engaged in a flurry of legislative activity, much of it at the instigation of President Roosevelt. During those three months, Congress passed more major legislation than at any other time in U.S. history, including the Emergency Banking Act,* the Economy Act,* the Civilian Conservation Corps* Reforestation Relief Act, the Federal Emergency Relief Act, the Agricultural Adjustment Act,* the Tennessee Valley Authority,* the Securities Act,* the National Employment System Act, the Home Owners' Refinancing Act, the Banking Act,* the Farm Credit Act,* the Emergency Railroad Transportation Act,* and the National Industrial Recovery Act. Compared to the Hoover administration, the early New Deal seemed, and was, bold and confident, and most Americans soon endowed Franklin D. Roosevelt with heroic status.

The so-called Second Hundred Days* in 1935–1936 only cemented the president's reputation. The Supreme Court's decision in 1935 and 1936 to outlaw the Agricultural Adjustment Administration* and the National Recovery Administration* had gutted the New Deal's recovery programs, which enraged Roosevelt and only committed him to more activism and a change in focus. At the heart of the early New Deal had been the idea of national economic planning and business-government cooperation, but the later New Deal had a different focus, which included antitrust activity, social reform, and Keynesian deficit spending. The later New Deal involved a shift to the left, indicated in such social reform legislation as the Social Security Act of 1935,* the National Labor Relations Act of 1935,* and the Wealth Tax Act of 1935,* and a new emphasis on Brandesian antitrust activity through such items as the Public Utility Holding Company Act of 1935.* In the presidential election of 1936,* FDR was reelected over Republican nominee Alf Landon* in a landslide.

Roosevelt's second term in office witnessed a shift in emphasis from the first. He all but abandoned the balanced budget rhetoric of the early New Deal in favor of the deficit spending philosophy of British economist John Maynard Keynes.* Roosevelt also gave a new boost to antitrusters in his Temporary National Economic Committee* hearings and new antitrust activity in the Department of Justice. But he also learned that there were limits to his popularity. In 1937, when he embarked on his court-packing scheme* to liberalize the Supreme Court, he ran into a political roadblock of opposition, even from supporters who resented many of the Court's anti–New Deal decisions. What FDR learned was that Americans did not want him tampering with the Court, even if they disagreed with it. In the election of 1938,* when he intervened in many primary elections to try and help defeat conservative Democrats, Americans again let him know that he had overstepped his bounds.

Some Republicans had high hopes of defeating Roosevelt when he decided to run for a third term in 1940, but events in Europe guaranteed FDR's reelection. Most Americans viewed Roosevelt as a father figure who had led the country through the pain of the Great Depression and had eased their suffering, and they trusted him to do the same in case of war. He was reelected in 1940 and again in 1944, dying in office on April 12, 1945. A grief-stricken nation mourned his passing.

SUGGESTED READINGS: James MacGregor Burns, *Roosevelt: The Lion and the Fox,* 1956; Paul Conkin, *The New Deal,* 1967; Frank Freidel, *Franklin D. Roosevelt: Launching the New Deal,* 1973; Frank Freidel, *Franklin D. Roosevelt: A Rendezvous with Destiny,* 1990; Joseph P. Lash, *Eleanor and Franklin,* 1971.

ROPER, DANIEL CALHOUN. Daniel Roper was born on April 1, 1867, in Marlboro County, South Carolina. In 1888 he graduated from Duke University and then spent the next four years teaching school, selling life insurance, and farming. In 1892, Roper won a seat as a Democrat in the state legislature. After a stint as the clerk for the U.S. Senate Committee on Banking and Commerce, Roper returned to the life insurance business and studied law part-time. In 1901 he received a law degree from the National University Law School in Washington, D.C.

Roper's connections in the Washington, D.C., political establishment served him well, and he parlayed them into a series of good career moves. He worked as clerk of the House Ways and Means Committee (1911–1913); first assistant postmaster general (1913–1916); vice-chairman of the U.S. Tariff Commission (1917); commissioner of the Internal Revenue Service (1917–1920); and president of Marlin-Rockwell Corporation (1920–1921). Between 1921 and 1933, Roper practiced law in Washington, D.C., and in 1933, President Franklin D. Roosevelt* named him secretary of commerce.

Roper spent his six years as secretary of commerce in a nearly impossible task—trying to drum up business support for what many businessmen considered to be antibusiness New Deal* legislation, such as the Securities Act of 1933,* the Banking Acts of 1933* and 1935,* the Securities Exchange Act of 1934, the Public Utility Holding Company Act of 1935,* the Wealth Tax Act of 1935,* and the National Labor Relations Act of 1935.* Still, through the Business Advisory Council* over which he presided, Roper reached out to the business community and brought them some reassurance about the New Deal's basic faith in the future of capitalism. Roper stepped down in 1938 and returned to the practice of law. He died on April 11, 1943.

SUGGESTED READINGS: Barry D. Karl, *Executive Reorganization and Reform in the New Deal: The Genesis of Administrative Management, 1900–1929,* 1963; Daniel C. Roper, *Fifty Years in Public Life,* 1942.

RURAL ELECTRIFICATION ADMINISTRATION. By the 1930s, there were two Americas, at least in terms of access to electricity. In cities and towns throughout the country, most Americans enjoyed electrical power systems in their homes, with the convenience of electric lights, home appliances, radios, and affordable heat. The major public utilities generated the power and constructed the delivery systems—poles and utility lines—to serve customers. Naturally, they preferred constructing such delivery systems in heavily populated areas, where the return on investment in terms of kilowatt hours of energy consumed would be high. Rural areas lagged behind in such service because the expense of constructing utility lines into sparsely populated areas was not cost-effective. A lone farm family living in a house several miles from their nearest neighbor would never be able to consume enough electricity to cover the up-front capital required to get the electricity into their home.

President Franklin D. Roosevelt* decided to do something about the problem. Using funds from the Emergency Relief Appropriation Act of 1935, Roosevelt issued Executive Order No. 7037 on May 11, 1935, establishing the Rural Electrification Administration (REA). The president named Morris Cooke, a long-time advocate of public power, to head the REA. In May 1936, Congress passed the Rural Electrification Act, which gave the REA statutory authority to function for ten years.

Since private power companies would not expand service into rural areas, the REA formed rural electric cooperatives. The REA extended low-interest, long-term loans to cooperatives that then built the delivery systems. The cooperatives then purchased electricity from private utilities. By 1939, the REA had helped form 417 rural electric cooperatives and had delivered electric power service to 268,000 homes. The REA continued to function, and by the 1950s, few homes in the United States were without electricity.

SUGGESTED READINGS: Jay L. Brigham, *Empowering the West: Electrical Politics before FDR*, 1998; D. Clayton Brown, *Electricity for Rural America: The Fight for the REA*, 1980; Thomas D. Isern, "Rural Electrification Administration," in James S. Olson, ed., *Historical Dictionary of the New Deal*, 1985; Ronald C. Tobay, *Technology as Freedom: The New Deal and the Electrical Modernization of America*, 1996.

RUSSO-FINNISH WAR, 1939–1940. Although the Soviet Union* had signed a nonaggression pact with Germany* in 1939, the Russians maintained no illusions about German aggressiveness or Adolf Hitler's intentions. To make sure that Hitler could not attack northern Russia, and especially Leningrad, by way of Finland, Soviet leader Joseph Stalin decided to conquer Finland. The fact that much of Finland had been Russian territory until the Treaty of Versailles in 1919 only gave Stalin a rationale for his aggression. In December 1939, to create a pretext for his invasion, Stalin petitioned the Finnish government, knowing full well that it would not agree, to grant the Soviet Union a huge swath of land in southeastern Finland. Stalin argued that he needed the territory to protect the Soviet Union from German attack. Finland refused, and in retaliation Stalin launched an air attack on Helsinki. The war was on.

Knowing that the Soviet army was on its way, the Finns dug in along the

"Mannerheim Line" on the Karelian Isthmus. The position was named after Baron Carl Gustav Mannerheim, who had engineered the Finnish defeat of the Bolsheviks in 1918. In 1939, Finnish military planners placed 125,000 Finnish troops along the Mannerheim Line, and they repulsed the first Soviet offensive, which consisted of 500,000 troops and 1,000 tanks, gaining headlines worldwide for their bravery and tenacity. In the United States, the Finns became popular "underdogs" in their battle against the "great Russian bear." The Finns then deployed ten-man cross-country ski brigades along the entire 700-mile Soviet-Finnish frontier, conducting a guerrilla war against the invaders. It was a brutal winter war fought in temperatures that often fell below fifty degrees Fahrenheit. Although Soviet troops outnumbered the Finns by five to one, the Finns held out for more than 3 months.

But in the end, the Finns could not prevail. With a population of only 3 million people, they could not stand up indefinitely to the Soviet Union's 150 million people. In February 1940, the Soviet Union unleashed a second massive offensive, and the Western powers, already allied to the Soviet Union in its war with Germany, could offer no assistance. On March 11, 1940, Finland signed a treaty ceding 10 percent of its territory to the Soviet Union. When the dead were counted, Finland had suffered a loss of 25,000 men to the Soviet Union's 250,000 dead.

SUGGESTED READING: Eloise Paananen and Lauri Paananen, *The Winter War: The Russo-Finnish Conflict, 1939–1940,* 1973.

S

SALT MARCH. For more than two centuries, the British had dominated the South Asian subcontinent, exercising imperial control over what would later become India, Pakistan, Bangladesh, Nepal, and Bhutan. But the seeds of discontent had already been sown, and in the 1930s, they blossomed into rebellion. The British Raj, as the imperial government was known, had long maintained a monopoly on salt production in India, levying a heavy tax on the necessity and reaping huge profits from its sale.

But for India's hundreds of millions of poor people, the salt monopoly and salt tax were burdens they despised. Late in March 1930, Mohandas Gandhi, the nationalist leader, decided to defy the salt monopoly in a public act of civil disobedience. After arranging for maximum press coverage, he walked 200 miles to Dandi on India's western coast. Arriving there on April 6, 1930, he broke the law and harvested salt from the ocean. Indians by the millions rallied to his symbolic act of protest, and throughout British India, similar acts of protest, marches, salt raids, work stoppages, riots, and boycotts took place. In the wake of the Salt March, British authorities arrested more than 60,000 Indians, including Gandhi, but the instability demonstrated how vulnerable the Raj was to mass protest.

SUGGESTED READING: Martin G. Green, *Gandhi: Voice of a New Age Revolution*, 1993.

SANGER, MARGARET. Margaret Sanger, one of the most influential women of her time, was born in Corning, New York, on September 14, 1879. Although her father became enamored of the single-tax ideas of Henry George and worked as a pro–single tax reformer, the family was poverty-stricken, and the eleven children had a difficult time growing up. Sanger decided early on that the family poverty was a result of too many children, and she became committed to the notion that birth control information was critically necessary for American women. She married in 1902 and tried her hand at housekeeping, but she had a restless streak, and when the family moved to New York City in 1902, Sanger became active in the radical union movement, working as an organizer for the Industrial Workers of the World.

Soon, however, Sanger left the union movement and began campaigning for sexual reform—sex education, family planning and birth control, and elimination of venereal diseases. Her crusade gave her a high profile and offended conservative elements of American society. In 1913, the U.S. Post Office refused to distribute the magazine *Call* because its lead article was composed by Sanger and dealt with syphilis. From that experience, Sanger decided that sexuality in America had become so stigmatized that real problems could not be solved because they could not even be discussed.

In 1914, Sanger founded the magazine *Woman Rebel* and dedicated it to promoting birth control education. The U.S. Post Office declared it unmailable and had Sanger indicted for violating the postal code. To avoid prosecution, she fled to Great Britain and the Netherlands, but her stay abroad only increased her education. In both countries, the political atmosphere was more hospitable to birth control education, and she learned how to be more politically effective. Sanger returned to the United States in 1914 and established a contraceptive advice center in Brooklyn. New York City police shut it down, but Sanger won a court decision reopening it as long as physicians were in charge. Throughout the country, she adopted the physician-directed approach to open other contraceptive advice centers.

In 1921, Sanger founded the American Birth Control League, which eventually evolved into the Planned Parenthood Federation of America. She established the Birth Control Clinical Research Bureau in New York. It was the first physician-staffed birth control clinic in the United States. During the years of the Great Depression, Sanger accelerated her effort. With massive unemployment afflicting the country, Sanger was even more convinced that women needed effective birth control information. By 1938, she had opened more than 300 birth control clinics throughout the United States.

Sanger also set her sights on overturning the Comstock Act of 1873, a federal law that had classified birth control information as obscene. Such legislation, Sanger believed, was absurd and an affront to the public health. In 1936, she succeeded when a federal court ruled that the mailing of birth control information to physicians could not be considered obscene. Sanger continued her crusade for the rest of her life, becoming a global leader in the movement for family planning and birth control. She died on September 6, 1966.

SUGGESTED READINGS: *New York Times*, September 7, 1966; James Reed, *From Private Vice to Public Virtue: The Birth Control Movement and American Society since 1830*, 1978; Margaret Sanger, *Margaret Sanger: An Autobiography*, 1938.

SCHALL, THOMAS DAVID. Thomas Schall was born in Reed City, Michigan, on June 4, 1878. He was raised in Campbell, Minnesota, and in 1902, he graduated from the University of Minnesota. Two years later, he received a law degree from the St. Paul College of Law. Although blinded in an electrical accident, he kept practicing law, and in 1914, he won a seat as a Republican in Congress. Ten years later, Schall won election as a U.S. senator. He loathed Franklin D. Roosevelt* and the New Deal* and accused the president of taking the country down the road to socialism and communism. Schall soon became guilty of gross hyperbole, accusing Roosevelt of being a drunkard, a philanderer, a radical, and a conspirator to destroy the American way of life. Schall died in an automobile accident on September 22, 1935.

SUGGESTED READINGS: *New York Times*, December 23, 1935; George Wolfskill and John A. Hudson, *All But the People. Franklin D. Roosevelt and His Critics, 1933– 1939*, 1969.

SCHECHTER POULTRY CORPORATION V. UNITED STATES

(1935). The National Industrial Recovery Act of 1933 was the linchpin of early New Deal* economic policy. The law established a new government agency— the National Recovery Administration* (NRA)—to address the problem of price deflation in the economy, which made corporate planning difficult, reduced business investment, and sliced into profit margins. The logic behind the NRA was that prices were falling because of industrial overproduction. The solution, therefore, was to cut industrial production, which supposedly would increase prices, raise profits, and stimulate the hiring of workers. The economic logic, of course, was badly flawed, since cutting industrial production would only lead to more unemployment.

Serious legal and political opposition also materialized against the NRA. Conservatives considered the National Recovery Administration an unacceptable increase in the power of the federal government, and they opposed the legislation on constitutional grounds. A host of lawsuits against the NRA found their way into the federal judicial system, and *Schechter Poultry Corporation v. United States* became the premier example. The NRA accused Schechter of violating several provisions of the agency's codes in their Brooklyn chicken processing business and levied a fine against them. In return, Schechter sued.

The case reached the U.S. Supreme Court and was decided, by a unanimous vote, on May 27, 1935. Writing for the Court, Chief Justice Charles Evans Hughes* declared the National Industrial Recovery Act unconstitutional. Hughes based his opinion on three principles. First, the existence of extraordinary economic conditions did not justify an attempt to enlarge the constitutional powers of the federal government. Second, the legislation delegated essential legislative powers to the executive branch, which violated the principle of separation of powers and amounted to "delegation run riot." Finally, the Schechter poultry operations were essentially a local matter, not a question of interstate commerce, and therefore Congress did not possess jurisdiction.

The *Schechter* decision gutted the early New Deal and enraged President

Franklin D. Roosevelt,* who soon launched his court-packing scheme* to re-organize and reform the federal judiciary. Although Roosevelt did not succeed in his crusade to restructure the federal court system, the controversy and political battle did allow him to replace the U.S. Supreme Court's conservative majority with more liberal justices who upheld the right of the federal government to regulate the economy.

SUGGESTED READING: 295 U.S. 495 (1935).

SCOTCH TAPE. In 1930, the Minnesota Mining and Manufacturing Company introduced to consumer markets "Scotch tape," a transparent adhesive tape made of cellulose. The company advertised the tape as a necessary product to seal up products wrapped in cellophane. They advertised it as "Scotch" tape because of the stereotype that the people of Scotland were especially thrifty and tried to save things. But the Du Pont Company quickly rendered the new product obsolete, for sealing up cellophane wrappers at least, by inventing heat-sealing cellophane. By that time, however, Americans had already found other uses for Scotch tape. At a time when incomes were down and most families were financially strapped, Scotch tape became useful for mending torn clothes, fixing up torn currency and documents, holding plaster to walls and ceilings, attaching photographs to frames and walls, and repairing toys. Minnesota Mining and Manufacturing could barely keep up with demand, and in 1935 the company introduced a small dispenser, which allowed consumers to pull out the tape and cleanly rip it across a serrated blade. By the end of the decade, Scotch tape had become an American institution.

SUGGESTED READING: Alfred Chandler, *Pierre S. Du Pont and the Making of the Modern Corporation*, 1971.

SCOTTSBORO CASE. It was not uncommon during the years of the Great Depression for unemployed men to hitch rides in railroad boxcars as they scoured the countryside looking for work. But in March 1931, riding the rails led to one of the century's most notorious criminal cases. Nine black men between the ages of thirteen and twenty hitched a ride on a train in Alabama, but during the trip, they got into a fight with a group of white youths. The white young men, after being ejected from the train, complained to the local sheriff, and at the next stop, deputy sheriffs arrested the nine blacks and two white women traveling with them. The women, perhaps worried about being prosecuted for prostitution, claimed to have been gang-raped by the blacks, and the deputies then hustled the accused rapists to the county seat in Scottsboro. Thus began the saga of the so-called Scottsboro boys.

They went on trial in April. Although the Sixth Amendment guarantees legal representation to indigent criminal defendants, the Scotttsboro boys received what can best be described as scandalously inadequate counsel. Also, the judge systematically excluded blacks from the jury, denying the defendants another dimension of their Sixth Amendment rights. Although the two women's stories were riddled with inconsistencies and physicians could find no physical evidence of rape, the first two defendants were convicted in a one-day trial after being given only a twenty-minute discussion with attorneys before the trial. Outside the courtroom, when the verdict was announced, 10,000 spectators cheered wildly and a brass band began playing marching music. In the next three weeks the other defendants, except the thirteen-year-old, were convicted. The judge declared a mistrial in his case. All the others were sentenced to death.

The case soon became a cause célèbre for civil rights advocates. Lawyers for the National Association for the Advancement of Colored People* (NAACP) joined the battle for the Scottsboro defendants, as did attorneys for the Communist Party. Attorneys for the NAACP and the communist-backed International Labor Defense worked up an appeal, and the case of *Powell v. Alabama** went to a higher court. The Alabama Supreme Court upheld seven of the convictions while reversing the conviction of the youngest defendant. The case then entered the federal courts. The case of *Powell v. Alabama* was argued before the Supreme Court on October 10, 1932. And on November 7, 1932, by a vote of 7 to 2, the U.S. Supreme Court reversed all of the convictions on the grounds that the defendants, by not having access to legal counsel, had been denied their Fourteenth Amendment right to due process.

The national controversy over the Scottsboro case ricocheted through the federal court system. On April 1, 1935, the Supreme Court decided the fate of Clarence Norris, one of the Scottsboro defendants who had been retried in the wake of the *Powell v. Alabama*, convicted again, and then sentenced to death. Norris's NAACP attorneys argued that because Alabama had systematically excluded African Americans from the trial jury and from the grand jury that had returned the indictment, they had not received a fair trial as dictated by the Fifth, Sixth, and Fourteenth Amendments to the Constitution. By a unanimous vote, the Court overturned the conviction, agreeing that Norris had been denied his rights to due process.

During the next several years, the Scottsboro defendants were tried again and again. By 1937, under intense political pressure and international scrutiny, the state of Alabama dropped charges against five of the young men. Several others were paroled from prison between 1937 and 1940. The last Scottsboro defendant was paroled in 1946. By that time the Scottsboro case had become one of the most notorious violations of civil rights in American history.

SUGGESTED READING: Dan T. Carter, *Scottsboro: A Tragedy of the American South*, 1979.

SECOND EXPORT-IMPORT BANK. See **EXPORT-IMPORT BANK**.

SECOND HUNDRED DAYS. The term "Second Hundred Days" was used first by journalists and then by historians to describe a flurry of legislative activity by Congress and the Roosevelt administration in the summer of 1935. On May 27, 1935, with Congress about to adjourn, the Supreme Court had handed down the *Schechter** decision, invalidating the National Industrial Recovery Act and dismantling the National Recovery Administration.* The Supreme Court's decision enraged President Franklin D. Roosevelt,* who decided to keep Congress in session and implement a dramatic series of New Deal* measures. That summer became known as the Second Hundred Days, named after the "Hundred Days"* when the New Deal began. During the Second Hundred Days, President Roosevelt implemented executive orders creating the National Resources Committee and the National Youth Administration.* Congress passed the National Labor Relations Act,* the Motor Carrier Act,* the Social Security Act,* the Banking Act of 1935,* the Public Utility Holding Company Act,* the Farm Mortgage Moratorium Act, the Wagner-Crosser Railroad Retirement Act,* the Guffey-Snyder Bituminous Coal Stabilization Act, and the Wealth Tax Act.* The Second Hundred Days marked a decidedly leftward shift in New Deal values.

SUGGESTED READING: William E. Leuchtenburg, *Franklin D. Roosevelt and the New Deal, 1932–1940*, 1963.

SECOND NEW DEAL. Journalists and historians have used the term "Second New Deal" to describe the burst of legislative activity that characterized the Franklin D. Roosevelt* administration from 1935 to 1939. The so-called First New Deal* focused on relief and recovery measures when the president and Congress tried to relieve the suffering of unemployment by creating such agencies as the Federal Emergency Relief Administration,* the Civil Works Administration,* the Public Works Administration,* and the Civilian Conservation Corps,* to end the depression through such agencies as the National Recovery Administration,* the Agricultural Adjustment Administration,* and the Tennessee Valley Authority*; to reconstruct the financial system through the Reconstruction Finance Corporation,* the Banking Act of 1933,* and the Emergency Banking Act of 1933*; and to strengthen labor standards through the National Industrial Recovery Act. Historians decided that the First New Deal ended in May 1935 when the Supreme Court handed down its decision in the *Schechter Poultry Corporation v. United States*,* invalidating the National Industrial Recovery Act and declaring the National Recovery Administration unconstitutional.

The Second New Deal then began, but its focus shifted. The change of focus resulted from the Supreme Court's conservative decisions, criticism of the New Deal* from the business community, and the persistence of the depression. At the core of the early New Deal was the idea of national economic planning and business-government cooperation, but the Second New Deal had a different focus, which included antitrust activity, social reform, and Keynesian deficit spending. The Second New Deal involved a shift to the left, indicated in such social reform legislation as the Social Security Act of 1935,* the National Labor Relations Act of 1935,* and the Wealth Tax Act of 1935,* and a new emphasis on Brandesian antitrust activity through such items as the Public Utility Holding Company Act of 1935* and the Temporary National Economic Committee* of 1937–1938. The Second New Deal also abandoned the balanced budget rhetoric of the First New Deal in favor of the deficit spending philosophy of British economist John Maynard Keynes.*

SUGGESTED READING: Arthur M. Schlesinger, Jr., *The Age of Roosevelt*, vol. III, *The Politics of Upheaval, 1935–1936*, 1960.

SECURITIES ACT OF 1933. The huge losses sustained by investors in the stock market crash* of 1929 convinced many politicians that the securities markets needed government regulation in order to prevent corporate abuses. The stock market in the 1920s had been characterized by fraudulent investment companies, high-pressure salesmanship, corruption, greed, dishonest securities disclosures, misrepresentation, margin buying, and highly inflated promises of guaranteed investment returns. In 1932, the Pecora Committee*—led by Ferdinand Pecora for Senator Peter Norbeck* of North Dakota—delved into the secrets of the securities industry. The hearings lasted for more than two years and exposed to public scrutiny just how corrupt the securities industry had become. Newspapers published headline after headline exposing the fraud, and by the time President Franklin D. Roosevelt* was inaugurated in March 1933, the public was more than ready for reform.

Late in March 1933, just three weeks after his inauguration, President Roosevelt called for reform legislation requiring full disclosure on all new securities issues, with the burden of responsibility resting on the seller, not the buyer. The eventual legislation that was drafted gave the Federal Trade Commission the power to investigate new securities issues and to postpone their sale if full disclosure had not taken place. The law—known as the Securities Act—was sponsored by Congressman Sam Rayburn* of Texas and Senators Joseph Robinson* of Arkansas and Duncan Fletcher of Florida. Congress passed the measure, and Roosevelt signed it on May 27, 1933.

The press referred to the legislation as the Fletcher-Rayburn Bill. Corporations issuing new stock as initial public offerings first had to file with the Federal Trade Commission all possible information about the prospective securities. Among the law's requirements were information about all commissions or discounts paid by the issuer to the underwriter, the names of people who held more than 10 percent of any other securities issued by that company, the names of the company's directors and officers, and detailed financial statements about the health and stability of the company. Hiding information or issuing bogus information carried criminal penalties. The Federal Trade Commission enjoyed quasi-judicial powers to investigate and to punish violators of the law. For the first time, the federal government had acquired real power over the securities industry.

SUGGESTED READINGS: Gary Dean Best, "The Securities Act of 1933," in James S. Olson, ed., *Historical Dictionary of the New Deal*, 1985; Michael Parrish, *Securities Regulation and the New Deal*, 1970; Donald A. Ritchie, *James M. Landis. Dean of the Regulators*, 1980.

SECURITIES AND EXCHANGE COMMISSION. When Congress passed the Securities Act of 1933,* investment bankers and Wall Street traders howled in protest. The law, they argued, was too punitive because of its criminal and civil penalties, which even included innocent mistakes and omissions. They also argued that the burdensome disclosure requirements would take too much time and money to implement. They insisted that the language of the bill was so vague that it subjected securities industries professionals to dangerous legal vulnerability. Finally, they had real concerns about the fact that the law essentially awarded legislative authority to an agency of the executive branch. They warned that the Securities Act would destabilize the securities markets and discourage the issuance of new securities, which would make it difficult for industrial concerns to acquire capital for investment. They also decried the great expansion of federal power that the legislation represented. Of course, there were some investment bankers who welcomed the Securities Act because they thought it would clean up the industry by driving unscrupulous competitors out of the market.

In 1934, New Deal* lawyers fine-tuned the language, and Congress passed new legislation—the Securities Exchange Act. It established a Securities and Exchange Commission (SEC) to replace the Federal Trade Commission as the governing federal agency in the securities markets. To reassure investment bankers and traders about their criminal liability, the language of the law was tightened and the disclosure and liability provisions of the Securities Act of 1933 were modified. President Franklin D. Roosevelt* appointed Boston banker Joseph P. Kennedy to head the SEC. Kennedy's leadership of the SEC was quite enlightened and helped revive private capital investment. He relied mostly on industry self-regulation and established consistent, industry-wide accounting rules, but at the same time he was not hesitant to investigate and prosecute fraud. James M. Landis, who had helped draft the bill that created the SEC, succeeded Kennedy as head of the agency in 1937. Some critics on the left claimed that the SEC was too pro-industry, while many Wall Street conservatives found it way too liberal. Like so much of the New Deal, the Securities and Exchange Commission followed a middle-of-the-road set of public policies.

SUGGESTED READINGS: Gary Dean Best, "The Securities Act of 1933," in James S. Olson, ed., *Historical Dictionary of the New Deal*, 1985; Michael Parrish, *Securities*

Regulation and the New Deal, 1970; Donald A. Ritchie, *James M. Landis. Dean of the Regulators*, 1980.

SECURITIES EXCHANGE ACT OF 1934. See **SECURITIES AND EXCHANGE COMMISSION**.

SENTINELS OF THE REPUBLIC. The Sentinels of the Republic was a right-wing, anti–New Deal,* and anti-Semitic political action group of the 1930s. It was founded by Alexander Lincoln and had its headquarters in Boston, Massachusetts. The group was financed largely by the Du Pont family and crusaded against such New Deal measures as the Social Security Act,* the Public Utility Holding Company Act,* and the Wealth Tax Act.* By the late 1930s, the Sentinels of the Republic blended into the pro-Nazi movement.

SUGGESTED READING: Arthur M. Schlesinger, Jr., *The Age of Roosevelt*. vol. III, *The Politics of Upheaval, 1935–1936*, 1960.

THE SHADOW. The Shadow was a popular radio crime melodrama that played weekly in prime time throughout the 1930s. It debuted on CBS on July 31, 1930, moved to NBC in 1932, returned to CBS in 1935, and finally became a program of the Mutual Network until its last broadcast on December 26, 1954. The creator of *The Shadow* was Walter B. Gibson. Part melodrama, part adaptation of real stories, the program revolved around the exploits of one Lamont Cranston, a brilliant social scientist and mind reader devoted to protecting the public from evil. Cranston enjoyed the "hypnotic power to cloud men's minds so that they cannot see him."

SUGGESTED READINGS: John Dunning, *On the Air: The Encyclopedia of Old-Time Radio*, 1998; Anthony Tollin, *The Shadow Scrapbook*, 1991.

SHAHN, BENJAMIN. Benjamin Shahn was born to a Jewish family in Kaunas, Lithuania, on September 12, 1898. The Shahns immigrated to the United States in 1906 and settled in Brooklyn, New York. When he was fifteen, Shahn apprenticed out to a commercial lithographer, attending art classes at night. Shahn rejected what he called the "passionless amorality" of abstract art and picked social themes for his work—paintings of Sacco and Vanzetti, striking workers, Middle America farmworkers, poor immigrants, and industrial workers in foundries and plants. Some critics accused him of being "didactic" or "preachy" in his art, but Shahn considered himself the artist of the masses and for the masses.

Mexican muralist Diego Rivera became enchanted with Shahn's work, and they came together to work on the *Man at the Crossroads* fresco for the RCA Building at Rockefeller Center in New York City. During the later 1930s, Shahn became the most prominent painter of the Federal Art Project* in the Works

Progress Administration.* His most memorable work for the Federal Art Project was the mural on immigration at the Jersey Homesteads housing project in New Jersey. Other memorable Shahn murals were completed at the Bronx Central Post Office in New York City and the Social Security Building in Washington, D.C. During World War II, Shahn designed posters for the Office of War Information. He died on March 14, 1969.

SUGGESTED READINGS: Howard Greenfield, *Ben Shahn: An Artist's Life*, 1998; *New York Times*, March 15–16, 1969.

SHANGHAI INCIDENT OF 1932. Many modern historians look to China* in the early 1930s to see the beginning stage of World War II. Japan* had invaded Manchuria* in 1931, and in response, the Chinese in Shanghai launched a boycott of Japanese-manufactured goods. Japan considered the boycott an affront to its sovereignty, and on January 28, 1932, Japan sent troops into Shanghai and bombed the city. The United States considered the invasion an act of war, and Secretary of State Henry L. Stimson* filed a vigorous diplomatic protest, demanded a Japanese withdrawal, and threatened to expand the U.S. military presence in Guam and the Philippines. On May 5, 1932, China and Japan signed an armistice ending the crisis.

SUGGESTED READING: Robert H. Ferrell, *American Diplomacy in the Great Depression: The Hoover-Stimson Foreign Policy, 1929–1933*, 1957.

"SHARE OUR WEALTH." See LONG, HUEY PIERCE, and SMITH, GERALD LYMAN KENNETH.

SHELTERBELT PROJECT. The so-called Shelterbelt Project was a personal favorite of President Franklin D. Roosevelt,* who had long maintained an interest in conservation and tree planting on the family estate at Hyde Park, New York. Ever since 1913, as part of the Department of Agriculture's "shelterbelt program," North Dakota farmers had planted belts of trees around their exposed fields to soil wind erosion. In 1934, Roosevelt tried to secure support for what he called the "Great Plains Shelterbelt," a vision of 3 billion trees planted on a 100-mile-wide strip of land extending from the Canadian border to central Texas. Within that swath of land, the U.S. Forest Service would plant tree belts 1-mile long and eight rods wide at half-mile intervals. In 1935, the Forest Service planted 125 miles of shelterbelts on land the Agricultural Adjustment Administration* had withdrawn from farm production.

The program did attract serious criticism from nursery owners and from eastern foresters, who felt the government program would compete with their interests. Eventually, the president only acquired a few million dollars for the program, but the money was used well, and by World War II, a total of 217 million trees had been planted on 232,212 acres.

SUGGESTED READING: Thomas R. Wessel, "Roosevelt and the Great Plains Shelterbelt," *Great Plains Journal*, 8 (January 1969), 57–73.

SHERLOCK HOLMES. *Sherlock Holmes*, based on the popular detective novels by Conan Doyle, debuted as a radio drama on October 20, 1930, on the Red Network. It remained on the air for the next sixteen years, moving back and forth from one network to another and attracting a celebrity cast, including Basil Rathbone, who played Sherlock Holmes in so many films. With his sidekick Watson, Holmes used his wits and his unparalleled deductive reasoning skills to solve crimes, and audiences loved it.

SUGGESTED READING: John Dunning, *On the Air: The Encyclopedia of Old-Time Radio*, 1998.

SHIPSTEAD, HENRIK. Henrik Shipstead was born on January 8, 1881, in Burbank, Minnesota. He graduated from St. Cloud State College and then in 1903 earned a degree in dentistry from Northwestern University. Between 1904 and 1920, Shipstead practiced dentistry in Glenwood, Minnesota, and became active in local politics. He was elected mayor of Glenwood in 1910, and in 1916, he won a term in the state legislature. In 1920, Shipstead moved to Minneapolis and joined the Farmer-Labor Party. He quickly earned a reputation as a progressive, and in 1922, he was elected to the U.S. Senate. In the Senate, he actively supported progressive causes, including the McNary-Haugen Bill, federal development of Muscle Shoals, and the 1924 presidential candidacy of Robert M. La Follette.* Shipstead was reelected to the Senate in 1928 and 1934. During the 1930s, he for the most part backed Franklin D. Roosevelt* and the New Deal,* joining forces with Democrats and progressive Republicans. When the Farmer-Labor movement disintegrated in the late 1930s, Shipstead joined the Republican Party. He was reelected to the Senate in 1940 but failed in his 1946 Senate bid. Henrik Shipstead died on June 26, 1960.

SUGGESTED READINGS: *New York Times*, June 27, 1960; Murray S. Stedman and Susan W. Stedman, *Discontent at the Polls: A Study of Farmer and Labor Parties, 1827–1948*, 1967.

SHOUSE, JOUETT. Jouett Shouse was born on December 10, 1879, in Woodford County, Kentucky. Shouse had eclectic interests. He studied at the University of Missouri and then took law courses at the University of Miami, but Shouse preferred business to law. Between 1898 and 1911, he ran several businesses in Lexington, Kentucky, but then moved out to Kansas, where he tried his hand at the cattle business. Shouse won a seat in the state legislature in 1912, and in 1914 he was elected as a Democrat to Congress. Shouse left Congress late in the Woodrow Wilson administration to work as assistant secretary of the treasury, and when President Warren G. Harding and the Republicans took over Washington, D.C., in 1921, Shouse joined a Washington, D.C., law firm.

Between 1928 and 1932, Shouse served as chairman of the Democratic National Committee, and he backed Governor Franklin D. Roosevelt's* 1932 run for the presidency. But once Roosevelt was in office, Shouse quickly grew disenchanted. The New Deal* was far too liberal for him and concentrated far too much power in the federal government. Deficit spending and massive bureaucracies frightened him, and he found himself more comfortable with the conservative views of the Wall Street crowd. In 1934, Shouse was a founding member of the anti-Roosevelt, anti–New Deal American Liberty League* (ALL), serving as the ALL's president until its dissolution in 1940. Shouse endorsed Republicans Alf Landon* and Wendell Willkie* for president in 1936 and 1940, respectively. Shouse remained in the private practice of law until his death on June 2, 1968.

SUGGESTED READINGS: *New York Times*, June 3, 1968; George Wolfskill and John A. Hudson, *All But the People. Franklin D. Roosevelt and His Critics, 1933–1939*, 1969.

SILVER PURCHASE ACT OF 1934. Ever since the 1880s and 1890s, midwestern and southern farmers and western miners had pitched currency expansion as the answer to deflation, and when the Great Depression of the 1930s pushed prices down, they resurrected the idea of expanding currency volumes through purchases of silver. During the 1920s, western mining and farming interests had suffered when agricultural commodity and metal prices declined while costs held steady. In the U.S. Senate, western senators—particularly Key Pittman* of Nevada, Burton K. Wheeler* of Montana, William Borah* of Idaho, and William King of Utah—argued that expanding the stock of monetary silver would ease the gold shortage, increase the money supply, raise silver prices, and increase farm purchasing power. U.S. government purchases of silver would also boost employment in western silver mines. Some of the proposals bordered on the ludicrous. Congressman Martin Dies of Texas demanded the export of all agricultural surpluses in exchange for silver. Senator Wheeler resurrected the old Populist proposal for free coinage of silver at the rate of sixteen to one. Congressman William Fiesinger of Ohio went even further, calling for the federal government to buy 50 million ounces of silver monthly until 1 billion ounces had been purchased.

President Franklin D. Roosevelt* found all of these proposals too radical, but he also understood political reality. Large numbers of Americans in the western states wanted some federal action on the silver question, and FDR needed to appease them. He approved Senator Elmer Thomas's* amendment to the Agricultural Adjustment Act of 1933,* which empowered the Department of the Treasury to exchange silver certificates for silver bullion. And to ratify the Silver Agreement the United States had signed at the London Economic Conference of 1933,* the president ordered the Treasury to purchase all newly mined domestic silver. Roosevelt also decided to sign the Silver Purchase Act of 1934, which ordered that the ratio of silver to gold in the money supply be increased until it reached one-third or until the price of silver hit $1.29 an ounce. Under the law, the Department of the Treasury would then issue silver certificates equal to the amount of silver purchased. The president would also nationalize silver stocks at a price not to exceed $0.50 per ounce.

Farm interests hailed the legislation, as did western mining interests, but the only real beneficiaries of the Silver Purchase Act of 1934 were miners and mining companies. The president had pursued the silver plan for political, not economic, reasons. After his experiences in 1933–1934 with the commodity dollar schemes of Irving Fischer* and George Warren,* he had no faith in monetary tinkering to stimulate the economy.

The Silver Purchase Act had little impact on the domestic economy, but it wreaked havoc overseas in countries whose monetary systems were based on the silver standard. Because silver prices in the United States were artificially high, silver moved from overseas markets to the United States. As those countries lost bullion to the United States, their own money markets destabilized.

SUGGESTED READING: John A. Breenan, *Silver and the First New Deal*, 1969.

SILVER SHIRTS. The Silver Shirts was an anti–Franklin D. Roosevelt,* anti–New Deal* fascist organization of the 1930s, led by William Dudley Pelley. Pelley launched the Silver Shirts within months of Adolf Hitler's rise to power in Germany* in 1933. The purpose of the Silver Shirts, Pelley claimed, was to destroy the "Dutch Jew Franklin Roosevelt" and the "Communist New Deal." For Pelley, the New Deal was nothing more than "the penetration of a predominantly Christian country and Christian government, by predatory, megalomaniac Israelites and their agents." Pelley kept up his crusade throughout the 1930s, but he was indicted for securities fraud as well. He was also convicted of sedition in 1942 and spent eight years in prison. Without his charismatic leadership, the Silver Shirts disappeared. Pelley died on July 1, 1965.

SUGGESTED READING: George Wolfskill and John A. Hudson, *All But the People. Franklin D. Roosevelt and His Critics, 1933–1939*, 1969.

SIMPSON, JOHN A. John Simpson, the champion of poor farmers during the 1920s and 1930s, was born on July 4, 1871, in Salem, Nebraska. In 1896 he graduated from the University of Kansas with a teaching degree and then spent four years in the public schools. Simpson then became an accountant for the state. In 1907, he got a job as a banker, and it introduced him to farm economics and farm politics. In 1917, he was elected president of the Oklahoma Farmers'

Union. Simpson spent the next fourteen years with the Oklahoma Farmers' Union, and in 1931, he was elected president of the National Farmers' Union.*

During the 1920s, Simpson had become increasingly politicized as he watched small farmers suffer the consequences of heavy debt burdens, overproduction, and falling commodity prices. Large commercial farmers, though pressured, seemed to survive the economic storm, but small farmers went bankrupt by the millions. Simpson especially resented the policies of the American Farm Bureau Federation,* which represented the interests of large commercial farmers. He made the National Farmers' Union the political organ of small family farmers.

With the advent of the New Deal,* Simpson backed the Agricultural Adjustment Administration,* even though he felt that it was primarily beneficial to large commercial farmers. He also urged upon President Franklin D. Roosevelt* a series of measures designed to relieve the mortgage and credit problems of small farmers. John Simpson died on March 15, 1934.

SUGGESTED READINGS: *New York Times*, March 16, 1934; William P. Tucker, "Populism Up-to-Date: The Story of the Farmers' Union," *Agricultural History*, 21 (1947), 198–208.

SINCLAIR, UPTON BEALL. Upton Sinclair, who became famous in the United States in 1906 with the publication of his novel *The Jungle*, was born on September 20, 1878, in Baltimore, Maryland. In 1897, he graduated from the City College of New York and then supported himself as a freelance writer. In 1906 the avowed socialist, who considered capitalism the source of evil in the modern industrial world, wrote *The Jungle*, which exposed to millions of readers the problems of the meatpacking industry in Chicago. Ironically, Sinclair's novel was designed as an exposé of the trials of immigrant life in America, but most American readers remembered little about that and a great deal about what went into the sausage. President Theodore Roosevelt read the novel, and partly as a result of an outpouring of public concern about meatpacking and food processing, Congress passed the Meat Inspection Act of 1906 and the Pure Food and Drug Act of 1906. Sinclair continued his writing career, although none of his later works earned him the notoriety of *The Jungle*. Among his other books before the onset of the Great Depression were *The Metropolis* (1908), *King Coal* (1917), *The Profits of Religion* (1918), *The Brass Check* (1919), *Mammonart* (1925), *Oil!* (1927), and *Boston* (1928).

When the country slipped into the Great Depression, Sinclair was convinced, as were so many other socialists, that capitalism would die of its own weight. He became politically active himself, running for governor of California as a Democrat in 1934 on a slogan of "End Poverty in California." His proposals were radical, including confiscation of excess wealth and state nationalization of major business enterprises. Sinclair lost the election, but he ran a good enough campaign to strike fear into Republican Governor Frank Merriam.

Sinclair then resumed his writing career. During the 1930s he wrote *Co-Op*

(1936), *The Flivver King: A Story of Ford-America* (1937), and *Little Steel* (1938). Between 1940 and 1953, he enjoyed huge commercial success with his "Lanny Budd" novels, beginning with *World's End in* 1940. In 1943 he won a Pulitzer Prize for his novel *Dragon's Teeth* (1942). By the time of his death on November 25, 1968, Upton Sinclair had become the dean of American letters.

SUGGESTED READINGS: William A. Bloodsworth, *Upton Sinclair*, 1977; Len Harris, *Upton Sinclair, American Rebel*, 1975; Upton Sinclair, *The Autobiography of Upton Sinclair*, 1962; Barbara Tyson, "Upton Beall Sinclair," in James S. Olson, ed., *Historical Dictionary of the New Deal*, 1985.

SMALL BUSINESS CONFERENCE OF 1938. See **NATIONAL SMALL BUSINESS MEN'S ASSOCIATION**.

SMITH, ALFRED EMMANUEL. Al Smith, the prominent Democrat during the 1920s, was born in New York City on December 30, 1873, to an Irish American family. Smith's neighborhood was Irish, Roman Catholic, working-class, and immigrant, and he absorbed and then radiated that culture. Smith's father died in 1873, and he had to quit school to go to work and support the family. Even as an adolescent, Smith became active in New York City's Fourth Ward, and in 1903, after earning considerable support in the Democratic Party, he won a seat in the state legislature. An excellent politician, Smith was dutiful in his attendance to constituent needs, loyal to party leaders, and particularly adept at legislative politicking. In 1911 he won election as majority leader of the state assembly, and in 1912 he became speaker of the assembly.

The Triangle Shirtwaist Fire of 1911 gave Smith a cause, and he became a strong advocate of social welfare legislation, workers' rights, abolition of child labor, workmen's compensation, and regulation of corporate monopolies. In 1918, Smith was elected governor of New York, failed in his 1920 reelection bid, and then won the governorship in 1922 and was reelected in 1924 and 1926. As governor, he promoted public housing for the poor, conservation, workmen's compensation, limits on child labor, public health programs, and public works jobs for the unemployed. He also became a national figure and the most prominent member of the Democratic Party.

In 1928, he won the Democratic nomination for president, and he ran against Republican Herbert Hoover.* But Smith faced two great obstacles in his bid for the presidency. First, Hoover and the Republicans took credit for the prosperity of the 1920s, and Smith had a difficult time criticizing them. Second, his Roman Catholicism and opposition to Prohibition proved to be a huge disadvantage in the South, where Democratic presidential candidates could usually count on solid support. Hoover won in a landslide. He then returned to private practice.

Franklin D. Roosevelt* had won the New York governorship in 1928, and he soon replaced Smith as the nation's most prominent Democrat. Smith grew jealous and then critical of Roosevelt, and when Roosevelt won the presidency in 1932, Smith's jealousy increased. Smith became permanently alienated from the New Deal* and a severe critic of Roosevelt, accusing the presidency of burdening the country with a huge bureaucracy and leading the country down the road to socialism. He became a leading figure with the anti-Roosevelt American Liberty League,* and in 1936 and 1940, he endorsed the Republican candidates—Alf Landon* and Wendell Willkie,* respectively—for the presidency. Roosevelt's triumphant reelections both times revealed just how far out of step with the public mood Al Smith had become. He died on October 4, 1944.

SUGGESTED READINGS: Oscar Handlin, *Al Smith and His America*, 1958; *New York Times*, October 5, 1944.

SMITH, ELLISON DURANT. Ellison Smith, the political nemesis of President Franklin D. Roosevelt* during the 1930s, was born on August 1, 1864, in Lynchburg, South Carolina. He was an unreconstructed southern Democrat who hated Republicans and the federal government and protected at all costs the interests of cotton farmers. In 1905, Smith had founded the Southern Cotton Association, which became a leading trade organization, and he was nicknamed "Cotton Ed" Smith because of his devotion to the cause. Smith was a member of Congress from 1896 to 1900, and in 1908, he won a seat in the U.S. Senate.

During the 1930s, the drift of the New Deal* contrasted sharply with Smith's race consciousness, class consciousness, and sectional pride. Smith's mind never left the bitterness of the Civil War and Reconstruction. Although he sat on the political fence during the early New Deal, Smith became an avowed opponent of the president after 1935. He opposed the Public Utility Holding Company Act,* the Wealth Tax Act,* and the court-packing scheme.* In the congressional elections of 1938,* the president personally campaigned in South Carolina against Smith, but the strategy backfired, and Smith was reelected by a landslide. Smith was reelected to another term in 1944, but he died on November 17, 1944.

SUGGESTED READINGS: *New York Times*, November 18–19, 1944; James T. Patterson, *Congressional Conservatism and the New Deal*, 1967.

SMITH, GERALD LYMAN KENNETH. Gerald L. K. Smith was born on February 27, 1898, in Pardeeville, Wisconsin. In 1917 he graduated from Valparaiso University and then attended Butler University in Indianapolis, Indiana. In Indiana, Smith became active in the Ku Klux Klan and its crusade against blacks, Jews, Catholics, and immigrants. In 1928 he moved to Shreveport, Louisiana, and became a Church of Christ minister, just as his father, grandfather, and great-grandfather had been. His career soon assumed a political dimension. Smith struck a responsive chord in his poor, working-class congregations by attacking the greed, wealth, and corruption of corporate America. Such themes resonated well in rural Louisiana. Smith then managed to get Governor Huey

P. Long* of Louisiana to stop all state foreclosure proceedings against poor people in northern Louisiana. In 1930, when Long won a seat in the U.S. Senate, Smith began writing speeches for him and became national director of Long's system of "Share Our Wealth" clubs. Although Share Our Wealth's proposals were vague, it attracted considerable loyalty among the rural poor because of its promises of government public works construction jobs and its promise to redistribute income.

After Long's assassination, Smith inherited his Populist mantle. Smith tried to seize control of "Share Our Wealth," but he had no influence or control over Long's political machine in Louisiana. Smith left Louisiana for Washington, D.C., where he joined Francis Townsend's* crusade for old-age pensions. Actually, Smith's politics were far more extreme than Townsend's. Smith said he wanted to rid the country of "Franklin Delano Jewsvelt" and his "Communist New Deal."

In 1936, Smith teamed up with Townsend's Old-Age Revolving Pensions, Ltd., and Roman Catholic Father Charles Coughlin's* National Union for Social Justice, another anti–New Deal* lobby. They formed the Union Party* and nominated Smith for president. The campaign self-destructed when Smith condemned Jews and Catholics and called for the organization of an army of white, young American men to arm themselves, march on Washington, D.C., and seize control of the federal government. The proposal struck most Americans as insane, and Smith's campaign died.

He then set about organizing a pro-fascist movement in the United States. Smith opposed U.S. entrance into World War II and organized the America First Party to promote isolationism. His pro-fascist newspaper *The Cross and the Flag* published Smith's ideas widely. In 1944, Smith ran for president as the nominee of the America First Party, with his campaign theme being "Create a white, Christian America." In 1947, Smith formed the Christian Nationalist Crusade, which called for the deportation of all Jewish Zionists, the deportation of all blacks back to Africa, and the destruction of all black and Jewish organizations. On April 15, 1976, Smith died in Glendale, California.

SUGGESTED READINGS: David H. Bennett, *Demagogues in the Depression. American Radicals and the Union Party, 1932–1936*, 1969; *New York Times*, April 16, 1976.

SMITH, KATE. Kate Smith was born on May 1, 1907, in Washington, D.C. Blessed with a powerful contralto singing voice, she worked the vaudeville circuits in the 1920s, often becoming the object of cruel jokes because of her weight. In 1930, an executive from Columbia Records heard her act and signed her to make a record. CBS Radio then made a star of Smith. In 1937, *The Kate Smith Show* became one of the most popular variety programs on radio, and in 1938, Irving Berlin* let her debut his new song "God Bless America," which became a Smith trademark. Smith became known as the "First Lady of Radio." Smith died on June 17, 1986.

SUGGESTED READINGS: *New York Times*, June 18, 1986; Kate Smith, *Upon My Lips a Song*, 1960.

SMOOT, REED. Reed Smoot, one of the Republican Party's most conservative figures in the 1920s and early 1930s, was born in Salt Lake City, Utah, on January 10, 1862. He graduated from Brigham Young Academy, later Brigham Young University, in 1879 and built a successful career in ranching, insurance, real estate, and banking. A devout Mormon, he became influential in the hierarchy of the Church of Jesus Christ of Latter-day Saints, being named an apostle in 1900. In 1902, Smoot ran as a Republican and won a seat from Utah in the U.S. Senate.

His election precipitated an enormous controversy in Congress when evangelical Protestants opposed his seating in the Senate on the grounds of his membership in the Mormon Church, which had so recently supported polygamy. The Senate investigated the case, but Smoot was finally seated. For the next thirty years, he served as a member of the Republican Old Guard, a body of conservatives who favored high protective tariffs, cuts in federal spending, tax breaks for the rich, and an isolationist foreign policy. Throughout the 1920s, Smoot chaired the powerful Senate Finance Committee, where he tried to promote his ideas.

With the advent of the Great Depression, Smoot's ideas quickly became anachronistic. As unemployment mounted in 1930 and 1931, demands for federal intervention, with relief and public works construction, intensified, but Smoot remained faithful to his conservative views, opposing almost all initiatives that would augment the power and size of the federal government. Like other conservative Republicans, Smoot lost political influence in those two years, even in Utah, a traditionally conservative state. When he ran for reelection in 1932, in spite of the fact that he was an apostle in the Mormon Church and most Utah voters were Mormon, Smoot lost. He retired to private life and his business interests. Reed Smoot died on February 9, 1941.

SUGGESTED READING: *New York Times*, February 10, 1941.

SNICKERS. In 1930, the Mars Company launched the Snickers candy bar, a candy bar consisting of nougat, caramel, and peanuts, all covered with thick milk chocolate, which sold at that time for 5¢. In spite of a weak economy, the candy bar was an immediate hit with consumers and soon became one of the company's most important products.

SUGGESTED READING: Lorraine Glennon, ed., *Our Times: The Illustrated History of the Twentieth Century*, 1995.

SNOW WHITE AND THE SEVEN DWARFS. Walt Disney's *Snow White and the Seven Dwarfs* was released in 1937 at Christmastime as the first full-length animated film in history. Disney adapted the story from one of the Grimms' fairy tales and fashioned an eighty-two-minute film out of it. Until *Snow White*, Disney's cartoons, or animated shorts, had featured animals like Mickey Mouse. *Snow White and the Seven Dwarfs* had people as the protagonists. Each of the seven dwarfs had a sharply defined personality, and the story was a classic tale of a virtuous young woman, an evil, wicked mother figure, and a happy ending with a rescue by a noble prince. The film received rave reviews and was a box-office smash, giving depression-battered Americans the escapist fare they so desperately needed.

SUGGESTED READING: Steven Watts, *Magic Kingdom: Walt Disney and the American Way of Life*, 1997.

SOCIALIST PARTY. The Socialist Party of America was founded in 1901, with Eugene V. Debs at its head. Debs remained at the helm until 1928, when Norman Thomas* succeeded him. In the presidential election campaigns of 1928, 1932,* and 1936,* Thomas called for nationalization of major American industries; increased federal public works construction and relief programs; minimum wage and maximum hours legislation for workers; government refinancing of farm and home mortgages; U.S. membership in the League of Nations; and federal systems of unemployment, old-age, and medical insurance.

Although Thomas was convinced that the Great Depression would usher in an era of socialism in the United States, most Americans had no interest in any political scheme that purported to take away people's private property. Thomas managed 267,835 votes in the presidential election of 1928 and then lost ground. He won only 881,951 votes in 1932 and 187,720 in 1936. In 1940, when he added isolationism to his socialism, he secured only 99,557 votes, proving the bankruptcy of socialism as a political philosophy in the United States. He simply could not overcome the boundless faith Americans had in the future, their respect for private property, and the popularity of New Deal* reforms.

SUGGESTED READINGS: David A. Shannon, *The Socialist Party of America*, 1955; Frank A. Warren, *An Alternative Vision: The Socialist Party in the 1930s*, 1974.

SOCIAL SECURITY ACT OF 1935. Ever since the early 1900s, social welfare advocates had called for the creation of a federal system of old-age insurance. By the 1920s, compulsory social insurance programs had become common in Europe, but bills submitted to Congress in the 1920s by Congressman William Connery of Massachusetts and Senator Clarence Dill of Washington failed. Too many Americans believed that family and local charities should take care of the elderly, not the federal government. The onset of the Great Depression after 1929 had intensified the demands, and in 1929 Abraham Epstein* established the American Association for Old-Age Security to promote a comprehensive federal insurance program. Pressure for a federal pension system became more politically compelling when Francis Townsend* established his Old-Age Revolving Pensions, Ltd., which campaigned for pensions and attracted substantial political support. In 1932 the American Federation of Labor* had endorsed the idea.

In June 1934, President Franklin D. Roosevelt* established the Committee on Economic Security,* headed by Secretary of Labor Frances Perkins,* to study the issue. The committee came up with a national system of federal old-age insurance financed by contributions from farm employers and workers. They also called for a federal-state system of unemployment insurance. Senator Robert Wagner* of New York and Congressman David Lewis of Maryland introduced the legislation to Congress. The bill inspired intense opposition. Conservative businessmen argued that the taxes would break them and lead the country down the road to socialism. Many southerners rejected the bill because it offered benefits to African Americans. Followers of Francis Townsend said the benefits were inadequate, far below the $200 per person per month Townsend had proposed. Such social welfare advocates as Abraham Epstein and Isaac Rubinow did not like the financing scheme. They preferred funding the program out of general revenues, not from taxes on workers and employers.

But the idea of old-age pensions enjoyed growing public support. Congress passed the law and President Roosevelt signed it on August 14, 1935. It established a Social Security Board to provide for unemployment compensation, old-age insurance, assistance to the destitute blind, and assistance for homeless, crippled, dependent, and delinquent children. The legislation established a federal-state system of unemployment compensation, financed by a federal tax on employer payrolls equal to 1 percent in 1936, 2 percent in 1937, and 3 percent thereafter. Each state administered its own program. The program for old-age and survivor's insurance was financed by equal taxes on employers and employees of 1 percent in 1937 and increasing to 3 percent by 1949. The money would accumulate in a national fund until January 1, 1942, when pensions would begin to be paid to people sixty-five years of age and older.

SUGGESTED READING: Roy Lubove, *The Struggle for Social Security 1900–1935*, 1968.

SOIL CONSERVATION ACT OF 1935. In 1934 and 1935, devastating droughts hit the Great Plains; and then rain, when it came, resulted in severe flooding and soil erosion. Midwestern farming interests began demanding federal action to deal with the problem, and Congress responded with the Soil Conservation Act of 1935. The law established soil conservation districts throughout the country, and using workers from the Civilian Conservation Corps* and later the Works Progress Administration,* a Soil Conservation Service in the Department of Agriculture conducted research on wind and water erosion and land-use planning, loaned funds to farmers to plant grasses and trees to hold down soil, and taught farmers how to employ strip cropping, terracing, and crop rotation techniques, all of which helped reduce soil erosion.

SUGGESTED READING: Richard Lowitt, *The New Deal and the West*, 1984.

SOIL CONSERVATION AND DOMESTIC ALLOTMENT ACT OF 1936. On January 6, 1936, in its *United States v. Butler** decision, the Supreme Court declared the Agricultural Adjustment Act of 1933* unconstitutional, which all but destroyed the New Deal's* farm recovery program. The Court ruled that the law's provisions placing federal controls on crop production and its tax on processors were unconstitutional. President Franklin D. Roosevelt* and the New Deal responded immediately, and Congress passed the Soil Conservation and Domestic Allotment Act. Roosevelt signed it into law on February 29, 1936. Instead of using a tax on processors to force reductions in production, the new measure used general revenues to take land out of production for "conservation" reasons. Everybody knew what Roosevelt was trying to do, and most farmers did not miss a check in the transition from one program to the other. The legislation authorized payments to farmers not to grow such "soil-depleting" crops as cotton, corn, tobacco, and wheat and to plant "soil-preserving" crops like alfalfa, clover, or hay. Another payment to farmers was authorized if they would purchase lime, potash, and phosphate fertilizers to restore soil fertility and to terrace their fields. In the end, the legislation did not succeed in really cutting the number of acres planted or the yields per acre. Large production increases in 1937 led to the Agricultural Adjustment Act of 1938.*

SUGGESTED READING: Dean Albertson, *Roosevelt's Farmer: Claude R. Wickard and the New Deal*, 1961.

SOKOLOFF, NIKOLAI. Nikolai Sokoloff was born on May 28, 1886, in Russia. A child prodigy, he was playing the violin with the Kiev municipal orchestra when he was only ten years old. Sokoloff immigrated to the United States in 1898, and in 1899, at the age of thirteen, he won a scholarship to study music at Yale. Sokoloff spent three years at Yale before becoming a violinist for the Boston Symphony Orchestra. In 1920, he became the Cleveland Orchestra's first conductor. He remained there for fifteen years, leaving only to become head of the Federal Music Project* in the Works Progress Administration* (WPA) in 1935. Under Sokoloff's direction, the Federal Music Project became the most successful of the WPA's art programs. Sokoloff left the Federal Music Project in 1939 and died on September 24, 1965.

SUGGESTED READINGS: William F. McDonald, *Federal Relief Administration and the Arts*, 1969; *New York Times*, September 25–26, 1965.

SOUTHERN TENANT FARMERS' UNION. During the 1930s, rural poverty became a terrible problem, and some New Deal* programs actually made matters worse for the poorest farm families. The Agricultural Adjustment Administration* (AAA) paid farmers not to grow in order to reduce crop surpluses, and although the Agricultural Adjustment Act of 1933* contained provisions to make sure that farm tenants saw some of that money, large landowners found ways to keep the bulk of the money for themselves. Also, by taking land out of production, the Agricultural Adjustment Administration increased unemployment among farm tenants, who no longer had land to work.

In 1934, the plight of poor tenant farmers in the South inspired Henry Clay East and Harry Leland Mitchell of Tyronza, Arkansas, to establish the Southern Tenant Farmers' Union (SFTU). Both men were socialists who had taken a suggestion from Socialist leader Norman Thomas* to found the group. The SFTU had a racial open-door policy, welcoming black and white tenant farmers into the union. In doing so, the SFTU inspired the wrath of white racists and large commercial farmers who feared losing their economic prerogatives.

At first, the SFTU concentrated on investigating and complaining about abuse of AAA policies by large commercial farmers, and planters reacted with hostility. SFTU organizers were harassed, beaten up, and arrested on charges of anarchy. Some were murdered. Hostility increased in 1935 when the SFTU urged its members to strike for higher wages for picking cotton. The SFTU implemented the strike during picking season when the planters were most vulnerable economically. The strike succeeded, and planters agreed to nearly double the pay of pickers.

The existence of the SFTU brought media attention to the problem of rural poverty, and in November 1936, President Franklin D. Roosevelt* established the Special Committee on Farm Tenancy to investigate the problem of rural poverty. As a result of the committee's report, Roosevelt proposed and Congress created the Farm Security Administration* in 1937. Later in the decade, the SFTU fell victim to jurisdictional disputes within its own membership. SFTU communists wanted to affiliate with the United Cannery, Agricultural, Packing, and Allied Workers of America, while socialists in the SFTU simply wanted to become an independent affiliate of the Congress of Industrial Organizations.* During World War II, the Southern Tenant Farmers' Union disintegrated.

SUGGESTED READINGS: David L. Chapman, "The Southern Tenant Farmers' Union," in James S. Olson, ed., *Historical Dictionary of the New Deal*, 1985; David E. Conrad, *The Forgotten Farmers: The Story of the Sharecroppers in the New Deal*, 1965; Donald H. Grubbs, *Cry from the Cotton: The Southern Tenant Farmers' Union and the New Deal*, 1971.

SOVIET UNION. When the Bolsheviks first assumed power after the Russian Revolution, the United States refused to extend diplomatic recognition to the Soviet Union, insisting that its communist ideology rendered the government illegitimate. The United States maintained that stance until 1933. By that time, the unprecedented downturn in the economy and the severe unemployment problem left the new Franklin D. Roosevelt* administration anxious to stimulate international trade. The United States extended diplomatic recognition to the Soviet Union in order to pave the way for improved trading relationships.

At the same time, Soviet Premier Joseph Stalin was consolidating his power. On December 1, 1934, Leonid Nikolaev, one of the dictator's most violent enforcers, assassinated Sergei Kirov, a leading member of the Communist Party who openly disagreed with Stalin. Although Stalin engineered the assassination, he feigned horror and gave Kirov a hero's funeral. At the same time, he used the assassination to blame so-called counterrevolutionaries, who simply happened to be his political rivals. Stalin instituted a series of high-publicity show trials, convictions, and executions, and he also used the killing of Kirov to launch what became known as the "Great Purge" of the Communist Party— mass killings of political rivals, would-be rivals, possible rivals, and future rivals, along with their families. Historians cannot find a bloodier example of political megalomania than the Great Purge.

The Great Purge lasted from 1935 to 1938, during which time Stalin's secret police arrested more than 5 million people. Most of them were summarily executed; other spent years in the "gulag," Stalin's massive system of forced labor camps and prisons. Most of those arrested were charged with plotting to assassinate Stalin and other top Soviet leaders, although the charges were trumped up. The entire country became gripped by a paranoia unprecedented in the history of the world.

By the late 1930s, as Adolf Hitler increased his power in Germany* and assumed aggressive military and diplomatic policies, Stalin became increasingly concerned about the possibility of war. Throughout history, Russia had suffered a series of disastrous invasions from the West, and Stalin wanted to provide the Soviet Union with a geographic edge in case a subsequent invasion ensued. Stalin was also interested in regaining territory that had been Russia's until after World War I. At the Treaty of Versailles, Latvia, Lithuania, Estonia, and Poland* had become independent countries, but before World War I, each had been partially or completely Russian territory. Stalin wanted them back. Doing so would also give him a geographic buffer between Germany and the Soviet Union. In 1939, Stalin signed the German-Soviet Non-Aggression Treaty, in which the two countries agreed not to launch military action against one another. The treaty was, of course, a cynical sham. Secret protocols permitted Germany, during a period of "territorial and political transformation," to occupy the western third of Poland and the Soviet Union to occupy the eastern two-thirds of Poland. Stalin wanted eastern Poland to stand as a buffer zone between western Russia and Germany in the event of a German invasion. And Adolf Hitler wanted a staging area in western Poland for an eventual German invasion of the Soviet Union. In September 1939, when Germany invaded and conquered

Poland, the secret protocols were implemented. The Soviet army quickly occupied eastern Poland.

In 1939, to protect the Soviet Union, especially Leningrad, from German aggression, Stalin launched the Russo-Finnish War.* The Finns put up a spirited defense, stalling the Soviet invasion and inflicting hundreds of thousands of casualties on the enemy. But in the end, Finland's 125,000 soldiers could not hold off the Soviet army. After three months, the Soviets Union finally overwhelmed the Finns, and Stalin had his buffer zone protecting the northwestern region of the Soviet Union from Germany. Even that, however, would eventually prove inadequate when Germany finally did invade in June 1941.

SUGGESTED READINGS: Allan Bullock, *Hitler and Stalin*, 1992; Adam Ulam, *Stalin: The Man and His Era*, 1973.

SPANISH CIVIL WAR. During the 1920s and 1930s, much of Europe slipped into the grip of totalitarianism. Benito Mussolini had already taken Italy* down the road to fascism, and in the Soviet Union,* Joseph Stalin had created a police state that would eventually liquidate tens of millions of its own people. In Germany,* Adolf Hitler and his National Socialist Party assumed an iron hand that would soon lead to the Holocaust and to World War II. For a time, it appeared that Spain would escape dictatorship and enthrone democracy. The Spanish people, depressed with being Europe's poorest country and frustrated with the incompetent rule of King Alfonso XIII and Prime Minister Primo de Rivera, were ripe for political change. In April 1931, the king called for municipal elections, and to his astonishment, Spanish voters selected antimonarchist candidates in overwhelming numbers. When Spanish military authorities refused to guarantee Alfonso's safety, the king abdicated and fled to France.

Elections were held in June 1931, and a liberal, Manuel Azana, became prime minister and moderate Niceto Alcala Zamora became president. Together they launched an ambitious program of school construction, legalized divorce, promised autonomy to Catalonia, and implemented legal measures to bring about a separation of church and state. Such reforms angered conservatives, and the liberal failure to implement genuine land reform alienated the Left. Over the course of the next several years, the political base supporting Spain's new and moderate democratic government slowly eroded. The liberal government also alienated large numbers of peasants in May 1932 when the national legislature outlawed parochial schools, prohibited the Jesuit order, and nationalized church property.

In November 1933, the Spanish Confederation of Autonomous Rights—a coalition of conservatives, monarchists, Catholics, and fascists, or falangists— won parliamentary elections and established a government committed to the destruction of Marxists, Masons, Separatists, and Jews. They also promised to restore the Roman Catholic Church to its privileged position in Spanish society.

Various socialist, communist, and separatist groups staged rebellions against the government. The rebellion in Asturias involved more than 50,000 people, and the government deployed General Francisco Franco, commander of Spain's foreign legion troops, to crush the insurrection. He did so ruthlessly, castrating captured rebel men and raping and mutilating rebel women. Any idea even resembling socialism or liberalism, let alone communism, was crushed.

A backlash soon set in, and when new elections were held in February 1936, the Popular Front, a coalition of liberals and socialists, took control of the government. Throughout the spring and early summer, Spain disintegrated into anarchy, with communists and fascists battling in the streets. Attacks on Catholic churches, assassinations, street riots, and factory seizures became all too common, and in July 1936, generals in the Spanish army, led by General Francisco Franco, rebelled. Franco entered Spain with his troops from Spanish Morocco. With financial backing from Adolf Hitler and Benito Mussolini, Franco attacked the government. The Soviet Union, aghast at the possibility of another fascist government in Europe, shipped money and supplies to the republic's defenders. Spain was soon engulfed in total civil war.

The bloody Spanish Civil War did not come to an end until March 1939 when Francisco Franco led an army of Nationalist troops into Madrid. His final triumph had actually begun the previous summer, when the Republican offensive along the Ebro River failed to overwhelm and break the Nationalist control of Catalonia. In January 1938 Franco had taken Barcelona, which broke the back of Republican resistance. The Soviet Union then terminated military and financial assistance to the Republicans, which doomed them. The fact that Franco's Nationalists also had complete air superiority over Republican forces guaranteed victory. Finally, in September 1938, when Great Britain and France signed the Munich Pact with Germany, giving Hitler a virtually free hand in Czechoslovakia,* the Republicans in Spain realized that the Western powers were not about to come to the assistance of their movement.

When the final death toll was counted, a total of 90,000 Nationalists had died in the civil war, along with 110,000 Republicans, with millions wounded. During the fighting, tens of thousands of civilians had either starved to death or been accidentally killed by collateral fire. Another 500,000 Spaniards had gone into exile. And in the wake of the Nationalist victory, Franco hunted down thousands of Republicans and prominent Republican sympathizers and had them executed.

But then Franco returned to a somewhat more moderate position than what his fascist colleagues in Germany and Italy had imposed. Although his Falange Party was the only legal party in Spain, Franco did not ruthlessly crush and eliminate all other political opposition, and he allowed the Catholic Church to regain some of its former political power. During World War II, Franco kept close ties to Adolf Hitler in Germany and Benito Mussolini in Italy, but he also proclaimed Spanish neutrality, wisely concluding that the civil war had drained the country of any desire for military adventurism.

SUGGESTED READINGS: Peter Pierson, *A History of Spain*, 1999; Michael Ugarte, *Shifting Ground: Spanish Civil War Exile Literature*, 1989.

SPECIAL COMMITTEE ON FARM TENANCY. See FARM SECURITY ADMINISTRATION.

STEAGALL, HENRY BASCOM.

Henry Steagall was born on May 19, 1873, in Clopton, Alabama. He earned a law degree from the University of Alabama and then practiced law in Ozark, Alabama. He was active in local Democratic Party politics and had a Populist streak that gave him some sympathy for the suffering of poor people. Steagall served one term in the state legislature, and in 1914, he won a seat in Congress. He held the seat for the next fourteen years.

Because of his concerns about rural poverty and farm credit, Steagall was assigned to the House Committee on Banking and Currency. He became an early advocate for a program of federal bank deposit insurance, and in 1932 he cosponsored the Glass-Steagall Banking Act, which expanded the definition of commercial paper eligible for rediscount by the Federal Reserve System. The law was designed to help address the liquidity problems that were contributing to the banking crisis.* As soon as Franklin D. Roosevelt* was inaugurated, Steagall pushed the Emergency Banking Act of 1933* through Congress, and two months later he sponsored the Banking Act of 1933,* which created the Federal Deposit Insurance Corporation.* Throughout the 1930s, Steagall faithfully supported most New Deal* programs, although he was somewhat uncomfortable with the centralization of power in the federal government and massive deficit spending. He died on November 22, 1943.

SUGGESTED READINGS: Jack Brian Key, "Henry B. Steagall: The Conservative as Reformer," *Alabama Review*, 17 (1964), 198–209; Jane A. Rosenberg, "Henry Bascom Steagall," in James S. Olson, ed., *Historical Dictionary of the New Deal*, 1985.

STEINBECK, JOHN ERNST.

John Steinbeck, perhaps America's most prominent literary figure during the 1930s, was born in Salinas, California, on February 27, 1902. He attended Stanford University sporadically between 1919 and 1925 and then lived for several years in New York City, where he tried his hand at writing fiction. After moving back to California, Steinbeck in 1929 published his first novel—*Cup of Gold*. A romantic piece of historical fiction based loosely on the life of Sir Henry Morgan, it was not exactly high-quality literature. His first real literary success came in 1935 with the publication of *Tortilla Flat*, a bittersweet comedy about farmworkers in Monterey, California. At that time, Steinbeck became active in the Cannery and Agricultural Workers Industrial Union, which was dominated by communists and gave Steinbeck his sense of class consciousness and sympathy for working-class people. His 1936 book *In Dubious Battle* was about a labor strike and attracted considerable literary and political attention. But Steinbeck was no ideologue. In *In Dubious*

Battle, he pilloried Communist Party organizers who simply used workers to advance their own political objectives.

In 1937, Steinbeck's book *Of Mice and Men* portrayed two poor migrant California farmworkers, one a retarded young man and the other his friend. Poverty-stricken and yet optimistic, they dreamed of getting some land of their own. It was, of course, a pipe dream and disintegrated when the retarded young man killed a woman who happened to be the daughter-in-law of the ranch boss. To protect his retarded friend from prosecution, the other young man shoots him.

After the release of *Of Mice and Men*, Steinbeck traveled widely through the valleys of central California, observing the plight of poor workers. Confined to shanty towns and living in homes made of cardboard or even in lean-tos, they suffered a numbing poverty, and Steinbeck wrote a series of newspaper articles about them. He decided to convert the stories into a novel—*The Grapes of Wrath**—which was published in 1939. It became a runaway bestseller and made Steinbeck's name a household word. The novel described one family— the Joads—of tens of thousands who abandoned Texas, Arkansas, and Oklahoma in the 1930s for California. Of course, Steinbeck became persona non grata to chambers of commerce in Arkansas, Oklahoma, and Texas and to the large commercial farmers in California. *The Grapes of Wrath* became an icon of the Great Depression.

Steinbeck continued to write and played out the role of cause célèbre in the United States. In 1962 he received the Nobel Prize for his work, even though most critics felt his work after the depression was mediocre. John Steinbeck died on December 20, 1968.

SUGGESTED READINGS: Donald V. Coers, "John Steinbeck," in James S. Olson, ed., *Historical Dictionary of the New Deal*, 1985; Warren French, *John Steinbeck*, 1961; Thomas Kiernan, *The Intricate Music: A Biography of John Steinbeck*, 1979.

STIMSON, HENRY LEWIS. Henry L. Stimson was born in New York City on September 21, 1867. In 1888 he graduated from Yale and then earned a law degree at Harvard. Between 1891 and 1899, he practiced law in New York with Elihu Root and then went out on his own. In 1906, President Theodore Roosevelt appointed Stimson U.S. attorney for the southern district of New York, a post that gave him a high political profile. Stimson failed in his 1910 bid for the governorship of New York, but in 1911, President William Howard Taft named Stimson secretary of war. During the 1920s, Stimson practiced law privately and accepted various diplomatic troubleshooting assignments from the Warren G. Harding and Calvin Coolidge administrations. He served as governor-general of the Philippines in 1928 and 1929, and in 1929, President Herbert Hoover* named Stimson secretary of state.

At the State Department, Stimson promoted the Good Neighbor Policy,* but his major challenge revolved around the 1931 Japanese invasion of Manchuria.*

Stimson condemned the invasion, and when Japan* established the puppet Manchukuo government in Manchuria, the United States refused to extend diplomatic recognition, a position that became known as the Stimson Doctrine. The
Japanese invasion had violated the Open Door Notes, the Nine Power Treaty of
1922, and the Kellogg-Briand Pact. But the Stimson Doctrine proved to be weak
and inconclusive, and Japan refused to withdraw from Manchuria. It had become
obvious to Japan that the United States did not like the invasion but would do
nothing militarily to force a Japanese withdrawal.

A Republican, Stimson returned to private life when Democratic President
Franklin D. Roosevelt* was inaugurated in 1933. In 1940, however, Roosevelt
brought him out of retirement to serve as secretary of war. Stimson's appoint-
ment allowed Roosevelt to take a bipartisan approach to foreign policy and then
World War II. Stimson served with distinction and retired in 1945. He died on
October 20, 1950.

SUGGESTED READINGS: Elting E. Morison, *Turmoil and Tradition: A Study of the
Life and Times of Henry L. Stimson*, 1960; *New York Times*, October 21, 1950; Henry
L. Stimson, *The Far Eastern Crisis*, 1936.

STOCK MARKET CRASH. During the 1920s, the stock market in the United
States underwent unprecedented, sustained growth, creating a speculative bubble
that burst in October 1929. An unusual infusion of cash drove stock market
prices ever higher during the early 1920s. Billions of dollars of corporate profits
from World War I found their way into the market, and when the Warren Harding administration (1921–1923) cut taxes on the rich, even more money flowed
into Wall Street. The decision of the Harding administration to pay off the
national debt removed U.S. Treasury securities from the money markets, and
the cash traditionally flowing there was rerouted to Wall Street. Finally, as the
market gained steadily in the early 1920s, many corporations foolishly invested
working capital there, as did many middle-class Americans, who removed
money from bank accounts and bought stocks. Finally, Americans borrowed
billions of dollars, often in margin purchases, in the form of broker loans to
buy even more stocks. The collective impact of such huge cash flows was enormous. The *New York Times* stock index stood at 65 in 1921 and jumped to 134
by the end of 1924, 180 at the end of 1926, 245 at the end of 1927, and 331
at the end of 1928. On August 31, 1929, the index peaked at 449.

The basic problem, however, was that market fundamentals did not justify
such gains. Corporate profits rose steadily, but modestly, during the 1920s, as
did dividends, but such modest dividend growth did not drive the huge capital
gains stockowners experienced. Also, investors had become accustomed to
double-digit annual gains and had become used to no bad stock market news.
The securities markets were extremely vulnerable. On October 23, 1929, the
stock market underwent a severe correction, with the *New York Times* index
falling from 415 to 384. The next day, in which historians remember as "Black
Thursday,"* the rout became a panic, with a record 12,894,650 shares changing

hands and the index plummeting to 372. On "Black Monday,"* October 28, the index dropped 49 points more, and on "Black Tuesday"* another 43 points. By mid-November 1929, the index hit 224. The crash had wiped out 50 percent of all asset values in just a few months. The slide continued intermittently for the next four years, with the index bottoming out at 58 in June 1932. The stock market crash, when combined with weaknesses in the banking system and chronic problems on farms, sent the entire economy into a tailspin that morphed into the Great Depression of the 1930s.

SUGGESTED READINGS: John Kenneth Galbraith, *The Great Crash 1929*, 1955; Robert Sobel, *The Great Bull Market: Wall Street in the 1920s*, 1968.

STONE, HARLAN FISKE. Harlan Fiske Stone was born on October 11, 1872, in Chesterfield, New Hampshire. In 1894 he graduated from Amherst College, and in 1898 he received a law degree from Columbia University. One year later, after opening his own law practice in New York City, Stone joined the law faculty at Columbia. Between 1910 and 1923, he served as dean of the law school at Columbia. In 1924—to restore credibility to the Justice Department in the wake of the Teapot Dome, Veterans' Bureau, and alien property custodian scandals—President Calvin Coolidge appointed Stone as attorney general of the United States. One year later, Coolidge nominated Stone to the U.S. Supreme Court.

Although his family background was conservative and Republican, he developed a pragmatic approach to life and to the law that defied ideological boundaries. At Columbia University, Stone had developed a reputation as a jurist who worked to defend civil liberties. He was also a believer in "sociological jurisprudence"—a judicial philosophy that rejected rigid adherence to legal tradition—and believed that the law was intimately connected to society and the economy and should evolve and adapt to changing circumstances. A Victorian liberal in philosophy, Stone criticized many federal court justices during the 1920s for being too conservative and too ready to protect property rights from legislative encroachment, whether at the state or federal level. The Constitution, for Stone, was a living document that had to be able to change.

On the Supreme Court, Stone soon became part of the dissenting liberal minority, aligned with Louis Brandeis,* Oliver Wendell Holmes, and Benjamin Cardozo.* The other justices—George Sutherland,* Willis Van Devanter,* William Howard Taft, and later Charles Evans Hughes* and Pierce Butler—were far more conservative and wedded to tradition, especially concerning government economic regulation of business. During the early years of the New Deal,* that conservative majority, over Stone's vigorous protests, declared unconstitutional a host of New Deal measures designed to relieve economic suffering. In Stone's opinion, the Constitution empowered the national government to deal with problems national in nature, and the power to govern must of necessity change accordingly to address current problems. Nor did he believe it was the judiciary's job to determine whether or not government problems were poorly designed or even feasible. When the economy entered the Great Depression, Stone became even more impatient with conservative Republican principles, even though he was a close friend of President Herbert Hoover.* He rejected completely all laissez-faire arguments and grew extremely frustrated when the Supreme Court invalidated so much of early New Deal legislation. Later in the 1930s, Stone became the leader of the liberal majority on the Supreme Court, and in 1941, President Franklin D. Roosevelt* named him chief justice. Harlan Fiske Stone died on April 22, 1946.

SUGGESTED READINGS: Alpheus Thomas Mason, *Harlan Fiske Stone: Pillar of the Law*, 1956; *New York Times*, April 23, 1946.

STUDS LONIGAN. *Studs Lonigan* was the title of James T. Farrell's depression-era fictional trilogy. The first volume—*Young Lonigan*—appeared in 1932. The second volume—*The Young Manhood of Studs Lonigan*—was published in 1934. *Judgment Day* came out in 1935. The novels revolved around the Irish American neighborhoods of Chicago—the pool halls, Roman Catholic parishes, saloons, and precinct stations that dotted the South Side and provided Irish Americans with their cultural and social infrastructure. Gritty, realistic, and sexually graphic, *Studs Lonigan* generated real controversy, but it also resonated with Americans in the Great Depression, who had seen their very way of life threatened. Among Irish Americans, according to *Studs Lonigan* at least, the traditional institutions of church, family, and school had disintegrated, leaving individuals bereft in a dangerous world.

SUGGESTED READINGS: James T. Farrell, *Young Lonigan*, 1932; *The Young Manhood of the Studs Lonigan*, 1934; *Judgment Day*, 1935.

SUDETENLAND. See CZECHOSLOVAKIA.

SUPERMAN. In 1938, Jerry Spiegel and Joe Shuster, two comic-book artists, came up with the idea for "Superman," an action hero for the comic book genre. Superman, a man of superhuman strength, had come to earth from a doomed planet to make sure that right triumphed over wrong and that justice was served. Pretending to be journalist Clark Kent, who worked for *The Daily Planet* in a city that closely resembled New York City, Superman thwarted criminals, monsters, and dictators. Spiegel and Shuster sold the rights to Superman to Action Comics, which published the first *Superman* comic book in 1938. The comic book was a runaway hit, and Action Comics eventually published thousands of different Superman stories and tens of millions of copies.

SUGGESTED READINGS: Michael Benton, *The Comic Book in America*, 1989; Will Jacobs and Gerard Jones, *The Comic Book Heroes*, 1985.

SUTHERLAND, GEORGE. George Sutherland was born in Buckingham-shire, England, on March 15, 1862. He was raised in Utah after his parents converted to the Mormon Church and immigrated to the United States. He attended Brigham Young Academy and the University of Michigan Law School. He practiced Law in Provo and Salt Lake City, Utah, where he became active in Republican Party politics. After terms in the territorial and then the state legislature, Sutherland was elected to Congress in 1900, and there his conservative, protectionist ideas flowered. In 1904, Sutherland was elected to the U.S. Senate, and he served two terms. In 1922, President Warren Harding appointed him as an associate justice of the U.S. Supreme Court.

By the 1930s, Sutherland was widely recognized as one of the most conservative of the so-called "Four Horsemen"*—a group of justices adamantly opposed to the expansion of the federal government's scope during the New Deal.* His judicial philosophy revolved around laissez-faire convictions and a commitment to substantive due process, both of which served to impose limits on governmental activism. Sutherland's conservatism, along with that of the other "Three Horsemen," triggered President Franklin D. Roosevelt's* assault on the federal judiciary in his court-packing scheme.* The plan stimulated enormous political opposition in Congress and was never implemented, but it did prompt some resignations, including that of George Sutherland in 1938. Sutherland died in Stockbridge, Massachusetts, on July 18, 1942.

SUGGESTED READING: *New York Times*, July 19, 1942.

SWING. "Swing" was a dance and musical form that appeared in the United States during the 1930s. It had its roots in New Orleans jazz, which during the years of Prohibition had spread to speakeasies throughout the country. When the Twenty-first Amendment repealed Prohibition in 1933, jazz seemed to lose some of its pop culture cache. Benny Goodman, a Chicago clarinetist, had a band with a small gig on the NBC Radio program *Let's Dance*. In 1935, Goodman took his band on the road, introducing Middle America to jazz. He was received casually at best until he arrived in Los Angeles, where mobs greeted his performances. In a matter of months, "swing" had become a pop culture phenomenon in the United States and Benny Goodman the country's most popular musician. Swing music was characterized by highly creative brass, woodwind, and rhythm musicians spontaneously playing off one another or working in a pure harmony. In 1938, swing reached its apogee when Goodman played Carnegie Hall in New York. Although critics labeled the music mediocre and boring, fans loved it, flocked the swing concerts, and bought records by the millions.

SUGGESTED READING: Fred Hall, *Dialogues in Swing*, 1989.

T

TALMADGE, EUGENE. Eugene Talmadge was born in Forsyth, Georgia, on September 23, 1884. After graduating from the University of Georgia, he became a schoolteacher, but after a year, he returned to the university and earned a law degree in 1907. He practiced law for several years and in 1918 became solicitor for the city court in McRae, Georgia. During the early 1920s, Talmadge became active in Democratic Party politics, championing the needs of poor cotton and corn farmers with a populist rhetoric. He became state agricultural commissioner in 1926 and governor of Georgia in 1933.

Talmadge soon staked out ground as a political enemy of the New Deal,* which he found way too liberal, too problack, and too prolabor. He considered the Agricultural Adjustment Act* and subsequent agricultural legislation to be "socialistic," and he considered Franklin D. Roosevelt* a near dictator. Talmadge was wedded to states' rights, and he felt the New Deal was concentrating too much power in the hands of the federal government. In the end, however, he proved too critical of Roosevelt, whom most Georgia voters supported. In 1938, Talmadge lost the Democratic primary for the U.S. Senate, but he won the governorship in 1940, only to lose it in 1942. Talmadge died on December 21, 1946.

SUGGESTED READING: William Anderson, *The Wild Man from Sugar Creek: The Political Career of Eugene Talmadge*, 1975.

TARZAN. Based on the popular novels by Edgar Rice Burroughs, *Tarzan* was a popular radio program during the 1930s. It first appeared in 1932 as a three-times-a-week, fifteen-minute syndicated series that revolved around the fictional exploits of a lone Englishman raised by apes in Africa. The voice of Tarzan was provided by a number of radio personalities, including James Pierce and Carlton KaDell. Between 1932 and 1935, more than 350 segments of Tarzan were produced.

SUGGESTED READING: John Dunning, *Tune in Yesterday: The Ultimate Encyclopedia of Old-Time Radio, 1925–1976*, 1976.

TAYLOR GRAZING ACT OF 1934. Throughout U.S. history, homesteading and relatively free use of the public domain had characterized federal government public policy. Over the years, the federal government had gradually allowed title to public domain land to shift from public to private hands, while permitting grazing on land still owned by the federal government. But the uncontrolled grazing on public lands had a price—deterioration of the range because of overstocking and cutthroat competition among livestock interests to get access to the grass. All attempts at federal planning, however, fell victim to interest group lobbying and appeals to states' rights.

But reform interests gained ground in the 1930s. The severe drought in the West exacerbated range environmental problems, and Congressman Edward Taylor of Colorado finally converted to the idea of planning. In 1934, he submitted what became known as the Taylor Grazing Act to Congress, and the bill enjoyed the backing of President Franklin D. Roosevelt,* Secretary of the Interior Harold Ickes,* and Secretary of Agriculture Henry Wallace.* The bill passed. It authorized the secretary of the interior to divide the West up into grazing districts and to then issue grazing permits to livestock owners, who would then pay fees for grazing rights. At first, a total of 80 million acres was parceled out into grazing districts, and each permit gave a stockman rights to the grass for ten years. A board composed of local stockmen advised the Department of the Interior on management of the program, and fees collected were to be used for range improvements. The Taylor Grazing Act was a landmark piece of legislation in the history of the federal government. No longer would the public domain be considered a "free" resource available to any businessman wishing to exploit it.

SUGGESTED READINGS: Wesley Calef, *Private Grazing and Public Lands: Studies of the Local Management of the Taylor Grazing Act*, 1960; Philip O. Foss, *Politics and Grass: The Administration of Grazing on the Public Domain*, 1960; Thomas D. Isern, "The Taylor Grazing Act of 1934," in James S. Olson, ed., *Historical Dictionary of the New Deal*, 1985; Roy M. Robbins, *Our Landed Heritage: The Public Domain, 1776–1970*, 1976.

TECHNOCRACY. The so-called Technocracy movement emerged in mid-1932 as a unique, if ineffectual, response to the Great Depression. Howard Scott was the leader of the movement. He argued that capitalism was dying because its increasingly efficient production led to decreasing manpower requirements in the economy, which had precipitated the Great Depression. With some backing from Columbia University, Scott conducted a study of the role of technology in the American economy. He eventually predicted the coming of an era of extraordinary prosperity after the collapse of capitalism because the country's natural resources and technological assets would be widely shared through what Scott called the distribution of "energy certificates." His ideas had no logic in economic reality, but his ideas generated considerable attention in a country desperate for answers to the depression. Scott's movement, however, collapsed in 1933 when he accused newly elected President Franklin D. Roosevelt* of leading the country down the road to fascism. At the time, FDR was the most popular man in the country, and Scott's accusations irritated most Americans. When journalists discovered that Scott had forged his academic credentials, he lost what little support he had left. Scott's organization—Technocracy, Inc.—survived until 1941, by which time it had become a protofascist group.

SUGGESTED READING: William A. Akin, *Technocracy and the American Dream: The Technocrat Movement 1900–1941*, 1977.

TEMPLE, SHIRLEY. The decade's most popular film star was a little girl who premiered in the 1934 film *Stand Up and Cheer*. With curly, reddish blonde hair, dimples, and an infectious smile, Temple sang and danced her way across the screen, and Americans flocked to theaters in record numbers. Between 1934 and 1937, she became Hollywood's top box-office draw, grossing $5 million a year and selling millions of lookalike Shirley Temple dolls to little girls. In films including *Bright Eyes* (1934), *The Little Colonel* (1935), *Heidi* (1937), and *Rebecca of Sunnybrook Farm* (1938), Temple perfected her persona as an adult in child's clothing who helped solve the problems of older people.

In the depression-era United States, Americans yearned for somebody to solve real problems of poverty and unemployment, and perhaps that need was fulfilled, on a fantasy level at least, in front of a movie beaming images of Shirley Temple. Critics charged that one Shirley Temple film mimicked another, and a few felt that the little, coquettish ingenue generated a bit too much sexuality. Audiences, however, could not get enough of Shirley Temple.

SUGGESTED READING: Shirley Temple Black, *Child Star: An Autobiography*, 1988.

TEMPORARY EMERGENCY RELIEF ADMINISTRATION. The Temporary Emergency Relief Administration (TERA) was established in September 1931 in New York by Governor Franklin D. Roosevelt.* With unemployment surpassing all predictions and hundreds of thousands of New Yorkers suffering, Roosevelt knew that the state government needed to provide relief programs, particularly since no such relief programs were forthcoming at the federal level from the Hoover administration. Harry L. Hopkins* headed the TERA. The TERA provided matching grants to local government agencies to provide relief to the unemployed. TERA issued bonds to generate its own revenues and encouraged cities to do the same to raise relief and public works construction revenues.

The TERA helped Governor Roosevelt project a political image as a caring reformer and contrasted sharply with Herbert Hoover's* image as a tight-fisted, insensitive conservative. Once Roosevelt was elected president in 1932, he used the TERA as a prototype for such New Deal* federal relief agencies as the Federal Emergency Relief Administration,* the Civil Works Administration,* and the Works Progress Administration.*

SUGGESTED READING: Robert Sherwood, *Roosevelt and Hopkins*, 1948.

TEMPORARY NATIONAL ECONOMIC COMMITTEE. Although the early New Deal* focused on national economic planning and cooperative relationships between the federal government and the business community as the best way to stimulate the economy and end the depression, the later New Deal became less visionary, more conservative, and increasingly interested in antitrust activity. Concern about monopoly and declining competition in the modern economy became a preoccupation of President Franklin D. Roosevelt* and the New Deal later in the 1930s. Some of FDR's closest advisers, including Thomas Corcoran* and Benjamin Cohen,* urged antitrust activities upon him, and the president agreed. In an April 29, 1938, message to Congress, he suggested the need for an investigation of antitrust activity and enforcement practices by the Department of Justice. In response, Congress established the Temporary National Economic Committee (TNEC).

Members of the TNEC included congressmen and representatives from the Securities and Exchange Commission,* the Federal Trade Commission, and the Departments of Justice, Commerce, Labor, and the Treasury. The committee members were all enthusiastic in their belief that economic concentration had gone too far in the United States and that the federal government needed to be more aggressive in its antitrust activities.

Between December 1938 and March 1941, the TNEC convened a series of fifteen hearings, investigating potential monopolies in the liquor, petroleum, construction, iron and steel, milk, poultry, and investment banking industries. But in the end, the TNEC achieved very little. Those industries were not controlled by visible, powerful monopolies, and antitrust activity did not enjoy universal support in Congress. The TNEC produced very few policy recommendations and served mostly to relieve President Roosevelt of political criticism from antitrusters. The TNEC ended up producing dozens of technical volumes of statistics but nothing of lasting public policy value.

After 1940, President Roosevelt's interest in antitrust activity flagged as well. The outbreak of World War II in Europe had stimulated the economy, and foreign policy issues crowded domestic concerns from the president's mind. The TNEC became an abstraction to him as World War II stimulated new levels of cooperation between private business and a big-spending federal government.

SUGGESTED READINGS: Robert M. Collins, *The Business Response to Keynes, 1929–1964*, 1981; Ellis W. Hawley, *The New Deal and the Problem of Monopoly: A*

Study in Economic Ambivalence, 1966; Dwight MacDonald, "The Monopoly Committee: A Study in Frustration," *The American Scholar*, 8 (1939), 295–308; Patrick D. Reagan, "The Temporary National Economic Committee," in James S. Olson, ed., *Historical Dictionary of the New Deal*, 1985.

TENNESSEE VALLEY AUTHORITY. The Tennessee Valley Authority, or TVA, remains today the most comprehensive economic development project of the federal government in U.S. history. The federal government had long owned a huge swath of land that included Muscle Shoals in northern Alabama, where the Tennessee River drops approximately 140 feet over a distance of thirty miles, creating enormous potential for hydroelectric power development. Early in the 1900s, the federal government constructed two dams and two nitrate plants at Muscle Shoals, but World War I erupted before those projects became operational and stalled more comprehensive projects, and during the 1920s the Muscle Shoals property became embroiled in political controversy.

Senator George Norris,* a progressive Republican from Nebraska, made development of Muscle Shoals his pet project. Private power companies afraid of the federal government generating cheap hydroelectric power in competition with them fought development of Muscle Shoals and called for the federal government to sell the land. Senator Norris kept submitting bills to Congress allowing the federal government to continue to develop the region, but when his bills survived committee and passed, they received quick vetoes from President Calvin Coolidge, who did not think it was the business of government to generate hydroelectric power in competition with private business. The debate over the project and whether it should be publicly or privately owned continued during the Herbert Hoover* administration.

But the onset of the Great Depression after 1929 boosted Norris's chances of success. The Tennessee River Valley was one of the poorest regions of the United States, and unemployment and economic plight there were worse than anywhere else in the country. When Franklin D. Roosevelt* took office as president in 1933, the chances of completing the Muscle Shoals project improved even more because he backed the idea and enjoyed widespread political support throughout the country. In April 1933, Roosevelt formally asked Congress for legislation establishing a federal agency to construct a comprehensive project at Muscle Shoals and along the entire Tennessee River Valley that would produce hydroelectric power and promote industrial and agricultural development through reforestation, flood control, and irrigation projects. Congress responded, and on May 18, 1933, the president signed a bill creating the TVA.

The TVA encountered bitter, ongoing opposition from the private power industry, which resented the cheap electricity TVA planned to generate. Wendell Willkie* of Commonwealth and Southern Company led the opposition of the utility companies. They accused the federal government of unfair competition, of trying to put them out of business, and they filed dozens of lawsuits. Although the TVA survived the lawsuits in the federal courts, the litigation forced a change of direction, and TVA began to place more emphasis on flood control and navigation than on power generation as its central mission. A different type of opposition came from property owners bitter about having their land condemned for flooding when the TVA built dams and created reservoirs. They also filed lawsuits. So did private fertilizer manufacturers who accused TVA of unfair competition. TVA also attracted criticism from other regions who claimed that the vast outpouring of federal funds attracted business from other areas into the Tennessee Valley.

In addition to external criticism, the TVA board was also characterized during the 1930s by bitter internecine, ideological warfare, and the political infighting reflected changes in the direction of the New Deal.* At first, the head of the TVA was Arthur Morgan, a former president of Antioch College. Morgan was a believer in the business commonwealth in which the federal government and the private business community engaged in cooperative economic planning. His views fit right in with the philosophy of the National Industrial Recovery Act of 1933 and the activities of the National Recovery Administration.* But the TVA's two other board members had decidedly different views. Harcourt Morgan championed the needs of large commercial farmers and was suspicious of big government. He wanted to place limits on the TVA, to curtail its activities. David Lilienthal, on the other hand, wanted the TVA to aggressively produce electricity and to compete directly with private companies. Only then would poor people enjoy low electricity prices. Both Harcourt Morgan and David Lilienthal opposed Arthur Morgan's belief in planning. By 1936 the battles on the TVA board had become public, with Lilienthal and Harcourt Morgan teaming up against Arthur Morgan, whose influence rapidly declined. At the same time, of course, the New Deal was abandoning the planning schemes it had emphasized in 1933–1935. In 1938, Harcourt Morgan became head of the TVA.

The bickering and external criticism, however, did not keep the Tennessee Valley Authority from transforming the Tennessee River Valley. A series of nine large dams were constructed on the Tennessee River, with dozens of smaller dams along its tributaries, and the Tennessee River actually became a series of large lakes with a 300-foot-wide channel that could be navigated by ships of 9-feet draft or less. The channel reached a total of 640 miles from Knoxville, Tennessee, to the Ohio River at Paducah, Kentucky. TVA became the most important economic and environmental force in the region. It was the largest producer of electrical power in the United States, and it manufactured chemicals for fertilizer; engaged in reforestation programs and projects to limit soil erosion; funded experimental farms to test fertilizers, crops, and new methods of production; constructed roads, bridges, and model cities; and developed enormous projects for irrigation and flood control.

SUGGESTED READINGS: Gordon R. Clapp, *The TVA: An Approach to the Development of a Region*, 1955; Wilmon H. Droze, *High Dams and Slack Waters: TVA Rebuilds a River*, 1965; Virginia F. Haughton, "The Tennessee Valley Authority," in James

S. Olson, ed., *Historical Dictionary of the New Deal*, 1985; Preston J. Hubbard, *Origins of the TVA: The Muscle Shoals Controversy, 1920–1922*, 1961; Marguerite Owen, *The Tennessee Valley Authority*, 1973; Ronald C. Tobay, *Technology as Freedom: The New Deal and the Electrical Modernization of America*, 1996.

THOMAS, ELMER. Elmer Thomas was born on September 8, 1876, in Green-castle, Indiana. In 1897 he graduated from Central Normal College, and three years later he earned a degree from DePauw University. Between 1900 and 1911, he practiced law in Lawton, Oklahoma, and between 1907 and 1920 he served in the state senate. In 1922 Thomas won a seat in Congress as a Democrat, and he was elected to the U.S. Senate in 1926. During the 1930s, Thomas served as a leader of the inflationary bloc of Congress—men who believed that the answer to the Great Depression was to inflate the currency, which they thought would bring about an increase in prices and stimulate an economic boom. Along with other farming interests and silver producers out West, he wanted to devalue the dollar. To appease those interests and to experiment with the commodity dollar ideas of economists like George Warren* and Irving Fischer,* Franklin D. Roosevelt* had Thomas draft the legislation in 1933 that permitted the president to devalue the dollar, monetize silver, and print more money. It was passed as an amendment to the Agricultural Adjustment Act.* Because of his support of Thomas's ideas, President Roosevelt enjoyed the support of the Oklahoma senator on other New Deal* issues. Thomas remained a member of the U.S. Senate until 1951. He died on September 19, 1965.

SUGGESTED READINGS: *New York Times*, September 20, 1965; James T. Patterson, *Congressional Conservatism in the New Deal*, 1967.

THOMAS, NORMAN. Norman Thomas was born on November 20, 1884, in Marion, Ohio. He briefly attended Bucknell College before going to the Princeton Theological Seminary, where he graduated in 1908. He then went to work for the East Side Settlement House in New York City and served as assistant pastor at Christ Church. In 1911, after being ordained a Presbyterian minister, he became pastor of the East Harlem Church. His experiences with immigrants soon convinced him that the capitalistic system would never address the needs of the poor because its profit motive was too overpowering. He found the vast gap between the rich and the poor in the United States to be offensive. Thomas joined the Socialist Party* of America. He openly opposed U.S. entry into World War I, and the political controversy surrounding his position forced him to resign the pastorate. He then became secretary of the Fellowship of Reconciliation, an antiwar, pacifist group.

Thomas then committed himself to promoting socialism in the United States. He helped found the American Civil Liberties Union in 1918, and in 1919 he established the League for Industrial Democracy. That same year, Thomas became an editor of the liberal journal *The Nation*. He was active in promoting the labor unrest of 1919–1920, and he openly denounced the federal government's activity in the Red Scare of 1919–1921. Thomas's profile in socialist circles became more and more prominent, and when Eugene Debs died, Thomas emerged as the most influential socialist in the country. He ran for president on the Socialist Party ticket in 1928, and when he ran again in 1932, he actually harbored hopes of victory, since the Great Depression had so damaged the economy. But American voters went with Franklin D. Roosevelt,* and Thomas lost to Roosevelt again in 1936, 1940, and 1944.

During the 1930s, Thomas actively campaigned for federal social welfare legislation, for more public works construction for the unemployed, and for relief of poor tenant farmers displaced by New Deal* acreage reduction programs. He constantly tried to push Franklin D. Roosevelt and the New Deal to move farther toward the left, and he kept up that pressure for the next thirty years. A bitter opponent of the Vietnam War, Norman Thomas died on December 19, 1968.

SUGGESTED READINGS: Harry Fleischman, *Norman Thomas: A Biography, 1884–1968*, 1969; Bernard K. Johnpoll, *Pacifist's Progress: Norman Thomas and the Decline of American Socialism*, 1970.

***THORNHILL V. STATE OF ALABAMA* (1940).** The case of *Thornhill v. State of Alabama* revolved around the rights of striking workers to picket a place of business. Alabama had passed a law allowing authorities to arrest strikers and charge them with loitering and becoming a public nuisance. Union officials filed a lawsuit, claiming that the state law was unconstitutional on the grounds that it robbed citizens of the right to peaceably assemble and freedom of speech. The U.S. Supreme Court heard the case and rendered its decision on April 22, 1940. The justices agreed with the workers and declared the state law unconstitutional.

SUGGESTED READING: *Supreme Court Reporter*, 60 (1940), 736–46.

TOBACCO ROAD. *Tobacco Road* was the title of Erskine Caldwell's* 1932 novel. The book revolved around the miseries of the Jeeter Lester family, poverty-stricken George sharecroppers who redefined the meaning of the dysfunctional family. The family lives on Tobacco Road, where they continuously make one bone-headed decision after another, keeping themselves in constant turmoil through their own self-inspired misadventures. Because of the Great Depression and the havoc it wreaked with the rural southern economy, Americans knew more about the plight of tenant farmers and sharecroppers than ever before. But whatever sympathy journalists generated for poor southerners evaporated in Erskine Caldwell's devastating portrait, since the Jeeters seemed fully capable of making all of their bad luck. In 1933, *Tobacco Road* became a successful Broadway play, guaranteeing that the term "Tobacco Road" would become a euphemism for rural poverty and squalor.

SUGGESTED READING: Erskine Caldwell, *Tobacco Road*, 1932.

TOWNSEND, FRANCIS EVERETT. Francis Townsend, who many historians consider to be a key player in the origins of Social Security, was born in 1866 outside Fairbury, Illinois. His family was poor and deeply religious and raised Townsend with a concern for the welfare of people less fortunate than he was. He tried his hand at farming in California but then moved to Omaha where he studied at the University of Nebraska Medical School. He graduated there in 1903 and then practiced medicine in Bear Lodge, South Dakota, for the next twenty years, except for a tour of duty as an army physician during World War I.

In 1923 Townsend opened a medical practice in Long Beach, California, but he had a difficult time making ends meet. Nearly seventy years old and destitute, he began speaking and writing articles for local newspapers urging the federal government to establish a program where senior citizens—over the age of sixty—received a monthly pension of $200. The message resonated with large numbers of people, and Townsend received more and more invitations to write and speak. He argued that the pension plan, to be financed by a tax on businesses, would pump purchasing power into the economy and end the depression.

In January 1934, Townsend joined hands with realtor Robert Earl Clements and turned his idea into a political movement. They founded Old-Age Revolving Pensions, Ltd., to promote the idea. With money coming in from supporters and subscribers to their newspaper—*The Townsend National Weekly*—the movement for a federal pension plan gained real momentum. They formed "Townsend Clubs" around the country, and by early 1935, the more than 3,000 clubs boasted of a membership of more than 500,000 people. The clubs lobbied for federal pensions.

At the time, only twenty-eight states had pension plans of any kind, ranging from $7.28 a month in Montana to $30 a month in Maryland. People listened. At the same time, Clements turned Old-Age Revolving Pensions, Ltd., into a profitable business. He marketed Townsend buttons, badges, banners, license plates, tire covers, radiator emblems, pictures, pamphlets, and songs. The newspaper had 300,000 subscribers by 1936 and turned an annual profit of $250,000.

In January 1935, Congressman John Steven McGroarty introduced the Townsend Plan to Congress, and supporters collected more than 20 million petition signatures backing the idea. President Franklin D. Roosevelt* considered Townsend a political threat, so he vigorously pushed the Social Security Act of 1935* as a means of silencing Townsend. It worked, even though Townsend participated in the ill-fated, anti-Roosevelt third-party Union Party* ticket in the presidential election of 1936.* In the end, Townsend lost much of his political base when he endorsed Republican candidate Alf Landon* for president.

Eventually, Congress decided to investigate Old-Age Revolving Pensions, Ltd., since Clements's tactics proved to be shady and ridden with fraud. Townsend refused to testify and was held in contempt of Congress, but President Roosevelt commuted the sentence. Townsend still had millions of Americans who admired him. He then slowly drifted into obscurity and died on September 1, 1960.

SUGGESTED READING: David H. Bennett, *Demagogues in the Depression: American Radicals and the Union Party, 1932–1936*, 1969.

TRACY, SPENCER. Spencer Tracy was born on April 5, 1900, in Milwaukee, Wisconsin. He served in the U.S. Navy during World War I. After the war, he attended Ripon College for several semesters and then moved to New York City, where he enrolled in the American Academy of Dramatic Arts. During the 1920s, he worked with touring theatrical groups, and in 1930, he signed a movie contact with William Fox* and first appeared in *Up the River*. During the 1930s, with Fox and MGM, Tracy rocketed to superstar status portraying rugged, independent, fair-minded men—the bedrock of America. He won best actor awards in two consecutive years: for his performance as Manuel, the Portuguese fisherman, in *Captains Courageous* (1937) and as Father Flanagan in *Boys Town* (1938). Tracy eventually made a total of sixty films and received Oscar nominations for *San Francisco* (1936), *Father of the Bride* (1950), *Bad Day at Black Rock* (1955), *The Old Man and the Sea* (1958), *Inherit the Wind* (1960), and *Judgement at Nuremburg* (1961). Tracy died on June 10, 1967.

SUGGESTED READINGS: *New York Times*, June 10, 1967; Larry Swindel, *Spencer Tracy: A Biography*, 1969.

TRANSATLANTIC FLIGHT. Ever since Charles Lindbergh's* famous solo flight from New York to Paris in 1926, the possibility of transatlantic flight had been a reality. But commercial passenger service across the Atlantic was quite another thing, and it did not become a reality until 1939. On June 28, 1939, Pan American Airways placed into service three Boeing Clipper seaplanes with transatlantic schedules and flight paths. On June 28, the *Dixie Clipper*, with twenty-two passengers, flew from Port Washington, New York, to the Azores, where it laid over a few hours before heading on to Lisbon, Portugal. The entire trip took twenty-two hours. The *New York Times* referred to the flight as the "aerial conquest of the last, and commercially most important, of the earth's oceans." The outbreak of World War II in 1939 interrupted commercial flights, but they resumed after the war.

SUGGESTED READINGS: *New York Times*, September 30 and October 1–2, 1939.

TRANSPORTATION ACT OF 1940. The Great Depression was a financial disaster for the country's railroads, who found themselves caught in a terrible economic squeeze because of increased competition from trucks, depressed freight rates and declining freight volume, and huge fixed costs because of enormous debt burdens. The Motor Carrier Act of 1935* had tried to address the problem of competition from the trucking industry by setting minimum freight rates, but it really did little to address the problem, other than enrage motor carriers. In March 1938 a conference was held among representatives of the Interstate Commerce Commission (ICC), the Reconstruction Finance Corporation* (RFC), and the Departments of Treasury, Agriculture, and Commerce to look at the problems facing railroads, and a Committee of Three was established under the leadership of ICC chairman Joseph Eastman.

The committee recommended that the RFC continue to make cheap equipment and credit loans to the railroads and that the ICC carry out a consolidation of the railroad industry to make it more efficient. The proposal immediately encountered the wrath of the railroad brotherhoods, which believed that the consolidation would eliminate too many jobs, and the railroad companies themselves, since many corporate entities would actually disappear. Eventually, the proposal was severely modified and passed as the Transportation Act of 1940. It gave the ICC control over coastal, inland waterways, and Great Lakes common and contract water-carriers, but it did little to address the railroad problem. The outbreak of World War II would eventually create huge demands for railroad freight and passenger service and temporarily solve many railroad problems, although those problems would reassert themselves after 1945.

SUGGESTED READING: Ari Hoogenboom and Olive Hoogenboom, *A History of the ICC: From Panacea to Palliative*, 1976.

TRAYLOR, MELVIN ALVAH. Melvin Traylor, one of the country's few Democratic, pro–New Deal* bankers during the 1930s, was born on October 21, 1878, in Breeding, Kentucky. After finishing high school, he moved to Texas, where he taught school for a while, studied law privately, and then practiced law. In 1904–1905, Traylor served as an assistant attorney in Hill County, Texas, and in 1906 he was appointed president of Citizens National Bank of Ballinger, Texas. During the next nine years, Traylor parlayed one banking job into another, moving steadily to positions of greater responsibility and more pay, and in 1919 he was appointed vice-president of the First National Bank of Chicago, one of the Midwest's premier financial institutions. He became president of First Chicago in 1920, and in 1925 he was elected president of the American Bankers Association.

Traylor always remembered his beginnings in the rural poverty of Kentucky, and he remained a loyal Democrat all of his life. In 1932, he ran as a darkhorse candidate for president, but when Governor Franklin D. Roosevelt* of New York won the nomination, Traylor enthusiastically supported him and cam-

paigned for him. Throughout 1933, Traylor served as an adviser to President
Roosevelt, assisting in the reconstruction of the nation's banking system. Melvin
Traylor died suddenly on February 14, 1934.

SUGGESTED READING: *New York Times*, February 15, 1934.

TUGWELL, REXFORD GUY. Rexford Tugwell, one of the New Deal's*
most influential economists, was born in Sinclairville, New York, on July 10,
1891. A brilliant student, he received bachelor's, master's, and Ph.D. degrees
in economics from the Wharton School of the University of Pennsylvania. Between 1920 and 1931, he taught economics at Columbia University and published prolifically. Among his major contributions were *The Economic Basis for
Public Interest* (1922), *The Trend of Economics* (1924), *American Economic
Life* (1925), *Industry's Coming of Age* (1927), and *Soviet Russia* (1928). He
became one of the country's premier experts in agricultural economics and a
strong proponent of national economic planning. Because of his friendship with
Professor Raymond Moley,* a political science professor at Columbia and adviser to Governor Franklin D. Roosevelt* of New York, Tugwell eventually
became a member of the "Brains Trust"* of academics who advised the governor
during his presidential campaign of 1932 and the transition to the White House
in 1932–1933.

In March 1933, Tugwell was appointed as assistant secretary of agriculture
under Secretary of Agriculture Henry Wallace,* but his real function was to
advise the president on economic matters. Tugwell had no faith in laissez-faire
and the balancing effects of the market, and he believed that the federal government needed to go beyond progressivism's antitrust and regulating agenda
to become the principal institution in the modern industrial economy, establishing production goals, allocating resources, and determining prices and wages.
Only then, Tugwell was convinced, would prices stabilize, full employment be
achieved, and the poor receive a decent lifestyle. His economic and political
philosophies were far too liberal for most Americans and for most people in the
Franklin D. Roosevelt administration, but Tugwell was nevertheless a powerful
voice for change and reform. He helped draft the Agricultural Adjustment Act
of 1933,* which tried to address the problem of agricultural overproduction and
falling commodity prices by paying farmers not to grow.

In 1934, the president named Tugwell undersecretary of agriculture, and one
year later, Tugwell became head of the Resettlement Administration,* a newly
created federal government agency designed to help the rural poor relocate to
other areas; to fund programs to reforest certain areas, build flood control systems, and prevent stream pollution and soil erosion; provide loans so that poor
farmers could buy land and farm equipment; and construct "Greenbelt towns"
of subsistence homestead communities that would provide low-income housing.
Real estate interests bitterly protested the Resettlement Administration, fearing
it would undermine rent prices, and large commercial farmers feared that it

would limit their access to cheap labor. Tugwell's unapologetic administration of the Resettlement Administration did not endear him to critics. In 1937, the new Farm Security Administration* assumed control of the Resettlement Administration.

Tugwell then left Washington, D.C., to become head of the New York City Planning Commission. In 1941 he became chancellor of the University of Puerto Rico but served for only a brief period of time because President Roosevelt named him governor of Puerto Rico. Tugwell spent World War II in Puerto Rico, and his 1946 book *The Stricken Land* analyzed the political and economic challenges facing the island. He then returned to academe as a professor of economics at the University of Chicago. During his tenure at Chicago, Tugwell wrote *The Place of Planning in Society* (1954), *A Chronicle of Jeopardy* (1955), and *The Democratic Roosevelt* (1957). He retired from Chicago in 1957 but continued to write and consult. Among his later books were *The Art of Politics* (1958), *The Brains Trust* (1968), and *Tugwell's Thoughts on Planning* (1975). Tugwell died on July 21, 1979.

SUGGESTED READINGS: Bernard Sternsher, *Rexford Tugwell and the New Deal*, 1964; *New York Times*, July 22, 1979; Duane Windsor, "Rexford Tugwell," in James S. Olson, ed., *Historical Dictionary of the New Deal*, 1985.

TWENTIETH AMENDMENT. Throughout U.S. history, each newly elected Congress first convened in session on March 4 after the previous November elections. Recently elected presidents also were inaugurated on March 4. That gave the old, lame-duck Congress nearly four months to continue in operation, even if voters had expelled them from office. Senator George Norris,* Republican of Nebraska, proposed a constitutional amendment allowing the new Congress to convene on January 3 and to inaugurate the new president on January 20. The last lame-duck session of Congress opened in December 1932 with 158 defeated members. Norris proposed the amendment on March 2, 1932, Congress passed it, and the Twentieth Amendment to the Constitution was ratified on February 6, 1933. President Franklin D. Roosevelt* was the first president inaugurated under the new amendment on January 20, 1937.

SUGGESTED READING: Alfred H. Kelly and Winfred A. Harbison, *The American Constitution*, 1970.

TWENTY-FIRST AMENDMENT. By 1932, the American experiment with Prohibition had become a profound failure. The Eighteenth Amendment had been ratified in 1919 and prohibited the manufacture and distribution of alcoholic beverages in the United States, but resistance to the amendment was widespread, and it became impossible to enforce the law. Organized crime moved into the breach, supplying to consumers a product that legitimate businessmen could not provide. Such lobbying groups as the Association against the Prohibition Amendment campaigned for repeal of the Eighteenth Amendment, and in the elections of 1928 and 1932* the Democratic Party agreed. After Franklin D. Roosevelt* won the presidential election of 1932, the Democratic-controlled lame-duck Congress submitted a proposed constitutional amendment to the states. The proposed Twenty-first Amendment to the Constitution repealed the Eighteenth Amendment. By December 5, 1933, the necessary thirty-six states had ratified it, and Prohibition was repealed.

SUGGESTED READING: Alfred H. Kelly and Winfred A. Harbison, *The American Constitution*, 1970.

TWO-THIRDS RULE. Between 1836 and 1936, the Democratic Party's presidential candidates had required a two-thirds majority of delegates to nominate a president. Among southerners, the two-thirds rule was all but sacrosanct because it gave them a virtual veto power over Democratic Party policy. It would prevent, they were convinced, a rehearsal of the Civil War and Reconstruction years when the North had run roughshod over the South. By the 1930s, however, the rule had become an anachronism, guaranteeing political infighting at the conventions, causing political disasters, such as the 1924 convention that had gone on for weeks and had required more than 100 ballots to nominate a candidate. In 1936, President Franklin D. Roosevelt* decided to change the rule, and it was relatively easy to do since his own renomination was a foregone conclusion. The delegates eliminated the two-thirds rule by voice vote. The change was highly symbolic of the rise of the urban North in the Democratic Party and the coming decline of the South.

SUGGESTED READINGS: Arthur M. Schlesinger, Jr., *The Age of Roosevelt*, vol. III, *The Politics of Upheaval, 1935–1936*, 1960.

TYDINGS, MILLARD EVELYN. Millard Tydings, the anti–New Deal* Democrat, was born on April 6, 1890, in Havre de Grace, Maryland. In 1910 he graduated from the Maryland Agricultural College and three years later earned a law degree from the University of Maryland. After a brief stint practicing law privately, Tydings won a seat in the state legislature but resigned it in 1917 to join the army. Tydings saw combat with the American Expeditionary Force in France. After the war, he regained his seat in the state legislature, and in 1922, he was elected to Congress. After two terms in Congress, Tydings was elected to the U.S. Senate.

A conservative Democrat, he fought President Franklin D. Roosevelt* and the New Deal at every opportunity. Tydings was committed to states' rights and a small federal government, and he felt FDR was taking the country down the road to big government centralized in Washington, D.C. He opposed the Agricultural Adjustment Act,* the National Industrial Recovery Act, the Tennessee Valley Authority,* Social Security,* and the National Labor Relations Act.* In

1938, Tydings was one of the conservative Democrats FDR targeted for defeat in the primary elections, and the president personally campaigned against him in Maryland. But Maryland voters in effect told Roosevelt to mind his own business by returning Tydings to the Senate. Tydings remained there until 1951. He died on February 9, 1961.

SUGGESTED READINGS: *New York Times*, February 10, 1961; James T. Patterson, *Congressional Conservatism in the New Deal*, 1967.

U

UNEMPLOYED COUNCILS. When the Great Depression put millions of people out of work, officials from the Communist Party of America saw an opportunity to gain real political strength. They sponsored thousands of demonstrations around the country and established local unemployed councils, all of them directed by the Communist-controlled Unemployed Councils of America. In 1931 the unemployed councils staged demonstrations in favor of unemployment compensation programs and hunger strikes to protest poverty in America. They also sponsored local demonstrations to make sure that relief agencies dispensed funds equitably and sometimes blockaded sheriffs' offices and judges' chambers in order to prevent evictions. Finally, the unemployed councils worked to organize workers into labor unions. In 1936, however, they lost most of their influence when the national office merged with the Workers' Alliance, a socialist organization.

SUGGESTED READING: Roy Rosenzweig, "Organizing the Unemployed: The Early Years of the Great Depression, 1929–1933," *Labor History*, 10 (1976), 37–60.

UNEMPLOYED LEAGUES. The plight of the unemployed had become a national trauma, and scandal, by 1931, and in the face of inaction on the part of the Herbert Hoover* administration, local governments and private groups tried to take matters into their own hands. In 1931 Carl Branin of the Seattle Labor College established the Unemployed Citizens' League (UCL) of Seattle. The group organized a drive—through barter, labor exchange, and private donations—that raised 120,000 pounds of fish, 10,000 cords of firewood, and eight carloads of fruit and potatoes. The fish, produce, and firewood were then distributed to the unemployed.

But as successful as the effort was, it had little long-term impact. Branin himself realized that for all the effort it had taken to raise the products, they supplied the needs of unemployed families for only a week or so. The unemployment problem was too vast for private action to ameliorate, and Branin decided that only direct political action would be required to address the nation's economic challenge.

Abraham Muste of the Conference on Progressive Labor Action (CPLA) had taken note of the UCL's energy. A socialist and pacifist, Muste wanted to develop a powerful working-class movement in the United States, one capable of taking over the federal government and implementing a socialist economy. Muste sent CPLA organizers throughout the country trying to replicate the UCL of Seattle. The plan was to organize local self-help programs and then move on to left-wing political organizations. Muste's organizers experienced some success among Pittsburgh steelworkers, Pennsylvania and West Virginia coal miners, and North Carolina textile workers. They staged demonstrations, sit-ins, petition drives, and picket lines to protest the suffering of the poor and the insensitivity of the rich in America.

In July 1933, 800 delegates from local unemployed councils met in Columbus, Ohio, and established the National Unemployed League (NUL). They claimed a membership of 150,000 people in thirteen states, but the NUL could never really sustain itself at the national level. New Deal* relief programs took some steam out of the movement, and Muste's own political meanderings hurt as well. His followers organized the American Workers Party and then the Trotskyite Workers Party, arguing incessantly about socialist theory and rendering themselves increasingly irrelevant. Unemployed League membership eroded steadily throughout the 1930s, and in 1936, the NUL joined with the Workers' Alliance, a socialist organization, and the Unemployed Councils, a communist-led organization, and formed the Workers' Alliance of America. The NUL then ceased to function at the national and local levels.

SUGGESTED READINGS: Roy Rosenzweig, "Radicals and the Jobless: The Musteites and the Unemployed Leagues," *Labor History*, 16 (1975), 52–77; Roy Rosenzweig, "Unemployed Leagues," in James S. Olson, ed., *Historical Dictionary of the New Deal*, 1985.

UNEMPLOYMENT. Economists still argue about the causes of unemployment during the 1930s, but most agree that the economy had become mired in a liquidity trap where underconsumption led to production declines, deflation, and layoffs. Around the industrial world, by 1930, more than 21 million people were out of work. The numbers of the homeless skyrocketed, and urban centers from New York City to London to Tokyo to Sydney became scenes of makeshift, cardboard homes, bread lines, begging, malnutrition, and suffering. Divorce rates fell because people could not afford to start up a new household, and so did birthrates. Suicide and desertion, on the other hand, jumped dramatically.

When President Franklin D. Roosevelt* came into office in March 1933, the unemployment rate in the United States exceeded 25 percent. And this was in an age when the vast majority of women did not work outside the home, meaning that nearly one in four American households was without an income. Also, there was no national program of unemployment compensation, social security, or welfare. In order to solidify his political support among the working classes, Roosevelt embarked on an ambitious program of unemployment relief through such government agencies as the Federal Emergency Relief Administration,* the Civil Works Administration,* the Civilian Conservation Corps,* and the Works Progress Administration.* The great contribution of the New Deal* to modern public policy is that the federal government assumed responsibility for guaranteeing full employment in the economy, and when the goal of full employment could not be met, the federal government was obligated to provide public sector jobs for those Americans out of work.

SUGGESTED READINGS: Anthony J. Badger, *The New Deal: The Depression Years, 1933–1940*, 1989; Paul Conkin, *FDR and the Origins of the Welfare State*, 1967.

UNION PARTY. By 1934, Franklin D. Roosevelt's* political honeymoon was over and the New Deal* began to attract criticism from the right and the left. Critics on the left—like Norman Thomas* of the Socialist Party* and Huey Long* and his Share Our Wealth crusade—accused Roosevelt of doing too little to relieve the suffering of the poor and the unemployed, while critics on the right, such as the National Association of Manufacturers,* charged him with creating a huge federal bureaucracy and leading the country down the road to socialism.

When Roosevelt looked at his critics, four of them in particular worried him politically: Huey Long and the Share Our Wealth plan; Francis E. Townsend* and Old-Age Revolving Pensions, Ltd.; Father Charles Coughlin* and the National Union for Social Justice; and William Lemke* and the Non-Partisan League. Gerald L. K. Smith* succeeded to the helm of Share Our Wealth in 1935 after Huey Long's assassination. Collectively, the critics proposed dramatic changes in the American political economy. Coughlin proposed the taking of monetary control from the hands of private bankers and the printing of vast amounts of paper currency through a new central bank. Smith called for government confiscation of large fortunes and the redistribution of those assets to poor people. Townsend wanted to establish a system of federal old-age pensions. Lemke proposed the printing of more paper currency and government programs to refinance home and farm mortgages.

What united the critics was a hatred of Franklin D. Roosevelt and the New Deal. In 1936, to oppose his reelection, they formed the Union Party and nominated William Lemke of North Dakota for president and Thomas C. O'Brien of Massachusetts for vice-president. They endorsed high protective tariffs, foreign policy isolationism, inflation of the currency, the refinancing of all home and farm mortgages, a federal system of old-age pensions, higher federal appropriations for work relief, high taxes on the rich and well-to-do, and vigorous federal antitrust action.

The Union Party was a complete fiasco. Smith's anti-Catholic, pro–Ku Klux

Klan rhetoric offended Charles Coughlin, who was a Roman Catholic priest, and in October 1936, when Smith called for the organization of a paramilitary group to overthrow the U.S. government, he was expelled from the Union Party. Francis Townsend then endorsed the candidacy of Republican Alf Landon.* The Vatican condemned the activities of Charles Coughlin. When the votes were counted, Lemke secured only 882,479 votes, compared to Landon's 16,674,665 and Roosevelt's 27,752,869. The Union Party then rapidly declined and officially dissolved in 1939.

SUGGESTED READING: David H. Bennett, *Demagogues in the Depression. American Radicals and the Union Party, 1932–1936*, 1969.

UNITED STATES V. BUTLER **(1936).** During the first "Hundred Days"* of the New Deal,* the Franklin D. Roosevelt* administration launched a concerted, if helter-skelter, crusade to ameliorate the effects of the Great Depression and to turn the economy around. Roosevelt was especially worried about hard times in rural America, where commodity prices had fallen below cost of production for many farmers. Most agricultural economists recognized overproduction as the key to the problem. The supply of farm products reaching the market was so huge that price levels were overwhelmed. To deal with the problem, Congress passed in 1933 the Agricultural Adjustment Act,* which established the Agricultural Adjustment Administration* (AAA). The AAA, by imposing processing taxes on middlemen, generated cash to pay farmers to reduce production or not to raise crops at all.

Conservatives, of course, were aghast at such an increase in the power and scope of the federal government. Many believed the legislation was unconstitutional. Food processors—canneries, packinghouses, and wholesalers—especially resented the tax they had to pay, and many of them sued. One case— *United States v. Butler*—reached the Supreme Court, which decided the case on January 6, 1936. In a 6 to 3 vote, the Court declared the law unconstitutional, arguing that regulating and controlling agricultural production was a state, not a federal, concern. As a result, the Agricultural Adjustment Administration violated the Tenth Amendment to the Constitution. The decision triggered a storm of controversy and quickly led to President Franklin D. Roosevelt's misguided attempt to "pack" the Supreme Court.

SUGGESTED READING: 297 U.S. 1 (1936).

U.S. CHAMBER OF COMMERCE. The U.S. Chamber of Commerce was established in 1912 to promote business cooperation and economic growth in the United States. Over the years, it evolved into the all-but-official voice of the American business community. At first, the Chamber of Commerce supported Franklin D. Roosevelt* and the New Deal,* particularly the initiatives of the National Industrial Recovery Act of 1933 and the National Recovery Administration.* Henry I. Harriman headed the Chamber of Commerce in 1933 and 1934, and he felt the New Deal was working to strengthen the banking system and helping to revive the economy.

But in 1935, relations between the Chamber of Commerce and the Roosevelt administration soured. Harper Sibley became head of the Chamber of Commerce, and the 1935 leftward shift of New Deal policy enraged and frightened Sibley. The Chamber of Commerce became decidedly anti-Roosevelt and anti–New Deal and openly opposed the National Labor Relations Act,* the Social Security Act,* the Walsh-Healey Public Contracts Act,* the Wealth Tax Act,* and the Banking Act of 1935.* At their 1936 convention, the Chamber of Commerce passed a formal vote of censure against Roosevelt and the New Deal and launched a pamphlet and speaking tour campaign against him. The chamber demanded balanced federal budgets as the answer to the Great Depression. Their view of Roosevelt only grew worse during the rest of the 1930s.

SUGGESTED READING: Robert M. Collins, "Positive Business Response to the New Deal: The Roots of the Committee for Economic Development, 1933–1942," *Business History Review*, 52 (1978), 369–91.

V

VALLEE, RUDOLPH. Rudy Vallee was born in Island Pond, Vermont, on July 28, 1901. Vallee was raised in Westbrook, Maine. After a brief stint in the navy during World War I, Vallee studied music at the University of Maine and Yale. An accomplished saxophonist, he began touring with his own band. His trademark greeting became "Heigh-ho, everybody." In 1929, NBC brought Vallee to radio with the *Rudy Vallee Show*, and it was a smash hit. Vallee played the saxophone and popularized the "crooner" style of singing. The show remained on the air throughout the 1930s, and Vallee became a national celebrity. Vallee left NBC in 1943 but remained in show business the rest of his life. He died on July 3, 1986.

SUGGESTED READINGS: John Dunning, *Tune in Yesterday: The Ultimate Encyclopedia of Old-Time Radio, 1925–1976*, 1976; *New York Times*, July 4, 1986.

VANDENBERG, ARTHUR HENDRICK. Arthur Vandenberg was born in Grand Rapids, Michigan, on March 22, 1884. He went into the newspaper business locally and successively became a journalist, editor, and publisher of the *Grand Rapids Herald*. A conservative Republican, Vandenberg was appointed to the U.S. Senate in 1928 to fill the seat vacated by the death of Senator Woodbridge N. Ferris. Although Vandenberg opposed most of the major New Deal* laws—including the Tennessee Valley Authority,* the Agricultural Adjustment Act,* the National Labor Relations Act,* the Fair Labor Standards Act,* the Wealth Tax Act,* and the Works Progress Administration*—he did not become ideological in his opposition and did not demonize President Franklin D. Roosevelt.* He even sponsored the legislation that became the Federal Deposit Insurance Corporation* provision of the Banking Act of 1933.*

Vandenberg's real interest was in foreign affairs, and here during the 1930s, he disagreed with the Roosevelt administration. An avowed isolationist, Vandenberg sided with Senator Gerald P. Nye* of North Dakota who led a major investigation of the munitions industry in 1934–1935. Vandenberg became a prominent member of the Senate Foreign Relations Committee and urged a cautious foreign policy on the president. But after Japan* bombed Pearl Harbor, Vandenberg supported the war effort wholeheartedly. In 1945, President Roosevelt appointed him as a delegate to the United Nations, which marked the beginning of Vandenberg's transition to an internationalist. He helped draft Article 51 of the UN charter, which endorsed collective defense arrangements to preserve international peace and security. Arthur Vandenberg died on April 18, 1951.

SUGGESTED READING: C. David Tompkins, *Senator Arthur H. Vandenberg: The Evolution of a Modern Republican*, 1970.

VAN DEVANTER, WILLIS. Willis Van Devanter was born in Marion, Indiana, on April 17, 1859. After graduating from the University of Cincinnati Law School in 1881, he joined his father's legal practice in Marion. Three years later, he ventured out on his own, moving to Cheyenne, Wyoming, where he became city attorney and later a territorial legislator and chief justice of the territorial court. In 1890 he returned to private practice, building a lucrative business with powerful corporate clients, particularly the Union Pacific Railroad. He was also active in Republican Party politics. In 1897, President William McKinley brought Van Devanter to Washington, D.C., as an assistant attorney general in the Department of the Interior. President Theodore Roosevelt named Van Devanter to the Eighth Circuit Court of Appeals in 1903. Van Devanter remained on the Eighth Circuit until 1910, when President William Howard Taft appointed him to the U.S. Supreme Court.

Van Devanter soon earned a reputation as the Court's leading conservative intellectual, a jurist committed to the notion that Congress's power under the commerce clause was limited to interstate commerce and matters directly related, not indirectly or tangentially related, to interstate commerce. He refused to acknowledge congressional authority to use the commerce clause or the taxing power to regulate labor-management relations or regulate business and industry.

During the years of the Great Depression and New Deal,* Van Devanter's belief in limited government made him part of the conservative majority that negated critically important congressional initiatives to ameliorate economic suffering. Journalists dubbed him one of the "Nine Old Men"* and a leading member of the "Four Horsemen"* who could always be counted on to uphold the needs of corporate America. In such decisions as *Railroad Retirement Board et al. v. Alton Railroad Company et al.* (1935),* *Schechter Poultry Corporation v. United States* (1935),* *United States v. Butler* (1936),* and *Morehead v. New York ex rel. Tipaldo* (1936), the Supreme Court overturned the central institutions of the New Deal and precipitated President Franklin D. Roosevelt's* decision to reform and reorganize the federal judiciary through his so-called court-packing scheme.* Although Congress never acted on the proposal, Roosevelt nevertheless prevailed. Van Devanter voluntarily stepped down from the

Court in 1937, and along with other resignations, the president was able to build a liberal majority. Willis Van Devanter died on February 8, 1941.

SUGGESTED READING: James O'Brien Howard, *Constitutional Doctrines of Mr. Justice Van Devanter*, 1937.

VANN, ROBERT LEE. Robert L. Vann, one of the most influential African Americans of his time, was born in Ahoskie, North Carolina, on August 27, 1879. He attended the Western University of Pennsylvania in Pittsburgh, where he edited the school newspaper. Vann graduated there in 1906 and then earned a law degree in 1909. He then served for a time as the legal counsel to *The Pittsburgh Courier*, a black newspaper. In 1918, he was named editor of the paper. Vann remained at the helm of *The Pittsburgh Courier* until his death in 1940.

Under Vann's direction, *The Pittsburgh Courier* became the most influential black newspaper in the country. In the process, Vann became the most prominent black journalist in the United States. In the presidential election of 1932* Vann, although a Republican, endorsed Franklin D. Roosevelt* and began the process that soon saw most African Americans becoming Democrats. Herbert Hoover* and the Republicans, Vann wrote frequently, had responded tepidly to the depression and did little while millions of people suffered. FDR then named Vann a special assistant in the Justice Department. In 1936, when he endorsed FDR again, Vann urged black people to "turn Lincoln's picture to the wall. That debt has been paid in full."

But Vann eventually grew disenchanted. He felt that he was being used as a token by the Roosevelt administration to attract the African American vote and that the New Deal* had done little to really help black people. In 1940, Vann returned to the Republican fold and endorsed Wendell Willkie* for president. Robert Vann died on October 24, 1940.

SUGGESTED READINGS: Andrew Bruni, *Robert L. Vann of the Pittsburgh Courier: Politics and Black Journalism*, 1974; *New York Times*, October 25, 1940.

THE VOICE OF FIRESTONE. A musical show of popular songs, classical music, show tunes, and marches, which premiered on NBC on December 3, 1928, *The Voice of Firestone* was one of the most popular programs on radio. Sponsored by Firestone Tire and Rubber, it occupied the Monday, 8:30 P.M. time slot for the next twenty-eight years.

SUGGESTED READING: John Dunning, *Tune in Yesterday: The Ultimate Encyclopedia of Old-Time Radio, 1925–1976*, 1976.

W

WADSWORTH, JAMES WOLCOTT, JR. James Wadsworth was born on August 12, 1877, in Geneseo, New York. In 1898 he graduated from Yale and served in the army during the Spanish-American War. After the war he farmed and ranched in the Geneseo area. In 1904, he was elected to the state legislature as a Republican, and he served until 1910. That year, Wadsworth moved to Texas to manage some large ranching properties there. In 1914, almost in absentia, he was elected to the U.S. Senate from New York, and he then left Texas. He served in the U.S. Senate until 1927, having failed in his reelection bid. Wadsworth returned to his ranching interests in New York, and in 1932, he was elected to Congress and kept his seat for nine terms. Throughout the 1930s, Wadsworth was a bitter opponent of Franklin D. Roosevelt* and the New Deal,* and he was a founder and leader of the American Liberty League,* an anti-Roosevelt lobbying group. Wadsworth believed wholeheartedly that the New Deal was antibusiness and anti-American, a protosocialist movement that would eventually destroy American life. Although he worked to build an effective anti–New Deal political coalition among southern Democrats and northern Republicans, his plans were stillborn. Roosevelt had captured the imagination and confidence of the American people. Wadsworth died on June 21, 1952.

SUGGESTED READINGS: *New York Times*, June 22, 1952; George Wolfskill, *Revolt of the Conservatives: A History of the American Liberty League, 1934–1940*, 1960.

WAGNER, ROBERT FERDINAND. Robert F. Wagner, a political icon for liberal Democrats in the first half of the twentieth century, was born on June 8, 1877, in Hesse-Nassau, Germany.* He was eight years old when the family emigrated from Germany, and they settled in New York City. Wagner became active as a young man in local ward politics and rose in the ranks of Tammany Hall's Democratic machine. In 1904 he won a seat in the state legislature, and by 1911 he was president pro tem of the state senate. In the state legislature, Wagner soon became known as an urban, progressive reformer interested in improving the lot of the poor and the working class. He believed in the rights of organized labor and of the role of state and federal government in stabilizing the economy.

In 1926, Wagner won a seat in the U.S. Senate, and his reputation as a pragmatic liberal only grew there. When the country slipped into the Great Depression, Wagner became an early advocate of federal legislation to provide relief to the unemployed. During the Herbert Hoover* administration, he submitted three bills to Congress on the issue. In 1930, Hoover signed a Wagner bill allowing the federal government to collect unemployment statistics, and in 1931 the president signed another bill establishing the Federal Employment Stabilization Board. Hoover vetoed another Wagner bill that would have reorganized the U.S. Employment Service. Several of Wagner's proposals for unemployment relief were implemented, however, in the Emergency Relief and Construction Act of 1932.*

When Franklin D. Roosevelt* was elected president in 1932, Wagner became a leading architect of the New Deal.* His commitment to unemployment relief was implemented in the Federal Emergency Relief Act of 1933, and the National Industrial Recovery Act of 1933 included Wagner's proposal for $3.3 billion in public works construction to assist the unemployed. Wagner also played the key role crafting the National Industrial Recovery Act's labor standards provisions and the National Labor Relations Act of 1935,* which guaranteed labor's right to collective bargaining. He was also very influential in securing passage of the Social Security Act of 1935.* Wagner served in the U.S. Senate until 1949. He died on May 4, 1953.

SUGGESTED READING: J. Joseph Huthmacher, *Senator Robert F. Wagner and the Rise of Urban Liberalism*, 1968.

WAGNER-CONNERY ACT. See **NATIONAL LABOR RELATIONS ACT OF 1935**.

WAGNER-COSTIGAN BILL. See **FEDERAL ANTY-LYNCHING BILL**.

WAGNER-CROSSER RAILROAD RETIREMENT ACT OF 1935. The Wagner-Crosser Railroad Retirement Act of 1935 was another name for the Railroad Retirement Act of 1935. See *RAILROAD RETIREMENT BOARD ET AL V. ALTON RAILROAD COMPANY ET AL.* (**1935**).

WAGNER-PEYSER ACT OF 1933. The Wagner-Peyser Act, or National Employment System Act, of 1933 established the U.S. Employment Service and authorized federal matching grants to states for establishing and maintaining employment offices. It was part of New York Senator Robert Wagner's* vision of a nationwide federal government employment service. It would match workers with available jobs on a national basis and, Wagner hoped, serve as a prerequisite to a national system of unemployment compensation. Throughout his administration, President Herbert Hoover* had blocked Wagner's attempts to implement such a program, but President Franklin D. Roosevelt* enthusiastically supported it. When the Social Security Act of 1935* was passed, it contained provisions for using the public employment offices as distribution points for unemployment compensation.

SUGGESTED READINGS: Paul Douglas and Aaron Director, *The Problem of Unemployment*, 1931; J. Joseph Huthmacher, *Senator Robert F. Wagner and the Rise of Urban Liberalism*, 1968.

WAGNER-STEAGALL HOUSING ACT OF 1937. With passage of the Wagner-Steagall Housing Act of 1937, the federal government first recognized housing as a social need and assumed some responsibility for providing it. Urban reformers, labor leaders, and social welfare advocates had long promoted public housing as a necessity in a modern industrial state, but their demands fell on deaf ears until the advent of the New Deal.* Once the country slipped into the Great Depression, the movement for public housing gained momentum because it would stimulate real estate and construction and provide jobs. Opposition came from rural areas, where politicians assumed they would receive none of the benefits. The Wagner-Steagall Housing Act became law on September 1, 1937.

The legislation established the U.S. Housing Authority within the Department of the Interior and appropriated $500 million for loans to promote low-cost housing construction. The U.S. Housing Authority could loan up to 90 percent of the cost of a housing project. Nathan Straus was appointed to head the U.S. Housing Authority, and to drum up rural support, he made sure that at least one-quarter of the agency's loans went to towns with less than 25,000 people. By 1940, the U.S. Housing Authority had made a total of $691 million in loans and had completed 344 projects with 188,045 units.

SUGGESTED READING: J. Joseph Huthmacher, *Senator Robert F. Wagner and the Rise of Urban Liberalism*, 1968.

WALLACE, HENRY AGARD. Henry A. Wallace was born on October 7, 1888, near the town of Orient in Adair County, Iowa. Intellectually precocious as a child, he began as a teenager a systematic study of plants, and at the age of sixteen, he began experimenting with seed corn, a step that would eventually make him one of the world's premier plant geneticists. In 1910, he graduated from Iowa State College in Ames, Iowa.

Wallace's father—Henry Cantwell Wallace—was a leading figure in American agriculture and publisher of *Wallace's Farmer*. The younger Wallace became editor of the journal in 1910 and remained in the post until 1933. In 1923, the younger Wallace's genetic experiments with corn produced the world's first commercially successful hybrid seed corn. To promote the invention, in 1926 he founded the Hi-Bred Seed Company and served as the company's president until 1933. Wallace's father served as secretary of agriculture in the Warren Harding administration. During the 1920s, Henry Agard Wallace became a strong exponent of federal action to address the farm problem. He supported the McNary-Haugen Bill, called on Presidents Calvin Coolidge and Herbert Hoover* to develop federal grain storage and marketing systems for farmers, and planned cuts in commodity production, which would help stem the problem of falling prices. When Wallace's father died in 1924, Henry Agard emerged as the most influential figure in American farm policy. In 1928, although he had been a lifelong Republican, Wallace endorsed Al Smith* for president.

In 1933, President Franklin D. Roosevelt* appointed Wallace to his cabinet as secretary of agriculture. In that position, Wallace presided over the New Deal's* cornucopia of farm programs, none of them more important than the acreage reduction agenda of the Agricultural Adjustment Administration.* Wallace remained at agriculture until 1940, when President Roosevelt selected him as his vice-presidential running mate. In 1944, Roosevelt replaced Wallace with Harry Truman as his running mate, and Wallace was appointed secretary of commerce. It was a short-term assignment because Wallace's politics were increasingly moving to the left, distancing himself from President Truman. Wallace left commerce in 1946.

In 1948, Wallace was becoming increasingly outspoken about the issue of civil rights and urged the federal government to pass legislation to end discrimination against black people. At the height of the Red Scare, he also became more vocal about his feelings that the United States should end the Cold War and reach a rapprochement with the Soviet Union.* In the election of 1948, Wallace bolted the Democratic Party and formed his own Progressive Party. He proposed a vigorous, expanded program of social welfare legislation, but his views were far too liberal for the vast majority of Americans. In the election, Wallace won only 2.4 percent of the popular vote, and President Truman was reelected. Wallace then returned to private life and his scientific experiments in plant genetics. He died on November 18, 1965.

SUGGESTED READINGS: Edward L. Schapsmeier and Frederick H. Schapsmeier, *Henry A. Wallace of Iowa: The Agrarian Years, 1910–1940*, 1968; Graham White and John Maze, *Henry A. Wallace: His Search for a New World Order*, 1995.

WALSH-HEALEY PUBLIC CONTRACTS ACT OF 1936. In May 1935, the Supreme Court rendered its decision in the *Schechter** case and declared the National Industrial Recovery Act unconstitutional. That automatically killed the labor standards, or wages and hours, provisions of the law as well. Labor leaders denounced the Court's decision, and Secretary of Labor Frances Perkins* decided that the least the federal government could do was enforce minimum wage and maximum hours regulations in companies receiving federal contracts. Senator David Walsh of Massachusetts and Congressman Arthur Healey, also of Massachusetts, sponsored the necessary legislation in Congress, and President Franklin D. Roosevelt* signed the Walsh-Healey Public Contracts Act on June 30, 1936.

The law required that all federal contractors had to pay their workers a minimum wage as established by the Department of Labor. Any contract for more than $10,000 required employers to pay overtime for more than eight hours of work a day or forty hours a week. Until Congress passed the Fair Labor Standards Act of 1938,* the Walsh-Healey Public Contracts Act was the federal government's key piece of labor standards legislation.

SUGGESTED READINGS: Milton Derber and Edwin Young, eds., *Labor and the New Deal*, 1957; Charles K. McFarland, *Roosevelt, Lewis, and the New Deal, 1933–1940*, 1970; *New York Times*, July 1–2, 1936.

WARBURG, JAMES. James Warburg, one of the few wealthy financiers in the United States to support Franklin D. Roosevelt* and the New Deal,* was born in Hamburg, Germany,* on August 18, 1896, to a wealthy, prominent family. In 1917 he graduated from Harvard University and joined the National Metropolitan Bank in New York City. Warburg soon found himself at the First National Bank of Boston and a prominent young man in Wall Street circles. In 1929, he was named president of the International Manhattan Company. But he did not fit the mold on Wall Street because of his political beliefs. A faithful Democrat, he eschewed laissez-faire and supported the notion that the federal government had an important role to play in stabilizing the money markets. In 1933, suspicious of newly elected President Franklin D. Roosevelt's monetary views, Warburg turned down FDR's offer to become secretary of the treasury.

But the president kept in close contact with Warburg and used him frequently as an economic adviser, particularly during the difficult months of 1933 when the banking system was being reconstructed. Warburg played a key role in drafting the National Industrial Recovery Act of 1933, the Emergency Banking Act of 1933,* and the Banking Act of 1933.* That same year the president appointed Warburg as a delegate to the World Monetary Conference in London.

But Warburg's suspicions of FDR's monetary views were confirmed late in 1933 when the president launched the ill-fated gold-buying scheme, an attempt to stimulate prices and the economy by manipulating the world price of gold. He was convinced that the so-called commodity dollar plan would undermine business confidence and restrict the flow of credit. Warburg and the president engaged in a vigorous debate over the issue, but FDR soon tired of it, deciding that Warburg was simply too bound to tradition. Warburg then left the administration. In the end, of course, Warburg had been right about the gold-buying, commodity dollar idea, and Roosevelt abandoned it in 1934.

By that time Warburg had become a vocal critic of the New Deal. His pamphlets *Hell Bent for Election* (1935) and *Still Hell Bent* (1936) accused FDR of being power hungry and likely to take the United States down the road to socialism and dictatorship. In the presidential primaries of 1936 Warburg served as an adviser to Frank Knox, a former Bull Moose Progressive, but when the Republican Party nominated Alf Landon,* Warburg returned to the New Deal camp. He apologized to the president, and FDR accepted, but Warburg had lost his influence over public policy. Warburg continued his successful business career, serving as president of the Bydale Company and later for years as director of the Polaroid Corporation. He died on June 3, 1969.

SUGGESTED READING: *New York Times*, June 4, 1969.

WAR OF THE WORLDS. A radio adaptation of H. G. Wells's science fiction novel *War of the Worlds*, *War of the Worlds* was broadcast on Sunday, October 30, 1938. Orson Welles, a twenty-three-year-old actor-producer-director at the Mercury Theater in New York City, planned the broadcast as a Halloween prank. The novel revolved around a Martian invasion of earth, and in the broadcast, Welles played it straight, handling it as a late-breaking, live news broadcast, complete with "late breaking bulletins," on-the-spot coverage, and live interviews. At the beginning of the broadcast, Welles had let listeners know that the program was fiction, but those who tuned in late did not know that. The broadcast made radio history. In a chain reaction, other radio stations picked up on the broadcast, and millions listened in. Panic occurred in some parts of the country. Welles later had to apologize for his antics, but the broadcast proved how powerful the radio had become in the development of pop culture and just how concerned Americans were about political and military tensions in Europe and the threat of war.

SUGGESTED READINGS: Hadley Cantril, *The Invasion from Mars: A Study in the Psychology of a Panic, with the Complete Script of the Famous Orson Welles Broadcast,* 1940; Barbara Leaming, *Orson Welles: A Biography,* 1985; *New York Times,* October 31 and November 1–2, 1938.

WARREN, GEORGE FREDERICK. George Frederick Warren was born in Harvard, Nebraska, on February 16, 1874. He was raised on the family's farm and then worked his way through the University of Nebraska, where he graduated in 1897 with a degree in farm management. He went on to earn a master's degree and the Ph.D. at New York State College of Agriculture at Cornell. After a year as a horticulturalist at the New Jersey Experiment Station, Warren returned to Cornell as an assistant professor of agronomy. In 1920, he became professor of agricultural economics at Cornell.

During the 1920s, Warren and his colleague at Cornell, Frank A. Pearson, had met Governor Franklin D. Roosevelt* of New York. Warren and Pearson coauthored the book *Prices* in 1933, in which they argued that the prices of wheat, cotton, tobacco, and other agricultural commodities rose and fell automatically because they were connected to the price of gold in relation to paper currency. It was possible, therefore, for public officials to set commodity prices by manipulating the price of gold. If the government bought gold in large amounts and then raised the price of gold gradually, the value of the dollar would fall and the prices of farm commodities would rise. Warren and Pearson called their theory the "commodity dollar."

President Roosevelt became enamored of the theory and in 1933 decided to try and implement it. He brought Warren to Washington as an economic adviser and gave him a job in the Department of Commerce. The critics of Warren proved to be correct. The 1933–1934 experiment with the commodity dollar through government gold-buying schemes failed, and Warren returned to Cornell. He died on May 24, 1938.

SUGGESTED READINGS: *New York Times*, May 25, 1938; James S. Olson, *Saving Capitalism: The Reconstruction Finance Corporation and the New Deal, 1933–1940*, 1988.

WARREN POTATO CONTROL ACT OF 1935. One of the great challenges facing the Agricultural Adjustment Administration* (AAA) in 1933–1934 was the number of farmers planting noncontract crops. For the AAA to have any hope of reducing production and boosting commodity prices, most farmers had to be participating in it. Only compulsory controls could stem the production tide. Congress had already passed the Bankhead Cotton Control Act* and the Kerr-Smith Tobacco Control Act,* and potato farmers in Idaho, Maine, Virginia, and North Carolina expected similar protections for themselves. Congressman Lindsay Warren of North Carolina, with the cosponsorship of Senator William Borah* of Idaho, submitted legislation to Congress, and the Warren Potato Control Act was passed on August 24, 1935. It imposed a burdensome tax on all noncontract potatoes, which made them noncompetitive in terms of price and therefore forced farmer participation.

SUGGESTED READINGS: Edwin G. Nourse, *Marketing Agreements under the AAA*, 1935; Van L. Perkins, *Crisis in Agriculture: The Agricultural Adjustment Administration and the New Deal*, 1969.

WEALTH TAX ACT OF 1935. The Wealth Act of 1935, also known as the Revenue Act of 1935, marked a different direction in New Deal* political and economic policy. In June 1935, President Franklin D. Roosevelt* proposed a major revision of the federal tax code. He was convinced that it was far too complex and actually contributed to the concentration of wealth in the United States. Roosevelt sought a modest redistribution of wealth through tax policies. Such tax policies, he thought, might stimulate the economy by putting money in the hands of working-class people and provide the necessary dollars to fund relief programs, which would also be spent by poor people. The proposal indicated that the president was drifting toward the left, a move stimulated by Supreme Court decisions that had dismantled several New Deal programs, rabid business opposition to New Deal policies, and political pressure from the likes of Father Charles Coughlin,* Francis Townsend,* and Huey Long.* Political support for the Wealth Tax also came from such old-line progressives as Senators William E. Borah,* Robert M. La Follette, Jr.,* Gerald P. Nye,* and Hiram M. Johnson. The American Federation of Labor* also backed the idea.

As first proposed, the measure was comprehensive and capable of curbing the transmission of great wealth from one generation to another. It called for inheritance and gift taxes, enhanced surcharges on large personal incomes, and the imposition of a major graduated tax schedule on corporations. FDR also proposed a constitutional amendment permitting the federal government to levy taxes on the interest earned from issues of state and local securities.

The Wealth Tax Act emerged from Congress much altered. It imposed a 12.5 percent rate on small corporations and a 15 percent rate on companies earning more than $50,000 annually. The law also imposed a 6 percent excess profits tax on earnings of more than 10 percent annually and 12 percent on earnings exceeding 15 percent. It did not include FDR's request for a constitutional amendment or an inheritance tax. In the end, the Wealth Tax Act achieved few, if any, of its objectives. It certainly did not redistribute wealth, and it raised little extra revenue for the federal government. Nevertheless, it was of great political significance. In an act of great hyperbole, conservatives proclaimed it unconstitutional and a form of class warfare, and liberals hailed it as a watershed in the history of public policy in that it at least declared the legitimacy of using the power of the federal government to decentralize wealth. Still, even after the legislation, the poor continued to be responsible for a disproportionate share of the tax burden.

SUGGESTED READINGS: Virginia F. Haughton, "The Wealth Tax Act of 1935," in James S. Olson, ed., *Historical Dictionary of the New Deal*, 1985; Ronald A. Mulder, "The Progressive Insurgents in the United States Senate, 1935–1936: Was There a Second New Deal?" *Mid-America*, 57 (1975), 106–25; Sidney Ratner, *American Taxation: Its History as a Social Force in Democracy*, 1942.

WEAVER, ROBERT CLIFTON. Robert Weaver, one of the most influential African Americans in the New Deal,* was born on December 29, 1907, in Washington, D.C. He earned a bachelor's degree from Harvard in 1929 and then a master's degree and the Ph.D. in 1931 and 1934, respectively. Secretary of the Interior Harold Ickes* used Weaver as an adviser on minority affairs, and as such, Weaver became a member of the so-called black cabinet.* In 1937 Weaver was named special assistant for the U.S. Housing Authority, a position he kept until 1940. Weaver later had a distinguished academic career at Columbia University and New York University, writing such well-received books as *Negro Labor: A National Problem* (1946) and *The Negro Ghetto* (1948). In 1954 he became deputy commissioner of the New York State Division of Housing. Between 1955 and 1959, he served as rent administrator for the state of

New York before joining the Ford Foundation. In 1961, President John F. Kennedy named him head of the Federal Housing and Home Finance Agency, and in 1966, Weaver became the first African American in history to serve in a presidential cabinet when Lyndon B. Johnson named his secretary of housing and urban development. Weaver served there for eight years, and in 1969 he left public service to become president of Bernard Baruch College. Robert Weaver died on July 17, 1997.

SUGGESTED READINGS: John B. Kirby, *Black Americans in the Roosevelt Era: Liberalism and Race*, 1980; Patricia Sullivan, *Days of Hope: Race and Diversity in the New Deal Era*, 1996.

WEST COAST HOTEL CO. V. PARRISH **(1937).** The U.S. Supreme Court decided the *West Coast Hotel Co. v. Parrish* case on March 29, 1937. The case revolved around a minimum wage law for women that the state legislature of Washington had passed. The law generated opposition from businessmen who did not want to pay a minimum wage and from feminists groups convinced that such gender labor restrictions only increased discrimination against women by resting on a belief in female inequality. In 1923, in *Adkins v. Children's Hospital*, the Court had overturned a minimum wage law for children, and opponents of the law felt that *West Coast Hotel* was a similar legal situation.

But the legal climate of opinion had changed dramatically between 1923 and 1937. President Franklin D. Roosevelt* had launched his attack on the conservative Court by proposing his court-packing scheme.* Although the attempt to reorganize the judiciary failed, it did prompt an ideological shift on the Court, and *West Coast v. Parrish* was the first example of the change. The judges overturned *Adkins* by a narrow 5 to 4 margin. The principle of freedom of contract, Chief Justice Charles Evans Hughes* wrote, was not unlimited, and government had the right to regulate the economy in the interests of the larger community. The chief justice also argued that the judiciary, except in the most extraordinary circumstances, ought to defer to the legislative branch in such matters. Justice Owen Josephus Roberts,* who usually could be counted on to vote with the conservative bloc, voted to uphold the minimum wage law. In doing so, he gave liberals an upper hand on the Court and made President Roosevelt's court-packing scheme moot. Journalists dubbed Roberts's decision the "switch in time that saved nine."

SUGGESTED READINGS: 300 U.S. 379 (1937); Charles A. Leonard, *A Search for a Judicial Philosophy: Mr. Justice Roberts and the Constitutional Revolution of 1937*, 1971.

"WET." The word "wet" was employed during the years of Prohibition to refer to an individual, especially a politician, who supported repeal of the Eighteenth

Amendment and relegalization of the manufacture and distribution of alcoholic beverages in the United States.

SUGGESTED READING: Norman H. Clark, *Deliver Us from Evil: An Interpretation of American Prohibition*, 1976.

WHEELER, BURTON KENDALL. Burton K. Wheeler was born in Hudson, Massachusetts, on February 27, 1882. In 1905 he graduated from the University of Michigan Law School and then opened a law practice in Montana. Wheeler served in the Montana state legislature from 1910 to 1913, when President Woodrow Wilson named him U.S. attorney for Montana. In 1922, Wheeler won a seat in the U.S. Senate. He soon earned a reputation as a progressive Democrat. His political philosophy would not let him endorse Democratic presidential candidate John W. Davis in 1924, and instead Wheeler accepted the vice-presidential nomination of the Progressive Party and ran on the ticket with Robert La Follette.* The party platform advocated vigorous antitrust action, public ownership of hydroelectric facilities and railroads, federal antiinjunction legislation to protect labor unions, federal guarantees of union collective bargaining rights, arms reductions, and a constitutional amendment to provide for elected federal judges with ten-year terms. But in the general election, the La Follette–Wheeler ticket managed only 16 percent of the popular vote. Wheeler was reelected to the Senate in 1928, 1934, and 1940.

Early in the 1930s, Wheeler became a strong supporter of President Franklin D. Roosevelt* and the New Deal,* and he was also a powerful voice for free coinage of silver and monetary inflation as an answer to the Great Depression. But Wheeler soured on Roosevelt later in the decade. The court-packing scheme* especially outraged Wheeler, who accused Roosevelt of dictatorial behavior. After 1937, Wheeler voted against every major piece of New Deal legislation. He was also a confirmed isolationist who felt that Roosevelt's internationalism would get the country into another war. In 1940, Wheeler contested the Democratic presidential nomination with Roosevelt, but to no avail. With the world drifting toward war, voters wanted to stay with the president they had grown to trust through such hard times. Wheeler opposed Lend Lease and the Selective Service Act of 1940 as proof that the United States was heading toward war. He was defeated in his 1946 bid for reelection. Wheeler returned to the practice of law in Washington, D.C. He died on January 7, 1975.

SUGGESTED READINGS: Kenneth C. MacKay, *The Progressive Movement of 1924*, 1947; *New York Times*, January 8, 1975; James T. Patterson, *Congressional Conservatism and the New Deal*, 1967.

WHEELER-HOWARD ACT. See **INDIAN REORGANIZATION ACT OF 1934**.

WHEELER-RAYBURN BILL. See **PUBLIC UTILITY HOLDING COM-PANY ACT OF 1935.**

WHITE, WALTER FRANCIS. Walter Francis White was born on July 1, 1893, in Atlanta, Georgia. He enjoyed a mixed racial ancestry, and although he could have passed as a white man, he lived as a proud African American. In 1916, White graduated from Atlanta University and found a job with the Atlanta Insurance Company. He also established an Atlanta chapter of the National Association for the Advancement of Colored People* (NAACP). In 1918, he moved to New York to work as assistant secretary of the national NAACP. White succeeded James Weldon Johnson in 1931 as secretary of the NAACP, and he remained at the post until his death in 1955.

During the 1930s, White invested most of his energies in promoting a Federal Anti-Lynching Bill* in Congress. Senators Edward Costigan of Colorado and Robert Wagner* of New York sponsored the legislation, which NAACP lawyers had drafted, but it never passed. Opposition from southern Democrats was too strong. Several of the NAACP's legal battles, however, like the fight to save the Scottsboro* boys, succeeded. White was outspoken in his demands for black voting rights, an end to Jim Crow segregation, a ban on poll taxes, and desegregation of the armed forces and public schools. The greatest factor limiting White's work, beyond the entrenched racism in white America, was the Great Depression's impact on NAACP finances. With its coffers badly depleted, White's opportunities to challenge racist institutions were quite limited. He kept the faith, however, and lived long enough to see the beginning of the Supreme Court's assault on Jim Crow. Walter White died on March 21, 1955.

SUGGESTED READINGS: Michael G. Dennis, "Walter Francis White," in James S. Olson, ed., *Historical Dictionary of the New Deal*, 1985; *New York Times*, March 22, 1955.

WHITE, WILLIAM ALLEN. William Allen White, perhaps the leading journalist of his time, was born on February 10, 1868, in Emporia, Kansas. He studied journalism at the University of Kansas, and in 1895 he purchased and began to edit the *Emporia Daily and Weekly Gazette*. He was a fine writer and had an eye for political detail, and his columns became widely syndicated. He also wrote a series of highly regarded political biographies and analyses, including *Strategems and Spoils* (1901), *The Old Order Changeth* (1910), *The Life of Woodrow Wilson* (1924), *The Life of Calvin Coolidge* (1925), and *Masks a Pageant* (1928). White specialized in politics and came at political issues from a position of moderate Republicanism.

The Great Depression and the politics of the 1930s put White in a difficult position. He greatly admired President Franklin D. Roosevelt* and considered him a gifted, dynamic leader. He also enthusiastically supported New Deal* relief, unemployment, Social Security, collective bargaining, labor standards, and progressive taxation legislation, and FDR jokingly referred to White as one "of my best friends three-and-a-half years out of four." He was also convinced that if the Republican Party was going to survive, it would have to dump its Old Guard and become more progressive. Nevertheless, in 1936 he endorsed Alf Landon* for president.

Later in the 1930s, White did become concerned about the drift of the New Deal. He found FDR's court-packing scheme* to be despicable, and he feared the government reorganization programs of the later New Deal. The federal government, White concluded, indeed had acquired too much power. But as the political situation in Europe deteriorated, White found himself again in FDR's camp, working to push the United States beyond a slavish devotion to isolationism. In 1940 he chaired the Committee to Defend America. William White died on January 29, 1944.

SUGGESTED READINGS: David Hinshaw, *A Man from Kansas: The Story of William Allen White*, 1945; *New York Times*, January 30, 1944.

WHITE HOUSE CONFERENCE ON THE EMERGENCY NEEDS OF WOMEN. In November 1933, at the urging of First Lady Eleanor Roosevelt,* President Franklin D. Roosevelt* convened the White House Conference on the Emergency Needs of Women. At the time, approximately 50,000 women nationwide were receiving assistance from the Federal Emergency Relief Administration* and the Civil Works Administration.* But Harry Hopkins estimated that another 400,000 to 500,000 women were in need. To meet their needs, the White House conference met under the direction of Ellen Woodward* and Mary Dewson.* Eleanor Roosevelt served as honorary chairwoman of the meetings and presided. Representatives from the League of Women Voters, the National Consumers' League, the American Red Cross, and the Women's Trade Union League met to discuss ways of securing more federal relief money, designing work relief jobs acceptable to women, particularly to those with small children, and generating more jobs in the private sector.

SUGGESTED READINGS: *New York Times*, November 20–22, 1933; Susan Ware, *Beyond Suffrage: Women in the New Deal*, 1981.

WHITNEY, RICHARD. Richard Whitney was born on August 1, 1888, in Beverly, Massachusetts. He came from a very old, very prosperous American family, and he attended Groton and Harvard. After graduating from Harvard in 1911, he went to work for J. P. Morgan and Company and then joined the Whitney family securities business. He became president of Richard Whitney & Company, a major Wall Street investment company. When the stock market crashed in 1929, Whitney was picked to head up the New York Stock Exchange, and he represented the industry during the Pecora Committee* investigations of 1930. Although the Pecora Committee uncovered fraud and stock manipulations as common practices in the industry, Whitney remained unapologetic, insisting that overall the industry was sound and honest. Whitney vigorously opposed federal regulation of the securities industry and spoke out against the Securities Act of 1933* and the Securities Exchange Act of 1934. Whitney resigned from the New York Stock Exchange in 1935 and returned to private business. But he soon got caught up in a Securities and Exchange Commission* investigation, which revealed that Whitney had personally engaged in embezzling funds from the New York Yacht Club and the New York Stock Exchange. He was convicted and served three years in a federal penitentiary. Whitney died on December 5, 1974.

SUGGESTED READINGS: *New York Times*, December 6, 1974; Michael Parrish, *Securities Regulation and the New Deal*, 1970.

WIGGIN, ALBERT HENRY. Albert H. Wiggin was born on February 21, 1868, in Medfield, Massachusetts. He went to work for the Commonwealth Bank in Boston after leaving high school. In 1891 Wiggin became a bank examiner for the office of the comptroller of the currency in the federal government. Politics cost him the job in 1893, however, when Grover Cleveland and the Democrats took control of the White House and swept Republicans from federal jobs. In 1893, Wiggin was hired by the third National Bank of Boston, and in 1897 he was appointed vice-president of Eliot National Bank. Wiggin moved to New York City to work for National Park Bank in 1899.

Five years later, however, he began his march down the road to financial prominence by organizing the Bankers' Trust Company of New York. In 1905 he was named vice-president of Chase National Bank. Wiggin became president of Chase in 1911 and chairman of the board in 1917. His tenure at Chase was marked by unprecedented growth. The bank's assets skyrocketed from $250 million to $2.5 billion, with Wiggins negotiating mergers and buyouts to generate the deposits.

After the stock market crash* of 1929, President Herbert Hoover* turned to Wiggin to rationalize the money markets and stem the panic, and Wiggin tried diligently to organize a private consortium of big money to stop the liquidation crisis, but the problem was simply bigger than the private sector. In 1931 he played a key role in forming the National Credit Corporation* to loan money to troubled banks, but that effort failed as well. Wiggins's career then cratered. The Rockefeller family purchased a controlling interest in Chase National Bank and forced Wiggin to resign when it became clear that he had engaged in risky speculative investments and mixed his personal assets with those of the bank.

Wiggin then became a target of the Pecora Committee* investigation in 1931. Congressman Ferdinand Pecora exposed corruption and fraud in the securities industry, and his investigators discovered that Wiggin had created dummy affiliated companies to help Chase avoid federal stock market regulations, had sold short on his own stock during the 1929 crash, and had dipped into Chase money to finance his own personal stock speculations. In the process, he became a symbol of the greed and irresponsibility that afflicted the stock market during the 1920s. Albert Wiggin died on May 21, 1951.

SUGGESTED READINGS: John Kenneth Galbraith, *The Great Crash 1929*, 1955; Matthew Josephson, *The Money Lords*, 1972; *New York Times*, May 22, 1951; Marjorie Wiggin, *New England Son*, 1949.

WILKINS, ROY. Roy Wilkins was born in St. Louis, Missouri, in 1901 and raised in Minneapolis, Minnesota. He graduated from the University of Minnesota in 1923, working his way through school by doing odd jobs and editing the St. Paul *Appeal*, an African American newspaper. He then moved to Kansas City, Missouri, to work on the staff of the *City Call*, another African American newspaper, and there he had his first experiences with segregation. Missouri's Jim Crow system raised his political consciousness, and he joined the local chapter of the National Association for the Advancement of Colored People* (NAACP). Wilkins was a patient, even-tempered man who despised discrimination, and he soon became a powerful influence in the national NAACP.

In 1931, Wilkins moved to New York City to work as assistant executive secretary to Walter White,* head of the NAACP. Three years later, he was named editor of the NAACP's official publication—*Crisis*. That year, he was arrested for the first time for leading a demonstration in Washington, D.C., against Attorney General Homer Cummings, who had refused to include lynching as a major crime in the United States. Throughout the 1930s, Wilkins kept up his crusade against the lynching of African Americans. In the 1940s, Wilkins fought for the desegregation of the armed forcs. He was the primary planner of the NAACP legal strategy that led to the famous *Brown v. Board of Education* decision in 1954. When Walter White died in 1955, Wilkins assumed the position of executive secretary of the NAACP. From that position, he was at the forefront of the NAACP's fight against segregation during the late 1950s and throughout the 1960s. Roy Wilkins resigned from his post as executive director of the NAACP in 1977. He died on September 8, 1981.

SUGGESTED READING: *New York Times*, September 9, 1981.

WILLIAMS, AUBREY WILLIS. Aubrey Williams was born into poverty in rural Springville, Alabama, in 1890. As a child he had to go into the cotton fields to earn money to supplement the family's poverty-level income, and the experience gave him a lifelong appreciation for the plight of poor people and the challenge of being black in the South. Although he was not an African American, he witnessed firsthand the numbing effects of racism and discrimination, and instead of incorporating the racism as part of himself, as did so many white southerners, Williams became committed to the idea of the social gospel and the need to treat poor people in general and black people in particular with respect.

During World War I, Williams worked for the Red Cross and fought for the French Foreign Legion, and that experience also gave him an appreciation for people of color. In 1922 he became executive secretary of the Wisconsin Conference of Social Work and committed himself to the battle against poverty, disease, and child abuse. He became convinced that the battle had to be fought on several fronts—the law, the state house, Congress, and in the public mind, where understanding of the causes of poverty in America seemed so limited. Williams was also a firm believer that the only effective form of public assistance was work relief, in which the indigent labored for their weekly stipend. Only then, he was convinced, could they retain a sense of dignity.

In 1932 and 1933, Williams worked for the Reconstruction Finance Corporation* (RFC) in Alabama and Mississippi after the Emergency Relief and Construction Act* gave the RFC a relief mission. After the inauguration of Franklin D. Roosevelt,* Williams became deputy to Federal Emergency Relief administrator Harry Hopkins.* Williams became a key figure in the Federal Emergency Relief Administration* and the Civil Works Administration,* and he worked diligently to make sure that black people received a share of the work relief programs. In 1935, Williams was appointed executive director of the National Youth Administration* (NYA) and deputy director of the Works Progress Administration* (WPA). He hired black staff members at the WPA and NYA and refused to segregate blacks in agency operations in the South. Williams's attitudes, of course, cost him political support among powerful southern congressmen, but he simply refused to let his principles become compromised by political concerns. He remained at the helm of the NYA until its demise in 1943.

Williams spent much of the rest of his life denouncing the Red Scare tactics of right-wing Republicans and southern Democrats and speaking in favor of civil rights for African Americans. He had a nobility about him that left a legacy of respect among those who knew him and knew of his influence. Aubrey Williams died in 1965.

SUGGESTED READINGS: Richard A. Reiman, "Aubrey Willis Williams," in James S. Olson, ed., *Historical Dictionary of the New Deal*, 1985; John A. Salmond, *A Southern Rebel: The Life and Times of Aubrey Willis Williams, 1890–1965*, 1983; Morton Sosna, *In Search of the Silent South*, 1977.

WILLKIE, WENDELL LEWIS. Wendell Willkie was born on February 18, 1892, in Elwood, Indiana. In 1913 he graduated from Indiana University and then earned a law degree there in 1916. He became a corporate attorney for Firestone Tire and Rubber Company in Akron, Ohio. Willkie also became active in local Democratic Party politics, where he displayed conservative but certainly not ideological attitudes. Willkie supported President Woodrow Wilson's attempt to get the United States in the League of Nations, and he condemned Ku Klux Klan influence in the Democratic Party during the 1920s. Willkie moved to New York in 1929 and became a partner in the law firm of Weadock and Willkie. His firm handled the account of the billion-dollar utility empire of Commonwealth and Southern Corporation, and in 1933, Willkie became president of the company.

He was a leader in the business community opposition to many New Deal* programs, especially the Tennessee Valley Authority* and the Public Utility Holding Company Act of 1935.* Although Willkie did not oppose government breakup of monopolies or regulation of companies to prevent abuses, he felt the New Deal had gone too far in actually breaking up efficient, well-run companies. He also spoke out against deficit spending, confiscatory taxes, and bureaucratic waste, all of which he thought the New Deal excelled in. In 1936, Willkie switched political allegiances and voted for Alf Landon.* Franklin D. Roosevelt* and the New Deal had simply gone too far beyond the reach of Willkie's Wilsonian progressivism.

In 1940, a coalition of anti-Roosevelt Democrats, Wall Street investors, and anti–New Deal journalists began pushing Willkie's candidacy for the Republican presidential nomination. He won the nomination on the sixth ballot at the Republican National Convention, and he selected Senator Charles McNary of Oregon as his running mate. Willkie built his campaign around a theme that accused President Roosevelt of vastly expanding the federal bureaucracy without ever really solving the depression and with letting the country's military defenses lapse into a state of unreadiness. He also hoped that the third-term issue might derail Roosevelt. No president had ever sought a third term in office, and Republicans anticipated victory.

The criticisms were certainly justified, but the Willkie-McNary ticket could not deal with the deteriorating international situation. The outbreak of World War II in Europe in 1939 had led to increased purchases of war goods in the United States, and millions of new jobs were being created. Most Americans could see the Great Depression slipping into the past. At the same time, Americans became loathe to switch leaders when war seemed on the horizon. Franklin D. Roosevelt had become almost a father figure to tens of millions of people, and Willkie could not compete with that image. When the votes were counted, FDR defeated Willkie 27,307,819 to 22,321,018, with 499 electoral votes to Willkie's 82. Wendell Willkie died on October 2, 1944.

SUGGESTED READINGS: Ellsworth Barnard, *Wendell Willkie: Fighter for Freedom*, 1966; Mary Earhart Dillon, *Wendell Willkie, 1892–1944*, 1952.

WINCHELL, WALTER. Walter Winchell was born in New York City on April 7, 1897. He quit school after the sixth grade and, with Jack Weiner and George Jessell, went to work at the Imperial Theater. The three friends formed a group of singing ushers and soon worked the local vaudeville circuit. Winchell joined the U.S. Navy during World War I, and after the war, he returned to vaudeville. In 1922, with no training in writing or journalism, Winchell became a reporter for the *Vaudeville News*, where he did theater reviews. Winchell moved to the *New York Graphic* in 1924, and five years later, he had his own syndicated column with the *New York Daily Mirror*.

To come up with celebrity gossip, Winchell at first spent a great deal of time in New York nightclubs, but he soon developed a system of contacts and sources that became the envy of journalism. He claimed the Stork Club as his unofficial office. Beginning in May 1930, Winchell had a daily evening radio show that trafficked in crime stories, celebrity gossip, and politics. Winchell's rapid-fire, staccato voice became his trademark, and because he was absolutely fearless, with millions of listeners, he became quite powerful. Despite his fractured syntax and penchant for making up words or changing the meaning of words, Winchell became the most popular journalist in the country. He regularly pilloried members of Congress but could not heap enough praise on President Franklin D. Roosevelt.* Late in the 1930s, Winchell took on Adolf Hitler and the "Ratsies" (Nazis), and during the 1950s, he was an outspoken backer of Senator Joseph McCarthy. Winchell remained on radio until 1955. Historians now look back on Walter Winchell as the father of broadcast celebrity gossip. Winchell died on February 20, 1972.

SUGGESTED READING: Neal Gabler, *Winchell: Gossip, Power and the Culture of Celebrity*, 1994.

THE WIZARD OF OZ. Based on the famous book by Frank Baum, *The Wizard of Oz* became an American film classic almost immediately upon its release in August 1939. It starred Judy Garland as Dorothy, Frank Morgan as the Wizard, Bert Lahr as the Cowardly Lion, Ray Bolger as the Scarecrow, and Jack Haley as the Tin Woodman, with Margaret Hamilton as the Wicked Witch. *The Wizard of Oz* was one of Hollywood's great musicals, with music by Harold Arien and lyrics by E. Y. Harburg. It was a Metro-Goldwyn-Mayer production directed by Victor Fleming.

Baum wrote the book during the 1890s, at the peak of the agitation over the suffering of American farmers and the rise of the Populist movement. Because of gross overproduction, commodity prices had fallen disastrously, and many farmers blamed the gold standard* for their plight. Populists advocated expansion of the money supply by the free coinage of silver, which they believed would bring about inflation and raise commodity prices. Opponents, of course, argued that abandoning the gold standard would constitute economic suicide for the United States.

In the story, which was put on film, Dorothy and her pet dog Toto are caught up from their Kansas farm in a tornado and carried to the mythical land of Oz, where she meets up with the Scarecrow, the Cowardly Lion, and the Tin Woodman, all of whom have a terrible problem. Dorothy just wants to find a way back to the Kansas farm and her Aunt Em, while the Cowardly Lion wants courage, the Tin Woodman wants a heart, and the Scarecrow wants a brain. They are advised to follow the Yellow Brick Road (the gold standard) to the Emerald City, where the Wizard of Oz solves all problems. The movie follows the four people as they sing and dance their way to Oz and encounter wicked witches, munchkins, apple-throwing trees, enchanted poppy fields, and the "horse of another color." When they reach the Emerald City, they discover that the Wizard is a hopeless, bumbling fraud. In the end, of course, because of their harrowing adventures, the Cowardly Lion learns that he possesses courage, the Tin Woodman realizes that he has a heart, and Scarecrow develops intelligence and brains. Dorothy wakes up from her dream to find herself back in Kansas.

The Wizard of Oz was one of the best movies in one of Hollywood's best years. It played to packed theaters and was the type of film that people enjoyed watching over and over again. With the advent of television in the 1950s, it continued to show up regularly on the small screen for Sunday evening viewing by families. Film historians look back on *The Wizard of Oz* as one of Hollywood's greatest achievements.

SUGGESTED READING: *New York Times*, August 18, 1939.

WOMEN'S REBELLION. Women's Rebellion was an upper-class, anti–New Deal* lobbying group during the 1930s. It was led by Sarah Oliver Huswit, who believed that President Franklin D. Roosevelt* was leading the country down the road to socialism and perhaps even communism. She called for disfranchisement of all federal relief workers and all welfare recipients. She even labeled FDR a "traitor to his class." Of course, most Americans loved Roosevelt and could have cared less about the Women's Rebellion.

SUGGESTED READING: George Wolfskill and John A. Hudson, *All But the People. Franklin D. Roosevelt and His Critics, 1933–1939*, 1969.

WOOD, ROBERT ELKINGTON. Robert Wood was born on June 13, 1879, in Kansas City, Missouri. In 1900, he graduated from the U.S. Military Academy at West Point and spent the next two years fighting against anti-American insurgents in the Philippines. He then did several stints in the quartermaster corps until he was appointed director of the Panama Railroad Company on construction of the Panama Canal. Wood lived in the Canal Zone from 1905 to 1915 and then left the military to become assistant to the president of General Asphalt Company. With the outbreak of World War I, Wood came back on active duty as acting quartermaster general of the U.S. Army. When the war ended, Wood was named vice-president of Montgomery Ward & Company. Five years later, he became president of Sears, Roebuck and Company. Wood served as president there from 1925 to 1939, when he became chairman of the board of Sears, Roebuck.

Unlike most big businessmen during the 1930s, Wood became active in New Deal* politics and issues. Although his basic attitudes were pro business, Wood had a modern view of political economy and believed that a complex, industrial society and economy needed an active central government. An early proponent of the trade association movement and the concept of industrial self-government, Wood supported the National Industrial Recovery Act of 1933 and the National Recovery Administration.* In June 1933 he became a member of the Business Advisory Council,* which advised the Roosevelt administration on business and economic matters. He was also a member of the Committee for the Nation to Rebuild Prices and Purchasing Power, an advocacy group committed to the "commodity dollar" ideas of Irving Fischer* and George Warren.*

After 1935, however, Wood soured on the New Deal. He became especially concerned about the demise of national economic planning, the later New Deal's new emphasis on antitrust activity, the massive regulation envisioned in such legislation as the Public Utility Holding Company Act of 1935,* and the antirich flavor of such laws as the Wealth Tax Act of 1935.* He was also a confirmed isolationist who believed that President Franklin D. Roosevelt's* internationalism would eventually bring the United States into another European war. In 1940 Wood was a leading figure in the establishment of the America First Committee, which promoted isolationism. Wood stepped down from Sears in 1954 and retired. He died on November 6, 1969.

SUGGESTED READING: *New York Times*, November 7, 1969.

WOODIN, WILLIAM HARTMAN. William H. Woodin was born in Berwick, Pennsylvania, on May 27, 1868. He studied for several years at Columbia University's School of Mines before accepting a position at his father's firm, the American Car and Foundry Company. Woodin proved to be a good businessman, and in 1916 he became president of the company. In 1922, he was selected as president and chairman of the board of the American Locomotive Company. Although he was a lifelong Republican, Woodin became friends with Franklin D. Roosevelt* during the 1920s when they both did charitable work for the Warm Springs Foundation, a group dedicated to the eradication of polio. Convinced that the Republican Party had not addressed the real problems facing the nation, Woodin endorsed Democratic candidate Al Smith* for president and FDR in 1932. The triumphant FDR picked Woodin as his secretary of the treasury. Woodin's ties to J. P. Morgan & Company made it a controversial nomination, but Woodin won Senate confirmation. Although ill health forced his resignation in January 1934, Woodin presided ably over the reconstruction of the banking system in 1933. He died on May 3, 1934.

SUGGESTED READING: *New York Times*, May 4, 1934.

WOODWARD, ELLEN SULLIVAN. Ellen Woodward was born in Oxford, Mississippi, on July 11, 1887. Her father, William Amberg Sullivan, had been a congressman and U.S. senator, and she acquired an interest in public affairs from him. She married Albert Young Woodward, an attorney and state legislator, but after his sudden death in 1925, she was appointed to complete his unfulfilled term in the state legislature. From 1926 to 1933, Woodward served as a member, and then as director, of the Mississippi State Board of Development, where she gained critical experience administering a variety of state public works, industrial, agricultural, and educational programs. Competent, efficient, charming, and politically connected, Woodward became one of the most influential women in the state.

In August 1933, Harry Hopkins* named Woodward to head the women's division of the Federal Emergency Relief Administration.* Her close relationship with Hopkins brought her into contact with First Lady Eleanor Roosevelt,* and the two women developed a close friendship. Woodward eventually succeeded to similar duties in the Civil Works Administration* and the Works Progress Administration* (WPA). At the WPA, she supervised the work of more than 500,000 women relief workers who were employed in such activities as household training, gardening, public health extension, canning, and rural library development. When Harry Hopkins left the WPA in December 1938, Woodward left as well and was appointed to the three-member Social Security Board, where she served until 1946. During those years, she crusaded for the extension of unemployment compensation and Social Security coverage to women workers and benefits for widows and dependent children.

From 1946 to 1953, Woodward headed the Office of Inter-Agency and International Relations of the Federal Security Agency.* When she retired in 1953, she was widely regarded as one of the most influential women in the Roosevelt administrations, third behind Secretary of Labor Frances Perkins* and First Lady Eleanor Roosevelt. Ellen Woodward died on September 23, 1971.

SUGGESTED READINGS: *New York Times*, September 24, 1971; Martha H. Swain, " 'The Forgotten Woman': Ellen S. Woodward and Women's Relief in the New Deal," *Prologue*, XV (1983), 201–14.

WORKS PROGRESS ADMINISTRATION. The greatest challenge facing public policymakers during the years of the Great Depression was unemployment.* During the Hoover administration and the early years of the Roosevelt administration, a variety of relief measures were implemented. The Federal Emergency Relief Administration* (FERA) was the first New Deal* relief agency, but critics charged that it was little more than a "dole" because recipients did not have to work for what they received. According to many Americans, a dole, or a welfare check, robbed people of their individual dignity and their incentive to work. More successful, as far as most Americans were concerned, were government relief projects that required recipients to work for the money they received. Such programs included the Public Works Administration,* the Civil Works Administration,* the Civilian Conservation Corps,* and the Works Progress Administration (WPA).

The WPA was by far the largest and most extensive of the New Deal's work relief agencies. President Franklin D. Roosevelt* established the WPA by executive order on May 6, 1935, to implement the dictates of the Emergency Relief Appropriation Act. The legislation appropriated nearly $5 billion, of which $1.4 billion went to the WPA. The WPA had a specific mission from the president to get out of the "relief business" and to help solve the unemployment problem through legitimate, useful government work programs. With the advent of the WPA, the FERA ceased operation. Harry Hopkins* headed the WPA, with Aubrey Williams* as his assistant and Ellen Woodward* in charge of the WPA's women's division.

Under Hopkins's direction, the WPA engaged in a great variety of work projects. It had two basic divisions. The nonconstruction division included the Federal Music Project,* which hired unemployed musicians to teach music in schools and community centers and to perform at public concerts; the Federal Theatre Project,* which hired unemployed actors, directors, and stage professionals to tour the country putting on plays and musicals; the Federal Dance Project,* which hired unemployed dancers and choreographers to teach dance and to stage dance productions; the Federal Art Project,* which hired unemployed artists as teachers and to paint murals on public buildings; and the Federal Writers' Project,* which hired unemployed teachers, librarians, and writers to conduct research, write oral histories, and serve as state and regional travel and business guides. WPA workers also served in libraries, community centers, schools, and health clinics. Eventually, more than 40,000 people were employed in the federal theater, music, art, dance, and writing projects. A total of 500,000 women were employed in such relief activities as household training, public and preventative health education, public gardening, school lunch preparation, canning, and child care.

The WPA construction division operated on a massive scale, and between 1935 and 1943, it constructed or improved 2,500 hospitals, 5,900 school buildings, 3,000 storage dams, 78,000 bridges, 1,000 airports, more than 10,000 public parks, and 650,000 miles of rural roads, sidewalks, park trails, and urban streets. At its peak, the WPA had 3.3 million people on the payroll.

Critics had a field day with the Works Progress Administration. Businessmen complained that the WPA provided unfair competition with them. Conservatives criticized the WPA for being a bureaucratic nightmare and ridiculed its activities as "boondoggling."* Some even said that its acronym stood for "We Piddle Around." Other conservatives complained that the WPA projects for writers, artists, actors, dancers, and musicians were too liberal and promoted social protest. Labor union leaders complained that the average WPA wage of $50 per month eroded wage levels in the economy at large.

In 1939, as part of the Reorganization Act,* the Works Progress Administration was renamed the Works Projects Administration* and transferred to the newly created Federal Works Agency.* When World War II erupted in Europe, the WPA quickly changed its focus to national defense projects, but rapidly rising employment in the private sector soon rendered its mission moot. In June 1943 the Works Progress Administration was eliminated.

SUGGESTED READINGS: Grace Adams, *Workers on Relief*, 1939; William F. McDonald, *Federal Relief Administration and the Arts*, 1969; Martha H. Swain, "The Works Progress Administration," in James S. Olson, ed., *Historical Dictionary of the New Deal*, 1985; Edward Ainsworth Williams, *Federal Aid for Relief*, 1939.

WORKS PROJECTS ADMINISTRATION. As part of the Reorganization Act of 1939,* the Works Progress Administration* was renamed the Works Projects Administration and placed under the jurisdiction of the new Federal Works Agency.* The new WPA's duties remained largely the same as the old WPA's.

WORLD DISARMAMENT CONFERENCE. The World Disarmament Conference convened in Geneva, Switzerland, on February 2, 1932, with representatives from fifty-nine countries working to reduce the global arms race. The sessions continued off and on well into 1934, but no progress was made. The Japanese invasion of Manchuria* in 1931, the Shanghai incident of 1932,* and the Franco-German rivalry complicated the conference, but it disintegrated when Adolf Hitler announced that—in defiance of the Treaty of Versailles—Germany* would rearm.

SUGGESTED READINGS: L. Ethan Ellis, *Republican Foreign Policy, 1921–1933*, 1968; Robert H. Ferrell, *American Diplomacy in the Great Depression*, 1967.

Y

YOUNG, OWEN. Owen Young was born in Van Hornesville, New York, on October 27, 1874. In 1894, he graduated from St. Lawrence University, and in 1896, he earned a law degree from Boston University. Young practiced law in Boston and specialized in the public utilities industry. Young became general counsel for General Electric in 1913, and in 1919, he organized the Radio Corporation of America (RCA), which assumed control of the radio patents of General Electric, American Telephone and Telegraph, and Westinghouse. In 1922, Young was named chairman of the board of Westinghouse.

As an active Democrat, Young's rising profile in corporate America gave him political caché as well. During the Warren Harding administration, he became deeply involved in the Dawes Plan to reorganize Germany's* reparations debts, and in 1929, he developed his own plan to further reduce those debts. Germany had been defaulting on its reparations payments in the 1920s, and the Allied nations had been defaulting on their World War I debt repayments to the United States. The cycle of default threatened to destabilize the world's money markets, and the Young Plan, which reduced German reparations to $8 billion, with a fifty-eight-year repayment period at a 5.5 percent annual interest rate, settled the markets temporarily until the Herbert Hoover* moratorium of 1931 and the Lausanne Conference of 1932* superceded it. Owen Young died on July 11, 1962.

SUGGESTED READINGS: Erik Barnouw, *A History of Broadcasting in the United States*, vol. 1, *A Tower in Babel: To 1933*, 1966; *New York Times*, July 12, 1962; Ida M. Tarbell, *Owen D. Young*, 1932.

YOUNG PLAN OF 1929. See YOUNG, OWEN.

Z

ZIEGFELD FOLLIES OF THE AIR. During the 1910s and 1920s, Florenz Ziegfeld was the most successful Broadway producer in the United States. His *Ziegfeld Follies* opened on Broadway in 1907 and sold out the theater for years. On April 3, 1932, Ziegfeld brought the *Ziegfeld Follies of the Air* to radio, where it debuted on CBS. It was a weekly, sixty-minute musical variety show starring Ziegfeld celebrities such as Fanny Brice, Billie Burke, Jack Pearl, and Will Rogers. What the show could not do, of course, was reproduce the lavish scenes and dance productions of the Broadway *Follies*. It remained on the air, off and on, until 1937.

SUGGESTED READING: Jack Dunning, *Tune in Yesterday: The Ultimate Encylcopedia of Old-Time Radio, 1925–1976*, 1976.

APPENDIX A: ACRONYMS

AAA	Agricultural Adjustment Administration
AALL	American Association for Labor Legislation
AAPA	Association against the Prohibition Amendment
AFBF	American Farm Bureau Federation
AFL	American Federation of Labor
AIDA	American Indian Defense Association
ALL	American Liberty League
BAC	Business Advisory Council
BB	Bureau of the Budget
BIA	Bureau of Indian Affairs
BPA	Bonneville Power Administration
CAA	Civil Aeronautics Authority
CCC	Civilian Conservation Corps
CCC	Commodity Credit Corporation
CIO	Committee for Industrial Organization; after 1938 the Congress of Industrial Organizations
CPLA	Conference on Progressive Labor Action
CRO	Citizen's Reconstruction Organization
CWA	Civil Works Administration
DAR	Daughters of the American Revolution
EHFA	Electric Home and Farm Authority
EIB	Export-Import Bank
FAP	Federal Art Project
FBI	Federal Bureau of Investigation
FCA	Farm Credit Administration
FCC	Federal Communications Commission

FCIC	Federal Crop Insurance Corporation
FDA	Food and Drug Administration
FDIC	Federal Deposit Insurance Corporation
FDP	Federal Dance Project
FDR	Franklin Delano Roosevelt
FEPC	Fair Employment Practices Committee
FERA	Federal Emergency Relief Administration
FFMC	Federal Farm Mortgage Corporation
FHA	Federal Housing Administration
FLA	Federal Loan Agency
FMP	Federal Music Project
FNMA	Federal National Mortgage Association
FPC	Federal Power Commission
FRB	Federal Reserve Board
FSA	Farm Security Administration
FSCC	Federal Surplus Commodities Corporation
FSLIC	Federal Savings and Loan Insurance Corporation
FSRC	Federal Surplus Relief Corporation
FTC	Federal Trade Commission
FTP	Federal Theatre Project
FWA	Federal Works Agency
FWP	Federal Writers' Project
GOP	Grand Old Party
HOLC	Home Owners' Loan Corporation
HRS	Historical Records Survey
IBA	Investment Bankers Association
ICC	Interstate Commerce Commission
IEC	Industrial Energy Commission
ILGWU	International Ladies' Garment Workers' Union
LIPA	League for Independent Political Action
NAACP	National Association for the Advancement of Colored People
NAM	National Association of Manufacturers
NBCC	National Bituminous Coal Commission
NCC	National Credit Corporation
NCL	National Consumers' League
NEC	National Emergency Council
NFHA	National Farmers' Holiday Association

NFU	National Farmers' Union
NIRA	National Industrial Recovery Act
NLB	National Labor Board
NLRB	National Labor Relations Board
NPA	National Progressives of America
NRA	National Recovery Administration
NRB	National Resources Board
NRPB	National Resources Planning Board
NSLRB	National Steel Labor Relations Board
NUL	National Unemployed League
NYA	National Youth Administration
PAB	Petroleum Administrative Board
PCA	Production Credit Association
PECE	President's Emergency Committee for Employment
PLPB	Petroleum Labor Policy Board
PNC	Progressive National Committee
POUR	President's Organization on Unemployment Relief
PWA	Public Works Administration
PWAP	Public Works of Art Project
RA	Resettlement Administration
RCA	Radio Corporation of America
REA	Rural Electrification Administration
RFC	Reconstruction Finance Corporation
SEC	Securities and Exchange Commission
STFU	Southern Tenant Farmers' Union
SWOC	Steel Workers Organizing Committee
TERA	Temporary Emergency Relief Administration
TNEC	Temporary National Economic Committee
TVA	Tennessee Valley Authority
UAW	United Automobile Workers
UCL	Unemployed Citizens' League
UMW	United Mine Workers
USDA	U.S. Department of Agriculture
USES	U.S. Employment Service
USHA	U.S. Housing Authority
WPA	Works Progress Administration

APPENDIX B: CHRONOLOGY

1929

February

11   The Committee on German Reparations meets in Paris to revise the Dawes Plan; Owen Young serves as chairman of the committee.

March

4   Herbert Hoover is inaugurated president of the United States.

July

21   France ratifies the debt settlement with the United States but insists that war debt payments to the United States be covered by German reparations payments.

October

7   Great Britain issues its invitation to the world's four other major naval powers to the London Naval Conference.

24   The securities markets in the United States begin the "Great Crash."

1930

January

21   The London Naval Conference convenes.

April

22   The London Naval Conference is concluded.

June

17   The Hawley-Smoot Tariff becomes law.

July

21   The Senate ratifies the London Naval Treaty.

November

4   In the elections, the Democrats seize control of the House of Representatives.

1931

February

26   President Hoover vetoes congressional legislation authorizing early payment of veterans' bonuses under the Adjusted Compensation Act.

March

3   President Hoover vetoes the Muscle Shoals Bill.

May

11   The Credit Anstalt Bank in Austria declares bankruptcy, triggering a global banking crisis.

June

20   President Hoover proposes a one-year moratorium on payments toward the Allied war debts and German reparations.

July

6   The Hoover moratorium goes into effect.

September

18   Japan invades Manchuria.

21   Great Britain abandons the gold standard.

December

10   The League of Nations forms the Lytton Commission to investigate the Manchurian crisis.

1932

January

4   The Japanese establish military control over south Manchuria.

7   The United States issues the Stimson Doctrine.

28   Japanese army and naval forces attack Shanghai in China.

February

2   The Geneva Conference convenes.
           President Hoover signs the Reconstruction Finance Corporation Act into law.

27   President Hoover signs the Glass-Steagall Banking Act into law.

March

3   Chinese forces are expelled from Shanghai.

23	The Norris–La Guardia Labor Relations Act becomes law.

May

2	The Supreme Court decides the *Nixon v. Congden* case.
31	Japan withdraws its troops from Shanghai.

June

16	At the Lausanne Conference, 90 percent of German reparations are canceled under the Young Plan.

July

21	The Emergency Relief and Construction Act becomes law.
22	The Federal Home Loan Bank Act becomes law.
29	Federal soldiers disperse the Bonus Army demonstrators in Washington, D.C.

September

15	Japan formally establishes the puppet state of Manchukuo in Manchuria.

October

4	The Lytton Report formally condemns Japan for its invasion of Manchuria but then proposes a settlement in which Manchuria is to become an autonomous state under Chinese sovereignty but Japanese control.

November

8	Franklin D. Roosevelt wins a landslide victory over Herbert Hoover in the presidential election.

December

15	Six Allied nations formally default on their war debts to the United States.

1933

February

6	The Twentieth Amendment to the Constitution is declared ratified.
24	The League of Nations formally adopts the Lytton Report.

March

4	Franklin D. Roosevelt is inaugurated president of the United States.
5	The president convenes Congress in an emergency special session to deal with the economic crisis.
6	President Roosevelt declares a nationwide bank holiday.
9	Congress passes the Emergency Banking Act.
27	By executive order, the president establishes the Farm Credit Administration.

31   The Civilian Conservation Corps Reforestation Act becomes law.

May

12   The Agricultural Adjustment Act becomes law.
            The Emergency Farm Mortgage Act becomes law.
            The Federal Emergency Relief Act becomes law.
            The London Economic Conference convenes.

18   Congress establishes the Tennessee Valley Authority.

27   The Securities Act, also known as the Fletcher-Rayburn Bill, becomes
            law.

June

6   The National Employment System Act, also known as the Wagner-Peyser
            Act, becomes law.

13   The Home Owners' Refinancing Act becomes law.

16   The Banking Act, also known as the Glass-Steagall Banking Act, be-
            comes law.
            The Emergency Railroad Transportation Act becomes law.
            The Farm Credit Act becomes law.
            The National Industrial Recovery Act becomes law.
            By executive order, President Roosevelt creates the Public Works Ad-
            ministration.

26   The Consumers' Advisory Board is appointed.

July

8   Harold L. Ickes is named federal administrator of Public Works.

9   The Cotton Textile National Industrial Relations Board is established.

11   By executive order, President Roosevelt creates the National Emergency
            Board.
            By executive order, President Roosevelt forbids the shipment of "hot oil."

30   The National Planning Board is established.

August

4   The Coal Arbitration Board is established.

5   The National Labor Board is established.

10   By executive order, President Roosevelt requires all government pur-
            chases to be made through suppliers cooperating with National Recovery
            Administration codes.

28   The Petroleum Administrative Board is established.

October

18   By executive order, President Roosevelt establishes the Commodity
            Credit Corporation.

November

9   By executive order, President Roosevelt establishes the Civil Works Administration.

17   By executive order, President Roosevelt establishes the National Emergency Council.

December

5   The Twenty-first Amendment to the Constitution is ratified.
Proclamation No. 2065 officially repeals the Eighteenth Amendment to the Constitution.

16   By executive order, the president authorizes the National Labor Board to investigate labor-management disputes and make recommendations for settlement.

19   By executive order, President Roosevelt establishes the Electric Home and Farm Authority.

21   The London Agreement on Silver of 1933 is ratified.

30   Jurisdiction over all state-chartered banks not members of the Federal Reserve System is restored to state banking authorities.

1934

January

30   The Gold Reserve Act becomes law.

31   The Farm Mortgage Refinancing Act becomes law.
Proclamation No. 2072 ends the "gold-buying" scheme and sets the price of gold at $35 an ounce.

February

2   By executive order, the president establishes the Export-Import Bank.

9   By executive order, the president authorizes the U.S. Army to carry the mail.

23   The Crop Loan Act becomes law.

March

7   By executive order, the president establishes the National Recovery Review Board.

12   The Second Export-Import Ban is established.

April

7   The Jones-Connally Farm Relief Act becomes law.

16   The Johnson-O'Malley Act becomes law.

21   The Bankhead Cotton Control Act becomes law.

27   The Home Owners' Loan Act becomes law.

May

2   Proclamation No. 2082 extends Title I of the Emergency Railroad Transportation Act for one year.

9   The Jones-Costigan Sugar Act becomes law.

18   The Department of Agriculture begins the Emergency Cattle Purchase Program.

24   The Municipal Bankruptcy Act becomes law.

June

6   The Securities Exchange Act becomes law.

7   The Corporate Bankruptcy Act becomes law.

12   The Reciprocal Trade Agreements Act becomes law.

18   The Indian Reorganization Act, also known as the Wheeler-Howard Act, becomes law.

19   The National Labor Relations Board is established.
                The Silver Purchase Act becomes law.

20   The Communications Act becomes law.

21   The Railway Labor Act, also known as the Crosser-Dill, Act becomes law.

26   By executive order, President Roosevelt establishes the National Longshoremen's Board.

27   The Railroad Retirement Act becomes law.

28   The Federal Farm Bankruptcy Act, also known as the Frazier-Lemke Farm Bankruptcy Act becomes law.
                By executive order, the president establishes the National Steel Labor Relations Board.
                By executive order, the president establishes the Committee on Economic Security.
                The Kerr-Smith Tobacco Control Act becomes law.
                The National Housing Act becomes law.
                The Taylor Grazing Act becomes law.

30   By executive order, the president establishes the Industrial Emergency Committee.
                By executive order, the president establishes the National Resources Board.

July

5   The National Power Policy Committee is established.

August

9   By executive order, the president "nationalizes" silver.

September

11   Proclamation No. 2098 extends the provisions of the Agricultural Adjustment Act.

26   The Textile Labor Relations Board is established.

December

11   By executive order, the president establishes Federal Prison Industries, Inc.

1935

January

7   The Supreme Court decides the *Panama Refining Company v. Ryan* case (293 U.S. 388).
             The Supreme Court decides the *Amazon Petroleum Corporation et al. v. Ryan* case (293 U.S. 388).

February

18   The Supreme Court decides the "Gold Clause Cases": *Norman v. Baltimore & Ohio Railroad Company* (294 U.S. 240); *United States et al. v. Bankers' Trust Company* (294 U.S. 240); *Nortz v. United States* (294 U.S. 317); *Perry v. United States* (294 U.S. 330).

22   The Connally Act becomes law.

April

8   The Emergency Relief Appropriations Act becomes law.

27   The Soil Conservation Act becomes law.

30   By executive order, the president establishes the Resettlement Administration.

May

6   By executive order, the president establishes the Works Progress Administration.
             The Supreme Court decides the *Railroad Retirement Board et al. v. Alton Railroad Company et al.* case (295 U.S. 330).

11   By executive order, the president establishes the Rural Electrification Administration.

27   The Supreme Court decides the *Louisville Joint Stock Land Bank v. Radford* case (295 U.S. 555).
             In what is remembered as "Black Monday," the Supreme Court decides the *Schechter Poultry Corporation v. United States* case (295 U.S. 495).

June

7   By executive order, the president establishes the National Resources
             Committee.

15   By executive order, the president reestablishes the National Labor Rela-
             tions Board.

26   By executive order, the president establishes the National Youth Admin-
             istration.

July

5   The National Labor Relations Act, also known as the Wagner-Connery
             Act, becomes law.

31   By executive order, the president extends the power of the National Labor
             Relations Board.

August

2   The Federal Art Project is established.
             The Federal Music Project is established.
             The Federal Theatre Project is established.
             The Federal Writers' Project is established.

9   The Motor Carrier Act becomes law.

12   By executive order, the president creates a new Electric Home and Farm
             Authority.

14   The Social Security Act becomes law.

23   The Banking Act becomes law.

24   The Warren Potato Control Act becomes law.

27   The Indian Arts and Crafts Board is created.

29   The Railroad Retirement Act, also known as the Wagner-Crosser Railroad
             Retirement Act, becomes law.

30   The Bituminous Coal Stabilization Act, also known as the Guffey-Snyder
             Coal Act, becomes law.
             The Wealth Tax Act becomes law.

September

21   By executive order, the president increases the spending limits of the
             Emergency Relief Appropriations Act of 1935.

November

16   The Federal Surplus Relief Administration is established.

December

21   By executive order, the president terminates the National Recovery Ad-
             ministration.

1936

January

6   The Supreme Court decides the *United States v. Butler* case (297 U.S. 1).

27   The Adjusted Compensation Act becomes law.

February

17   The Supreme Court decides the *Ashwander v. Tennessee Valley Authority* case (297 U.S. 288).

29   The Neutrality Act becomes law.
         The Soil Conservation and Domestic Allotment Act becomes law.

March

8   The Federal Dance Project is established.

18   The Supreme Court decides the *Carter v. Carter Coal Company* case (198 U.S. 238).

April

3   By executive order, the president increases the spending limits of the Emergency Relief Appropriations Act of 1935.

6   The Supreme Court decides the *Jones v. SEC* case (298 U.S. 1).

20   The Rural Electrification Act becomes law.

May

1   The Alaska Reorganization Act becomes law.

June

15   The Flood Control Act becomes law.

20   The Federal Anti-Price Discrimination Act, also known as the Wright-Patman Act, becomes law.

26   The Oklahoma Indian Welfare Act becomes law.

30   The Walsh-Healey Public Contracts Act becomes law.

November

17   The Special Committee on Farm Tenancy is established.

1937

February

7   President Roosevelt sends his court-packing bill to Congress.

March

29   The Supreme Court decides the *West Coast Hotel v. Parrish* case (300 U.S. 379).

April

12   The Supreme Court decides the *National Labor Relations Board v. Jones & Laughlin Steel Corporation* (301 U.S. 1).

26   The Guffey-Vinson Bituminous Coal Act becomes law.

May

27   The Columbia River Anti-Speculation Act becomes law.

June

29   The Emergency Relief Appropriations Act becomes law.
            The Railroad Retirement Act becomes law.

July

22   The Bankhead-Jones Farm Tenancy Act becomes law.

August

5   The National Cancer Institute Act becomes law.

11   The Miller-Tydings Act becomes law.

20   The Bonneville Power Administration Act becomes law.

September

1   The Farm Security Administration is established.
            The Wagner-Steagall Housing Act becomes law.

2   The Pittman-Robertson Act becomes law.

October

27   By executive order, President Roosevelt transfers all federal housing projects to the U.S. Housing Authority.

1938

February

10   The Federal National Mortgage Association is established.

11   The Small Business Conference convenes.

16   The Agricultural Adjustment Act becomes law.
            The Federal Crop Insurance Act becomes law.

June

16   The Temporary National Economic Committee convenes.

22   The Chandler Act becomes law.

23   The Civil Aeronautics Act becomes law.

25   The Fair Labor Standards Act becomes law.
            The Food, Drug, and Cosmetic Act becomes law.

1939

April

3   President Franklin D. Roosevelt signs the Reorganization Act.

July

1   The reorganization of the executive branch of the federal government is
                implemented.
                The Federal Loan Agency is established.
                The Federal Security Agency is established.
                The Federal Works Agency is established.
                The National Resources Planning Board is established.

August

2   The Hatch Act becomes law.

November

4   The Neutrality Act becomes law.

1940

April

22   The Supreme Court decides the *Thornhill v. State of Alabama* case (310
                U.S. 88).

July

19   A second Hatch Act becomes law.

August

22   The Investment Advisers Act becomes law.
                The Investment Company Act becomes law.

September

18   The Transportation Act becomes law.

1941

February

3   The Supreme Court decides the *United States v. Darby* case (312 U.S.
                567).

June

25   By executive order, the president creates the Fair Employment Practices
                Committee.

November

24   The Supreme Court decides the *Edwards v. People of the State of Cali-
                fornia* case (314 U.S. 160).

December

7   Japan bombs Pearl Harbor.

GENERAL
BIBLIOGRAPHY

Akin, William E. *Technocracy and the American Dream: The Technocrat Movement, 1900–1940.* 1977.

Allen, Frederick Lewis. *Since Yesterday.* 1939.

Allswang, John. *The New Deal in American Politics.* 1978.

Badger, Anthony J. *The New Deal: The Depression Years, 1933–1940.* 1989.

Barber, William J. *From New Era to New Deal: Herbert Hoover, the Economists, and American Economic Policy, 1921–1933.* 1985.

Barnard, Rita. *The Great Depression and the Culture of Abundance.* 1995.

Bernstein, Irving. *Turbulent Years: A History of the American Worker, 1933–1941.* 1970.

Bernstein, Michael A. *The Great Depression: Delayed Recovery and Economic Change in America, 1929–1939.* 1987.

Bird, Caroline. *The Invisible Scar.* 1966.

Braeman, John, ed. *The New Deal.* 1975.

Brinkley, Alan. *The End of Reform: New Deal Liberalism in Recession and War.* 1995.

———. *Liberalism and Its Discontents.* 1998.

Burner, David. *Herbert Hoover: A Public Life.* 1979.

Burns, James MacGregor. *Roosevelt: The Lion and the Fox.* 1956.

Carter, Paul. *The Twenties in America.* 1968.

Chambers, Clarke A. *Seedtime of Reform: American Social Service and Social Action, 1918–1933.* 1963.

Chandler, Lester V. *American Monetary Policy, 1928–1941.* 1971.

———. *America's Greatest Depression, 1929–1941.* 1970.

Collins, Robert M. *The Business Response to Keynes, 1929–1964.* 1981.

Conkin, Paul. *The New Deal.* 1967.

Daniels, Jonathan. *The Time between the Wars: Armistice to Pearl Harbor.* 1966.

Davis, Joseph S. *The World between the Wars, 1919–39: An Economist's View.* 1975.

Dickinson, Matthew. *Bitter Harvest: FDR, Presidential Power, and the Growth of the Presidential Branch.* 1997.

Fausold, Martin L. *The Presidency of Herbert C. Hoover.* 1985.

Fraser, Steve, and Gary Gerstle, eds. *The Rise and Fall of the New Deal Order, 1930–1980.* 1989.

Freidel, Frank. *Franklin D. Roosevelt: A Rendezvous with Destiny.* 1990.

Friedman, Milton, and Anna Schwartz. *The Great Contraction, 1929–1933*. 1965.
Galbraith, John Kenneth. *The Great Crash 1929*. 1955.
Garraty, John A. *The Great Depression*. 1987.
Gordon, Collin. *New Deals: Business, Labor, and Politics in America, 1920–1935*. 1994.
Graham, Otis, Jr. *Encore for Reform: The Old Progressives and the New Deal*. 1967.
Hawley, Ellis W. *The Great War and the Search for a Modern Order: A History of the American People and Their Institutions, 1917–1933*. 1979.
———. *The New Deal and the Problem of Monopoly: A Study in Economic Ambivalence*. 1966.
Hearnes, Charles R. *The American Dream and the Great Depression*. 1977.
Hicks, John D. *Republican Ascendancy, 1921–1933*. 1960.
Himmelberg, Robert F. *The Origins of the National Recovery Administration: Business, Government, and the Trade Association Issue, 1921–1933*. 1976.
Irons, Peter. *The New Deal Lawyers*. 1982.
Karl, Barry. *The Uneasy State*. 1983.
Kennedy, David. *Freedom from Fear: The American People in Depression and War, 1929–1945*. 2000.
Ketchum, Richard M. *The Borrowed Years, 1938–1941: America on the Way to War*. 1989.
Kindleberger, Charles. *The World in Depression*. 1973.
Lash, Joseph P. *Dealers and Dreamers: A New Look at the New Deal*. 1988.
Lekachman, Robert. *The Age of Keynes*. 1966.
Leuchtenburg, William E. *Franklin D. Roosevelt and the New Deal, 1932–1940*. 1963.
Marks, Frederick, III. *Wind and Sand: The Diplomacy of Franklin Roosevelt*. 1988.
Mason, Alpheus Thomas. *The Supreme Court from Taft to Warren*. 1958.
May, Dean. *From New Deal to New Economics*. 1982.
McElvaine, Robert S. *Down & Out in the Great Depression*. 1983.
———. *The Great Depression. America, 1929–1941*. 1984.
McFarland, Charles K. *Roosevelt, Lewis, and the New Deal, 1933–1940*. 1970.
McGovern, James. *And a Time for Hope: Americans in the Great Depression*. 2000.
Mitchell, Broadus. *Depression Decade. From New Era through New Deal, 1929–1941*. 1947.
Nash, George. *The Life of Herbert Hoover*. 1983.
Pells, Richard H. *Radical Visions and American Dreams: Culture and Social Thought in the Depression Years*. 1973.
Perkins, Dexter. *The New Age of Franklin D. Roosevelt, 1932–1945*. 1957.
Potter, Jim. *The American Economy between the World Wars*. 1974.
Romasco, Albert U. *The Politics of Recovery: Roosevelt's New Deal*. 1983.
Rosen, Elliot A. *Hoover, Roosevelt, and the Brains Trust: From Depression to New Deal*. 1977.
Rosenof, Theodore. *Dogma, Depression, and the New Deal: The Debate of Political Leaders over Economic Recovery*. 1975.
———. *Economics in the Long Run: New Deal Theorists and Their Legacies, 1933–1993*. 1997.
Scharf, Lois. *To Work and to Wed: Female Employment, Feminism, and the Great Depression*. 1980.
Schwarz, Jordan A. *The Interregnum of Despair: Hoover, Congress, and the Depression*. 1970.

————. *The New Dealers: Power Politics in the Age of Roosevelt*. 1993.

Sitkoff, Harvard. *A New Deal for Blacks: The Emergence of Civil Rights as a National Issue*. Vol. I, *The Depression Decade*. 1978.

Sobel, Robert. *The Great Bull Market: Wall Street in the 1920s*. 1968.

Stein, Herbert. *The Fiscal Revolution in America*. 1969.

Stevenson, Elizabeth. *Babbitts and Bohemians: The American 1920s*. 1967.

Sullivan, Patricia. *Days of Hope: Race and Diversity in the New Deal Era*. 1996.

Taylor, Graham D. *The New Deal and American Indian Tribalism: The Administration of the Indian Reorganization Act, 1934–1945*. 1980.

Temen, Peter. *Did Monetary Forces Cause the Great Depression?* 1976.

Terkel, Studs. *Hard Times: An Oral History of the Great Depression, 1929–1940*. 1984.

Terrell, Tom, and Jerrold Hirsch, eds. *Such as Us: Southern Voices of the Thirties*. 1978.

Thomas, Gordon, and Max Morgan-Witts. *The Day the Bubble Burst: The Social History of the Wall Street Crash of 1929*. 1979.

Wandersee, Winifred D. *Women's Work and Family Values: 1920–1940*. 1981.

Ware, Susan. *Beyond Suffrage: Women in the New Deal*. 1981.

————. *Holding Their Own: American Women in the 1930s*. 1982.

Warren, Harris Gaylord. *Herbert Hoover and the Great Depression*. 1959.

Watkins, T. H. *The Great Depression: America in the 1930s*. 1991.

Westin, Jeane. *Making Do: How Women Survived the '30s*. 1976.

Wicker, Elmus R. *Federal Reserve Monetary Policy, 1917–1933*. 1966.

Wilson, William H. *Coming of Age: Urban America, 1915–1945*. 1974.

Yunay, Yuval. *The Struggle over the Soul of Economics: Institutionalists and Neoclassical Economists in America between the Wars*. 1998.

INDEX

Page numbers for main entries in the dictionary are set in **boldface** type.

About the Author

JAMES S. OLSON is Professor of History and Department Chair at Sam Houston State University. He is the author of more than forty books, including *Historical Dictionary of the 1970s* (Greenwood, 1999), *Historical Dictionary of the 1960s* (Greenwood, 1999), and *Historical Dictionary of the 1950s* (Greenwood, 2000).

For Reference